QUANTITATIVE ECONOMIC HISTORY

QUANTITATIVE ECONOMIC HISTORY

Edited by

N. F. R. Crafts, N. H. Dimsdale, and S. Engerman

CLARENDON PRESS · OXFORD
1991

Oxford University Press, Walton Street, Oxford OX2 6OR

Oxford New York Toronto
Delhi Bombay Calcutta Madras Karachi
Petaling Jaya Singapore Hong Kong Tokyo
Nairobi Dar es Salaam Cape Town
Melbourne Auckland

and associated companies in
Berlin Ibadan

Oxford is a trade mark of Oxford University Press

Published in the United States
by Oxford University Press, New York

British Library Cataloguing in Publication Data
Data available

Library of Congress Cataloging in Publication Data
Data available

Printed in Northern Ireland at The Universities Press (Belfast) Ltd

CONTENTS

INTRODUCTION

By N. F. R. CRAFTS, N. H. DIMSDALE, *and* S. ENGERMAN

THIS collection of articles on quantitative economic history first appeared in *Oxford Economic Papers* in December 1987 and December 1988. It contains ten articles covering a wide range of topics in economic history with a strong quantitative content. Eight of the papers examine nineteenth-century data and the remaining two relate to the inter-war period. Five papers fall broadly into the area of labour economics. There are three papers on industrial economics and the final two papers are concerned with money and macroeconomics. The editors were keen to publish papers which draw upon historical data sets, where the resulting analysis is likely to be of interest to both economists and economic historians.

Both Eichengreen and Hatton and Bailey make use of *The New Survey of London Life and Labour* in their studies of unemployment and of female participation in inter-war Britain. Nicholas and Shergold use the records of convicts transported from Britain to Australia in the early nineteenth century to examine the nature of the early Australian labour force and factors explaining migration within Britain during the Industrial Revolution. Treble draws on the records of the decisions of Conciliation Boards on wage determination in the British coal industry during the late nineteenth century to carry out a detailed study on wage behaviour in the industry. Williamson uses a wide range of historical sources in his assessment of the working of factor markets during the early nineteenth century.

The industrial papers are concerned broadly with the measurement of productivity. Foreman–Peck uses the British Railway Returns to assess efficiency in the railway system during the mid-Victorian era, while Millward and Ward use data on costs and output in the British gas industry to compare the costs of public and private production at the end of the nineteenth century. Davis, Gallman, and Hutchins conduct a detailed comparison of productivity and profits in the British and American whaling fleets in the early nineteenth century. They analyse the data using index numbers rather than the direct estimation of cost functions which is attempted in the two previous papers.

Finally, there are two papers on macroeconomic and monetary questions. Calomiris examines the determination of prices and exchange rates in the United States from 1862 to 1878, when the gold standard was suspended, using a comprehensive set of data to test the underlying theoretical model. Gorton carries out a thorough analysis of causes of panics under the US National Banking System from 1863 to 1914. These two papers use time series analysis and other quantitative techniques to examine questions which have been discussed previously by other writers using a less sophisticated approach.

Eichengreen examines the argument of Benjamin and Kochin (1979) that unemployment in inter-war Britain was largely voluntary and can be attributed to the provision of generous state unemployment benefits. He uses a microeconomic approach drawing data from *The New Survey of London Life and Labour* carried out at the London School of Economics in 1929–31. The survey was intended to be a successor to Charles Booth's previous survey of Victorian London. It was carried out in a thorough and painstaking way, but the limitation of the sample to London is unfortunate, since employment in the capital was not representative of the country as a whole, as there was an emphasis on services and light consumer goods and exclusion of the major staple industries.

The ratio of benefits to male earnings, the replacement ratio, is a key variable in the analysis, but causes difficulties of measurement, since the earnings of the unemployed must be imputed. Eichengreen overcomes the problem of estimating the imputed wage due to selection bias by using an instrumental variable approach. He first estimates an earnings function for all male workers, both employed and unemployed. The estimated values from the equation are used in the denominator of the replacement ratio, while in the numerator the unemployment benefits of both employed and unemployed are imputed. The earnings function is of interest in its own right, showing male earnings rising with age and peaking in the late forties. Earnings are higher for married than unmarried men and decline in families with a large number of children.

Probit regressions are then estimated for unemployment which is explained by a vector of age variables, a vector of family characteristics, and the constructed replacement ratio. The probability of unemployment is found to be lowest for men aged 35–44 and rises in both directions as age moves from this range. Risk of unemployment rises particularly in the 55–9 age group, while single adults face a higher risk of unemployment than married men. Being a head of household reduces the probability of unemployment and the presence of children increases it.

The replacement ratio was not statistically significant in affecting unemployment for all male workers. However, Eichengreen finds an important difference between householders and other workers. The employment decisions of the former were not affected by the replacement ratio, but this did not apply to the latter group. It appears that secondary workers adjusted their decision on employment in accordance with the generosity of unemployment benefits, but their impact on the whole sample was slight, since 77 per cent of workers were heads of households.

Eichengreen calculates counterfactual unemployment rates for 1930–1 assuming the replacement ratio of 1913 and concludes that only 20 per cent of inter-war unemployment in Britain can be attributed to increased unemployment benefits. This result contrasts with an estimated contribution of 30–50 per cent in the work of Benjamin and Kochin (1979). The result of the analysis of survey data is to reduce the estimated impact of benefits on unemployment, but not to eliminate it. This conclusion is consistent with more recent studies of the inter-war labour market by Dimsdale, Nickell, and Horsewood (1989), who find little impact of benefits on real wages and unemployment in an analysis of quarterly data.

In the second paper on inter-war Britain Hatton and Bailey study the factors influencing the participation of women in employment. They analyse two sets of data, the first drawn from *The New Survey of London Life and Labour* (*NSLLL*), the same source as used by Eichengreen in the previous paper, and the second from the 1931 Census. During the inter-war period female employment was concentrated among single women and was chiefly confined to a narrow range of occupations, such as domestic service and employment in textiles. Although female participation rose in the inter-war period, the main growth occurred after 1938.

Hatton and Bailey draw a random sample of 1356 households from the *NSLLL*. The first stage in the analysis is the estimation of a female earnings function, which is needed to impute the wages of non-participants. The predicted values of earnings for the whole sample are included in the participation equation. Women's earnings depend upon age and upon location dummies which reflect the occupational structure of different labour markets. The participation equation which is estimated as a probit regression shows participation rising to the 18–19 age group and declining in the 25–34 group, with a further decline from age 45 and upwards. There are major differences between the participation of household heads and that of wives and others. For household heads participation peaks in the 45–54 age group, whereas for wives and others the peak is at age 18–19. The withdrawal of wives from the labour force came after marriage rather than with the birth of children. There is some evidence of an added worker effect, that is of the unemployment of the male head of household prompting married women to seek employment. Women's predicted wages are not statistically significant, possibly because job opportunities were a more important factor than the wage rate. There is, however, evidence of a negative effect of household income on participation.

In the second part of the paper female participation is examined using Census data; this is less detailed than the London survey but allows for the greater degree of variation in regional participation rates. The sample includes 144 County Boroughs or equivalent urban areas. As in the previous equation, participation is related to demographic and financial variables, but in addition variables reflecting the industrial composition of different regions are included. These are found to play an important role in accounting for regional variations in participation. Female employment opportunities rose with local employment in textiles and personal services and declined with employment in mining, metals, and transport. More surprisingly, regional employment in commerce and professions also discouraged female participation. The wage rate, proxied by male wages in building, becomes statistically significant when industrial employments are included, implying a wage elasticity of 0.54. Overall the results from the 1931 Census are comparable with those reported from the 1971 Census, except that industrial employment effects were stronger and the range of regional variation in participation rates was wider in the inter-war period.

Nicholas and Shergold examine the factors influencing migration in Britain during the Industrial Revolution using a new data source. The database for their study consists of indents giving detailed information on 10,000 men and women tried in British courts and transported to New South Wales from 1817 to 1839. The indents can be interpreted in two ways: first, as providing socio-economic data about the characteristics of the early Australian labour force; and second, as furnishing evidence on the causes of migration within Britain. The indents included convicts who were migrants, as indicated by county of conviction differing from county of birth, and non-migrants, whose place of birth and conviction were similar. The sample therefore provided details on the characteristics of migrant and non-migrant convicts.

Nicholas and Shergold claim that their sample of convicts is representative of the English working class, with a distribution of skills which is comparable to that found in the 1841 Census. If the skills and literacy of the transportees were typical of the British labour force, they should not be regarded as being drawn from a criminal underclass, as claimed by some historians. Rather, because of their endowments of skill and literacy, the convicts made a valuable contribution of human capital to the new colony, particularly since the majority were male and in the productive age group of 16–25.

The second element in the paper is the analysis of the determinants of migration within Britain from place of birth to place of conviction. A logit model is estimated, where the probability of migrating depends on age, sex, marital status, skill, and industry of employment. The probability of migrating is found to increase with skill and literacy. Females were more mobile than males, perhaps reflecting the opportunities for employment in domestic service, while marriage appears to have reduced mobility. Urban workers had a lower probability of migrating than rural workers because of their greater opportunity for local employment.

The paper shows how the data derived from the indents can be used to examine factors affecting migration. However, this conclusion depends on the validity of the authors' claim that their sample is representative of the British labour force.

Williamson starts from the conventional view that there were major distortions in the British labour market during the Industrial Revolution which showed up in the form of high urban/rural wage differentials combined with limited migration. More recently Crafts (1985) has pointed to the rapid release of labour from agriculture and Williamson confirms that migration was occurring at a relatively rapid pace. He then turns to the wage gap which he finds to be more than 100 per cent in the South of

England and lower in the North, but still 70 per cent for the country as a whole. Arguing that migration should respond to differentials in real rather than money wages, he corrects urban wages for higher living costs, largely on account of higher urban rents. Adjustments are also made for the disamenities of urban living, proxied by differentials in population size, density, and infant mortality, with a further correction for poor relief payments to Southern agricultural labourers. The outcome of these adjustments is an average real wage differential of 18 per cent for England, rising to 40 per cent in the Southern counties. While the wage gap does not disappear, it is greatly reduced when measured in real terms.

The impact of the wage gap on the economy is assessed using a partial equilibrium approach, followed by a simulation in a general equilibrium model set out in Williamson (1985). The deadweight loss arises from the higher real wage in industry relative to agriculture, limiting industrial employment and output in comparison to the situation with a perfect labour market. In Fig. 1 the wage gap BC limits industrial employment to OL. If wages were equated in the two sectors industrial employment would rise to OP at the market clearing wage of EP. The increase in national income with the elimination of the wage gap arises because the loss of agricultural output LCEP is less than the gain in industrial output LBEP by the triangle CBE, assuming unchanged relative output prices in a partial analysis. This area measures the deadweight loss due to the wage gap which Williamson computes to be 1.5 per cent of 1831 national income.

While the gain in terms of national income is not great, there are important distributional effects as the wage gap depresses industrial profits relative to agricultural rents, which could have adverse effects on capital accumulation, if investment were largely financed from the reinvestment of profits.

Williamson then introduces imperfections into the capital market, assuming that the required rate of profit in industry is 2.4 times greater than in

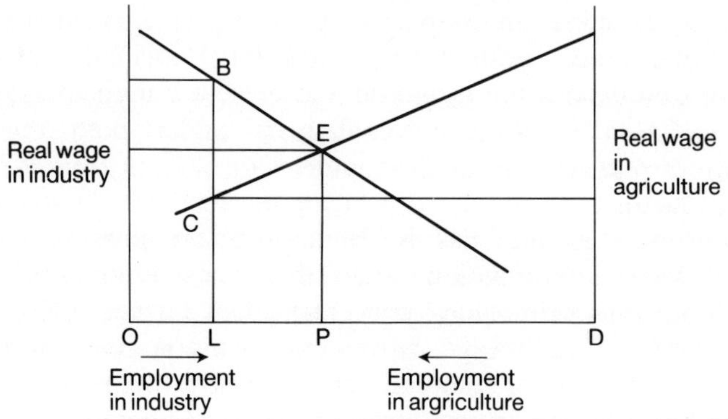

FIG. 1 The wage gap in industry and agriculture: a partial equilibrium approach

agriculture. In his general equilibrium model the removal of the wage gap raises national income by 3 per cent, which is increased to 7 per cent when combined with the elimination of capital market imperfections. The upshot of the discussion is that factor distortions were important, particularly when the consequences for industrial profits and accumulation are taken into account. The main distortions arise in the capital rather than the labour market. The dynamic and sectoral effects are larger than a simple calculation of the static deadweight loss for the aggregate economy suggests.

Williamson's paper is stimulating and serves to raise many questions. One key query is in regard to the assumption of a much higher rate of return in industry than in agriculture, while the assumption of much higher rates of reinvestment of profits than rents requires more empirical support. The paper thus provides a most useful agenda for future research within a consistent framework.

Treble returns to a question which has been widely discussed by economic historians, the process of wage determination in the British coal industry in the late nineteenth century. There was widespread use of product price sliding scales to adjust the wages of coalminers. Since wage rates were tied to the price of the product, sliding scales were similar to the share contracts recently advocated by Weitzman (1984) as a means of reducing fluctuations in employment. During the 1890s there was a movement away from sliding scales towards wage determination by Conciliation Boards. It was intended that the Boards would reduce the automaticity of the sliding scale and allow factors other than the price of coal to affect wages, a conclusion which has been questioned by writers on the industry such as Rowe (1923).

Treble draws on the extensive records maintained by the district Conciliation Boards to examine the relationship between wages and product prices. Using these data he estimates the relationship implicit in decisions on wages. He finds this to be piecewise linear, that is wages vary directly with coal prices within upper and lower limits. Movements in coal prices which lie outside these limits do not affect wages, but within the limits the Boards effectively operated sliding scales.

Treble then examines the impact of price movements on the wage risk borne by miners under both sliding scales and Conciliation Boards. Two measures of ex-ante risk are proposed and these are used to assess the risk of wage variation incurred by coalminers under both regimes. The introduction of maxima and minima under Conciliation Boards is found to be the main factor reducing the risk facing the workers. Treble argues that the comparison of ex-ante risk is the appropriate measure for assessing methods of wage determination rather than considering actual outcomes upon which previous writers have concentrated. A further analysis is needed to take account of real wage movements. This is relevant to Treble's analysis in that the upper limit on wage adjustment became increasingly burdensome upon miners in real terms in the period before the outbreak of the First World War, when the general price level was rising. Conciliation

Boards may have contributed to poor labour relations in the coal industry at this time on account of the upper limit on wage adjustment.

The next two papers, by Foreman-Peck and Millward and Ward, are concerned with industries which enjoyed a high degree of natural monopoly. Foreman-Peck explores the efficiency of the British railway system, while Millward and Ward compare the relative efficiency of private and public gas generation.

Foreman-Peck shows that British railway policy did not evolve a satisfactory way of regulating natural monopoly. Contemporary discussions included consideration of granting franchises for routes and the separate ownership of tracks and rolling-stock to promote a measure of competition within the industry, but neither suggestion proved to be of practical significance. In the main part of the paper a translog cost function is estimated from cross-section data drawn from the Railway Returns for 1865. The results suggest that cost reductions could have been achieved from longer hauls and by reducing the number of trains run. Costs could also have been reduced by higher freight and passenger loads per train. There is therefore evidence that traffic could have been managed so as to reduce costs. The problem here is that frequency of service might have been reduced, so causing consumers some inconvenience. Unless these welfare losses are shown to fall short of the potential reduction in costs, it is difficult to assess the charge of inefficient operation.

In the final section of the paper Foreman-Peck documents the higher level of capital costs per mile in the British system in an international comparison across twelve countries. Had construction costs been lowered to the international level, return on capital could have risen from 3 to 4 per cent. Railway costs could have been reduced by about 15 per cent, raising GNP by 0.75 per cent without allowing for any increase in traffic as a result of these cost reductions. Foreman–Peck therefore questions the wisdom of Victorian policy towards the regulation of railways in view of the apparently more satisfactory results achieved overseas.

In analysing the relative costs of private and public production of gas in late nineteenth-century Britain, Millward and Ward raise an issue which is fundamental to the current debate over the privatization of nationalized industries. They analyse a sample of 35 gas undertakings of which 19 were owned by local authorities and 16 were privately owned, including 3 large London gas companies. The data, derived from the *Gas World,* include statistics on costs and output. Using this data set Millward and Ward estimate a general translog cost function and test for differences in cost between privately and publicly owned enterprises. Equations are estimated for factor shares, from which it appears that the demand for inputs is negatively related to their prices. Although the relevant coefficients are correctly signed, they are generally lacking in statistical significance. The factor share equations do not reject homotheticity of the production function, that is factor proportions do not vary with output with constant input prices. In the second stage the dependent variable is adjusted for the effect of factor prices, allowing the impact of scale and technology on costs to be estimated. The results reject homogeneity of the production function, indicating the presence of economies of scale up to a production of 1.3 m. cubic ft., which is in excess of the sample mean of lm. cubic ft. for all provincial undertakings, excluding the London companies. Thus in the provinces there were unexploited economies of scale but for the London companies an increase in output would have raised costs.

Publicly owned undertakings had lower average costs than private firms, but this was largely explained by lower input prices and reduced distribution costs because of greater density of consumers. They also had more modern plants, but overall there was no statistically significant difference between the costs of the two types of undertaking. This result contrasts with the finding of Foreman-Peck and Waterson (1985) that private firms had lower costs in electricity generation in inter-war Britain.

In the third industrial study, Davis, Gallman, and Hutchins examine competition between the British and American whaling fleets in the early nineteenth century. At the beginning of the period the British fleet was dominant and enjoyed government bounties as well as tariff protection. In 1816 there were 150 British whalers at sea and only two American ships. However, by 1842 the American fleet had risen to 700 ships and the British fleet had shrunk to 30 vessels.

There were differences in techniques of production between British and American whalers. The British used larger ships and employed relatively larger crews, but their average voyage length was shorter, partly on account of bounties being paid per voyage. The Americans undertook preliminary refining of blubber on board and included in their crews skilled artisans who could carry out repairs at sea.

Total factor productivity in the two fleets is compared using superlative index numbers rather than by estimation of cost functions as in the previous two papers. The developments in index number theory arise from the work of Caves, Christensen, and Diewart (1982) and are of particular importance to economic historians. The index numbers can readily be calculated from data on inputs and output prices and quantities, which enable measures of productivity to be derived. On the assumptions of perfect competition and constant returns, the resulting index numbers approximate to a translog production function, so avoiding the econometric problems of direct estimation. The authors argue that the last two assumptions are satisfied for the whaling industry. Comparisons of total factor productivity are made on the basis of three different assumptions about the input of capital and labour in the two fleets to take account of the longer periods at sea of American whalers.

The computed indexes show wide variation from year to year but point to the overall superiority of the American fleet, which was more productive in all three variants of input measurement. Comparisons of relative productivity are supported by comparisons of profitability which confirm the higher financial returns to the American industry. In a counterfactual analysis it is suggested that, if the British government had withdrawn both bounties and tariffs and the price of whale oil had been at the US level, the British whaling industry would have been eliminated in direct competition with the American fleet. In reality, the main threat to British whalers was the growing competition from coal oil and coal gas, which were increasingly substituted for whale oil in street lighting after 1820.

The two concluding papers of the collection are concerned with the macroeconomic behaviour of the American economy in the nineteenth century. Calomiris examines the determination of prices and the exchange rate during the Greenback era and Gorton investigates the causes of banking panics under the National Banking System.

Calomiris questions the interpretation of price and exchange rate movements during the Greenback era of 1862–78 by Friedman and Schwartz (1963) who argue that the issue of Greenbacks raised the price level and reduced the exchange rate. He supports the view associated with Wesley Mitchell (1903) that expectations about the timing of the resumption of specie payments and about the course of fiscal policy were the main determinants of the exchange rate and the price level. Calomiris draws on the work of Sargent and Wallace (1984), who show how a continuing budget deficit generates expectations of inflation and of future monetary growth. He examines the institutional features of the money supply during the period of suspension of the gold standard. The US government was unable to control the supply of high-powered money, since the National Banks were empowered to issue their own banknotes, which were perfect substitutes for Greenbacks. The supply of National Bank notes depended upon the profitability of their issue, against the required holding of government bonds and reserves by the Banks. Calomiris shows that Bank profits were inversely related to the expected rate of inflation and then derives an equation for expected inflation. He points out that the domestic price level at the expected date of resumption was directly related to expected international prices measured in gold. The course of prices was determined from this terminal price level and expected inflation, which, given the real rate of interest, also determined the nominal interest rate. Fiscal policy changes were important in influencing expectations about the timing of resumption. However, the issue of Greenbacks did not have any effect on the supply of high-powered money or the price level, since a larger stock of Greenbacks reduced the profitability of note issue by the National Banks, leaving the aggregate stock of high-powered money unchanged.

In the second part of the paper the theoretical model is tested. The model assumes that markets for goods and financial assets are efficient, and in particular that the foreign exchange market takes full account of expectations about government policy in determining the exchange rate. Calomiris provides evidence to support the claim that the exchange rate is close to being a random walk, which is consistent with the market being efficient and reacting only to unexpected news. In the bond market expectations of deflation prior to the return of the gold standard are implied by the lower yield on securities denominated in Greenbacks than in gold.

In the final section of the paper Calomiris examines the evidence for changes in government financing influencing the exchange rate and for the exchange rate influencing prices, using a ten equation system of vector autoregressions. Since first differences are taken of monthly data, it is hardly surprising that the results show a low degree of statistical significance. The reported F tests are all less than unity and the correlations among the variables are also low. Hence Calomiris's attempts to draw conclusions from the results of his VAR analysis must be treated with some scepticism, despite the plausibility of his basic model.

Gorton asks whether it is correct to regard banking panics as random events caused by changes in the attitudes of economic agents which are unrelated to the real economy. Against this random interpretation of panics, he contrasts his own view that they are the outcome of a systematic process arising from changing perceptions of risk which are related to the business cycle. He argues that depositors lack the information to discriminate between the risks borne by individual banks, and therefore assess risk on the basis of aggregate data. When perceived risk reaches a critical level risk-averse depositors withdraw their deposits and switch into cash, so producing a run on the banking system. Gorton develops a model explaining the behaviour of depositors both during and outside periods of panic, which supports his thesis that panics are systematic rather than random or 'sunspot' phenomena.

He models the currency–deposit ratio using a 'cash in advance' inventory model developed from earlier work by Tobin and Baumol. Holdings of currency relative to bank deposits depend upon expected returns and perceived risk plus linear and quadratic time trends. Expected returns include both the interest payable on deposits and expected losses to depositors. Perceived risk depends upon the covariance between changes in consumption and factors affecting the risk of depositors. This covariance will not in general be constant over time. The expected losses of depositors are related to bankruptcies, measured by the liabilities of failed businesses, pig iron production, and the commercial paper rate, while perceived risk is measured by the covariance between changes in pig iron production, as a proxy for changes in consumption, and the liabilities of failed non-financial businesses and the commercial paper rate. Considerable ingenuity is shown in the development of monthly proxies for the variables in the currency–deposit ratio equation. The outcome is an estimated model which accounts for cash holding both during and outside periods of panic, in that dummy variables included in months of panic are not found to be statistically significant.

Further analysis shows that perceived risk reaches a critical or threshold value before a panic occurs and that the critical value is not reached at other times. Panics tended to correspond with large values of the cyclical component of the liabilities of failed business. This appears to be a general feature of US panics from 1865 to 1914, supporting Gorton's view that panics are a systematic element in the business cycle.

The pre-1914 pattern does not, however, hold so well in the inter-war period when the National Banking System had been superseded by the Federal Reserve. A counterfactual suggests that the panic of 1920 would have been more severe under the National Banking System but that bank failures in the early 1930s would have been greatly reduced compared to actual experience under the Federal Reserve. This is an interesting result which requires further analysis. Gorton has produced a thorough and stimulating paper which is a model of its kind.

Having reviewed the contributions to this volume, it is now opportune to consider what they reveal of the state of the 'new economic history' after some thirty years or so of its existence. In particular, it seems useful both to reflect on the use of economics in historical studies and also on the potential for economic history to contribute to modern economics.

The most obvious feature of these papers is that they reflect the increasing maturity of cliometrics and its evolution beyond the first phase of the 1960s and 1970s, so well surveyed in Wright (1971) and McCloskey (1978). In his survey Wright stressed that the 'distinctive contribution of the New Economic History has not been so much the use of "econometrics" but the use of *economics*' (1971, p. 416); and he noted that relatively few papers employed even elementary regression methods. McCloskey justifiably argued that in the literature of that time 'economic theory, especially the theory of price, is the defining skill of cliometricians, as of other economists. A cliometrician is an economist applying economic theory (usually simple) to historical facts (not always quantitative) in the interest of history (not economics)' (1978, p. 15) and he was happy to report that 'the conclusions have often been variations on the theme "The Market, God Bless It, Works . . ." (1978, p. 21).

These descriptions of the field are now much less apposite, as this volume shows. Much work in the area is now heavily reliant on fairly sophisticated quantitative methods and the use of economics is more eclectic and less dominated by simple price theory. For instance, the econometric models used by the authors here include ARIMA, VAR, Logit, and translog production functions, techniques which are of quite recent diffusion amongst economists and are particularly congenial to investigators without strong priors. Moreover, the papers by Foreman-Peck, Millward and Ward, and Williamson all report results which would run counter to intuitions derived from the simple competitive model.

We regard these tendencies towards greater eclecticism and letting the data speak as largely healthy and as reducing the very real danger, forcibly voiced by Solow, that 'economic history is as much corrupted as enriched by economic theory' (1986, p. 21). Furthermore, it is noticeable that by now there is much greater use of insights from traditional historical literature grounded in close observation of the workings of institutions in practice *together* with those from economic analysis rather than the pursuit of revisionism based on an imperialism of elementary economic theory, as tended to be the case in extreme examples of the new economic history in the past, such as Benjamin and Kochin (1979). Thus, Hatton and Bailey and also Eichengreen in this volume provide accounts of aspects of the inter-war labour market which are much more likely to be persuasive to historians than was that of Benjamin and Kochin because they encompass more of the historical evidence.

We believe that this volume is a further demonstration that economics can make a positive contribution to understanding the past beyond that envisaged by McCloskey through exploiting insights from recent developments in economic theory, embracing modern quantitative methods and (sometimes ingeniously) analysing the often very rich historical data sources. Good examples of these aspects of the value of economics to economic history can be found in the papers of Calomiris, Treble and Nicholas, and Shergold.

A further slightly less obvious benefit of the value of the new economic history which underlies several of these papers, which in the field as a whole has probably been of still greater importance, is in the construction of historical data. Thus, in the British case major additions to the stock of knowledge have come in the form of series of estimates for national income back to 1855 (Feinstein, 1972), the money supply back to 1870 (Capie and Webber, 1985) and English population back to 1541, 260 years before the first census (Wrigley and Schofield, 1981).

Thus the scope for economics to add value in historical study is both considerable and well on the way to being realized. By contrast, the usefulness of history to economists is far from being adequately appreciated, although there are major returns to be reaped. This unfortunate situation comes about for several reasons and has had self-perpetuating tendencies, although, as this volume suggests, amelioration may yet be possible.

Economic history can have value for economists in at least three ways: by offering a valuable array of data with which to investigate economic hypotheses further; by providing an important body of evidence relevant to current policy issues; and, perhaps most singularly, by making apparent that model specification, choice of appropriate policy rules, and policy instruments are all highly dependent on political and institutional circumstances.

The studies in this volume should whet the appetite of those economists interested in using historical data for empirical work. Indeed some of the authors would describe themselves as economists rather than economic historians, which illustrates the point that barriers to entry are not insurmountable, although equally it should be obvious that the quality of the work published here has been based on a non-negligible investment in learning about the availability and shortcomings of historical sources.

The results of several of these papers bear out the point that the historical record contains much of substantive interest for policy-orientated economists. For example, the Foreman-Peck and Millward and Ward papers relate to the economics of regulation; while the Calomiris and Gorton papers have insights bearing upon monetary and fiscal policy, and both also underline the message that changes in institutional arrangements have significant policy implications and that the past contains a much wider range of institutional and policy configurations than can be researched by confining oneself to the present.

Nevertheless, it must be acknowledged that relatively little use of history is made by those interested in present-day policy questions. This is so even when events occur which clearly could be illuminated by informed discussion of historical parallels, like the stock market crash of 1987. Professional economists have typically never been taught what *they* would find useful to know about the past; on the contrary, at some stage, they probably have had to undergo a course in economic history organized in such a way as completely to put economists off the subject.

Moreover, economic historians, in seeking to impress their own peer group, have tended to pursue research programmes and to present findings driven by a historiographic menu rather than a policy menu. Accordingly economists tend to underestimate what history has to offer them.

In sum, the past ten years have seen substantial progress made in quantitative economic history with major improvements in the quality of analysis and the building up of a large inventory of research findings. The maturity of these second-phase papers, as compared with those surveyed by McCloskey and by Wright, is evident in this collection. There is, however, much work to be done by economic historians in developing effective strategies for fulfilling the potential of the subject in improving the human capital of economists.

On a more optimistic note, it is clear that there are important opportunities for a 'third phase' of new economic history. Recent developments in time-series econometrics and in both the macro- and microeconomic analysis of strategic and opportunistic behaviour enhance the pay-offs from working with historical data. In particular, there seems to be much scope for exploring the implications of ideas such as 'credibility', 'agency problems', 'tit-for-tat', etc.

This would seem to be especially true for twentieth-century studies, which clearly will predominate in the third phase of new economic history as the nineteenth century did in the first phase. The analysis of government policy, the performance of large firms, industrial relations, and the mixed economy will inevitably loom larger. The need is already apparent for new economic historians now to develop and utilize 'new business history' and 'new labour history' rather than relatively to neglect these types of economic history, as has been the tendency hitherto.

For example, the internal workings of firms can be treated more seriously, greater effort can be put into the analysis of industries' development and less to biographies of particular firms, bargaining models can be deployed to examine productivity levels within firms, and government–industry relations can be examined in an explicitly game-theoretic framework. Historical case studies would seem much more useful than was believed by economists brought up in the structure, conduct, performance paradigm of industrial economics and would also seem to be a valuable way of getting an empirical handle on Olson's (1982) fascinating suggestion that long-established democracies tend to develop sclerotic tendencies as economic growth is impeded by interest groups.

The implication of such developments is likely to be a further retreat from new economic history's original love affair with the invisible hand but a much more truly historical approach than was characteristic of the first phase.

In the meantime the editors are more than happy to publish the present collection of papers which both provide interesting explorations of historical data and also reflect the high standards and maturity of new economic history in the late 1980s.

REFERENCES

BENJAMIN, D. and KOCHIN, L. (1979), 'Searching for an Explanation for Unemployment in Interwar Britain', *Journal of Political Economy,* 87, 441–78.

CAPIE, F. and WEBBER, A. (1985), *A Monetary History of the United Kingdom,* (London: Allen and Unwin).

CAVES, D. W., CHRISTENSEN, L. R. and DIEWART, W. E. (1982), 'Multilateral Comparisons of Output, Input and Productivity Using Superlative Index Numbers', *Economic Journal,* 92, 73–86.

CRAFTS, N. F. R. (1985), *British Economic Growth during the Industrial Revolution* (Oxford: Clarendon Press).

DIMSDALE, N. H., NICKELL, S. J. and HORSEWOOD, N. (1989), 'Real Wages and Unemployment in Britain during the 1930s', *Economic Journal,* 99, 271–92.

FOREMAN-PECK, J. and WATERSON, M. (1985), 'The Comparative Efficiency of Public and Private Enterprise in Britain: Electricity Generation between the World Wars', *Economic Journal,* Supplement to vol. 95.

FRIEDMAN, M. and SCHWARTZ, A. J. (1963), *A Monetary History of the United States 1867–1960* (Princeton: Princeton University Press).

MCCLOSKEY, D. N. (1978), 'The Achievements of the Cliometrics School', *Journal of Economic History,* 38, 13–28.

MITCHELL, W. C. (1903), *A History of the Greenbacks* (Chicago: Chicago University Press).

OLSON, M. (1982), *The Rise and Decline of Nations* (New Haven: Yale University Press).

ROWE, J. W. F. (1923), *Wages in the Coal Industry* (London: P. S. King and Son).

SARGENT, T. J. and WALLACE, N. (1984), 'Some Unpleasant Monetarist Arithmetic', in B. Griffiths and G. E. Wood (eds.), *Monetarism in Britain* (London: Macmillan), 15–41.

SOLOW, R. (1986), 'Economics: Is Something Missing?', in W. N. Parker (ed.), *Economic History and the Modern Economist* (Oxford: Blackwell), 21–9.

WEITZMAN, M. L. (1984), *The Share Economy* (Cambridge, Mass.: Harvard University Press).

WILLIAMSON, J. G. (1985), *Did British Capitalism Breed Inequality*? (London: Allen and Unwin).

WRIGHT, G. (1971), 'Econometric Studies of History', in M. D. Intrilligator (ed.), *Frontiers of Quantitative Economics* (Amsterdam: North Holland).

WRIGLEY, E. A. and SCHOFIELD, R. S. (1981), *The Population History of England, 1541–1871: A Reconstruction* (London: Arnold).

Oxford Economic Papers 39 (1987), 597–623

UNEMPLOYMENT IN INTERWAR BRITAIN: DOLE OR DOLDRUMS?

By BARRY EICHENGREEN

INTERWAR Britain remains one of the principal testing grounds for competing theories of macroeconomic fluctuations. To Keynesians, Britain's interwar experience provides incontrovertible evidence in support of their vision of pervasive involuntary unemployment due to insufficient aggregate demand. Indeed, British unemployment in the Great Depression was the crucible with which the Keynesian view of demand failure was forged. For nearly 50 years, this Keynesian interpretation has informed the literature on labor market dynamics in the 1930's, and interwar unemployment continues to be invoked as a classic illustration of the social costs of inadequate fiscal and monetary management.

Until recently, there was little dissent from the Keynesian interpretation of interwar Britain's unemployment experience.[1] New Classical theories of the labor market, according to which unemployment temporarily exceeds its natural rate when real wages are unexpectedly high, were applied almost exclusively to the United States.[2] It seemed impossible to reconcile New Classical theories of intertemporal substitution with recorded unemployment rates that between 1921 and 1938 scarcely dipped below double-digit levels. In a series of recent articles, Benjamin and Kochin (1979a, 1979b, 1982) have argued, however, that these sustained high levels of unemployment are explicable on equilibrium grounds once the existence and effects of Britain's exceptionally generous unemployment insurance system are taken into account. They argue that large numbers of workers voluntarily opted for unemployment because the generosity of the dole reduced the opportunity cost of idleness.[3] Although Keynesians have conceded that some

* This paper is part of a project on unemployment in interwar Britain, for which the Earhart and National Science Foundations provided financial support. I thank the Librarian of the London School of Economics and Political Science for access to materials from the New Survey of London Life and Labour. Many individuals have assisted in the course of this project; in connection with this paper I am grateful to Andy Warner for research assistance and to Nancy Williamson for programming advice.

[1] See for example Howson (1981), Kirby (1981) or Tomlinson (1981).

[2] The seminal article is of course Lucas and Rapping (1969). Subsequent contributions to the literature are surveyed in Altonji (1982).

[3] To measure the generosity of the unemployment insurance scheme, Benjamin and Kochin (1979a) construct an index of benefits for a hypothetical family of four and divide by Chapman's (1953) index of average wages. They find that the replacement rate rose from 24 percent in 1921 to 37 percent in 1922. After 1922 it never fell below 40 percent, approaching 60 percent by the end of the interwar period. They argue, moreover, that the average may understate incentives on the margin. Workers in low wage industries may have received benefits that exceeded their net earnings from employment (Benjamin and Kochin, 1979a, p. 525). The other dimension of the insurance system's generosity was the proportion of the unemployment spell over which benefits might be drawn. For much of the interwar period, there was little effective waiting period and little risk that benefits would be exhausted. Hence the typical spell of unemployment was almost totally covered.

small portion of interwar unemployment may be explicable on these grounds, few have sympathy for the notion that the insurance system contributed significantly to the magnitude of the problem.[4]

Two forms of evidence buttress the claim that the generous provision of unemployment benefits added significantly to unemployment. The first is based on a comparison of adult male unemployment rates with those for juveniles and women. Since juveniles were eligible for far less generous benefits and had lower recorded unemployment rates than adults, the contrasting experience of the two groups is taken as evidence that the dole served as a disincentive to work. For the years 1924–35, when overall unemployment averaged 14.6 percent, juvenile unemployment averaged only 5.0 percent. Mirroring changes in the level of benefits, the unemployment rate roughly doubled at age 18 and rose by a further 50 percent at age 21.

The problem with these official statistics is that they may reflect the incentive to register at an Employment Exchange, and hence the tendency to be recorded as unemployed, more than actual labor market status. Among unemployed juveniles, only those who had previously made the 20 to 30 weekly contributions needed to qualify for benefits had a strong incentive to lodge their employment books at an Employment Exchange.[5] Some of the ineligible may have registered nonetheless in order to make use of the Employment Exchange's placement service, but estimates of the share of unemployed juveniles who found jobs in this way suggest that any such tendency was slight.[6] Moreover, some of the eligible may have refused to register to avoid having to attend a Junior Instruction Centre, a burden not imposed upon adults.[7]

[4] Witness Collins (1982, pp. 371–72), "There is little dispute that the provision of an insurance scheme has some effect; any discussion is over whether the effect is significant."

[5] Moreover, juveniles were not eligible to draw benefits under supplementary insurance schemes designed for individuals who had exhausted their regular benefits. The 1914 Insurance Act required 10 contributions, the 1920 Act 12. The second Act of 1924 raised this number to 30 and mandated that they take place within the preceding two insurance years (which began each July). The basis for the insurance system's day-to-day operation was the worker's employment book, in which insurance contributions and benefits were recorded. When an insured person became unemployed, he retrieved this book from his employer and lodged it with the Employment Exchange. Upon obtaining work the individual transferred his book from the Exchange to his new employer, who added contribution stamps weekly so long as the individual remained in his employ.

[6] Roker and Scott (1926), p. 64, in their study of boys in Bermondsey, found that only five percent of the school leavers surveyed obtained jobs through the Exchange.

[7] Diepenhorst (1931), pp. 60–61. London Advisory Committee for Juvenile Employment (1931) provides information on the extent of this practice. Benjamin and Kochin dispute this claim, citing data from the 1931 Census. Census unemployment rates for boys and girls aged 16 to 17 were 7.6 and 6.8 percent, respectively, while the insurance figures for the corresponding months were 7.9 and 7.1 percent, respectively. They note and dismiss the objection that the Census figures list as unemployed only wholly unemployed individuals, excluding those on

A similar debate surrounds the interpretation of the unemployment statistics for women. Until 1931 women were eligible for benefits subject to the same restrictions as men. But as the insurance system's financial position deteriorated, the authorities grew increasingly concerned that recently married women, whose normal tendency was to withdraw from the labor force upon marriage, were continuing to draw benefits despite no intention of remaining in the labor market. In October 1931 Parliament adopted the Anomalies Regulations, requiring married women, as a prerequisite for drawing benefits, to have made 15 weekly contributions since marriage and eight over the preceding six months, or to demonstrate that they were both actively seeking work and had a reasonable chance of acquiring a position. The recorded unemployment rate among women fell sharply following the adoption of these regulations, which Benjamin and Kochin (1979a, p. 463) take as evidence of the impact on unemployment of increasing stringency in the provision of benefits.

The problem with this interpretation, as Collins (1982, p. 372) notes, is that the change in the recorded unemployment rate for women following adoption of the Anomalies Regulations may simply indicate that fewer women, finding themselves eligible for benefits, bothered to register as out of work. Following adoption of the regulations, they may have dropped off the register rather than dropping back into employment.[8]

Given these problems, Benjamin and Kochin's hypothesis stands or falls on their second form of evidence, which derives from regression analysis. Using annual observations for the period 1920–1938, they regress the Ministry of Labour's unemployment rate on the replacement rate (the ratio of benefits to wages) and a proxy for macroeconomic conditions. On the basis of a positive partial correlation between the replacement rate and the level of unemployment, and a coefficient which differs significantly from

[8] Benjamin and Kochin (1982, p. 416) ultimately concede that the evidence on married women "does not necessarily demonstrate that the system reduced employment."

Footnote 7 (*continued*)

temporary layoff. In contrast Garside (1979) questions whether the Census provides a representative picture of juvenile unemployment.

An additional problem is that factors other than the insurance system may have contributed to the divergent unemployment experiences of juveniles and other workers. Juveniles were concentrated to an unusual extent in industries characterized by lower than average unemployment rates. Benjamin and Kochin raise the possibility that the low observed unemployment rates in industries employing many juveniles simply reflect the insurance system's effects. In contrast, Heim (1984) argues for the importance of factors specific to the industries in which juveniles were concentrated and largely unrelated to the operation of the insurance system. She presents evidence that firms establishing plants in the new industries of the interwar years (motor cars, rayon, household appliances, etc.; see von Tunzelmann, 1982) preferred to employ workers other than prime-age males with previous experience in industry, such as juveniles and women. This argument suggests that the unemployment rate for juveniles may have been lower than that for prime-age males for reasons having to do with the structure of labor demand rather than the impact of the insurance system on labor supply.

zero at standard confidence levels, Benjamin and Kochin reject the null hypothesis that unemployment insurance was unrelated to unemployment.[9] They infer that interwar unemployment would have fallen by a third to a half had the replacement rate been held at 1913 levels.[10]

A variety of questions were raised subsequently about these statistical results. First, a number of critics have expressed reservations about the adequacy of the data.[11] For example, where the numerator of Benjamin and Kochin's replacement rate is statutory weekly benefits for a hypothetical family of four (husband and wife with two dependent children), the denominator is not wages for adult male household heads (for which no time series is available) but Chapman's (1953) index of average weekly wages of men, women and juveniles. Dividing benefits for the male head of a household of four by an index of wages earned on average by men, women and juveniles tends to overstate the replacement rate. Second, Cross (1982) among others has suggested that the correlation between unemployment and the replacement rate may reflect causation running from the former to the latter, insofar as the authorities responded to political or financial pressures by adjusting benefit levels. If so, it is invalid to interpret this unadjusted correlation as evidence of benefit-induced unemployment. Third, Omerod and Worswick (1982) among others have noted that Benjamin and Kochin's results are altered when the sample period is redefined. Such problems have led a number of critics to emphasize the general difficulty of convincingly testing models of individual choice using aggregate statistics. As Metcalf, Nickell and Floros (1982, p. 395) put the point, "[i]t seems unlikely, to say the least, that robust and accurate estimates of labor supply responses can be obtained satisfactorily from short aggregate time series."

Many readers will agree that empirical studies of interwar unemployment

[9] The basic regression (with t-statistics in parentheses) is:

$$U = 5.19 + 18.3(B/W) - 90.0(\log Q - \log Q^*)$$
$$(2.64)\quad (4.46)\qquad (-8.30)$$
$$R^2 = 0.84 \quad DW = 2.18$$

where U is the official unemployment rate in percentage points, from Department of Employment and Productivity (1971, p. 306); B is weekly benefits payable to an adult male with one adult and two child dependents, in shillings, from Burns (1941, p. 368); W is average weekly earnings of full-time employees, in shillings, from Chapman (1953, p. 27); Q is net national product at constant 1938 factor cost, from Feinstein (1972, Tables 15–16); and $\log Q - \log Q^*$ is deviations of the natural log of output from its trend value, as in Benjamin and Kochin (1979a, pp. 452–453).

To gauge the robustness of this result, Benjamin and Kochin replace the level of unemployment with its natural logarithm, omit the first years of the sample (which were marked by exceptionally large changes in the ratio of benefits to wages), add a time trend, use gross domestic product in place of gross national product, and construct the output variable in a variety of ways.

[10] These calculations are based on unweighted average of the figures in Benjamin and Kochin's (1979a) Table 1.

[11] See for example Hatton (1979) or Metcalf, Nickell and Floros (1982).

based on aggregate time series have reached the point of diminishing returns.[12] These aggregates are many steps removed from the individual level where decisions were made and the effects of the Great Depression felt. Progress in identifying the statistical significance and economic importance of the unemployment insurance system's effects ultimately requires more and better data, disaggregated ideally to the household level.

In this paper I report the results of research along these lines. The analysis makes use of a survey of working-class London conducted principally in the years 1929–31 at the London School of Economics. A sample drawn from some 27,000 case record cards completed in the course of this survey is used to analyze the relationship between insurance benefits and unemployment. In this paper attention is restricted to adult males.[13]

The results contrast with Benjamin and Kochin's view. After controlling for other characteristics of individuals, I find a generally positive but small association between unemployment incidence and the replacement rate. Although for adult males as a whole one cannot reject the null hypothesis of no association, one can use the standard errors of the coefficients to construct upper- and lower-bound estimates of the contribution to unemployment of increasingly generous insurance benefits. That contribution is small in the context of the Great Depression. Even more revealingly, disaggregating between household heads and other adult males identifies very different degrees of association between the probability of unemployment and the level of benefits. Among household heads, for whom the elasticity of labor supply should be relatively low, the effect of a change in the replacement rate on the probability of unemployment is essentially zero.[14] In contrast, among other adult males (referred to here as secondary workers), for whom the opportunity costs of leisure and search should rise relatively slowly and the elasticity of labor supply should be correspondingly high, the impact of a change in the replacement rate on the probability of unemployment is, in half the equations estimated, both statistically significant and economically important. But since such individuals comprise a small share of the adult male labor force, the overall impact of benefits on unemployment remains small. It would appear that Benjamin and Kochin's army of the voluntarily unemployed was essentially a squadron of secondary workers.

I. The data

The investigation providing the basis for the analysis in this paper was conducted at the London School of Economics starting in 1928. Known as

[12] A survey of recent contributions which is generally sympathetic to this conclusion is provided by Hatton (1985).

[13] One reason for treating the groups separately is that exit is likely to represent a more important option for juvenile and female workers, therefore requiring a more complicated multinominal regression analysis of labor market status. An analysis of juvenile unemployment which makes use of the New Survey can be found in Eichengreen (1987).

[14] Modern estimates of these elasticities are surveyed by Killingsworth (1983).

"The New Survey of London Life and Labour," it was designed as a sequel to Charles Booth's (1889–1903) study of the social and economic condition of the working class in Late Victorian London. Given the metropolitan region's subsequent expansion, it was decided to add to the region surveyed by Booth the minimal fringe of suburban areas needed to produce a unit whose economic character was roughly comparable to that of the County of London in 1891.[15] With the addition of Acton and Willesden to the west, Hornsey to the north, and Leyton, West Ham, East Ham and Barking to the east, the resulting unit encompassed 106,000 acres, nearly 150 percent the size of the County of London but still only a quarter of the region designated Greater London in the 1931 Census. It is from this region that the sample used in this paper is drawn.

The investigators' sampling strategy was to interview one household in 60.[16] They first identified the population to be sampled by assembling information on the residences of working-class households. Lists of inhabited buildings obtained from Borough Offices were checked for completeness and supplemented as necessary by addresses obtained from Parliamentary Registers and School Attendance Officers' Lists. Residences were then selected by street number, and investigators were engaged to arrange and conduct interviews.

Investigators were provided detailed instructions on completion of the survey record card.[17] Where more than one household resided at an address, information for each was recorded on a separate card. All persons who habitually slept in the tenement were to be listed, starting with the household head. Residents were classified as wage-earners or non-earners, with persons described as unemployed or temporarily incapacitated placed in the former category. Unemployed persons were defined as those wage-earners (as opposed to dependent or retired persons) who had not worked in the last week because of lack of employment or temporary ill health. Individuals who worked the entire previous week but reported themselves as unemployed for a part of the week in which the survey was taken were not classified as unemployed. There is no evidence that investigators used an independent test, such as time since a person's last job or amount of search activity in which he or she engaged, to reclassify individuals as out of the labor force. A special effort was made to obtain information on regular occupation, full-time hours, earnings, and social

[15] This description of survey procedures draws on Appendices I and III of Volume 3 of the New Survey.

[16] To insure that information was obtained for a minimum of 500 households in each borough, larger sampling factors were applied in smaller boroughs. In Bethnal Green, for example, the sampling factor was one in 20.

[17] Each investigator was provided detailed instructions on procedures to follow when difficulties arose. In the event that a building on an interviewer's list was uninhabited, instructions were provided on substituting an adjoining structure. Under no circumstances was it permissible to substitute a neighboring household if the residents at a specific address proved uncooperative. Instead the investigator was instructed to pay repeated visits.

insurance coverage. For the vast majority of individuals, this information was secured through interview, but where no response was obtained, estimated earnings were inputed at the central survey office on the basis of other information.[18]

For the employed, both a normal or full week's and the most recent week's earnings were recorded on the card. Where an individual received tips, bonuses and other variable earnings, their average amount and the amount received in the most recent week were recorded under separate headings. Earnings were entered gross of National Health and Unemployment Insurance deductions and of transportation costs to and from work, along with separate entries for these items. Income from other sources was entered with listings for income from lodgers, rooms sublet, property, pensions, poor relief, charitable sources, gifts from relatives and unemployment insurance benefits.

Compared to other social surveys of interwar Britain, the sample design and execution appear to have been closely supervised.[19] While problems of unrepresentativeness should not be underestimated, the random nature of the addresses selected, the strict instructions provided investigators, and the practice of paying repeated visits until information was secured together minimize the likelihood that responses were obtained disproportionately from households which were easily contacted. It seems likely, for example, that overrepresentation of unemployed persons, who were most likely to be home if the interviewer called during the day, was not a serious problem.

For this study, I drew a ten percent sample of case record cards from the New Survey collection. The survey record cards are filed by borough, and within each borough bear a sequential identification number. The sampling procedure was simply to select each tenth card.[20]

The strength of this data set is the exceptional detail it provides on the social and economic circumstances of individual households—detail unmatched by previous sources used to study the interwar labor market. Of particular relevance to the present investigation, the New Survey permits exploration of the possibility that the association of unemployment benefits with unemployment differed by individual circumstance. One can control, for example, for differences in family size and composition. It is not necessary to select one index of wages or unemployment benefits as representative of British workers. Thus, the data used here are free of the problems created when the replacement rate is constructed for a "repre-

[18] It is possible to distinguish entries obtained at interview from those added at the central office on the basis of notations provided on the cards. The analysis reported below was replicated omitting individuals for whom earnings were imputed, with no significant change in the results.

[19] For an illuminating comparison, see the criticisms of the social survey of York conducted by Seebohm Rowntree in 1950 in Atkinson, Maynard and Trinder (1983).

[20] The sampling procedure, the coding, and the characteristics of the data set are described in detail in Eichengreen and Freiwald (1985).

sentative" family or when a single index of wages is used to analyze the experience of both men and women.[21] They go some way toward meeting Garside's (1979) objection that any coefficient on the replacement rate based on aggregate time series estimation will be biased by the omission of family characteristics that were both correlated with the replacement rate and otherwise associated with unemployment.

The data utilized here, it must at the same time be acknowledged, are not without their limitations. The major departure from a random sample of the population of Greater London is the omission of all but the working class. The official cutoff for working-class wage earners was £250 in annual earnings.[22] Although the ostensible justification was to insure comparability with Booth's earlier survey of working-class London, this procedure may also have reflected an element of expediency since middle-class households were less inclined than their working-class counterparts to volunteer information. This type of censoring may exaggerate the influence of unemployment benefits over the aggregate unemployment rate, since the missing middle and upper classes were comprised relatively heavily of self-employed and non-manual workers with earnings in excess of £250 annually who were ineligible for benefits, and of recipients of relatively high wages and therefore relatively low replacement rates.

A second limitation of the data set is its exclusive focus on London.[23] On the side of labor supply, Greater London, compared to England and Wales, was inhabited by a smaller proportion of children under 15, of males aged 15 to 20, and of individuals of both sexes over the age of 65. Conversely, there was an unusually high proportion of both males and females in the prime earning years of 20 to 45. On the side of labour demand, London was distinguished by the relative unimportance of the staple trades and the dominance of distribution, personal service and light industry engaged in the manufacture of consumption goods.[24] Two correlates of this industry

[21] See for example Collins (1982), Cross (1982) and Metcalf, Nickell and Floros (1982).

[22] In practice, information on occupation was also used to determine working-class status. Thus, publicans, shopkeepers, shop managers and supervisors, police inspectors and those in professional and clerical occupations were ranked as middle class, while the self-employed, small employers, street traders, shop assistants and police sergeants were ranked as working class. Shopkeepers were demoted to working class if their incomes were definitely less than £250, while shop assistants and the self-employed were promoted to middle class if their incomes definitely exceeded this amount. In addition, Jewish households also appear to have been excluded, due presumably to difficulty in obtaining their cooperation. See Eichengreen and Freiwald (1985).

[23] A more detailed discussion of the London labor market and its characteristics can be found in Eichengreen (1986).

[24] The leading sources of employment were building, engineering and metal-working, furnishing and woodworking, clothing, boot and shoe manufacture, dock labor and domestic service, which together occupied almost half of London's working population. See Smith (1930), Vol. 2, Chapter 1.

mix were an exceptionally small scale of enterprise and a relatively low level of mechanization.[25]

While unemployment rates in London were highest in many of the same depressed industries with the highest unemployment rates elsewhere, unemployment there exhibited certain distinctive characteristics. An unusually large share of unemployment in London took the form of repeated short spells associated with the system of casual or short-period engagements in industries where the demand for labor was irregular.[26] Unemployment in London was further distinguished by its pronounced seasonal fluctuation. One source of seasonal unemployment was the unusually important building trade, in which the volume of employment was sensitive to seasonal variations in climate. Another was the traditional London "season," which affected employment in the jewelry, tailoring, dressmaking and catering trades.[27] Yet the amplitude of its fluctuation does not disguise the fact that unemployment in London persistently remained below the national average. According to the 1931 Census, unemployment in London County was 9.8 percent and in Greater London 8.5 percent at the same time it averaged 11.5 percent in England and Wales and 12.0 percent for the whole of Britain.[28] A similar differential is evident in the statistics generated by the unemployment insurance system.[29]

Clearly, it cannot be argued that the situation in London was representative of the nation as a whole. Its relatively buoyant labor market and the almost total absence of the depressed staple trades suggest that the prevalence of involuntary unemployment was probably less in London than in other parts of the country. For this reason also, estimates of the share of unemployment attributable to voluntary motives should probably be interpreted as upper bounds.

A third limitation of the data set is the absence of information on a number of variables of interest. While each person's age is provided, no information was solicited on years of schooling, labor force participation or service with the current firm. There is no alternative to employing age and

[25] The 1921 Census classified 42 percent of London enterprises as factories, defined as establishments with power-driven mechanical equipment, in contrast to 48 percent for Britain as a whole. There was a tendency over the course of the decade, in London as elsewhere, toward increased mechanization; thus by 1929 the percentage of factories in total establishments had risen by this definition to 54 percent in London and 58 percent in the nation. Smith (1930), Vol. 2, p. 6.

[26] On the short duration of unemployment spells in London, see Singer (1939). The classic instance of casual employment, as it was known, was the docks, where traditional practice was to engage workers for a day or even less at a time.

[27] The "season" had its origin in the summer Parliamentary session, although by the Edwardian period it had simply become customary for the wealthy to return to London from their country homes in February or March.

[28] 1931 Census, England and Wales, Industry Tables 2 and 6; Scotland, Industry Table 15.

[29] The Ministry of Labour unemployment rate for June 1931 was 11.2 percent in the Administrative County and City of London, in contrast with 21.1 percent for Great Britain as a whole. See Ministry of Labour (1934), p. 53.

that component of earnings which cannot be predicted on the basis of other available information as proxies for these characteristics. Similarly, although a space is provided on the survey record card for each wage-earner's occupation, for unknown reasons this variable was not systematically recorded. Occupation or industry of employment was provided only for a minority of the workers in the sample.[30]

Table 1 displays some basic characteristics of the sample of adult males, distinguishing household heads from others and the employed from the unemployed. The unemployment rate in the sample is 8.6 percent, which can be contrasted to the Ministry of Labour's average rate of 9.6 percent for adult males in the Administrative County of London over the period 1929–31 and the 1931 Census unemployment rate for males 21 and over in Greater London of 10.1 percent.[31] Unemployment among household heads is slightly lower than among other male adults. Many of those in the other-adult-males category are grown children residing at home; not surprisingly, their average age is little more than half that of the household heads. While there is a lesser incidence of illness among non-household heads, presumably reflecting their youth, there appears to be a greater incidence of sickness among the unemployed than the employed be they household heads or others.

Different types of income are associated with the incidence of unemployment in very different ways. For the sample as a whole and for both subgroups, the normal full week's earnings of the employed exceed those of the unemployed, signalling the possibility that individuals with high unemployment risks possess characteristics associated with relatively low productivities or which otherwise render them undesirable workers from the employer's point of view. Adjusting earnings for other measured characteristics of individuals should attenuate the relationship of earnings to unemployment risk, but since both unemployment risk and earnings are likely to be influenced also by unmeasured characteristics, some association may remain. Note in contrast that there is no consistent pattern of association between wealth, nonwage income and unemployment. While unemployed household heads have more nonwage income (defined as total family income from sources other than the wages and unemployment benefits of all household members) than do their employed counterparts, the opposite is true for other adult males.

[30] For an analysis of occupational structure in interwar London, see Eichengreen (1986).

[31] The Ministry of Labour figures, for males aged 18 and over, are calculated by dividing number of unemployed persons on the registers at the end of each quarter of the calendar year by the number of insured persons as of July of that year. See London County Council (various issues). The Census estimate, persons out of work as a percentage of the occupied, are taken from the Occupation tables, which do not separately list numbers of 18 to 20 year olds out of work.

TABLE 1
Characteristics of the Sample

Males Variable	All Adult Males			Household Heads			Other Adult		
	All	*Employed*	*Unemployed*	*All*	*Employed*	*Unemployed*	*All*	*Employed*	*Unemployed*
Age	38.2	38.2	38.0	42.6	42.6	43.1	23.4	23.4	23.1
Percent Ill	1.6	1.5	3.3	2.1	1.9	3.8	0.4	0.2	1.9
Percent Residing in Owned Home	2.7	2.9	1.0	3.5	3.7	1.3	0.2	0.2	0.0
Percent with Working Spouse	5.1	4.9	7.6	6.7	6.3	10.2	0.0	0.0	0.0
Percent with Unemployed Spouse	0.2	0.1	0.5	0.2	0.2	0.6	0.0	0.0	0.0
Full week's Earnings (shillings per week)	55.2	55.9	47.2	59.3	60.0	51.0	41.6	42.1	36.3
Nonwage Income (shillings per week)	4.3	4.1	6.6	4.0	3.7	7.2	5.1	5.2	4.7
Other Family Income* (shillings per week)	26.9	26.5	31.5	19.3	19.0	23.8	52.2	52.1	53.7
Percent Unemployed	8.6	0.0	100.0	8.3	0.0	100.0	9.6	0.0	100.0
Children in Household	1.3	1.3	1.2	1.3	1.3	1.2	1.3	1.3	1.3
Number	2,440	2,230	210	1,879	1,723	156	561	507	54

* Other than wages and benefits of current worker only.
Source: See text.

II. Earnings and unemployment benefits

Analyzing the association between unemployment incidence and replacement rates requires measures of both earnings and unemployment benefit entitlements for the wage-earners in the sample.

While two measures of wage income are available for the employed—full week's and last week's earnings—only the former exists for the unemployed. If the same measure is to be used for all wage-earners, there are two alternatives. One is to use data for the currently employed to estimate a relationship between last week's earnings and observable characteristics of individuals, and to use that relationship to impute the last week's wage to the unemployed. The other is to use the information provided on full week's earnings for both the employed and unemployed.

In fact, both procedures are likely to mislead. Using the ordinary-least-squares (OLS) relationship between current earnings and personal characteristics of the employed to impute current earnings to the unemployed will yield a biased estimate of the imputed wage due to selectivity bias, as documented in recent studies of women's labor supply decisions.[32] The problem is typically of the form:

$$W = \alpha X_\omega + \epsilon_\omega \tag{1}$$

$$E = \beta X_E + \gamma W + \epsilon_E \tag{2}$$

where W is a measure of earnings, E is employment status (hours of labor supplied in studies of labor force participation, employed versus unemployed in the present context), and X_ω and X_E are vectors of personal characteristics associated with these variables. α, β and γ are parameters. Since by assumption W affects E but not vice versa, so long as the disturbances to the two equations (ϵ_ω and ϵ_E) are uncorrelated, the system is recursive and OLS estimates of equation (1) could be used to impute wages to nonworking women or unemployed men for use in estimating equation (2). In practice, the two disturbances are certain to be correlated. This will be the case whenever there is a correlation between unmeasured factors that affect employment status and unmeasured factors that affect earnings. Recall, for example, that the New Survey provides no information on seniority. If layoffs followed an inverse seniority rule but earnings rose with seniority, the two disturbance terms would be positively correlated. Since individuals with unmeasured characteristics negatively associated with earnings will tend to be included among the sample of the unemployed while individuals with unmeasured characteristics positively associated with earnings will not, selectivity would cause OLS estimation of equation (1) on the subsample of the employed to yield biased predictions of earnings for the currently unemployed.

[32] Early recognition of this problem appears in Heckman (1976), and the subsequent literature is surveyed by Killingsworth (1983).

It seems preferable, therefore, to use full week's wages for both the employed and unemployed, despite the sacrifice of information on part-time employment. But an OLS regression of employment status on this measure of earnings and other characteristics still fails to yield an unbiased measure of the relationship. The source of the problem is the same as before: the employment-status equation is part of a system in which employment status is determined by earnings and other characteristics, while earnings are also determined by those characteristics. That system will only be recursive in the sense that earnings are exogenous to the employment status equation if the two disturbance terms are uncorrelated. For the reason just described (both earnings and employment status depend on similar unmeasured characteristics), this is unlikely to be the case.[33]

I adopt the simplest solution to estimating simultaneous systems, namely instrumental variables. The predicted value of *W* derived from an earnings function such as equation (1), estimated on the entire sample, is substituted for the observed value of *W* in equation (2). Assuming the exogeneity of variables on the right-hand side of equation (1), OLS estimates of the earnings function will suffice.

Table 2 reports the earnings functions for the entire sample and for subsamples of household heads and other adult males. Following Becker (1975) and Mincer (1974), earnings are regressed on age, age squared, and a variety of household characteristics. The results in Table 2 appear to be the first earnings functions estimated for interwar Britain. The equations explain a respectable share of the variation in the dependent variable (judged on the basis of other historical studies of earnings patterns), seem theoretically plausible and are generally consistent with historical estimates for other countries.[34] Further work might include comparisons across countries and across different historical periods. Here I focus on basic features of the results.

In all equations, earnings rise with age before peaking in the late forties. Individuals for whom there was an indication of ill health earn less than the healthy. Single household heads (bachelors and widowers) earn less than their married counterparts. Relationships similar to these have been found both for the nineteenth century United States and for many countries in the post-World War II era. The standard interpretation of the marital differential is that single individuals have fewer financial obligations and family responsibilities and therefore feel less need to expend the effort required to obtain high earnings. It has been suggested, in addition, that employers confer higher wages or preferential treatment regarding promotion upon married men on grounds of need. In addition, in Table 2 there is a negative association between the presence of many children and the level of earnings. A popular explanation for such a result is that men with large

[33] Again, see Killingsworth (1983), p. 152.
[34] See for example Eichengreen (1984).

TABLE 2
Earnings Functions for Adult Males (dependent variable is full week's earnings)

Variable	*All Adult Males* (*i*)	*Household Heads* (*ii*)	*Nonhousehold Heads* (*iii*)
Constant	−4.562	29.142	−42.116
	(3.38)	(5.27)	(8.05)
Age	3.085	1.617	5.018
	(0.17)	(0.25)	(0.50)
Age Squared	−0.033	−0.018	−0.612
	(0.002)	(0.03)	(0.01)
Unmarried	−7.269	−8.500	−16.583
	(1.58)	(1.60)	(17.88)
Illness	−15.403	−15.753	−18.902
	(3.09)	(3.17)	(12.59)
One child	0.910	0.945	−1.362
	(1.03)	(1.20)	(1.96)
Two Children	0.271	0.016	2.033
	(1.19)	(1.36)	(2.37)
Three or More Children	−2.442	−2.375	0.676
	(1.13)	(1.33)	(2.12)
Lives in Owned Home	4.146	4.673	−1.712
	(2.42)	(2.44)	(25.15)
Spouse Unemployed	−8.795	−9.001	
	(9.75)	(9.74)	—
Spouse Works	−4.799	−6.102	
	(1.81)	(1.84)	—
Nonwage Income	−0.052	−0.024	−0.052
	(0.013)	(0.02)	(0.03)
R^2	0.18	0.08	0.20
Number of Observations	2,440	1,879	561

Source: See text.
Note: Ordinary least squares regressions with White-corrected standard errors in parentheses.

numbers of children possess characteristics which render them relatively unattractive employees. Failure to control fertility may have been taken as a signal of unreliability. Alternatively, workers with dependents may have been less mobile than average and found it difficult to move to secure higher-paid employment. But such an argument should apply also to some degree to heads of households containing one or two children, compared to childless persons, and Table 2 contains no evidence to this effect. High wage workers appear less likely to be married to women who are also in the labor market, pointing to the labor-supply decisions of women as an important topic for research.

The predicted value of earnings derived from these equations provides the denominator of the replacement rate to be used in regression analysis.

An estimate of the numerator is available for the unemployed in the form of benefits reported to Survey investigators. For the employed, benefit entitlements must be imputed on the basis of other information. The amounts received by those qualifying for benefits can be imputed on the basis of age, sex and family composition.[35] For example, a male household head 21 years or older might be entitled to 17 shillings weekly for himself, to 7 shillings for a nonworking spouse, and to 2 shillings for each dependent child. This much is straightforward, given the available information. The problem is determining who qualified. In 1920 nearly all manual workers as well as non-manual workers earning less than £250 per annum were brought under the insurance system's compass. Exceptions included those engaged in agriculture, private domestic service and education and those employed by the public authorities, the railways and the utilities.[36] Exceptions were also made for share fishermen, wives or husbands employed by their spouses, unpaid employees and individuals engaged in work provided by the Poor Law authorities. Those individuals in the sample engaged in covered occupations can be identified by the presence of an insurance contribution. However, some contributors may still have been ruled ineligible for benefits for failure to make the required number of weekly contributions, to satisfy the waiting period requirement (having experienced three days' unemployment in six consecutive working days within the last ten weeks), to genuinely seek work or to pass the means test.[37] There is no way of determining on the basis of the survey record cards whether a currently employed person, upon losing work, might have been denied benefits for these reasons. This problem, which similarly plagues all recent attempts to estimate the effects of unemployment benefits, admits of no easy solution. However, by the end of the 1920s, the means test had been eliminated, while in 1930 the genuinely-seeking-work provision was weakened to provide for disqualification only if the claimant had without good cause refused suitable employment offered by the Employment Exchange or had failed to carry out written instructions provided by an Exchange official. By shifting the onus of proof onto the Ministry of Labour, the stringency of the

[35] Under the interwar system, benefits were a function of age, sex, and family size and composition but not of earnings when previously employed.

[36] Some of these groups, such as railroad employees, had their own out-of-work benefit schemes.

[37] For most of the interwar period, any three days of unemployment occurring in six consecutive working days were regarded as continuous unemployment, and a pair of such three-day periods, occurring within three to ten weeks of one another, could be combined to constitute a six-day period of continuous unemployment. As Burns (1941, pp. 102–105) notes, this provided workers and employers alike an incentive to arrange temporary layoffs so as to continuously satisfy the waiting period requirement. The liberal nature of this continuity rule was subject to considerable criticism. The Royal Commission on Unemployment Insurance recognized that the system tended to subsidize casual and intermittent laborers who customarily worked no more than one or two days per week, but who paid in contributions and therefore received benefits for days when not ordinarily employed. The Anomalies Regulations of 1931, which restricted benefits to days normally constituting a full work week, eliminated many such practices. See Industrial Relations Counselors (1934).

requirement was considerably reduced. Moreover, the problem of insufficient weekly contributions is likely to have applied primarily to 16 year olds who are excluded from the subsample analyzed here. Arguably, for most of the sample period, this inability to control for disqualification should not be a major problem.[38]

In addition, the value of benefits changed slightly in 1930. The changes were small in magnitude: of the adult males in the sample, they applied only to the benefits received by 18 year olds, which rose from 10 to 12 shillings per week, and to the supplement for adult dependents, which rose from seven to nine shillings. That the changes were small does not mean, however, that they were inconsequential. Unfortunately, few of the survey record cards list the date of interview. Therefore, two values for the benefit variable were imputed, one based on the lower entitlements prevailing before October 1930, the other based on the more generous values prevailing thereafter. These alternative values can then be compared with the actual benefits reported by the unemployed. For unemployed persons reporting benefits, one or the other imputed value matches the reported value almost without exception, which serves to reassure that the imputation is accurate. The distribution of reported values suggests that roughly half the interviews were conducted before the change in statute in 1930 and half thereafter. The major discrepancy between the imputation and the amounts listed as received by the unemployed is in cases where no benefits are reported. While the absence of benefits could reflect employment in an uncovered occupation or disqualification of a claim, the incidence of missing benefits is so great that it must predominantly reflect nonreporting. Therefore, imputed benefits are used in a place of actual benefits not just for the employed but also for the unemployed. Not only does this eliminate any timing problems that might be created by comparing benefits reported for one period with imputations based on statute for another, but insofar as disqualification occurred it will tend to exaggerate the benefits received by unemployed persons, again permitting the association between unemployment benefits and unemployment estimated below to be treated as an upper bound.

This measure of the replacement rate varies from 0.39 when pre-1930 benefits are imputed to 0.42 when post-1930 benefits are used instead. It contrasts with Benjamin and Kochin's series which ranges from 0.50 to 0.54 between 1929 and 1931. The difference is largely attributable to the fact that no benefits have been imputed here to employed individuals not covered by the system.

[38] Between 1922 and 1931, the disqualification rate fluctuated between 10 and 20 percent, figures considerably inflated by the fact that the same individuals applied repeatedly for benefits following disqualification. Moreover, many of those failing the means test found their benefits reduced but not eliminated.

III. Replacement rates and unemployment

Table 3 displays the bivariate relationship between unemployment and the replacement rate, distinguishing household heads from other adult males. The two variants of the constructed replacement rate use pre-1930 and post-1930 statutory benefits. Here the reported full week's wage, not the fitted value, is used in the denominator. Grouping wage-earners by income category has much the same effect as using the predicted wage in the analysis of individual cases, in that it tends to filter out (in this case by averaging together) the impact on earnings and replacement rates of unmeasured attributes of individuals. The advantage of this approach, compared to that described in Section II, is that the results do not hinge on the adequacy of a particular earnings function. The disadvantage is that it is impossible to control for other observable aspects of the individual's economic position likely to be correlated with unemployment risk.

These results provide a first indication that the association between unemployment benefits and unemployment differed significantly between primary and secondary workers. Among household heads, there is no obvious correlation. In contrast, among other adult males unemployment incidence tends to increase as the replacement rate rises, from 7.8 or 9.0 percent in the lowest replacement rate category to 13.0 or 13.3 percent in the highest.[39] However, this increase is smoother when pre-1930 rather than post-1930 replacement rates are used, and there appear to be large numbers of unemployed individuals ineligible for benefits, which casts doubt on the robustness of the unemployment-replacement rate relationship even for nonhousehold heads.

As noted, these tabulations do not control for other measured characteristics of individuals likely to be associated with the incidence of unemployment. Table 4 therefore reports probit regressions relating unemployment to a set of observed characteristics including the replacement rate, now calculated as the ratio of the imputed unemployment benefit to the predicted wage. Except for benefits and wages, the variables considered are the same as in Eichengreen (1986), where patterns of unemployment in interwar and postwar London were compared. Following Nickell (1980), a vector of age variables is included to capture any relationship between human capital endowments and unemployment incidence. Following Mincer and Polacheck (1974), a vector of family variables is included to capture determinants of the reservation wage.

The results for household heads tell a consistent story. Unemployment by age traces out a u-shaped pattern. Unemployment risk is lowest for workers in their prime earning years, between the ages of 35 and 44. It then rises with movement away from this age group (in both directions). However, it peaks not among the very oldest workers but among those aged 55–59.

[39] When all individuals with replacement rates above 0.6 are grouped together, there is no rise in the unemployment rate compared to the 0.2 to 0.4 and 0.4 to 0.6 brackets.

TABLE 3
Percentage Unemployed and Replacement Rates

I. Household Heads					
	Pre-1930 Replacement Rates (RR)				
	$0 \leq RR < 0.2$	$0.2 \leq RR < 0.4$	$0.4 \leq RR < 0.6$	$0.6 \leq RR < 0.8$	$0.8 \leq RR$
Unemployment Rate	15.8	6.7	7.9	13.6	2.4
	Post-1930 Replacement Rates				
	$0 \leq RR < 0.2$	$0.2 \leq RR < 0.4$	$0.4 \leq RR < 0.6$	$0.6 \leq RR < 0.8$	$0.8 \leq RR$
Unemployment Rate	15.8	7.5	7.4	9.4	4.7
II. Nonhousehold Heads					
	Pre-1930 Replacement Rates (RR)				
	$0 \leq RR < 0.2$	$0.2 \leq RR < 0.4$	$0.4 \leq RR < 0.6$	$0.6 \leq RR < 0.8$	$0.8 \leq RR$
Unemployment Rate	23.3	7.8	9.2	9.5	13.3
	Post-1930 Replacement Rates				
	$0 \leq RR < 0.2$	$0.2 \leq RR < 0.4$	$0.4 \leq RR < 0.6$	$0.6 \leq RR < 0.8$	$0.8 \leq RR$
Unemployment Rate	22.0	9.0	8.2	5.4	13.0

Source: See text.

TABLE 4
Determinants of Unemployment (dependent variable is employment status)

Variable	*All Adult Males* Pre-1930	*All Adult Males* Post-1930	*Household Heads* Pre-1930	*Household Heads* Post-1930	*Nonhousehold Heads* Pre-1930	*Nonhousehold Heads* Post-1930
Constant	−1.864	−1.882	−1.786	−1.904	−5.734	−4.624
	(0.13)	(0.14)	(0.15)	(0.16)	(20.59)	(20.55)
Replacement Rate	1.426	1.411	−0.025	1.180	4.099	0.456
	(0.84)	(0.97)	(1.17)	(1.12)	(2.26)	(2.74)
Age 18–24	0.229	0.197	0.521	0.500	2.631	2.989
	(0.13)	(0.13)	(0.20)	(0.20)	(20.58)	(20.53)
Age 25–29	0.319	0.329	0.305	0.300	2.958	3.182
	(0.14)	(0.14)	(0.16)	(0.16)	(20.58)	(20.54)
Age 30–34	0.221	0.227	0.148	0.151	3.333	3.398
	(0.14)	(0.14)	(0.15)	(0.15)	(20.58)	(20.53)
Age 45–54	0.109	0.102	0.126	0.127	−7.708	−7.531
	(0.13)	(0.13)	(0.13)	(0.13)	(37.83)	(37.79)
Age 55–59	0.417	0.399	0.431	0.425	−1.141	−0.749
	(0.17)	(0.17)	(0.17)	(0.18)	(125.2)	(124.1)
Age ≥ 60	0.362	0.353	0.327	0.378	−1.186	−0.254
	(0.16)	(0.16)	(0.17)	(0.17)	(49.47)	(60.33)
One Child	0.143	0.130	0.205	0.177	—	—
	(0.10)	(0.10)	(0.12)	(0.12)		
Two children	0.047	0.138	0.185	0.251	—	—
	(0.11)	(0.13)	(0.14)	(0.15)		
Three or More Children	0.125	0.138	0.094	0.156	—	—
	(0.11)	(0.12)	(0.14)	(0.15)		
Sickness	0.360	0.341	0.289	0.242	−0.314	−1.133
	(0.25)	(0.25)	(0.26)	(0.27)	(1.26)	(1.70)
Unmarried	0.365	0.387	0.383	0.380	7.83	8.156
	(0.13)	(0.13)	(0.14)	(0.14)	(33.90)	(33.86)
Residual Wage	−0.009	−0.009	−0.009	−0.009	−0.131	−0.012
	(0.002)	(0.002)	(0.002)	(0.002)	(0.004)	(0.004)
Lives in Owned Home	−0.498	−0.510	−0.491	−0.497	—	—
	(0.32)	(0.32)	(0.32)	(0.32)		
Non-wage Income	0.002	0.002	0.003	0.003	0.003	0.015
	(0.001)	(0.001)	(0.002)	(0.002)	(0.003)	(0.003)
Log Likelihood	−687.6	−688.0	−512.6	−512.0	−164.1	−164.4
Conditional Mean Adjustment Factor	0.147	0.147	0.139	0.141	0.104	0.108
Number of Observations	2,440	2,440	1,879	1,879	561	561

Source: See text.

Note: Probit estimates with standard errors in parentheses. Dichotomous dependent variable takes on a value of unity for the unemployed. Columns labelled "Pre-1930" use the imputed replacement rate for the years up through 1930; those labelled "Post-1930" use replacement rates based on revised statutes.

Contemporary investigators and subsequent observers also noted that those aged over 45 and under 25 tended to be overrepresented in the pool of the unemployed.[40] The popular explanations for the rising incidence of unemployment among older workers emphasize pay relativities across workers and over time.[41] While productivity may eventually begin to decline with age, firms nonetheless find it difficult to pay workers with more seniority less than their more junior counterparts, or to reward workers with real wage cuts for their continued service with the firm. Thus, when an occasion arises to render workers redundant, the firm selects older employees whose productivities are lowest relative to their wages. Alternatively, younger and older workers may face similar risks of termination, but older workers may have a lower probability of finding a new position. Constantine (1980) has argued that lower reemployment probabilities provide much of the explanation for rising unemployment incidence among older men in interwar Britain, while Ministry of Labour (1930) evidence on unemployment incidence suggests that this factor provides at least part of the explanation for the differential. The apparent decline in unemployment among those sixty and older probably reflects the tendency of the elderly to withdraw from the labor force upon losing work.

To explain unemployment among males aged 18 to 24, contemporaries cited the problem of dead-end jobs. The structure of pay and jobs is said to have dictated that wages rise faster than warranted by productivity alone during a worker's late teens and early 20's. Apprenticeship was one source of pay structure. So long as a young worker was apprenticed, his earnings and the cost of his labor remained low. But upon completing apprenticeship at age 18 or 21, union contracts or labor-market conventions stipulated that his earnings increase discretely.[42] The wages of many younger workers not involved in apprenticeship also increased at ages 18 and 21, presumably to maintain pay relativities between skilled and unskilled workers. High rates of unemployment among males aged 25 to 29 were sometimes viewed as a result of the inability of workers in their early 20's to reestablish themselves in the labor market after loss of their dead-end jobs.[43] Some Ministry of Labour studies in the 1920s attributed the high risk of unemployment in this age bracket to the fact that the labor force participation of these workers had been interrupted or delayed by service in the armed forces.

[40] A study of claimants to benefit aged 16 to 64 on the registers of Employment Exchanges as of 16 September 1929 showed that more than 9 percent of men in the 55 to 59 year old age bracket and 12 percent of those in the 60 to 64 year old bracket claiming benefit had been continuously unemployed for at least 52 weeks, compared with 5.5 percent of men of all ages. In contrast, only 1.8 percent of those in the 18 to 24 year old age bracket had been unemployed for so long a time. See Ministry of Labour (1930).

[41] See discussions provided by Morley (1922) and Riddle (1984).

[42] It is difficult to obtain quantitative information on the extent of such practices. A graphic portrayal of their impact is Greenwood (1933).

[43] Constantine (1980), p. 24. See also Gilson (1931).

Single adult males appear to have faced a higher risk of unemployment than otherwise comparable married workers, as Morley (1922) also concludes. One of the more surprising relationships links the number of children in the household to the unemployment risk of its head. Compared to childless households, there is a higher incidence of unemployment among the heads of households containing one or two children. While evidence for households with three or more children points in the same direction, it is impossible to reject the hypothesis that unemployment incidence among the heads of such households is no different than for heads of childless households.[44] The popular explanations for these findings are those invoked in Section II's discussion of earnings-family size relationships: that failure to control fertility is taken by employers as a signal of unreliability or, alternatively, that wage-earners with dependents are less mobile than average and therefore find it difficult to relocate to secure employment. Since the second of these interpretations may hinge more on the presence of children than their numbers, it is tempting to conclude that the immobility explanation was more important during the interwar years.

Table 4 suggests also that adult male heads of households receiving relatively high levels of income from sources other than earnings or unemployment benefits ran the greatest risk of unemployment. Not surprisingly, those who owned their homes rather than renting, a status which can be taken to measure permanent income, financial reserves and therefore past employment stability, had an unusually low current risk of unemployment.[45]

The critical results concern the coefficients on earnings and unemployment benefits. Table 4 summarizes the results when reported full week's earnings are partitioned into a predicted component, based on the earnings functions in Table 2, and a residual component associated with the unmeasured characteristics of individuals. To construct the replacement rate, the predicted component is entered as a ratio to the imputed unemployment benefit. The residual component of earnings enters with a negative sign that is uniformly significant at the 99 percent confidence level. Consistent with the assumptions motivating the econometrics, it appears that unmeasured characteristics of individuals associated with unusually high earnings were also associated with unusually low risk of unemployment. The results for the coefficient on the replacement rate are less robust. For the sample as a whole, the partial correlation between unemployment and the replacement rate is positive, as search theory would lead one to expect, but it is impossible to reject that the coefficient is zero at standard confidence

[44] Further disaggregation did not turn up a well-defined association between the probability of unemployment and number of additional children.

[45] This finding is replicated by Nickell (1980) for postwar Britain and interpreted in terms of socioeconomic group.

levels.[46] On this basis it does not appear that the generosity of the dole had much impact on the overall unemployment rate. Considering the subset of household heads can eliminate even the positive coefficient. As in Table 3, among households heads there is no clear association between the generosity of the dole and the incidence of unemployment.

The results are different for other men.[47] Two points emerge. First, the level of statistical significance depends on the variant of the imputed unemployment benefit used, again highlighting the sensitivity of estimates of the extent of benefit-induced unemployment to methodological assumptions. Nonetheless, unemployment incidence among other men is positively and, in some instances, significantly related (at the 90 percent level) to the magnitude of the replacement rate.[48] Compared to the equations for household heads, the impact of a change in the replacement rate on the probability of unemployment can be large. It would appear that secondary workers were more responsive than household heads to the incentives provided by increasingly generous unemployment benefits. Many such men were second or third wage earners in households containing several members engaged in market work. It is plausible that the opportunity cost of idleness was lower on the margin for secondary workers whose families did not depend so heavily on their individual paychecks. In other words, they could afford to be responsive to the incentives to engage in additional search provided by an increasingly generous level of unemployment benefits.

What do these results imply for the contribution of unemployment benefits to the level of unemployment? Answering this question requires one to assume a counterfactual replacement rate. Benjamin and Kochin (1979) attempt to estimate the level of unemployment that would have prevailed between the wars had unemployment benefits remained at the lower levels of 1913. Using the methods described above, they estimate the

[46] Since the residual component of earnings has a stronger effect than the replacement rate, and since the two influences work in the opposite directions, when actual rather than predicted earnings is used as the denominator of the replacement rate, the effect of the residual component dominates, reversing the sign of the replacement rate, whose negative coefficient is statistically significant at standard confidence levels. This confirms the importance of removing that component of earnings associated with unmeasured characteristics before estimating the impact of the replacement rate on unemployment.

[47] Since most of these individuals are adult children living in their parents' households and since nearly all of them are single, including all the family variables, notably the number of children, gave rise to extremely large standard errors on the latter and problems of multicolinearity. Hence the estimated equations reported here drop those family variables. Alternative equations, not reported here, including the entire vector of family variables yielded virtually identical coefficients on the variables of interest.

[48] Compared to pre-1930 benefits, post-1930 benefits were relatively generous for 18 year olds, who had low unemployment rates compared to older workers. By raising the replacement rates of a category of low-unemployment-rate workers, this minor change in imputation considerably reduces the unemployment rate-replacement rate correlation. The difference caused by using post-1930 benefits in place of pre-1930 benefits highlights the difficulty of making any definitive statement about the effect of unemployment benefits.

TABLE 5
Actual and Counterfactual Unemployment Rates Assuming 1913 *Replacement Rates*

	Household Heads	*Nonhousehold Heads*	*Adult Males*
Actual	8.3	9.6	8.6
Counterfactual			
Best Estimates			
Variant I	8.3	4.5	7.4
Variant II	6.1	9.0	6.8
Lower Bounds			
Variant I	4.0	0.0	3.1
Variant II	2.0	1.9	2.0
Upper Bounds			
Variant I	12.6	10.1	12.0
Variant II	9.5	16.1	11.0

Source: See text.

1913 replacement rate for the head of a representative household of four as 0.27, or little more than half of 1929–31 levels.

In an attempt to construct estimates comparable to theirs, the counterfactual unemployment rates reported in Table 5 are calculated on the assumption that the replacement rate for household heads was reduced to 0.27. Benjamin and Kochin offer no estimate of the 1913 replacement rate for single males upon which counterfactual calculations can be based. From statute it is clear by how much benefits would have fallen but, in the absence of separate wage rates for secondary workers, estimates of the replacement rate remain difficult to obtain. Since the replacement rate for other adult males implied by the New Sample survey is 90 percent that for household heads, I multiply Benjamin and Kochin's family-of-four replacement rate of 0.27 by 0.9 to obtain 0.24, which is used as the 1913 benchmark for other adult males in the calculations that follow. Other counterfactual replacement rates would yield other counterfactual unemployment rates but, for reasons that will be evident momentarily, would not alter the thrust of the results.

Table 5 reports counterfactual unemployment rates on the assumption that replacement rates had been held at 1913 levels. The best estimates are those derived using the point estimates of the coefficient on the replacement rate in Table 4. These show that the unemployment rate among household heads is changed little if at all but that the unemployment rate for other adult males can be quite considerably reduced. Since household heads comprise 77 percent of the sample of adult males, the overall adult male unemployment rate falls only moderately, from 8.6 to 7.4 percent in the case of variant I replacement rates and to 6.8 percent in the case of variant

II. While this change is non-negligible, its magnitude and its concentration among secondary workers convey a different impression than Benjamin and Kochin's results. By this measure, no more than a fifth, rather than Benjamin and Kochin's third to a half, of interwar unemployment was attributable to the generosity of the insurance scheme. And household heads, upon whose earnings so many wives and children depended for subsistence, show relatively little responsiveness to variations in the replacement rate.[49]

Basing conterfactuals on the point estimates of the coefficients on the replacement rate alone conveys a false sense of precision. One of the advantages of basing calculations on results like those in Table 4 is precisely that they facilitate sensitivity analysis. Increasing and decreasing these coefficients by two standard errors yields the lower and upper-bound estimates reported in Table 5. The first point to note is the extreme sensitivity of the calculations to plausible changes in parameters. It is appropriate, therefore, to treat the evidence here on the relationship of benefits to the unemployment rate with considerable caution. But it is important to note also that this exercise in sensitivity analysis does not overturn the conclusion that the largest changes in unemployment rates are those experienced by non-household heads.

The reader who has patiently followed the tale to this conclusion will be painfully aware of the slips betwixt cup and lip. As already noted the social survey from which the data are drawn are subject to limitations. The calculations made with the resulting data set, in particular the imputation of unemployment benefit entitlements, have limitations as well. Despite these caveats, however, the microeconomic data upon which the analysis in this paper is based bring the investigator infinitely closer to the level at which economic decisions affecting employment status were made. Ultimately, they yield a coherent picture of the magnitude and incidence of benefit-induced unemployment—one which is broadly consistent with the impressions of many contemporary observers. Finally, they suggest an agenda for research on the economic response to the Great Depression of other secondary workers such as women and juveniles—research that might be based on the kind of survey data utilized here.

IV. Conclusion

The findings of this paper will not please adherents to extreme views, for they indicate neither that interwar unemployment was largely a voluntary phenomenon nor that it was entirely involuntary. They suggest that those workers who could best afford to respond to the incentives of the dole did so and that others did not. Other recent investigators have cited statements by

[49] The Pilgrim Trust calculated that 250,000 long-term unemployed were responsible for 170,000 wives and 270,000 young children. Mitchell (1985), p. 105.

contemporary observers such as Edwin Cannan who believed that interwar unemployment was heavily voluntary, and by modern economists who refuse to admit that the argument has any validity. In light of this paper's results, it is fitting that I cite the opinion of another contemporary, known for his eclecticism and empirical judgment, who held to the intermediate view that emerges from this paper: that while both the dole and other factors contributed to interwar interwar unemployment, the influence of the latter predominated. To Cannan he responded:

> "The second cause [for unemployment Professor Cannan] gave was that with better unemployment pay there is not quite the same pressure that there used to be on the individual unemployed man to secure employment . . . . I do not believe that it is possible to make a plausible case for supposing that when unemployment was 12 percent, such factors as were mentioned by Professor Cannan were predominant ones . . . . When we have got unemployment down to 4 or 5 percent, then there are other causes which also have to be tackled by other methods, but, if you have a financial factor responsible for the difference (say) between 5 and 12 percent, then it is an enormous cause of immense poverty, immense suffering, and it is a matter which is well worth bending our energies to get rid of."[50]

University of California, Berkeley.

REFERENCES

ALTONJI, J. (1982), "The Intertemporal Substitution Model of Labor Market Fluctuations: An Empirical Analysis," *Review of Economic Studies* XLIX, pp. 785–824.

ATKINSON, A. B., MAYNARD, A. K. and TRINDER, C. G. (1983), *Parents and Children: Income in Two Generations,* London: Heinemann Educational Books.

BECKER, G. (1975), *Human Capital,* Chicago: University of Chicago Press.

BENJAMIN, D. and KOCHIN, L. (1978a), "Searching for an Explanation for Unemployment in Interwar Britain," *Journal of Political Economy* 7, pp. 441–478.

—— (1979b), "What Went Right with Juvenile Unemployment Policy Between the Wars: A Comment," *Economic History Review* new ser. 32, pp. 523–528.

—— (1982), "Unemployment and Unemployment Benefits in 20th Century Britain: A Reply to our Critics," *Journal of Political Economy* 90, pp. 410–436.

BOOTH, C. (1889–1903), *Life and Labour of the People of London,* 17 vols., New York: AMS Press (reprint).

BURNS, E. (1941), *British Unemployment Programs, 1920-38,* Washington, D.C.: Social Science Research Council.

CHAPMAN, A. L. (1953), *Wages and Salaries in the United Kingdom, 1920-1938,* Cambridge: Cambridge University Press.

COLLINS, M. (1982), "Unemployment in Interwar Britain: Still Searching for an Explanation," *Journal of Political Economy* 90, pp. 369–379.

CONSTANTINE, S. (1980), *Unemployment in Britain Between the Wars,* London: Longmans.

CROSS, R. (1982), "How Much Voluntary Unemployment in Interwar Britain?" *Journal of Political Economy* 90, pp. 380–385.

DEPARTMENT OF EMPLOYMENT AND PRODUCTIVITY (1971), *British Labour Statistics: Historical Abstract 1886–1968,* London: HMSO.

[50] Keynes (1924), reprinted in Keynes (1981), pp. 182–84.

DIEPENHORST, I. N. T. (1931), *Juvenile Unemployment and How to Deal With It,* Amsterdam: Drukkerij Holland.

EICHENGREEN, B. (1984), "Experience and the Male–Female Earnings Gap in the 1890s," *Journal of Economic History* XLIV, pp. 822–834.

—— (1986), "Unemployment in Interwar London: A Microeconomic Perspective," *Journal of Interdisciplinary History* 17, pp. 335–338.

—— (1987), "Juvenile Unemployment in 20th Century Britain: The Emergence of a Problem," *Social Research* 54, pp. 273–301.

EICHENGREEN, B. and FREIWALD, S. (1985), "From Survey to Sample: Labor Market Data for Interwar Britain," *Historical Methods* 18, pp. 125–136.

FEINSTEIN, C. (1972), *National Income, Expenditure and Output of the United Kingdom, 1855-1965,* Cambridge: Cambridge University Press.

GARSIDE, W. R. (1979), "Juvenile Unemployment Between the Wars: A Rejoinder," *Economic History Review* new ser. 32, pp. 529–532.

GILSON, M. B. (1931), *Unemployment Insurance in Great Britain,* New York: Industrial Relations Counselors.

GREENWOOD, W. (1933), *Love on the Dole,* London: J. Cape.

HATTON, T. J. (1979), "Unemployment in Interwar Britain: A Role for the Dole?" Unpublished manuscript: University of Essex.

—— (1986), "The Analysis of Unemployment in Interwar Britain: A Survey of Research," *Journal of Economic Studies* (forthcoming).

HECKMAN, J. (1976), "The Common Structure of Statistical Models of Truncation, Sample Selection, and Limited Dependent Variables and a Simple Estimator for Such Models, *Annals of Economic and Social Measurement* 5, pp. 475–492.

HEIM, C. (1984), "Structural Transformation, the Demand for New Labor and Uneven Development in Advanced Economies: The Case of Interwar Britain," *Journal of Economic History* XLIV, pp. 485–495.

HOWSON, S. (1981), "Slump and Unemployment," in R. Floud and D. McCloskey, eds., *The Economic History of Britain Since 1700,* Cambridge: Cambridge University Press, Vol. II, pp. 265–285.

INDUSTRIAL RELATIONS COUNSELORS, INC. (1934), *An Historical Basis for Unemployment Insurance,* Minneapolis: University of Minnesota Press.

KEYNES, J. M. (1924), "Mr. J. M. Keynes's Speech," from International Labour Office, *Studies and Reports,* Series C (Unemployment), No. 9, Geneva: ILO, reprinted in *The Collected Writings of John Maynard Keynes,* Vol. 19, *Activities, 1922–29*, ed. Donald Moggridge, Cambridge: Cambridge University Press, 1981.

KILLINGSWORTH, M. (1983), *Labor Supply,* Cambridge: Cambridge University Press.

LONDON ADVISORY COMMITTEE FOR JUVENILE EMPLOYMENT (1930), *Sixth Annual Report, 1929*, London: HMSO.

LONDON COUNTY COUNCIL (1930–32), *London Statistics,* London: P. S. King.

LUCAS, R. and RAPPING, L. A. (1969), "Real Wages, Employment and Inflation," *Journal of Political Economy* 70, pp. 721–754.

METCALF, D. NICKELL, S. and FLOROS, N. (1982), "Still Searching for an Explanation of Unemployment in Interwar Britain," *Journal of Political Economy* 90, pp. 386–399.

MINCER, J. (1974), *Schooling, Experience and Earnings,* New York: National Bureau of Economic Research.

MINCER, J. and POLACHECK, S. (1974), "Family Investments in Human Capital: Earnings of Women," in T. W. Schultz, Ed., *Economics of the Family,* New York: Columbia University Press, pp. 397–429.

MINISTRY OF LABOUR (1930), "Analysis of the Unemployment Record of Claimants Aged 18 to 64 on the Register of Employment Exchanges on 18 March 1929 and 16 September 1929," *Ministry of Labour Gazette* 38, pp. 6–7.

—— (1934), *Twenty-First Abstract of Labour Statistics of the United Kingdom,* London: HMSO.

MITCHELL, M. (1985), "The Effects of Unemployment on the Social Condition of Women and Children in the 1930s," *History Workshop* 19, pp. 105–127.

MORLEY, F. (1922), "The Incidence of Unemployment by Age and Sex," *Economic Journal* 32, pp. 477–488.

NICKELL, S. J. (1980), "A Picture of Male Unemployment in Britain," *Economic Journal* 90, pp. 776–794.

OMEROD, P. A. and WORSWICK, G. D. N. (1982), "Unemployment in Interwar Britain," *Journal of Political Economy* 90, pp. 400–409.

RIDDLE, S. M. (1984), "Age, Obsolescence and Unemployment: Older Men in the British Industrial System, 1920–1939," unpublished.

ROKER, P. and SCOTT, H. C. (1926), "Juvenile Unemployment in West Ham," *Economica* VI, pp. 58–77.

SINGER, H. W. (1939), *Unemployment and the Unemployed,* London: P. S. King.

SMITH, H. L. (1930–34), *New Survey of London Life and Labour,* London: P. S. King.

TOMLINSON, J. (1981), *Problems of British Economic Policy 1870–1945,* London: Methuen.

VON TUNZELMANN, N. (1982), "Britain's 'New Industries' Between the Wars: A New 'Development Block'?" in Charles Kindleberger and Guido di Tella, eds., *Economics in the Long View: Essays in Honor of W. W. Rostow,* London: Macmillan, vol. 3, pp. 1–49.

Oxford Economic Papers 39 (1987), 624–640

INTERCOUNTY LABOUR MOBILITY DURING THE INDUSTRIAL REVOLUTION: EVIDENCE FROM AUSTRALIAN TRANSPORTATION RECORDS*

By STEPHEN NICHOLAS *and* PETER R. SHERGOLD

THE BRITISH industrial revolution has attracted much attention from economic historians not only because it was first, but also because of the lessons successful industrialisation offered follower nations. The British model suggested that successful industrialisation required agriculture to yield abundant labour and natural resources for employment and production to the growing industrial sector. Yet it is surprising, and disturbing, how little we know about the extent and nature of labour mobility during the most rapid years of British industrialisation (see Tranter, 1981 for a recent survey). The age-sex profile, human capital endowments (skill and literacy), marital status, occupations and urban-rural location of migrants are unknown. Indeed, it was not until 1851 that the census recorded data on the counties of birth of persons residing in each English county, so that even the source and destination counties of industrial revolution migrants are lost to history.

However, geographic migration has been accorded a major place in the industrialisation process. Using aggregate population data, Deane and Cole (1975, p. 119) found that many of the industrial centres were heavily dependent on migration from those surrounding counties which had experienced high natural increases in population. Cheshire and Lancashire, for example, relied on migration for almost 30 per cent of the estimated increases in population between 1801 and 1831.[1] Recently, Williamson (1985a, 1985b) has confirmed that British rural-urban migration rates were large by the standard of contemporary Third World industrial revolutions. Using the 1851 census to reconstruct city immigration flows, Williamson (1985a) found that migration was as important as natural increase in accounting for urban population growth before 1850. Unfortunately what we know of migration, and the migrant, rests either on data from the post-1851 censuses extrapolated backwards to the industrialisation period or is derived from small local studies, many of which deal with the pre-industrial period. For example, local data on migration to Preston in 1851 allowed Anderson (1974) to test wave (two-step) migration—in which the

* Kris Corcoran provided research assistance. Ronger Tonkin, Glenn Withers, Bruce Chapman and J. J. Pincus provided helpful comments. All remaining errors are the authors'.

[1] Deane and Cole's (1975, pp. 108–9) estimates are upper bounds since they implicitly assume that all urban migrants died on arrival and had no children.

same individual moved to urban areas in progressive steps—and to measure distance travelled. He found that wave migration explained little of Preston's population growth, concluding that most migrants moved short distances of less than 30 miles. For an earlier period, Tranter (1967) identified high rates of mobility for the Bedfordshire parish of Cardington while confirming Anderson's finding that most movement was short distance. Drawing on marriage, tax and baptism records for the 17th and early 18th centuries, Laslett (1965), Buckatzasch (1951), Ooserveen (1974), Cornwall (1967) and Chambers (1972) discovered that high levels of mobility over short distances was also a feature of these earlier periods. But the evidence remains fragmentary and ambiguous. Using ecclesiastical court depositions, Cressey (1970) found 69 per cent of all migrants into Stepney and Whitechapel moved more than 50 miles between 1580 and 1640. The small sample sizes, their questionable representativeness and the emphasis on the pre-industrial revolution period caution against generalising these local study results to the period after 1780.

In contrast, much of what historians have discovered of internal migration comes from data taken from the 1851, and later, censuses. Using these statistics gravity flow migration models have been estimated. Inter-county gravity models hypothesise that migration was directly related to population size in the origin and destination counties and inversely correlated with distance (see Greenwood, 1975 for a survey). To make the models operational behavioural variables, such as wage rates, unemployment levels and weather were introduced to proxy income differentials, transport costs and non-monetary psychic costs. The gravity flow models estimated from the 1851 and 1861 census suggested that migrants responded to economic factors with a pronounced sensitivity to costs imposed by distance. But the sign and significance of the wage and opportunity variables were sensitive to model specification, reflecting the *ad hoc* use of different proxy variables across equations (Greenwood Thomas, 1973; Vedder and Cooper, 1974). Certainly there is a danger in extrapolating these results backwards to the industrial revolution period. Greenwood and Thomas (1973, p. 92) have warned, for example, that there had already been a significant labour transfer from agricultural to non-agricultural pursuits by 1851 and emigration now offered a major alternative to internal migration.

For the industrial revolution period, neither the local studies nor the econometric models based on aggregate census data can answer the question of how selective migration was in terms of skill, literacy and age or whether migration tended to increase or narrow regional disparities. Reconstructing city immigration flows by age from the 1851 census and birth-death rates, Williamson (1985b) showed that urban migration displayed an age selectivity bias. However, such demographic reconstructions of migration are first steps. As Williamson acknowledges, until demographic influences are married to economic push-pull factors the causes of migration remain hidden. The problem is that individual migrant behaviour can be variously interpreted. Rural-urban migration might have attracted the innovative and ambitious farmers; equally it might have swept the rural failures into the cities (Crafts, 1978; Bouvier *et al.*, 1976; Moreland, 1982). It might have done both. Migration, then, remains an important, but elusive, variable in the industrialisation phase of British growth.

This paper utilises a new data source to analyse the individual socio-economic characteristics of over 10 thousand potential industrial revolution migrants. Our methodology is overtly econometric. The causes of inter-county labour mobility between 1780 and 1840 depend on the interpretation of the statistical results from our economic migration model. Specifically, we address three basic questions: what migrant characteristics determined the decision to migrate; what socio-economic factors explained long versus short distance migration; and to what extent were labour markets regional?

I

The data base we employ comprised 10,151 men and women tried in English courts and transported to the colony of New South Wales, Australia, between 1817 and 1839. In all some 160,000 convicts were shipped to the Australian colonies, of whom about 16 per cent were women. Our sample is from the 80,000 sent to New South Wales from the First Fleet in 1788 to the end of transportation in 1840. Transportation continued in Van Diemen's Land until 1852, by which time 67–69,000 convicts had arrived, and in Western Australia, until 1868, with a total intake of 97,000 male transportees. The convict indents which accompanied each convict ship to New South Wales provide complete data on age, urban-rural location, sex, occupation, conjugal status, literacy, county of birth and trial and crimes for 6,684 men and women. All migration considered in this paper was intercounty, defined as workers born in a different county than place of trial. Before 1840 the trial of a crime was conducted in the county in which the offence was committed before magistrates' courts, Courts of Quarter Session or the Assizes held in each county (Jenks, 1935). We assume that crimes were committed in the offenders' county of residence.[2] Convicts were selected for transportation on the basis of their length of sentence, age and health, and on the seriousness of their crime and their prison behaviour. These factors were independent of mobility.

We provide several tests to show that the convict sample was representative of the English working class. First, the occupational structure of the convict sample and the 1841 English census were both coded using Armstrong's (1972) skill-social class scheme; 1—professional, 2—intermediate, 3—skilled, 4—semiskilled and 5—unskilled. Classes 1 and 2 (which accounted for less than 3 per cent of the 10,151 cases in the sample) were excluded from the analysis, restricting the sample to class 3–5 men and

[2] While violations to this assumption will no doubt occur, the violations are likely to be random and not systematic.

women. A chi-square test showed no significant difference between the skill-social class distribution of the convict sample and the English working class population in the 1841 census, although the convict sample had a slightly higher proportion of unskilled category 5 workers than did the census. Spearman's rank correlation between 83 occupations identified in both the 1841 census and the convict indents was 0.714. The major difference was that farmers and farm labourers were markedly under-represented amongst the transportees, reflecting an urban bias in the convict sample.

An alternative assessment of the representativeness of the convict sample involved a comparison of the transported convicts with offenders left at home. Recent work by historians (for example Rude, 1985; Jones, 1982; Philips, 1977) has rejected the idea of a criminal or dangerous class, born and bred to a life of crime and operating as organised gangs. Even in London, reputed to be the centre of professional crime and dangerous districts, Rude (1985) found no case for the existence of a 'criminal class'. The studies show that the great majority of crime was committed by ordinary men and women, who worked at jobs normally but also stole articles on occasion. There can be little doubt that the transportees were typical of such British criminals. Compared to Black Country offenders, transported convict workers had a similar occupational breakdown—58.8 and 53.4 per cent unskilled and semiskilled, 38.4 and 43.6 per cent skilled and 2.8 and 2.9 per cent middle and upper classes respectively. The rank correlation between the occupations of transported male convicts and of male prisoners held in British gaols at the 1841 census was 0.908. They had committed the same types of offences, less than 3 per cent against persons and the rest property offences, overwhelmingly larcency (Philips, pp. 141–67).

On the bases of these tests, it seems fair to argue that the convict sample was coincident with the broad skill-social class mix of the convict population at home which itself did not differ significantly from the rest of the working population. The convict sample differed from the English working population only by having an age distribution biased towards those age groups most 'at risk' to migration and against those engaged in rural occupations. In contrast to the 1841 census population in Table 1, the age structure of the samples of transported convicts and Black Country offenders approximated that of Baines' hypothetical female migrants for 1846 which he reconstructed from the 1851 census.[3] In these major respects, the convict sample was reasonably representative of working men and women in England most at risk to migration between 1817 and 1839.

Even before the onset of rapid growth, the British population was mobile; but most studies argue that short distance intracounty mobility, commonly less than 20 miles, was most typical (Laslett, 1965; Buckatzasch, 1951;

[3] Since Baines' (1972) estimate is net of returns, a hypothetical age structure of current immigrants based on the census data should be adjusted downward from these levels.

TABLE 1
Age distribution of the sample population

Age Distribution (in years)	*1841 Census (i)*	*Convict Sample (ii)*	*Hypothetical 1841 Female Migrants (iii)*	*Black Country Offenders (iv)*
≤20	47	32	35	29
20–29	18	48	50	46
30+	35	20	15	25

Sources: (i) Great Britain, 1841 *Census*; (ii) Convict indents; (iii) Baines (1972, p. 134), (iv) Philips, (1977, p. 160).

Ooserveen, 1974; Cornwall, 1967). Greater distance mobility is evident in the convict indent sample. In part this reflects the fact that intracounty migration cannot be identified. Our observed lifetime moves are not a sample of all moves, but only intercounty moves. The greater distance travelled may also reflect the measure of distance used in our study. Neverthless, movers totalled 3,225 cases, or about one third of the sample, showing a high incidence of intercounty mobility during industrialisation by the sample population. Such a high proportion of intercounty movers suggests a major break from the pre-industrial pattern. In one sense this is a minimum estimate, since hidden within the 'stayers' would be movers who had returned to reside in their county of birth. Distance moved was calculated for each individual by road mileage in 1821 between the largest town in the source and destination county. Over half of all intercounty movements took place over distances greater than 74 miles, a sharp contrast with pre-industrial short distance mobility. Longer distance mobility was confirmed by an alternative measure. Calculating distance in terms of adjacent and non-adjacent county mobility, 51 per cent of the movers migrated to nonadjacent counties. London drew 21 per cent of all movers, a high proportion of whom came from surrounding counties.

Table 2 summarises the micro data on literacy, skill-social class, age, marital status and sex for each individual from the convict indents.

TABLE 2
Summary of socio-economic characteristics of convicts

Characteristics	*Mean*	*Standard Deviation*
Literacy	0.739	0.439
Skilled	0.430	0.495
Semiskilled	0.291	0.454
Marital Status	0.290	0.454
Male	0.919	0.273
Age	25.500	8.540
Total Sample 10,151		

Source: Convict indents.

Urban-rural location and type of industry (agriculture, mining, manufacturing, transport, dealing, industrial, public and domestic service, building and labour not elsewhere defined) were also available for each individual. No data exist for occupation-specific wages, income or unemployment rates during the industrial revolution period. However, various intercounty economic variables were available, including the 1827 agricultural labourer's wage differential (Bowley, 1898), the average 1801 and 1851 urbanisation rate differential (Law, 1986), the 1831 population differential and the average 1839–42 Registrar-General's literacy rate differential. Bowley's agricultural wage rates are imperfect measures of intercounty income potential, especially when much migration was rural-urban. Unfortunately, no evidence in this period points clearly to whether agricultural and nonagricultural wage rates were correlated, although for a much later period agricultural and nonagricultural wage rates were not found to be highly correlated (Greenwood and Thomas, 1973).

II

Our data provide a sharply contrasting interpretation of the convict settlers' contribution to Australia's colonial development to that of the current historiography.[4] Thirty years ago Manning Clark (1956) suggested that the nationalist interpretation of the convict settlers as 'innocent and manly' unfortunates fighting for freedom and social justice grossly distorted Australia's past. Clark argued that those transported to New South Wales could not be typified as poor rural workers pushed into poaching by enclosure and economic exigency; still less were they Chartists or Whiteboys, Captain Savings or Tolpuddle Martyrs, imprisoned for their political convictions. The transported convicts were not helpless victims of a repressive and cruel British society, but persistent thieves engaged in a life of crime.

Clark's conclusions have gained support from the statistical analysis of the convicts' crimes. Exhaustively sampling the indents, Robson (1965) and Shaw (1966) presented detailed breakdowns by type of crime and cross-tabulations by offence and age, sex, nationality and length of sentence. Combined with selective qualitative data on individual convicts and with the old historiography on an English criminal class, the statistical work was used to identify the transportees as professional and habitual criminals, recruited from a distinct class and trained to crime from the cradle. This interpretation of the transportees as members of a criminal class has served to shortcircuit analysis of the economic impact of transported labour on Austrialian growth, and reinforce untested assumptions about the inefficiency of convictism as a system of production. Based on their criminality, historians have viewed the convicts as, quite literally, good for

[4] This section draws on Nicholas (1988).

nothings. Shaw (1966, p. 164) described them as 'ne'er-do-wells . . . quite unable to earn an honest living'. Robson (1965, p. 158) agreed, arguing that the only real trade most convicts possessed was thieving; the transportees, according to Clark (1962, pp. 243–4), had an innate aversion to labour. It was hardly surprising that hardened criminals, without workplace skills or the experience of regular employment, were driven or terrorised into labour by the lash. The coercive and brutal nature of convictism condemned it as an inefficient labour system.

Australian historians have dismissed the convict settlers, in Benjamin Franklin's evocative phrase applied to British criminals transported to America, as 'human serpents'. We assess them as human capital, relying on the indents for data on occupational skill and literacy. Utilising these neglected data, our statistical analysis suggested that the convicts were not qualitatively different from the English labour force, endowing Australia with a unique reservoir of human capital. The evidence on occupational status recorded in the indents for each convict was reliable. It was entered in surprising detail, with over one thousand separate occupations. The regional occupations cross-tabulate well with the convicts' county of trial: most cutlery makers were tried in Sheffield, knitters and stockingmakers in Nottingham, potters in Staffordshire and weavers in Lancashire. Linking the English occupations of our sample convicts with their occupations in the 1828 Australian census revealed that 44% of all convicts in the colony were performing jobs which utilised their English skills. This is a remarkably high percentage given the very different structures of the English and New South Wales economies, and the fact that agricultural labourers were seriously underrepresented amongst the convicts. Finally, over one third of all offences were work-related, defined as crimes against masters and stealing tools and goods, which indicated that a high proportion of the transportees were labouring in their stated occupations. The indent data on previous convictions lend support to the proposition that the convicts were ordinary working men and women: 59% of the English transportees were first offenders, hardly consistent with being members of a criminal class.

Occupation status alone does not fully describe the human capital that convicts brought to Australia. The convicts had literacy levels equivalent to those for the English labouring population. Measured by a questionnaire, 74% of the English convicts could read, or read and write compared with 65% of the English population who could sign the marriage register. Even allowing for large measures of error in the convict indents, the fact that the two measures of literacy are not identical and the higher proportion of males and urban workers in our sample, the convicts' literacy levels confirm a significant investment in education by the workers transported to Australia. The quality of the convicts as workers can also be assessed through the data on age and gender. The convicts were overwhelmingly male, and three-quarters were aged between 16 to 35, the most productive age group. (See Table 2). Convicts and ex-convicts never accounted for less than 85% of the male workforce; unlike free migrants, the convicts brought no dependents and few (less than 5%) returned home. The absence of dependents, low levels of natural population growth due to the skewed sex distribution and the large numbers of male convicts and ex-convicts meant New South Wales was unique in having about 65% of the population in the male workforce (Butlin, 1985). Never again would the percentage be so favourable.

The growth performance of colonial Australia was highly correlated with the quality and quantity of its convict and ex-convict workforce, whose skills were supplied by Britain. Butlin's (1986) estimates of current price domestic product and, after 1828, real product, suggest rapid growth before 1840, consistent with our evidence of a workforce with a significant investment in human capital. It is hard to believe that an inefficient labour system, resting on the twin pillars of coercion and a workforce of professional criminals, could have to promote such growth. The convicts' contribution to Australian economic growth undermines the old interpretation of the convicts as a criminal class, supporting our contention that the convicts were broadly representative of the working class at home, and a suitable data set with which to analyse migration in industrialising England.

III

The empirical literature on migration has been split between aggregate models, focusing on economic differentials between locations, and models of individual migrant chacteristics, usually derived from survey data. Both approaches, however, share the common theoretical approach of individual utility maximisation. Migration is an investment which increases the productivity of human capital. The returns to the investment are usually measured by interdestination wage and economic opportunity variables. The investment's real costs, such as the costs of moving and information, and nonpecuniary psychic costs, including separation from family and community, are measured by education, skill and personal migrant characteristics. We assume the individual decision-maker, i, choses to move, $j = 1$, or not to move, $j = 2$, depending on his individual attributes, S_i, on alternatives from a set of choice attributes, X_{ij}, and on some model of individual choice and behaviour. The representative individual's utility function can be written:

$$U_{ij} = \bar{U}(X_{ij}, S_i) + \varepsilon(X_{ij}, S_i) = \beta Z_{ij} + e_{ij} \quad (1)$$

where Z_{ij} is a vector of functions of the characteristics X_{ij} and attributes S_i, β is a vector of alternative-specific parameters, and e_{ij} is a random variable representing random individual behaviour, unobserved factors and measurement error. (See Judge *et al.*, 1980 and Fomby *et al.*, 1984 for the basic model.)

Since the utilities are stochastic, the choice of moving or staying occurs with some probability. Assuming that the explanatory variables vary by alternative, McFadden (1974a; 1974b) has shown the general random utility function (1) can be represented as a conditional logit model. But, our data vary across individuals, not alternatives. By allowing the explanatory variables to have differential impacts upon the odds of choosing to move or stay the coefficient vector is made alternative specific and the selection probabilities are given by,

$$P_{ij} = \exp(\beta_j X_{ij}) \Big/ \sum_{j=1}^{J} \exp(\beta_j X_{ij}) \tag{2}$$

where J equals the number of possible alternatives in the choice set. (Judge *et al.*, 1980, p. 598; Maddala, 1983, pp. 42–3). The logit model provides a convenient functional form for the theoretical model of migration as an investment in human capital. Following common practice, the explanatory variables enter the logit model by intuitive appeal, proxying the arguments in the utility function. For the industrial revolution period, the choice of exogenous variables was constrained by the data. But the work-related characteristics of the potential migrants are important variables in the decision to migrate in so far as that decision is based on human capital considerations. These characteristics may also be related to nonpecuniary factors in the migration decision.

IV

The coefficients of the logit equations are reported in Table 3. The constant represents an unskilled individual in Model 1; an unskilled individual aged 38 years or older in Model 2; and an unskilled individual in agriculture, mining, building or transport in Model 3. The positive and significant skill and literacy coefficients in Model 1 indicate that the probability of moving increases with education and training. Education, proxied by literacy, allowed individuals to adapt more easily to alternative locations, reducing the nonpecuniary psychic costs of leaving family and community. Further, education reduced the real costs of information. The positive skill coefficients are explained by the lower job search costs and greater job opportunities for individuals with general training. An alternative way to show the same results is to evaluate the predicted probabilities of moving for skill and literacy. In Table 4 the higher probabilities of moving for the skilled and educated (with sex, marital and age calculated at their means) bear out the influence of human capital on the migration decision. Migration was a self-selecting process.

The negative value for MARITAL is associated with the higher real costs of moving for married as opposed to single individuals, although the coefficient was not significant. This may reflect the fact that the variable was ambiguous, including both those who had migrated without their spouse and those who had married after migration. SEX has a negative (and significant)

TABLE 3
Logit equations for stayers–movers[1]

	Model 1	*Model* 2	*Model* 3
SEX (0 = female,	−0.49	−0.50	−0.24
1 = male)	(−5.30)	(−5.42)	(−2.17)
MARTIAL (0 = single,	−0.10	−0.12	−0.10
1 = married)	(−1.41)	(−1.64)	(−1.30)
EDUC (0 = illiterate,	0.35	0.34	0.35
1 = literate)	(5.39)	(5.19)	(5.44)
SKILLED	0.28	0.27	0.47
	(4.06)	(4.03)	(4.39)
SEMISKILLED	0.22	0.22	0.28
	(3.04)	(2.92)	(2.55)
AGE	0.02		0.01
	(4.30)		(3.15)
AGE DUMMY 1 (≤22)		−0.34	
		(−3.04)	
AGE DUMMY 2 (23–38)		0.01	
		(3.04)	
LOC (0 = rural,			−0.24
1 = urban)			(−4.20)
IND 1 (manufacturing)			−0.16
			(−1.96)
IND 2 (dealing, industrial			0.39
and public service)			(4.25)
IND 3 (domestic service,			0.17
other labourers)			(1.50)
CONSTANT	−1.23	−0.66	−1.46
	(−8.70)	(−4.35)	(−8.27)
X^2	109.89	122.35	165.20
D.F.	6	7	10
Sample Size	6684	6684	6684

[1] Asymptotic *t*-ratios given in parentheses.

impact on the likelihood of migrating. Our results provide weak support (noting that females account for just six per cent of the sample) for Ravenstein's suggestion that females were more migratory than males.[5] The higher female mobility rate may reflect the higher proportion of rural-urban life time moves by women employed in domestic service. AGE has a slightly different interpretation in our model than in most migration studies due to the nature of the data. Since age at time of the move is unknown, the older an individual, *ceteris paribus,* the greater chance of having moved. This is confirmed by the probability of moving increasing with age in Model 1 where age enters as a continuous variable and in Model 2 where age categories are utilised.

[5] Ravenstein (1885) excludes persons who ultimately emigrate and these were most likely to be male, thus his female migration rate is biased upwards.

TABLE 4
Predicted probabilities of moving for skill and literacy characteristics

Model	*Predicted Probabilities*
Table 3 Model 1	
Skilled and literate	0.414
Unskilled and illiterate	0.232
Unskilled and literate	0.300
Skilled and illiterate	0.332
Table 8 Married Model 1	
Skilled and literate	0.420
Unskilled and illiterate	0.213
Unskilled and literate	0.280
Skilled and illiterate	0.335
Table 8 Single Model 1	
Skilled and literate	0.347
Unskilled and illiterate	0.198
Unskilled and literate	0.257
Skilled and illiterate	0.275

Model 3 includes two further explanatory variables, location and type of industry. The rural-urban dummy has a negative and significant effect on the probability of moving, reflecting the fact that the greater job opportunities of urban locations discourage urban workers from moving. There are significant differences between industrial sectors in the probability of moving. Workers in dealing, industrial service and public service (IND2) had the highest odds of moving while domestic service and labour not elsewhere classified (IND3) had a lower, but positive, probability of migrating. Workers in manufacturing (IND1) had a negative (and significant) probability of moving, indicating a disincentive to separate from the most rapidly expanding industrial sector. The constant included the industry categories, agriculture, mining building and transport.

The log likelihood chi-square statistic for the logit equations in Table 3 allowed the null model, with all the coefficients equal to zero, to be rejected. An alternative test of the 'goodness' of the logit models compares the predicted probability of moving, evaluated at the mean, with the share of the sample that moved. In Table 5, the predicted probabilities are very close to the sample share that moved, confirming the 'goodness' of the predictions of the model.

Conditional on moving, Table 6 analyses the intercounty movers in terms of short and long distance movement. Movement over distances less than 60 miles was considered short, with about 80 per cent of all short distance intercounty movers migrating less than 42 miles. In contrast half of all long distance movers migrated in excess of 120 miles and 75 per cent more than 90 miles. The reference group was unskilled workers in agriculture, mining, building and transport. SEX, MARTIAL, EDUC and AGE—the human capital determinants of the move-nomove decision—do not impact on the

TABLE 5
Model predicted probabilities of moving evaluated at mean

Model		*Share Moving*	*Predicted Probabilities of Moving*
Table 3	Model 1	0.30	0.32
	Model 2	0.30	0.30
	Model 3	0.30	0.28
Table 6	Model 1	0.50	0.49
	Model 2	0.50	0.51
	Model 3	0.50	0.52
Table 7	Model 1	0.30	0.27
	Model 2	0.30	0.30
	Model 3	0.32	0.31
	Model 4	0.32	0.25
Table 8	Model 1	0.30	0.29
	Model 2	0.27	0.26
	Model 3	0.32	0.32
	Model 4	0.26	0.24

distance decision significantly in Model 1. When these variables were dropped from Model 1, on the basis of likelihood ratio tests, the coefficients remained stable.[6] Model 2 shows that skill had a positive and significant impact on distance moved, proxying job search costs and employment opportunities. The coefficient for DIFFW, the difference in wage levels between counties, supports the hypothesis that income differences between source and destination locations encouraged individuals to maximise their returns from human capital by moving longer distances to higher earning areas.

Employment opportunities were measured by LOC (rural-urban location), DIFFE (intercounty education differentials), DIFFP (intercounty urbanisation differentials), and DIFFU (intercounty urbanisation differentials). Higher urbanisation and higher education levels in source counties discouraged long distance movement. The variables suggest that migrants were sensitive to differentials in intercounty economic opportunities when making their decision to move. DIFFP and LOC were positive but not significant. While the size of the coefficients were very small, Model 3 shows there was little justification for dropping either LOC or DIFFP from the model. The industry variable IND3, domestic service and labour not elsewhere defined, showed a greater likelihood of moving long distances than IND2, dealing, industrial and public source, which was also positive and significant or IND1, manufacturing, which is positive but insignificant. The reference

[6] As expected from the stability of the coefficients, the correlation matrix showed no significant correlation between independent variables.

TABLE 6
Logit equations for short–long distance migration[1]

Variable	*Model* 1	*Model* 2	*Model* 3
SEX (0 = female,	−0.10		
1 = male)	(−0.51)		
MARITAL (0 = single,	−0.18		
1 = married)	(−1.46)		
EDUC (0 = illiterate,	0.01		
1 = literate)	(0.08)		
SKILLED	0.49	0.51	0.52
	(2.97)	(3.17)	(3.21)
SEMISKILLED	0.41	0.43	0.42
	(2.27)	(2.43)	(2.36)
AGE	0.01		
	(1.85)		
LOC (0 = rural,	0.17	0.16	
1 = urban)	(1.63)	(1.59)	
DIFFW	0.13	0.13	0.17
	(3.57)	(3.61)	(5.61)
DIFFE	−0.01	−0.01	−0.01
	(−2.37)	(−2.31)	(−2.22)
DIFFP	0.0002	0.0002	
	(1.87)	(1.92)	
DIFFU	−0.01	−0.01	−0.01
	(−3.06)	(−3.09)	(−2.98)
IND 1 (manufacturing)	0.20	0.19	0.20
	(1.38)	(1.37)	(1.40)
IND 2 (dealing, industrial and public service)	0.50	0.54	0.56
	(3.39)	(4.16)	(4.33)
IND 3 (domestic service, other labourers)	0.64	0.67	0.67
	(3.50)	(3.74)	(3.72)
CONSTANT	−0.90	−0.73	−0.67
	(−3.18)	(−4.18)	(−3.97)
X^2	73.37	69.50	63.96
D.F.	14	10	9
Sample Size	1991	1991	1991

[1] Asymptotic *t*-ratios given in parentheses.

group, agriculture, mining, building, and transport had the lowest probability of moving long distances.

Next, extensions (and complications) to the simple models are considered by dropping some of the restrictive assumptions. Using regional dummies for the Home Counties, Midlands, the industrial North, the South West and the fringe (Cornwall, Devon, Northumberland, Durham and Westmorland) Model 1 in Table 7 indicates significant regional differences. For each geographic area with more than 1200 observations separate logit equations were estimated. Coefficients in Table 7 which were significantly different (at the 5 per cent level) from those of the aggregate Model 3 in Table 3, are

TABLE 7
Logit equations for regions

Variable	Model 1 Regions	Model 2 Home	Model 3 Midlands	Model 4 North
SEX (0 = female, 1 = male)	−0.21 (−1.88)	−0.18* (−0.90)	−0.39 (−1.39)	−0.54* (−2.44)
MARITAL (0 = single, 1 = married)	−0.10 (−1.37)	−0.05 (−0.35)	−0.15 (−0.96)	−0.17 (−1.24)
EDUC (0 = illiterate, 1 = literate)	0.35 (5.28)	0.50 (4.07)	0.21* (1.48)	0.38 (3.18)
SKILLED	0.44 (4.12)	0.45 (2.57)	0.55 (1.80)	0.23* (1.13)
SEMISKILLED	0.27 (2.33)	0.11 (0.58)	0.34 (1.06)	0.11 (0.52)
AGE	0.01 (2.97)	0.004* (−0.58)	0.02* (2.38)	0.01 (1.92)
LOC (0 = rural, 1 = urban)	−0.21 (−3.59)	−0.44* (−4.24)	−0.08* (−0.58)	−0.23 (−2.11)
HOME COUNTIES	−0.60 (−5.37)			
MIDLANDS	−0.39 (−3.28)			
NORTH	−0.66 (−5.88)			
SOUTH-WEST	−0.12 (−0.94)			
IND 1 (manufacturing)	−0.15 (−1.81)	−0.06* (−0.34)	−0.39* (−1.96)	−0.17 (−1.20)
IND 2 (dealing, industrial and public service)	0.38 (4.13)	0.26 (1.57)	0.31 (1.39)	0.35 (1.99)
IND 3 (domestic service, other labourers)	0.14 (1.17)	−0.07 (−0.37)	0.49* (1.56)	−0.21* (−0.90)
CONSTANT	−0.96 (−4.71)	−1.34 (−4.34)	−1.39 (−3.13)	−1.15 (−3.71)
X^2	228.29	63.31	34.06	58.33
D.F.	14	10	10	10
Sample Size	6684	2231	1286	2085

[1] Asymptotic *t*-ratios given in parentheses.
* Significant difference between the coefficient and those in the Aggregate Model Table 3.

marked with an asterisk. Even a cursory glance at Table 7 confirms the presence of significant differences in the decision to migrate between the regional models and the national logit. Of course, this result is consistent with much of the historical literature (for example Pollard, 1978 and Mathias, 1972) which suggest regional labour markets during the industrialisation period. However, inter-regional differences were not so great as to nullify the use of the aggregate national data. Most of the regional differences occur in the location and industry-type variables which are expected to vary due to industry-specific location and different urbanisation rates across counties. Importantly, the signs on the regional independent variables usually agree with those in the aggregate model. For example, regional skill and literacy variables still impact strongly on the probability of moving, but to a greater or lesser extent than the national variables. Therefore, the socio-economic factors influencing the migration decision tended to have the same impact on the migration decision across space. The predicted probabilities evaluated at the mean performed well and are reported in Table 5.

Our original model specification allowed only the constant term to be shifted by MARITAL and SEX, constraining the coefficients to be the same for all individuals. To check for different coefficients between males and females and single and married individuals, the sample was stratified by marital status and sex. Few of the changes in the coefficients of the logit subsamples were significant, giving us confidence in the use of the aggregate data.[7] Interestingly, the size of the married coefficients for skill and education tended to be larger than those for single individuals. This result, lost in the aggregate model, presumably reflects both the older age of married individuals with a larger stock of human capital and a different risk preference. For married and single individuals, the probabilities of moving for skill and literacy are given in Table 4 and the predicted probabilities in Table 5.

V

There is very limited knowledge on the causes of internal migration in England during the industrial revolution. Census statistics are of little value prior to 1851. Thus the convict indents which provide place of birth and trial of English men and women transported to the penal colony of New South Wales provide a unique and rich data source on the socio-economic characteristics of intercounty migrants. The convict sample was found to be broadly representative of the English urban working class most at risk to migration. Using socio-economic variables on each individual, the logit models showed that the probability of moving was relatively high for skilled, literate individuals and low for the unskilled and illiterate worker. Migration was a self-selecting process and the internal migrant was not simply chaff from the rapidly changing rural economy.

The movers were economically advantaged in terms of their human

[7] We estimated models with an intercept dummy and interactive slope dummies for SEX, although the results are not reported here. While the intercept dummy was significant, the slope dummies were not, indicating no significant variation between male and female coefficients. However, the skill and literacy variables were highly correlated with their slope dummies, making the estimates inefficient. This problem was largely due to the data which presented only a relatively small number of female observations. The results are available on demand.

capital and intent on migration which further enhanced that advantage. This is demonstrated by the greater probability that long distance movement (as opposed to short distance) depended on wage differentials and job opportunities between counties and on job search costs. The results suggest a workforce sensitive to improving the economic returns to their human capital. Of course, movement was not wholly pecuniary, but pecuniary factors were importantly correlated to movement in a systematic way. Labour markets displayed regional biases. But (although the size of the coefficients for the various regions differed significantly) the sign and significance of the human capital and economic opportunity proxies were uniform across regions. Generally, in their decisions to migrate, workers heeded labour market signals and maximised their investments in human capital by migrating.

University of New South Wales & University of Reading
Office of Prime Minister, Canberra.

REFERENCES

ANDERSON, M. (1974). "Urban Migration in Nineteenth Century Lancashire: Some Insights into Two Competing Hypotheses" in M. M. Drake, ed., *Historical Demography: Problems and Projections,* Open University Press, Milton Keynes.

ARMSTRONG, W. A. (1972). "The Use of Information About Occupations" in E. A. Wrigley, ed., *Nineteenth Century Society: Essays in the Use of Quantitative Methods for the Study of Social Data,* Cambridge University Press, Cambridge.

BAINES, D. (1972). "The Use of Published Census Data in Migration Studies" in E. A. Wrigley, ed., *Nineteenth Century Society: Essays in the Use of Quantitative Methods for the Study of Social Data,* Cambridge University Press, Cambridge.

BOUVIER, L. *et al.* (1976). "Towards a Framework for the Analysis of Differential Migration" The Case of Education" in A. H. Richmond and D. Kubat, eds. *Internal Migration; The New World and the Third World,* Sage Publications, California.

BOWLEY, A. L. (1898). "The Statistics of Wages in the United Kingdom During the Last Hundred Years", *Journal of the Royal Statistical Society,* 61.

BUCKATZSCH, E. J. (1951). "The Constancy of Local Population and Migration in England Before 1800", *Population Studies,* 5.

BUTLIN, N. (1985). "White Human Capital in Australia, 1788–1850", Department of Economic History, Working Paper No. 32, Australian National University.

BUTLIN, N. (1986). "Contours of the Australian Economy 1788–1860", *Australian Economic History Review,* XXVI.

CHAMBERS, J. D. (1972). *Population, Economy and Society in Pre-Industrial England,* Clarendon Press, Oxford.

CLARK, M. (1956). "The Origins of the Convicts Transported to Eastern Australia, 1787–1852", *Historical Studies: Australia and New Zealand,* 7.

CLARK, M. (1962). *A History of Australia,* I, *From the Earliest Times to the Age of Macquarie,* Melbourne University Press, Melbourne.

CORNWALL, J. (1967). "Evidence of Population Mobility in the Seventeenth Century", *Bulletin of the Institue of Historical Research,* XL.

CRAFTS, N. F. R. (1978), "Enclosure and Labour Supply Revisited", *Explorations in Economic History,* 15.

CRESSEY, D. (1970). "Occupations, Migration and Literacy in East London, 1580–1640", *Local Population Studies,* 5.

DEANE, P. and COLE, W. (1975). *British Economic Growth 1688–1959,* Cambridge University Press, Cambridge.

FOMBY, T. B., CARTER-HILL, R. and JOHNSON, S. R. (1984). *Advanced Econometric Methods,* Springer-Verlag, N.Y.

GREENWOOD, M. and THOMAS, L. (1973). "Geographic Labour Mobility in Nineteenth Century England and Wales", *Annals of Regional Science,* VII.

JENKS, E. (1935). *The Book of English Law,* John Murray, London.

JONES, D. (1982). *Crime, Protest, Community and Police in Nineteenth Century Britain,* Routledge, London.

JUDE, G. *et al.* (1980). *Theory and Practice of Econometrics,* Wiley, New York.

LASLETT, P. (1965). *The World We Have Lost,* Methuen, London.

LAW, C. M. (1986). Private communication of urbanisation rates based on the definitions given in Law. C. M. (1967). "The Growth of Urban Population in England and Wales, 1801–1911", *Transactions of the Institute of British Geographers,* No. 41.

MADDALA, G. S. (1983). *Limited-Dependent and Qualitative Variables in Econometrics,* Cambridge University Press, Cambridge.

MATHIAS, P. (1972). *The First Industrial Nation: The Economic History of Britain, 1700–1914,* Methuen, London.

MCFADDEN, D. (1974a). "Conditional Logit Analysis of Qualitative Choice Behaviour' in P. Zarembka, ed., *Frontiers in Econometrics,* Academic Press, N.Y.

MCFADDEN, D. (1974b). *Urban Travel Demand: A Behavioural Analysis,* North Holland, Amsterdam.

MORELAND, R. S. (1982). "Population, Internal Migration and Economic Growth: An Empirical Analysis", *Research in Population Economics,* 4.

NICHOLAS, S. (ed) (forthcoming 1988). *The Convict Workers: England, Ireland and New South Wales,* Cambridge University Press, Sydney.

OOSERVEEN, K. (1974). "Hawkshead (Lancs.) Mobility as Shown by the Reconstruction of the Parish from the Register", *Local Population Studies,* 12.

PHILIPS, D. (1977). *Crime and Authority in Victorian England,* Croom Helm, London.

POLLARD, S. (1978). "Labour in Great Britain", in P. Mathias and M. M. Postan, eds., *The Cambridge Economic History of Europe,* Vol. 1, *The Industrial Economies: Capital, Labour and Enterprise,* Part II Cambridge University Press, Cambridge.

RAVENSTEIN, E. G. (1885). "The Laws of Migration", *Journal of the Royal Statistical Society,* Part 1, 48.

REEDE, G. (1985). *Crime and Victim: Crime and Society in Early Nineteenth Century England,* Clarendon Press, Oxford.

ROBSON, L. (1965). *The Convict Settlers of Australia,* Melbourne University Press, Melbourne.

SHAW, A. G. L. (1966). *Convicts and the Colonies,* Faber and Faber, London.

TRANTER, N. L. (1967). "Population and Social Structure in a Bedfordshire Parish; The Cardington Listing of Inhabitants, 1782", *Population Studies,* 21.

TRANTER, N. L. (1981). "The Labour Supply, 1780–1860", in R. Floud and D. McCloskey, eds., *The Economic History of British Since 1700,* Vol. 1, Cambridge University Press, Cambridge.

VEDDER, R. and COOPER, D. (1974). "Nineteenth Century, English and Welsh Geographic Labour Mobility: Some Further Evidence", *Annals of Regional Science,* VIII.

WILLIAMSON, J. (1985a). "The Urban Transition During the First Industrial Revolution: England 1776–1871", Harvard Institution for Economic Research Discussion Paper 1146, April.

WILLIAMSON, J. (1985b). "City immigration, Selectivity Bias and Human Capital Transfers During the British Industrial Revolution", Harvard Institution for Economic Research Discussion Paper 1171, July.

Oxford Economic Papers 39 (1987), 641–678

DID ENGLISH FACTOR MARKETS FAIL DURING THE INDUSTRIAL REVOLUTION?*

By JEFFREY G. WILLIAMSON

I. Two competing views

DID FACTOR markets fail during the English industrial revolution? Did distortions in factor markets serve to starve industrial firms for finance and suppress accumulation there? Did urban-rural wage gaps, inelastic city labor supplies and the lack of integrated labor markets serve to drive up the cost of labor in the cities thus choking off the rate of industrialization? With regards to labor market failure, the literature is of two minds.

Labor markets did fail

An extensive traditional literature takes the view that migrants were reluctant to move, wage gaps were large, and regional labor markets were fragmented.

A century ago, Earnst Ravenstein (1885, 1889) published his classic work on internal migration, subsequently augmented by Arthur Redford (1926) and Alex Cairncross (1949, 1953). Ravenstein asked how many migrated, when they migrated, who migrated, where they migrated from, and where they migrated to. The same questions dominate modern migration studies. Thus, for example, the literature has been busy substantiating Ravenstein's and Redford's observation that the majority of migrants went only a short distance, and often by steps. Such observations have encouraged the belief that workers failed to move to the highest wage areas and thus that the perfect labor market thesis must fail.

There is an equally long tradition among British labor historians that there was a multiplicity of labor markets between 1750 and 1850, that regional labor markets were very poorly integrated, and that local autonomy reigned (Pollard, 1978). The labor-markets-failed view also leans heavily on the evidence that wage gaps were pronounced during the industrial revolution. Indeed, E. D. Hunt (1973) reported an enormous amount of regional wage variation well into the late 19th century.

Labor markets did not fail

Nick Crafts has recently argued that English labor was released from agriculture early and fast, implying that this factor reallocation contributed

* The research in this paper has been supported by an NSF grant as part of a project entitled *Coping With City Growth*. The paper has been aided by the effective research assistance of Erin Page and Miles Kimball, and by the comments of George Boyer, Brad DeLong, Barry Eichengreen, Robert Fogel, Larry Goulder, Carol Heim, Peter Lindert, Donald McCloskey, Cynthia Taft Morris, Mark Rosenzweig, Kenneth Snowden, David Weir and the Cornell, Harvard and Michigan Economic History Workshops.

to significant economy-wide productivity gains. This labor release by English agriculture at an early stage of development (Crafts, 1985, p. 2) implies economy-wide productivity gains to the extent that labor had higher marginal productivity in industry. Indeed, this kind of reasoning is central to such development economists as Simon Kuznets (1971) and Hollis Chenery and Moshe Syrquin (1975), as well as to the growth accounting of Edward Denison (1967, 1974). Crafts feels that by 1840 factor markets were fairly well integrated (Crafts, 1985, pp. 3 and 7), although wage gaps between agriculture and industry were still pronounced (Crafts, 1985, p. 68). Comparisons with other early developers have persuaded Crafts that England's relative factor market integration and early labor release was important to her early success.

My own work has documented that emigration rates from the English countryside rose dramatically after the French Wars, reaching very high levels by the 1840s (Williamson, 1985b). Indeed, the rates of rural emigration were higher than in the Third World where, it has been argued, there is "over-urbanization" (Kelley and Williamson, 1984).

Others have shown that migrants were responsive to labor market signals (Nicholas and Shergold, 1985a, 1985b), and that the elasticity of migration to earnings differentials were no smaller than those found in other economies, past and present (Greenwood and Thomas, 1973; Vedder and Cooper, 1974).

In short, this revisionist literature suggests that English labor markets linking city and countryside were well integrated and at least as successful in transferring labor to the dynamic urban sectors as those in developing countries which have followed England's example.

Making an assessment

Ravenstein-like documentation of migrant flows or Hunt-like documentation of nominal wage gaps is not nearly enough to test the labor-markets-failed hypothesis. While costs of migration in the pre-railway age may have generated wage gaps between surplus and deficit regional labor markets, stability in those gaps over time could imply a well integrated national labor market. And even if wage gaps rose over time, such evidence could not be viewed as unambiguous support for the view that imperfect labor markets were succumbing to the disequilibrating shocks of unbalanced growth across the industrial revolution. After all, rising nominal wage gaps—especially between town and countryside—may simply have reflected the relative rise in the cost of city life, including the disamenities associated with crowding and high density. Furthermore, short distance moves need not shed any light at all on the labor-market-failure hypothesis. Workers need only move at the margin, and the statement holds for the marginal worker as well as for the marginal move.

Even if labor markets were in disequilibrium during the First Industrial

Revolution, did it matter in any important quantitative sense? If so, how did it matter? What was the impact of the alleged labor market failure on English growth, accumulation and industrialization? Neither of the two competing views has posed these questions. Rather, the debate has focused on the distinctly uninteresting question: Were labor markets perfect? Of course they were not perfect. The interesting question, it seems to me, is whether the imperfections were large enough to matter.

This paper will offer some answers to these questions by focusing on wage gaps between city and countryside. It will also assess the impact of capital market distortions. Section II will review the evidence on rising nominal wage gaps and the rural emigration response across the First Industrial Revolution, the magnitudes placed in comparative perspective. Section III constructs urban-rural cost of living differentials, where the critical ingredient turns out to be rents. Sections IV and V add on the influence of poor relief and urban disamenities, so that the nominal wage gaps for 1831 can be converted to real wage gaps. The real wage gaps are much smaller, but they hardly disappear. Section VI makes a simple comparative static assessment of the quantitative importance of these wage gaps by computing the deadweight loss associated with the labor market failure. The figures turn out to be fairly small.

Why, then, has the fuss over labor market failure persisted for so long? I think the answer lies with the employment, distribution and accumulation effects associated with the labor market failure. Section VII introduces these issues in partial equilibrium. Section VIII then uses general equilibrium to compare the quantitative impact of labor market failure with capital market failure. The results are striking: it appears that the traditional literature is correct, labor markets *did* fail, but capital market failure was even more pronounced. Both served to constrain English industrialization during the First Industrial Revolution to less than optimal rates.

II. Labor market disequilibrium and migration response: the evidence for failure

Rising nominal wage gaps

Elsewhere I have shown (Williamson, 1986a, Table 1) that the gap between the annual nominal earnings of unskilled non-farm and farm laborers rose sharply across the first half of the 19th century. The evidence suggests that the nominal wage gap did not begin to rise during the English industrial revolution until well after the French Wars. Indeed, the index suggests that wartime conditions served to erode the wage gap. Since the conflict caused a contraction in foreign trade and a rise in the relative price of grains, agriculture was favored. Under such conditions, it is hardly surprising that the wage gap would tend to collapse as labor demands were relatively strong in the countryside. With the end of the wars, however, the pace of industrialization accelerated and agriculture resumed its long run relative demise (Williamson, 1984). Thus, the derived demand for labor shifted dramatically towards urban sectors. If labor market disequilibrium was ever to appear in England, the times were certainly ripe for it after about 1820. Trends in the wage gap would appear to reflect those disequilibrating forces since it rises sharply to a peak in 1851. The gap never reaches its mid-19th century peak again.[1] Thus, if we are looking for evidence of labor market failure, the 1830s, 1840s and 1850s are clearly the place to start.

How big was the rural-urban wage gap during these three decades? Hunt and Crafts both contend that the wage gap is best captured with the available evidence by comparing agricultural wages with unskilled in the building trades (Hunt, 1973, p. 5; Crafts, 1982, p. 64). We can construct the gaps for the North and South of England separately, and since many have argued that the English labor market was regionally segmented (Pollard, 1978, pp. 103–4; 1981, p. 902), it might be wise to do so. Table 1 estimates these nominal wage gaps for the 1830s. In the South of England, the wage gap was indeed very large: annual unskilled wages in the London building trades exceeded those of farm laborers in the southern counties by an enormous factor, 106.2 percent. These nominal gaps include the influence of seasonal unemployment in both city and countryside, but they exclude poor relief payments. As we shall see below, the addition of poor relief payments to the labor earnings of able-bodied would serve to diminish the size of the gap in the South, but not by much. For the North of England, the wage gap was much smaller: annual unskilled wages in the five towns of Coventry, Huddersfield, Newcastle, Macclesfield and Manchester exceeded those of farm laborers in the northern counties by 36.3 percent.

Table 1 also implies that those big wage gaps in the South of England were less a function of lower rural wages in the South compared to the North, and more a function of the high urban wages in London compared with northern towns. Indeed, Section V will present some evidence which suggests that the gap between northern and southern farm wages can be explained largely by more generous agricultural poor relief down South. The source of those big wage gaps in the South of England were, therefore, high London wages.

We shall offer some explanations below for the regional difference in the size of the wage gaps, but for the moment it should suffice simply to note that a weighted average of the two regions yields an all-England nominal gap of 73.2 percent.

[1] Based on somewhat different data, Bellerby (1956, Table 45, p. 33; 1953, p. 135) has also documented similar trends. Comparing nominal agricultural wages with *average* industrial wages, he finds a peak wage gap in the 1850s, declining for the remainder of the century followed by a rise again between the 1880s and the 1900s. Based on Brassey and Gilboy, Colin Clark (1957, p. 530) also finds a peak in 1851, but he believes the late 18th century gaps to have been even higher.

TABLE 1
Nominal Wage Gaps in the 1830s

Region	*Annual Wages* (£)	*Description and Source*
London 1831	48.07	Laborers in the building trades (for bricklayers, plasterers and masons), 21.75 sh./week. Assumes 44.2 weeks worked per year. Mayhew estimated that 30 percent of London's workers in the building trades were unemployed during slack seasons. If the slack season is taken as 6 months, then weeks worked per year is 26 + (0.7)26 = 44.2. See G. Jones (1971), p. 41 and Boyer, 1985, p. 28. The weekly wages are from Bowley (1900a), p. 83.
Northern Towns 1838–40	36.38	Laborers in the building trades, average summer weekly wages, weighted average of Coventry, Huddersfield, Newcastle, Macclesfield, and Manchester, where weights are 1841 population (PP 1843, vol. 22, p. 10). Also assumes 44.2 weeks worked per year. The weekly wages are from Bowley (1900b), pp. 300–310.
Rural South 1833	23.31	Agricultural laborers, average weekly wage (excluding poor relief payments) across 21 shires, where we assume 44.2 weeks worked per year in grain-growing counties of the Southeast, and 48 weeks worked per year in Southwest. The counties are: Middlesex, Surrey, Kent, Sussex, Hants, Berks, Oxford, Herts, Bucks, Northampton, Hunts, Beds, Cambs, Essex, Suffolk, Norfolk, Wilts, Dorset, Devon, Cornwall and Somerset. The weekly wages range from 8.50 to 13.08 sh., and they are taken from Bowley (1900a), end table, col. 8.
Rural North 1837	26.70	Agricultural laborers, average weekly wage (excluding poor relief payments) across 18 shires, where we assume 48 weeks worked per year. The counties are: Glou, Heref., Salop, Staffs, Worc, Warwick, Leic., Lincs, Notts, Derby, Cheshire, the three Yorks, Durham, Northumb., Cumb., Westmore. The weekly wages are from Bowley (1900a), end table, col. 11.
Southern Wage Gap:	106.2%	
Northern Wage Gap:	36.3%	
Average (Weighted) Wage Gap:	73.2%	

Sources: The average wage gap is computed from a weighted average of the North and South wages, where the weights are 1841 county populations (Mitchell and Deane, 1962, p. 20), London and 41 northern towns (*Parliamentary Papers,* 1843, vol. 22, Preface, p. 10).

The wage gap is computed as the difference between urban and rural relative to the rural wage.

Migration response

Rural emigration appears to have responded to the labor market disequilibrium produced by the unbalanced growth associated with the industrialization spurt after c1820. In contrast with the conventional wisdom that English rural labor was reluctant to move and thus failed to respond vigorously to the wage gaps (Redford, 1926, pp. 84 and 94; Pollard, 1978, pp. 103–115), the rates of emigration from the English countryside rose dramatically after the French Wars and reached what appear to be very high levels by the 1840s.

With the exception of the war-induced good times for English agriculture between 1801 and 1806, Table 2 shows that rural emigration took place at every point across the century 1776–1871. After the French Wars, the rates of rural emigration were high by almost any standard. While they ranged between 0.87 and 2.10 percent per annum after 1816, they ranged between 0.97 and 1.21 percent per annum in the Third World in the 1960s and 1970s

TABLE 2
Rural Emigration Rates in England and Wales, 1776–1871

Period	*Rural Population at Starting Year* (000) (*1*)	*Rural Emigration Over 5 Years* (000) (*2*)	*Annual Rates of Rural Emigration* (%) (*3*)
1776–1781	4,995	211	0.86
1781–1786	5,106	125	0.50
1786–1791	5,168	143	0.56
1791–1796	5,372	207	0.79
1796–1801	5,559	226	0.83
1801–1806	5,736	−53	−0.18
1806–1811	6,005	311	1.07
1811–1816	6,268	181	0.59
1816–1821	6,572	281	0.87
1821–1826	6,895	397	1.19
1826–1831	7,174	399	1.14
1831–1836	7,399	364	1.01
1836–1841	7,575	442	1.20
1841–1846	7,740	583	1.57
1846–1851	7,776	646	1.73
1851–1856	7,699	571	1.54
1856–1861	7,745	594	1.60
1861–1866	7,821	780	2.10
1866–1871	7,663	746	2.05
Long Period Averages:			
1776–1816			0.63
1816–1831			1.07
1831–1851			1.38
1851–1871			1.82

Source: Williamson (1985b), Table 5, Panel B, pp. 23–24.

(Kelley and Williamson, 1984, Table 3-13, p. 93). More important to the issues at hand, however, the rate of rural emigration rose sharply over the period, especially after the French Wars. The average emigration rate between 1776 and 1816 was only 0.63 percent per annum. Furthermore, there was considerable instability in the rate over these four decades of modest industrialization and stop-go during wartime, and there is no evidence of significant upward trend. The same was true of wage gaps. After 1816, the emigration rates surged upwards consistently, as did wage gaps. By the 1840s, the emigration rate was 1.65 percent per annum, or about two and a half times the pre-1816 rate. By the 1860s, the rate was 2.08 percent per annum, or more than three times the pre-1816 rate.

The 1830s seem, therefore, to lie in the middle of a dramatic epoch of high and rising emigration from the countryside at precisely the time when wage gaps were also high and rising, thus offering a strong inducement to potential migrants.

A comparative assessment

Were these wage gaps large? Since all industrializing countries find it difficult to cope with the economic shocks associated with industrial revolutions, wage gaps are a manifestation of factor market disequilibrium that both economic historians and development economists have come to expect during such episodes of dramatic growth and transformation. Did English labor markets fail by the standards of other industrial revolutions?

Table 3 offers a partial answer. Here we compare English experience with that of nineteen Third World economies in the 1960s and 1970s, and with that of seven 19th century developing economies. The English wage gaps are adjusted for seasonal unemployment while the others are not, but in most other dimensions the underlying calculations are similar. Each of these estimates attempts to focus on homogeneous labor, unskilled labor's wages being used throughout.[2] Indeed, unskilled wages in the building trades are used in all of the Third World estimates, and they also seem to have been used in most of the 19th century estimates as well. Furthermore, wage supplements and poor relief are excluded throughout.

[2] There is no shortage of studies in both the historical and development literature which appeal to various, and inappropriate, proxies of labor market disequilibrium. The most famous is by Simon Kuznets (1966) who uses average labor productivities to infer the resource allocative gains from the demise of agriculture. Of course, it is marginal labor productivities which matter, and average productivities are likely to be a very poor proxy for the marginal productivities given the far higher human and physical capital intensities which prevail outside agriculture. Additional examples are offered by those who compare average industrial wages with agricultural wages. Since industry averages include skilled labor which embody human capital, such wage gaps exaggerate the size of the labor market disequilibrium. Let me simply cite two fine examples of historical studies which use this approach. One is offered by Bellerby's otherwise excellent work on the British farm sector (Bellerby, 1953, p. 135; 1956, pp. 233–234), which figures importantly in Eric Jones' impressive survey of the agricultural labor market in England (E. Jones, 1964, p. 328). The second is illustrated by Mazumdar's (1973, p. 495) classic study of the Bombay textile industry.

TABLE 3
Nominal Wage Gaps for Unskilled Labor: Some Comparative Data

Observation	*Wage Gap (%)*	*Description and Source*
South of England 1830s	106.2	Table 1
North of England 1830s	36.3	Ibid.
All England 1830s	73.2	Ibid.
Third World 1960s–70s	41.4	Squire (1981), Table 30, p. 102. As with the English data, these are also based on unskilled in urban construction and agriculture. They also exclude payments in kind and wage supplements. There are 19 countries underlying this average (excluding four cases of negative gaps): Guatemala, Chile, Pakistan, Ivory Coast, Morocco, Mexico, Cameroon, Uruguay, Argentina, Panama, Sri Lanka, Kenya, Tunisia, Malawi, Trinidad and Tobago, Venezuela, Costa Rica, Tanzania and Malaysia.
19th C Developing Nations	51.2	Clark (1957), Table II, pp. 526–531. Agricultural wages include payments in kind, while unskilled urban wages seem to be for general laborers. The countries included are: Argentina 1872; Australia 1887; Denmark 1872; France 1892, 1801; Hungary 1865; Japan 1887; and US 1890, 1820–29. Clark also reports figures for the UK where the average 1843–1869 = 37.3%, well below our estimate for the 1830s.

Notes: Throughout, the percentage unskilled wage gap is computed as the difference between urban and rural relative to rural wage.

Based on Table 3, it appears that wage gaps in the North of England were a little smaller than those typical of the Third World and the rest of the developing 19th century world economy. The wage gaps in the South of England, however, far exceeded those typical of developing countries. If we are looking for relative failure in labor markets, the South of England is where we are most likely to find it. And the South of England was sufficiently important to the total labor market that on average English wage gaps were indeed comparatively large.

III. Going from nominal to real wage gaps: cost-of-living differentials

These nominal wage gaps must be deflated before the efficiency of the English labor market in the early 19th century can be assessed. Indeed, we now know that living costs were considerably higher in the large cities (Crafts, 1982; Williamson, 1986a). Part of the explanation, of course, lies with dwelling rents.

Rents were higher in the cities primarily due to land scarcity, although construction costs may also have been higher given higher nominal city wages. Furthermore, as urbanization took place across the industrial revolution, urban land got even scarcer and labor-intensive products like dwellings rose in relative cost (especially in the absence of significant productivity advance in the building trades), thus increasing the relative cost of new urban housing. Indeed, estimates from some Black Country towns, from Leeds, and from Trentham in Staffs suggests that city rents rose in real terms at about 30 percent each decade between the 1790s and the 1840s (Williamson, 1986a, Table 5). There is reason to believe, therefore, that some portion of the rise in the nominal wage gap between the 1790s and the 1850s was driven by rising city rents and thus by the rising relative cost of living in the city.

By how much did urban rents exceed rural rents? It turns out that we have very good information documenting the differential. In the early 1830s, the Manchester Statistical Society initiated a set of housing surveys which were quite remarkable. The first of these involved 4,102 families in a working class district of Manchester (1834, covering the police divisions of St. Michael's and New Cross). To augment their sample and to make comparative judgments possible, the Society then surveyed rural districts outside of Dudley, followed by similar surveys of Rutland and Northumberland. By the 1840s, statistical societies in London, Bristol, Leeds and elsewhere were replicating the work of the Manchester group. Each of these studies was surprisingly detailed, including information on the size and quality of the dwellings surveyed as well as the districts in which they were located—e.g., the number of families per privy, quality of drainage, distance to water supply and its quality, persons per room, and so on. The information on the quality of these dwellings is sufficiently detailed that the rents quoted in Table 4 can be viewed as applying to fairly homogeneous housing between cities, towns, and the countryside. However, since most of the rural rents are for dwellings which include small gardens and pig sties, Table 4 probably understates the size of the urban-rural rent differential.[3] I have not been able to secure the necessary data to estimate through hedonic regressions the value of those rural perquisites, so I have no evidence of the quantitative magnitude of the understatement.

The high cost of city rents in the 1830s and 1840s is certainly confirmed by the evidence in Table 4. London rents for the working class were about two and a half times those prevailing in the rural South, and the same was true of Manchester compared with the rural North. Furthermore, there was considerable variance between cities, generally higher the bigger and more

[3] It might be argued that city rents are understated for another reason—disamenities. High rents reflect land scarcity, land scarcity breeds crowding, and crowding tends to create pollution, crime and other environmental "bads". Shouldn't house rents at some urban "bad" location reflect these disamenities in the form of lower rents? Classical urban economics suggests this is so, but we will instead explore the impact of urban "bads" directly on employment decisions and thus on wages, rather than indirectly through residential decisions and thus on rents.

TABLE 4
Urban and Rural Dwelling Rents, 1834–1851

Region	*Annual Rent (£)*	*Date*	*Source and Notes*
London	9.42		Unweighted average of the following:
St. George's, Hanover Sq., Inner Ward	11.06	1843	JSSL, 6(1843): 1465 families of the "poorest localities" of the Ward.
St. George's, East End	9.32	1845	JSSL, 11(1848): 1954 working class families.
St. Margaret's and St. John's, Westminister	7.89	1840	JSSL, 3(1840–41): 5366 working class families.
Northern Towns	7.01		Weighted average (using 1841 population) of the following:
Manchester	7.58	1834	BAAS, 9(1839): 4102 working class families in police division of St. Michael's and New Cross.
Black Country Towns	7.80	1815–1850	Barnsby (1971), p. 236, covering the period 1815–1850.
Leeds	6.67	1838/39	JSSL, 2(1839–40): 61,212 working class persons in eight wards.
Macclesfield	6.06	1842	"Local Reports," p. 246: 8,902 tenements or cottages.
Stockport	6.65	1842	"Local Reports," p. 246: 14,925 tenements or cottages.
Newcastle	4.78	1842	"Local Reports," p. 246: 2,888 tenements or cottages.
Stoke-upon-Trent	5.55	1842	"Local Reports," p. 246: 8,737 tenements or cottages.

Rural North	3.13		Weighted average (using 1841 population) of the following:
Rural North Midlands	3.11	1839–1851	"Local Reports," pp. 133–137, 153, 186–190, 250 and Caird (1967), p. 474: Lincs, Staffs, Derby, Notts.
Rural North	3.00	1851	Caird (1967), p. 474: Northumb.
Rural Northwest	3.15	1839–1851	"Local Reports," pp. 186–190; 227–228 and Caird (1967), p. 474: Cumb., Ches., Salop, Lancs.
Rural South	4.03		Weighted average (using 1841 population) of the following:
Rural East	3.74	1839–1851	"Local Reports," pp. 133–137 and Caird (1967), p. 474: Norfolk, Suffolk, Camb., Essex, Hunts.
Rural West	3.69	1839–1851	"Local Reports," p. 15 and Caird (1967), p. 474: Cornwall, Worc., Devon, Wilts., Hereford.
Rural Home Counties	3.37	1851	Caird (1967), p. 474: Surrey, Bucks, Berk.
Rural Southeast	5.43	1839–1851	"Local Reports," pp. 36–40 and Caird (1967), p. 474: Sussex, Hampshire, Kent.
Rural South Midlands	3.68	1839–1851	"Local Reports," pp. 96–137, 153 and Caird (1967), p. 474: Leic., Northamp., Rutland, Glouc.

Notes: These attempt to control for dwelling quality. They are "average" in quality and space, although the rural dwellings normally included a garden and/or pig sty, thus implying an understatement of the true cost of housing in the city, which did not have such prequisities. JSSL refers to the *Journal of the Statistical Society of London*; BAAS to the *British Association for the Advancement of Science*; and "Local Reports" to *Local Reports on the Sanitary Condition of the Labouring Population of England* (July 1842).

TABLE 5
Regional Cost of Living Differentials in the 1840s (London = 100)

	(1)	(2)	(3)	(4)
	Crafts' Economiser		*Williamson's Geometric Weights*	
Region	*Rural Rent Weights*	*Urban Rent Weights*	*London Weights*	*Northern Town Weights*
London	100.0	100.0	100.0	109.0
Northern Towns	94.7	95.4	91.3	100.0
North Midlands Rural	90.2	83.0	82.6	89.9
North Rural	90.1	82.9	82.2	89.9
Northwest Rural	87.4	80.6	81.4	88.3
East Rural	93.7	86.1	86.6	92.7
West Rural	95.9	87.9	87.0	92.8
Home Counties Rural	96.5	88.5	87.3	93.3
Southwest Rural	93.4	85.7	89.9	96.3
South Midlands Rural	90.7	83.6	84.0	89.6
Northern Rural	na	na	82.1	89.5
Southern Rural	na	na	86.8	92.7
Urban-Rural Differential:				
North	na	na	9.2	10.5
South	na	na	13.2	16.8
All England	na	na	10.9	13.6

Source: Cols. (1) and (2) are from Crafts (1982), Table 6, p. 62 where his rural and urban budget weights for rents are 0.065 and 0.15 respectively. Cols. (3) and (4): the prices of provisions are from *ibid.*, Table 2, p. 55, the same prices used by Crafts to construct his Economiser; rents are taken from Table 4; and the budget weights are from Williamson, (1985a), Appendix Table A.1, p. 210, where northern rural rent weights are 0.083, southern rural rent weights 0.085, and urban rent weights 0.191.

1841 population weights used to construct northern and southern rural. See Table 1 for sources.

dense the city. The variance seems to have been far less between rural locations, suggesting that it was indeed city land scarcity and nominal wage costs facing the building trades that determined the structure of dwelling rents across England.

Table 5 offers regional cost-of living differentials by adding our new rent estimates to Crafts' provision prices, and by applying what I view to be more appropriate budget weights. While the difference between Crafts' "Economiser" indices and my geometric weight indices is not great, the new figures do suggest somewhat larger rural-urban cost-of-living differentials. In short, the cost-of-living for unskilled workers was 13.2 percent lower in the rural South than in London, while it was 10.5 percent lower in the rural North than in the northern towns. For England as a whole, it was 12.3 percent lower (the average of columns 3 and 4).

These cost-of-living differentials are too small to account for anything but a modest share of the nominal wage gaps observed, so we must in addition look elsewhere for explanations.

IV. Going from nominal to real wage gaps: urban disamenities

What about the poor quality of urban life? Didn't urban employers have to pay a premium to attract potential rural emigrants to locations of poorer environmental quality? Recent work of mine (Williamson 1981, 1982) attempted to assess the value of these ghastly urban disamenities by estimating hedonic earnings equations on urban parish wages reported in the 1834 Poor Law Inquiry.[4] The exercise was successful, making it possible to place a value on disamenities incurred when migrating from a relatively pleasant village environment (e.g., Sweet Auburn) to a very unpleasant big city environment (e.g., Sheffield). According to these estimates, it required a wage premium of 7 to 13 percent to compensate workers for the inferior urban environmental standards in the North of England, although no compensation was required in the South (Williamson 1982, p. 234).

These estimates can be improved in three ways. First, we now have the better regional deflators in Table 5 which presumably will improve the quality of the parish real wage estimates used in the hedonic regressions. Second, it has been suggested that ordinary least squares is inappropriate in estimating the hedonic equations since one of the key disamenity proxies, the infant mortality rate, is itself a function of the real wage. If so, then instrumental variables may be a better econometric device to apply to the data. In what follows, therefore, I will report both the ordinary least squares and the instrumental variables estimates. Third, the marginal disamenities package may have been misspecified. The cost of the package was calculated as

$$\text{COST} = \text{B1DDEN} + \text{B2DPOP} + \text{B3DINFM}$$

where DDEN refers to the difference in density between some typical rural village and large city, DPOP refers to the difference in population size, and DINFM refers to the difference in infant mortality. The B_j are weights which emerge from the hedonic regression. COST was then expressed as a percentage of the village unskilled wage. I have been persuaded, however, that COST should include the influence of DINFM only since density is simply another (and poorer) proxy for urban disamenities and since population size is simply an index of city living costs and perhaps even labor market disequilibrium. Thus, the remainder of this paper will calculate the cost of the disamenity package as

$$\text{COST} = \text{B1DINFM}.$$

[4] To repeat, these hedonic earnings equations are estimated on *urban* parish wages; that is, they are estimated on intra-urban wage gaps among large cities and small market towns, not on farm-urban wage gaps. The estimated urban disamenities premium is assumed to apply to the farm-urban comparisons, but it may, of course, understate them.

TABLE 6
Calculating the Urban Disamenities Premium for the 1830 s

Item	*North*	*South*	*Notes*
Average rural wage (w)	12.114 sh.	13.699 sh.	Weekly wage in 11 southern rural parishes and 6 northern rural parishes underlying the 66 parishes in the regressions reported in Williamson, 1986a, Appendix Table 1, weighted by population size, and deflated by cost of living.
ΔINFM	92.34	69.19	Difference in infant mortality rate per 1000 between rural parishes noted above and 10 southern urban parishes plus 6 northern urban parishes underlying the regression reported in Williamson, 1986a, Appendix Table 1, weighted by population size.
$\text{COST}_1 = \hat{\beta}_1 \Delta\text{INFM}$	1.480 sh.	1.107 sh.	The estimate $\hat{\beta}_1 = 0.0160$ is from Appendix Table 1, OLS, and we take it to be the same in both regions.
$\text{COST}_2 = \hat{\beta}_2 \Delta\text{INFM}$	3.630 sh.	2.720 sh.	The estimate $\hat{\beta}_2 = 0.0393$ is from Williamson, 1986a, Appendix Table 1, instrumental variables, and we take it to be the same in both regions.
$\text{PREMIUM}_1 = (\text{COST}_1 \div w) \times 100$	12.22%	8.08%	The average for all England is 9.7%, using 1841 population weights.
$\text{PREMIUM}_2 = (\text{COST}_2 \div w) \times 100$	29.97%	19.86%	The average for all England is 23.9%, using 1841 population weights.

Source: See text for a description of the method.

The new urban disamenity regressions are summarized elsewhere (Williamson, 1986a, Appendix Table 1). Table 6 reports the disamenities premium as a percent of rural real wages. The premium was higher in the North of England—ranging between 12 and 30 percent, than in the South of England—ranging between 8 and 20 percent. The larger nominal wage gaps down South cannot be explained by larger urban disamenities in London, since the northern towns were environmentally worse. For England as a whole, the urban disamenities premium ranged between 10 and 24 percent.

In short, city employers had to pay a higher nominal wage for two reasons—they were expensive places to live and they were environmentally unpleasant places to live. It appears that environmental forces were at least as important a quantitative influence as high living costs in contributing to the nominal wage gap.

V. Accounting for the wage gap

Adding poor relief payments

One final adjustment remains. As Karl Polanyi (1944), Arthur Redford (1926) and so many others have pointed out, prior to 1834 and the passage of the new Poor Laws, poor relief served to augment the wage income of agricultural laborers, especially in the grain-producing South of England. Since able-bodied farm laborers were being supported during slack season, and since those payments are not included in the nominal wage earnings estimates reported in Table 1, they must somehow be added. If we fail to do so, the true wage gap will be overstated, especially in the South of England, where, as we have seen, market wage gaps were the greatest.

Fortunately, George Boyer (1985) has recently constructed some estimates that seem to fit our needs nicely. Boyer had to face two problems in constructing estimates of the extent to which farm laborers' incomes were augmented by relief payments. First, he had to estimate the share of a parish's relief expenditures which actually went to agricultural laborers and their families (in contrast with the non-able-bodied poor). Boyer believes that a share ranging between 33 and 50 percent is most plausible. To err on the conservative side, and given that not all rural laborers received relief, we have used Boyer's 33 percent estimate in what follows. Second, poor relief expenditures were correlated with grain specialization. Thus, parishes in the East, Southeast, and Home County regions were the heart of Speenhamland, while those in the West and South Midlands had much less generous relief, and those to the North had little relief (of able-bodied) at all. We shall, as a result, assume no agricultural relief (of able-bodied) in the rural North, and take the levels in the West and in the South Midlands to have been only about one quarter of the main Speenhamland counties.

Based on Boyer's data, it appears that poor relief payments increased the incomes of unskilled rural labor by about 10.5 percent over their wage earnings in the Speenhamland counties, by about 7.1 percent in the South of England as a whole, and by about 4.4 percent in England overall (Williamson, 1986a, Appendix Table 2).

Were wage gaps illusory?

Table 7 offers a final accounting of the wage gap in the 1830s. After adjusting for the fact that cities were expensive, that cities were environmentally unattractive and required some compensation for the "bads" prevailing there, and that poor relief was used to augment workers' incomes in the countryside during slack season, much of the wage gap disappears. This is especially true of the South of England where city living costs were so high (London rents in particular) and where rural relief was more significant. Thus, while the nominal wage gap between London and the rural South was an enormous 106.2 percent, the true real income gap ranged between 39.5 and 54.7 percent. That is, the gap down South is cut by more than a half when it is measured properly. In the North of England, the wage gap tends to evaporate entirely when it is measured properly. Here the nominal gap was 36.3 percent, while the true real income gap was 8.7 percent or less. The wage gap and labor market failure appears to have been solely a southern problem. For England as a whole, the nominal wage

TABLE 7
Decomposing the Nominal Wage Gap

Item	*The Wage Gap (in %)* South	North	All England
(1) Nominal wages	106.2	36.3	73.2
(2) Adjusted by cost of living	79.0	21.9	52.1
(3) Also adjusted by rural poor relief of able-bodied	67.1	21.9	46.1
(4) Also adjusted by disamenities premium for city life			
(4a) Premium 1	54.7	8.7	33.2
(4b) Premium 2	39.5	−6.2	17.9

Source: Row (1) is taken from Table 1. Row (2) is derived by applying the cost of living deflators in Table 5 to the nominal wages in Table 1. Row (3) is based on Boyer, (1985), Table 1 and discussed in the text, where poor relief payments to rural laborers is added onto real wages. Row (4) is derived by inflating these rural real wages by the disamenity premium estimates in Table 6.

gap was 73.2 percent, while the true real income gap was far less, ranging between 17.9 and 33.2 percent.

Much of the wage gap *was* illusory, but it fails to disappear entirely. Spatial labor market disequilibrium *was* an attribute of the First Industrial Revolution. Yet, the labor market disequilibrium in England in the 1830s no longer looks unique. That is, after all of these necessary adjustments to the nominal wage gap are made, the true English wage gap now looks very much like the experience of other 19th century developing countries, and even like the contemporary Third World.

VI. The quantitative importance of labor market failure: deadweight losses

The issues

How badly did labor markets fail during the First Industrial Revolution? Economic historians typically attack this question in one of two ways. First, they seek evidence of open unemployment, of disguised unemployment, or of wage gaps between workers of comparable skill, since (most) theory suggests that such evidence offers clear symptoms of market failure. Second, they seek evidence of institutional or government intervention which (most) theory tells us will generate evidence of market failure, such as labor unions and monopsony power. Since every economy exhibits such evidence, one is never sure how to interpret such descriptive histories. How would we recognize significant labor market failure when presented with such evidence?

Lurking behind each of these histories is an implicit counterfactual: If there had been an optimal allocation of labor in England in the 1830s, by how much would national income have been raised? Would industrialization have taken place much more rapidly? And who would have gained the most by the elimination of the labor market failure?

Since the efficiency of unfettered markets is an article of faith to so many neoclassical economists, and since the pervasiveness of imperfections and their contribution to market failure is an equally strong article of faith to their critics, we must proceed with caution. I propose to adopt the null hypothesis of the Chicago School, namely no appreciable increment in aggregate economic welfare could have been achieved had wage gaps disappeared and had the distribution of labor been optimal in England in the 1830s.[5]

The Chicago School null hypothesis strikes me as a harsh test of the efficient operation of English labor markets. After all, we are assuming, like most development economists, that the real wage gaps documented in Table 7 reflect disequilibrium. They may not. First, they may reflect the real (as opposed to psychic) costs of moving. Second, they may reflect our inability to fully control for differences in the quality of labor (even among young, unskilled males), immigration to the city having selected individuals with attributes which had real economic value to city employers. Third, they may reflect urban employers' attempts to minimize turnover, in which case the cost of an efficiency unit of labor may in fact have been equalized between sectors even though measured wage gaps persisted. Fourth, higher urban wages may simply reflect lower life expectancies in the cities, the higher "spot" wage necessary to generate similar discounted earnings over lifetimes. Fifth, the higher male adult wage may simply compensate for more limited earnings opportunities for current or expected family members. I suspect that none of these factors was very important since the city workers being considered were largely young, unmarried and unskilled day laborers in the building trades. Finally, higher wages in urban employment may reflect greater job uncertainty or the cost of job search. This latter view is the essential contribution of the Todaro model (Todaro, 1969; Harris and Todaro, 1970), applied so extensively to Third World labor markets. Indeed, Sidney Pollard (1978, pp. 902–3) believes that it is applicable to 19th century England as well. "Good" city jobs are defined here as high paying and with a relatively high degree of employment certainty. Thus, Todaro stresses the role of "casual" employment in the urban service sector as a holding area for the reserve army of immigrants who have come to the city in the anticipation of getting the more attractive jobs. Certainly Mayhew (1861) made much of London's traditional urban service sector and unskilled casual labor has played an important part in 19th century labor

[5] Berry and Sabot (1978), pp. 1200 and 1230. I have found their stimulating survey of labor market performance in developing countries very useful in organizing my own thoughts about England in the 1830s.

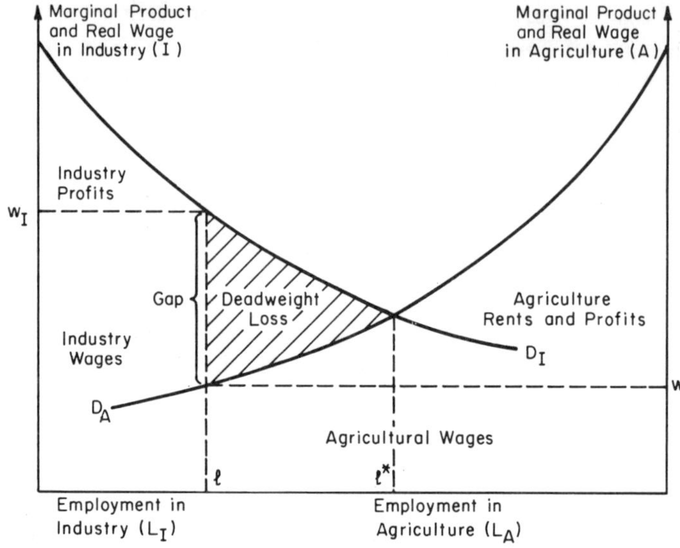

FIG. 1. "Partial" general equilibrium analysis of wage gaps in two sectors.

histories since.[6] The key here, of course, is that there may have been higher uncertainty attached to unskilled casual work in the city (like the building trades), and that the measured wage gaps reflect some compensation for such uncertainty.[7] If so, we have another argument for the view that the measured wage gaps in Table 7 may not reflect labor market disequilibrium at all.

Thus, the Chicago School null hypothesis is a harsh standard by which to judge the efficiency of English labor markets in the 1830s.

"Partial" general equilibrium analysis: deadweight losses

How can the Chicago School null hypothesis be tested? I propose first to implement empirically the analysis in Fig. 1. This familiar diagram shows employment distribution between agriculture and non-agriculture in the presence of wage gaps. Given wages in the two sectors, and given the two derived labor demand functions, then the deadweight loss associated with labor market failure is the shaded area in the diagram. In the presence of the failure, national income is simply the sum of the areas under each of those two derived demand curves, up to employment at *l*. If the wage gaps

[6] Williamson (1985c), p. 8. I should add that the paper just cited does not find any evidence in support of the Todaro hypothesis when confronted with data drawn from the 1851 British Census.

[7] The issue here is not *predictable* seasonal unemployment. Such factors are already embedded in the wage earnings estimates in Tables 1 and 7.

were eliminated, migrants would have left agriculture for non-agricultural employment, and employment would have been optimally distributed at l^*. National income would have been increased by the shaded area, or by the elimination of the deadweight loss.[8] Since we have already constructed the real wage estimates for the two sectors (e.g., the wage gaps in Table 7), and since Deane and Cole (1962, Tables 31 and 37, pp. 143 and 166) supply estimates for labor force distribution and national income for 1831, all that remains is to guess at alternative values of the labor demand elasticities in the two sectors. We shall consider a range of estimates. Assuming a Cobb-Douglas production function in agriculture, and given the price elasticity of demand for agricultural goods, then Marshall's formula yields the elasticity of demand for labor in agriculture.[9] If one views the English economy as relatively closed to trade, then the elasticity is 0.68. If instead one views the English economy as relatively open to trade, then the elasticity is more like 1.10. I find the latter assumption more attractive, but both will be utilized so that we can be assured that our results are robust. For non-agriculture I rely on a wide range of contemporary estimates from 20th century America—0.25, 0.75 and 3.0.[10] Once again, this range is sufficiently broad to give us assurance that our results are robust, although I favor the middle value of 0.75 given the importance of non-tradables in the non-agricultural bundle and their likely low price elasticity of demand.

Table 8 summarizes the results of the experiment. Three initial wage gaps are postulated. If the reader feels uneasy with my estimates of urban disamenities, but accepts the rural/urban price deflators, then he will favor the wage gap of 52.1 percent. I favor the conservative estimate of the size of the urban disamenity premium, so a wage gap of 33.2 percent seems more relevant to me. No doubt the Chicago School among my readers will favor the larger urban disamenity premium estimate and therefore the lower wage

[8] Donald McCloskey performed a similar experiment to assess the impact of improved capital markets between 1780 and 1860. However, he did not focus on the issue of optimal resource allocation. See McCloskey (1981, pp. 118–119).

[9] Given a Cobb-Douglas production function in agriculture, and assuming the economy to be closed to trade, the elasticity of demand for agricultural labor is written

$$(1-\theta_{LA}) + \theta_{LA}(\varepsilon_A) = \eta_{LA}$$

where θ_{LA} is labor's share and ε_A is the price elasticity of demand for agricultural goods. Estimates for these two parameters for 1821 can be found in Williamson (1985a, Appendix D).

I should emphasize that the typical "partial" general equilibrium analysis of distortions ignores the interaction between factor markets and product markets. Thus, if the removal of a distortion causes labor emigration from agriculture, then agricultural output should contract, and agricultural prices should tend to rise, unless the small country case is invoked. The opposite is the case, of course, in industry. The analysis in this paper includes these interactions between factor and product markets.

[10] Estimates of the elasticity of demand for labor in manufacturing can be found in the survey by Hammermesh and Grant (1979, Table 2, pp. 526–528).

TABLE 8

Assessing the Deadweight Loss of Labor Market Disequilibrium in 1831: "Partial" General Equilibrium in Two Sectors, Agriculture and Non-Agriculture

(1)	(2)	(3)	(4)	(5)	(6)	(7)	(8)	(9)	(10)	(11)	(12)
	Labor Demand Elasticities		*Emigrants*		*Deadweight Loss*		*Average Wage (£)*		*% Change In*		
Initial Wage Gap (%)	η_A	η_{NA}	*Number (000)*	*Share of Agricultural Labor Force (%)*	£(000)	*Share of Nat'l Income (%)*	*In Disequilibrium*	*In Equilibrium*	*Agricultural Wage*	*Average Wage*	*% Increase In Non-Agricultural Employment*
52.1	0.68	0.25	262.2	14.6	1857	0.55	37.51	34.00	26.1	−9.4	4.9
52.1	0.68	0.75	368.2	20.5	2722	0.80	37.51	37.76	40.0	0.7	6.8
52.1	0.68	3.00	430.5	24.0	3272	0.96	37.51	40.32	49.5	7.5	8.0
52.1	1.10	0.25	330.3	18.4	2295	0.68	37.51	32.43	20.2	−13.5	6.1
52.1	1.10	0.75	516.1	28.7	3762	1.11	37.51	36.67	36.0	−2.2	9.6
52.1	1.10	3.00	642.0	35.7	4850	1.43	37.51	40.28	49.3	7.4	11.9
33.2	0.68	0.25	180.7	10.0	814	0.24	33.69	31.51	16.8	−6.5	3.3
33.2	0.68	0.75	256.8	14.3	1193	0.35	33.69	33.82	25.4	0.4	4.8
33.2	0.68	3.00	303.1	16.8	1438	0.42	33.69	35.37	31.2	5.0	5.6
33.2	1.10	0.25	227.2	12.6	1010	0.30	33.69	30.49	13.1	−9.5	4.2
33.2	1.10	0.75	360.9	20.1	1662	0.49	33.69	33.05	22.6	−1.9	6.7
33.2	1.10	3.00	456.4	25.4	2164	0.64	33.69	35.18	30.5	4.4	8.5
17.9	0.68	0.25	104.6	5.8	254	0.07	30.59	29.45	9.2	−3.7	1.9
17.9	0.68	0.75	150.4	8.4	372	0.11	30.59	30.66	13.7	0.3	2.8
17.9	0.68	3.00	179.3	10.0	449	0.13	30.59	31.47	16.7	2.9	3.3
17.9	1.10	0.25	131.2	7.3	316	0.09	30.59	28.89	7.1	−5.6	2.4
17.9	1.10	0.75	212.0	11.8	521	0.15	30.59	30.22	12.1	−1.2	3.9
17.9	1.10	3.00	272.9	15.2	684	0.20	30.59	31.32	16.1	2.4	5.1

Sources and Notes: The initial (real) wage gaps are taken from Table 7, "All England," for three cases: 52.1%, cost of living adjusted only; 33.2% and 17.9%, cost of living plus poor relief plus two alternative city disamenities premia adjustments. The labor demand elasticities assumed in the experiments are discussed in the text. The calculations implement Figure 1, and we require the following additional initial values for 1831: $L_A = 1.8$ million, $L_{NA} = 5.4$ million (Deane and Cole, 1962, Table 31, p. 143); and national income = £340 million (Deane and Cole, 1962, Table 37, p. 166). I have bracketed what seems to me the "best guess" among all of these experiments.

gap of 17.9 percent. I have bracketed in Table 8 the case which I think is the "best guess", but most of the findings are robust across all cases.

What do we find? In no case does the deadweight loss exceed 1.5 percent of 1831 national income, while the "best guess" estimate is more like 0.5 percent, a tiny number.[11] It hardly seems possible to develop a case for English labor market failure on the basis of such estimates. Nor is it possible to argue that labor market failure of this sort played a significant role in constraining English growth during the industrial revolution. A corollary is that any improvement in labor market efficiency after 1831 cannot have contributed much to growth performance over the remainder of the 19th century, Edward Denison, Simon Kuznets and development economists notwithstanding.[12] Nor is this evidence very kind to a similar thesis offered by Nick Crafts. In his recent book, Crafts (1985, p. 2) has argued that English agricultural labor was released early and fast, and that this factor reallocation contributed significantly to economy-wide productivity gains. If the labor market disequilibrium generated by the industrial revolution up to 1831 implied only a tiny deadweight loss, how could the elimination of that loss contribute much to overall growth thereafter or even before?

Table 8 deals with two sectors split along agricultural and non-agricultural lines. Since agriculture employed only about a quarter of the labor force in 1831 (1.8 million out of 7.2 million), perhaps it is inevitable that the deadweight loss would be small. Furthermore, the wage gaps documented in Table 7 might be viewed by some to apply to rural versus urban employment, not just agricultural versus non-agricultural employment, and rural employment was a far larger share of total employment, in fact more than half (4 million out of 7.2 million). Yet, when the two sectors are split along rural and urban lines the largest deadweight loss is still no bigger than 2.5 percent of national income, and the "best guess" figure is only 0.6 percent (Williamson, 1986a, Appendix Table 3).

So far labor market failure during the First Industrial Revolution doesn't seem to have cost the average Englishman very much, and an optimal allocation of labor would have added very little to aggregate economic welfare. Why, then, do British economic historians make such a fuss over the lack of a fully integrated national labor market?

[11] Small deadweight losses are typical in the applied public finance and labor economics literature, so these results for English wage gaps in 1831 should come as no surprise. Thirty years ago, Leibenstein (1957) was able to report seven studies where such deadweight loss calculations were performed, and in no case did any of them exceed 1 percent of national income. Similar findings were reported in the early 1970s by Dougherty and Selowsky (1973). More recently, Shoven and Whalley (1984) have shown the same.

[12] In a series of publications on the "sources of growth", Denison has argued that the reallocation of labor from low to high productivity sectors contributed in large measure to rapid growth in post World War II Japan (Denison and Chung, 1976, Chp. 5) and in much of post World War II Europe (Denison, 1967, Chps. 18 and 21). He did so by invoking the Kuznets Effect (Kuznets, 1966), a statistical approach which ignores the economics embedded in Figure 1. This tradition is carried to late 19th Century Britain by Matthews et al. (1982, Chp. 9).

VII. The quantitative importance of labor market failure: distribution and accumulation effects

Who lost and who gained?

While the deadweight loss associated with labor market failure estimated so far is trivial, distributional incidence is another matter entirely. Figure 2 tells us exactly who gains and who loses. With the disappearance of wage gaps, and with the emigration of labor from agriculture, wages would have risen in agriculture and fallen in industry. Given no change in capital, land or technology in either of the two sectors, it follows that rents (plus profits) in agriculture would have diminished and profits in industry would have increased. Profits in industry would have risen by ABHC, an increase in their producers' surplus. Rents (or, more likely, farmers' profits) in agriculture would have fallen by EHGF, a decrease in their producers' surplus. It is not clear, however, how common labor would have fared. Laborers gain in agriculture but lose in industry for an ambiguous net change of DGFE minus ABDC. The net change in the wage bill will be influenced by relative labor demand elasticities: if they are lower in agriculture, workers gain; if they lower in industry, workers lose.

Table 9 offers some estimates of who gained and who lost from labor market failure based on the "best guess" case in Table 8. The estimates make it quite clear that the offsetting distributive effects of labor market failure were far greater than the overall efficiency losses. Farmers and/or landlords gained much from labor market failure (9.85 million £) while

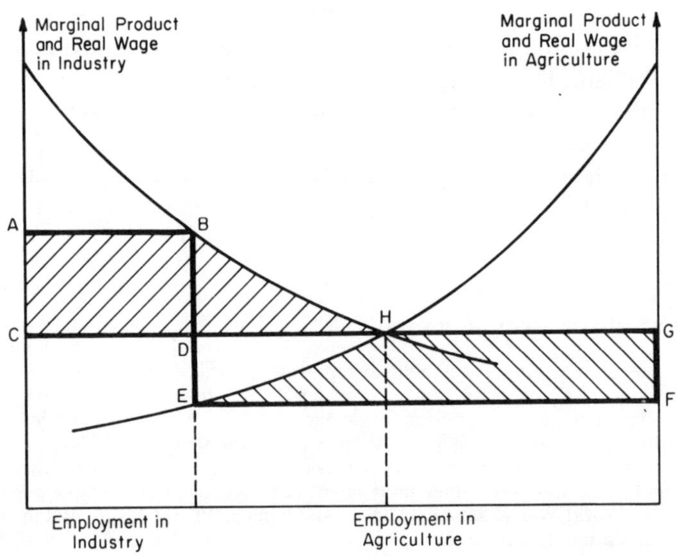

FIG. 2. "Partial" general equilibrium analysis of wage gaps: who gains and who loses?.

TABLE 9
Who Gained and Who Lost From Labor Market Failure? Some Estimates for 1831

Item	*Figure 2 Notation*	*Gains (+) and Losses (−) (Millions £s)*	*Share in 1831 National Income*
Change in Wage Bill	ABDC minus DGFE	+4.554	+1.3%
Change in Industry Profits	minus ABHC	−16.066	−4.7
Change in Agricultural Rents	plus EHGF	+9.850	+2.9
Change in National Income	BHE	−1.662	−0.5

Note: This example uses the "best guess" case in Table 8, where the wage gap = 33.2%, $\eta_A = 1.1$, and $\eta_{NA} = 0.75$.

capitalists lost even more (16.066 million £). Furthermore, these gains and losses appear to have been a significant share of total non-wage incomes: agricultural rents (plus profits) may have been augmented by as much as 34 percent by the labor market failure while profits in industry may have been reduced by as much as 20 percent.[13]

These big numbers are, of course, only tentative estimates, but they suggest that we need to know far more about the causes of the labor market failure. They also suggest that the calculation of deadweight losses may be the least interesting means of assessing factor market failure.

Industrialization and accumulation responses

The example also suggests how misleading comparative static deadweight loss calculations can be when assessing the importance of market failure to growth, accumulation, and industrialization. While it is true that the elimination of the deadweight loss would have augmented national income only by about 0.5 percent—about a year's worth of growth in per capita income according to Crafts' growth estimates (Crafts, 1985, Table 2.11, p. 45), it must have tended to choke off industrial employment by much more. In the absence of the labor market failure, non-agricultural employment would have been augmented by 6.7 percent—almost four years' worth of employment growth according to Deane and Cole's employment figures for the 1830s (Deane and Cole, 1962, Table 31, p. 143).

Furthermore, to the extent that the classical saving postulate holds (Marglin, 1984, pp. 324–328), industrial capital accumulation was also

[13] These calculations rely on Deane and Cole's (1962, Table 37, p. 166) estimates of 1831 value added in agriculture (79.5 million £) and in non-agriculture (260.5 million £). Labor's share in agricultural value added is assumed to be 0.51, while in industry it is assumed to be 0.63 (Williamson, 1985a, p. 241). Thus, the calculations take non-labor income to be about 39 million £ in agriculture and about 96.4 million £ in non-agriculture.

choked off by labor market failure. That is, if the reinvestment rate out of industrial profits was far higher than out of rents (and farmers' profits), then aggregate savings were lower in the presence of labor market failure, and so too must have been the rate of accumulation economy-wide. Even if the classical saving postulate did not hold, imperfect capital markets would have ensured that the rate of accumulation in *industry* would have been lower given the lower profits in the presence of labor market failure. This, after all, is the central premise of the classical labor surplus model (for its modern guise, see W. A. Lewis, 1954).

The finding that labor market failure significantly augmented agricultural rents at the expense of industrial profits certainly has its attraction. After all, most of us now agree that England achieved only modest rates of accumulation during the First Industrial Revolution (Williamson, 1984; 1985a, Chp. 11), even when compared with the rest of Europe (Crafts, 1985, p. 64). One of the explanations for this has been that English capital markets failed to innovate those changes which would have made external finance more accessible to industrial firms (Mokyr, 1985, pp. 33–38). Now we have another explanation, namely that labor market failure served to choke off industrial profits and thus accumulation.

VIII. Factor market failure in general equilibrium

Other forces making for too many farmers

There were other forces at work which tended to make English agriculture too big in the 1830s. Imperfect capital markets starved industry for funds, driving a wedge between rates of return in industry and agriculture. Since the industrial capital stock was, therefore, too low, industrial jobs were fewer than they would have been had capital markets been perfect. There were too many workers in agriculture on that score as well.[14] Which of these two forces had the biggest allocative and distributional impact on the English economy in the 1830s—labor market failure or capital market failure?

Capital market failure has long been a staple in the literature on the English industrial revolution, and it has an equally long tradition in contemporary development economics (McKinnon, 1973). As Postan (1935, p. 71) put it, "the reservoirs of savings were full enough, but

[14] In addition, commercial policy served to encourage more labor (and capital) to stay in agriculture than would have been the case under free trade. Tariffs served to take away incentive for industrial expansion as domestic prices were twisted to favor agriculture and to hurt industry. Since by 1840 there were duties on raw cotton, timber, copper and other raw materials, "the effective rate of protection for factors of production specialised in manufacturing was slightly negative" (McCloskey, 1980, p. 307; and Capie, 1983, pp. 12–18). And, of course, there were the Corn Laws. Susan Fairlee (1969, Table 3, p. 106) estimates that the Corn Laws served to increase grain prices some 20 percent above what they would have been under free trade in the 1830s. Surely this policy by itself meant there were too many farmers in England around 1831.

conduits to connect them to the wheels of industry were few and meagre." This view was so common even in the early 19th century, that the Classical Economists took it for granted that industrial profits and their reinvestment were the central determinants of accumulation and industrialization. Indeed, this view persists even today in growth paradigms which invoke the Cambridge Savings Equation (Marglin, 1984, pp. 324–328), as well as in the labor surplus model favored by development economists (Lewis, 1954).

The capital-market-failure thesis is not without its critics. Crouzet, for example, doubts that capital market failure played a very important role in the First Industrial Revolution, even in the 18th century:

> the eighteenth century capital market seems, to twentieth century eyes, badly organized, but the creators of modern industry do not seem to have suffered too much from its imperfection . . . English industry . . . seems to have overflowed with capital (Crouzet, 1965, pp. 187–188).

True, self-finance was the rule in English industry during the industrial revolution, but one wonders to what extent this result was induced by a capital market failure which made external finance so scarce. As Joel Mokyr has recently put it

> the question should be whether the Industrial Revolution in Britain would have occurred faster and more efficiently if financial constraints had been less stringent (Mokyr, 1985, p. 38).

The literature on capital market failure during the First Industrial Revolution seems to suffer the same shortcomings that we have already found in the labor market failure literature. Not enough attention has been paid to evidence of capital scarcity that really matters, namely: Was the rate of return to capital far higher in industry than in agriculture? Here, precision is impossible. McCloskey suggests that rates of return on industrial capital may have been as much as three times that of agriculture, 5 percent per annum in the latter and 15 percent in the former (McCloskey, 1981, p. 119). Based on scraps of evidence taken from the mid-19th century, the rates in industry appear to be more like two and a half times that of agriculture, still a wide discrepancy.[15] If more perfect capital markets had been able to eliminate these rate of return differentials, would the allocative

[15] F. M. L. Thompson (1963, p. 251) estimates the rate of return on industrial capital in 1846 to have been 8–9 percent. Paul David (1975, pp. 264–265) uses Thompson's data on estate improvements between 1847 and 1879 to get a rate of return on agricultural capital of 3.6 percent. Thompson himself feels that between 1846 and 1853 there were "no measureable returns" in agriculture (Thompson, 1963, p. 249). David also estimates the rate of return to agricultural mechanization to have been 2–4.5 percent between 1846 and 1853. Taking the rate of return to industrial capital at about 8.5 percent (Thompson's 8–9 percent in 1846), and the rate of return to agricultural capital at about 3.25 percent (David's 2–4.5 percent in 1851), then the ratio was about 2.4, the figure reported in the text and used in subsequent calculations. It might be relevant to note that the United States had very similar rate of return differentials between industry and agriculture in 1850 (James and Skinner, 1985, p. 528, gross returns to fixed capital).

gains have been significant? McCloskey (1981, pp. 118–119) doesn't think so, although his estimates are much too low since he doesn't allow labor to chase after capital as the latter gets reallocated. Even if McCloskey is right, shouldn't we also explore the implications of capital market failure for distribution, industrialization and accumulation? Deadweight loss calculations, as we have seen above, may miss the point.

A general equilibrium assessment

I propose to offer answers to these questions by appealing to a simple computable general equilibrium model. A variant of the model has been used elsewhere (Williamson, 1985a). As the Appendix makes it clear, the model has been modified, but its basic attributes are the same. It is a four sector model composed of agriculture, industry, services and mining. There are four social classes who supply inputs to the production process (landlords supplying agricultural land, capitalists and farmers supplying capital, common labor supplying unskilled labor, and the labor aristocracy supplying skills). The economy is a net importer of agricultural products and raw materials, and a net exporter of manufactures. The prices of the three tradables—raw materials, agricultural products and manufactures—are taken to be set by world market conditions and commercial policy, while the non-tradables—services and the products of the mines—are determined endogenously by domestic demand and supply. The model was designed to deal with comparative static issues only, but it is ideal for making exactly the kinds of distributional and resource allocative assessments posed above. It can be used to assess the impact of factor market failure on sectoral employment (were there too many farmers?), on national income (how big was the deadweight loss?), on industrialization (was industrial output constrained?), and on distribution (were profits, and thus accumulation, too low?). Those readers who are suspicious of such models may be appeased, at least in part, by the discovery that, where comparisons are relevant, most of the results of the simple partial equilibrium analysis above are reproduced in the more complex general equilibrium exercise below. Magnitudes, however, are bigger.

Table 10 presents the main findings under the assumption that capital is "quasi-mobile" between sectors; that is, imperfect capital markets drive a wedge between rates of return inside and outside agriculture, but capital migrates to the highest returns until that wedge is re-established (where industrial rates of return are 2.4 times that of agriculture). The assumption of capital "quasi-mobility" implies a long run assessment of the impact of factor market failure. I believe this is the appropriate assumption. Otherwise, capital is not allowed to chase after labor, and the impact of the labor market failure will be understated. Table 10 assesses the impact of an elimination of labor market failure (the 1831 "best guess' real wage gap is allowed to disappear), and an elimination of capital market failure (the ratio

TABLE 10

The Impact of Factor Market Failure: Assuming Capital "Quasi-Mobile"

Impact	(1) *Eliminating the Wage Gap and Labor Market Failure*	(2) *Eliminating the Rate of Return Gap and Capital Market Failure*	(3) *Eliminating Both Gaps and Labor plus Capital Market Failure* ($\neq$ (1) + (2))
A. *Agriculture*			
Percent Rise in Agriculture Output (Constant Prices)	−20.4%	−56.1%	−69.6%
Emigrants from Agriculture as a Percent of Agricultural Labor Force	−39.0	−51.4	−57.9
B. *Non-Agriculture*			
Percent Rise in Non-Agricultural Output (Constant Prices)	+13.4	+35.8	+39.8
Percent Rise in Non-Agricultural Employment (Unskilled Labor Only)	+15.5	+20.4	+23.0
Percent Rise in Non-Agricultural Profits (Nominal)	+11.2	+64.6	+78.1
C. *Manufacturing*			
Percent Rise in Manufacturing Output (Constant Prices)	+24.1	+63.6	+73.4
Percent Rise in Manufacturing Employment (Unskilled Labor Only)	+25.3	+40.6	+47.2
Percent Rise in Manufacturing Profits (Nominal)	+23.6	+114.7	+141.8
D. *Economy-Wide Increase in Real GNP*	+3.3	+8.2	+7.0

Notes: See text. Column (3) does not add the entries in (1) and (2), but rather reports the impact of the joint change.

TABLE 11
The Impact of Labor Market Failure Assuming Capital Immobile

Impact	*Eliminating the Wage Gap and Labor Market Failure*
A. *Agriculture*	
Percent Rise in Agricultural Output (Constant Prices)	−10.5%
Emigrants from Agriculture as a Percent of Agricultural Labor Force	−29.5
B. *Non-Agriculture*	
Percent Rise in Non-Agricultural Ooutput (Constant Prices)	+5.5
Percent Rise in Non-Agricultural Employment (Unskilled Labor Only)	+11.7
Percent Rise in Non-Agricultural Profits (Nominal)	+5.5
C. *Manufacturing*	
Percent Rise in Manufacturing Output (Constant Prices)	+11.0
Percent Rise in Manufacturing Employment (Unskilled Labor Only)	+16.7
Percent Rise in Manufacturing Profits (Nominal)	+10.8
D. *Economy-Wide Increase in Real GNP*	+0.6

Notes: See text and Table 10.

of industrial to agricultural rates of return is reduced to 1 from the 2.4 figure prevailing in the late 1840s). Table 11 presents the findings under the assumption that capital is completely immobile between agriculture and nonagriculture (although mobile within nonagriculture). The table therefore offers a shorter run assessment of the impact of the elimination of wage gaps. I believe this is an inappropriate assumption for the reasons given above. Consider the results reported in Table 10 first.

To begin with, the results listed in each column of Table 10 should satisfy economic intuition. The elimination of the wage gap, for example, tends to create labor scarcity in agriculture, output contracts, and employment contracts even more, since the relative scarcity of labor rises. Symmetrically, output expands in nonagriculture, and employment expands even more, since the relative scarcity of labor falls. The impact on output in the two sectors exceeds that attributable to employment changes alone since, of course, capital is allowed to chase after labor and the higher returns. Profits rise in nonagriculture, but by less than output. The explanation is a bit more subtle. Since the capital-labor ratio tends to fall in nonagriculture as the relative scarcity of labor falls, one would have thought that the rate of return to capital there would rise and thus that profits would rise by even more given that the capital stock has been augmented. But the rise in profits is somewhat less than expected since the prices of the nontradables (services and mining) decline. In any case, profits do rise with the elimination of the wage gaps, a result we found in the partial equilibrium analysis as well. Manufacturing output by itself gets an even bigger boost from the elimination of the wage gaps, primarily because, given the small-country assumption, the price of output remains stable there. Finally, and perhaps least interesting, real GNP increases with the elimination of the deadweight losses associated with labor market distortions.

Now consider the magnitudes. The deadweight losses reported in Table 10 are considerably higher than they were in the partial equilibrium case reported in Table 8 (3.3 versus 0.49 percent of GNP), primarily because capital is allowed to chase after labor in the general equilibrium case. (The deadweight losses are much smaller in the capital immobile case of Table 11, 0.6 percent of GNP, almost exactly the partial equilibrium result.) These deadweight losses associated with labor market failure are hardly trivial, to be sure, but they are considerably smaller than those associated with capital market failure (8.2 percent). Thus, the impact of capital market failure on the English economy in the 1830s was far greater than the impact of labor market failure.[16]

Of course, this is only a simple model of the English economy, and many of the parameters embedded in it are only guesses, so the empirical results reported in Table 10 should be viewed as suggestive rather than definitive. Nonetheless, the results are striking.

First, the results suggest that nonagricultural employment in general, and manufacturing employment in particular, must have been seriously choked off by factor market failure up to the 1840s. While England's industrialization performance was certainly impressive after the French Wars, it would have been far more impressive in the absence of these domestic factor market distortions. Indeed, nonagricultural employment would have been 23 percent higher. If that increase is stretched over the two decades 1821–1841, it implies that nonagricultural employment growth would have been about 3 percent per annum, not the 2 percent per annum actually achieved (Deane and Cole, 1962, p. 143). Manufacturing output would have been 73.4 percent higher. And if that increase is stretched over the period 1815 to 1841, it implies that industrial output growth would have been about 5.2 percent per annum, not the 3.1 percent per annum actually achieved (Harley, 1982, p. 276, "Divisia"). Thus, factor market distortions seriously inhibited industrialization in England after the French Wars, although capital market failure was the more serious constraint.

Second, these distortions had important distributional implications. Profits in nonagriculture would have been much higher (by 78.1 percent), and

[16] Note that the combined effects of labor market and capital market failure in Table 10 are *not* additive. Albert Fishlow and Paul David (1961) alerted us to that possibility some time ago. That is, perfect labor markets are a partial remedy for capital market failure and perfect capital markets are a partial remedy for labor market failure. However, Table 10 also shows that the deadweight losses associated with eliminating both factor market failure is *less* than that of eliminating capital market failure alone. That result is impossible in theory, but it has appeared in fact due to difficulties in handling non-linearities in the solution. I am exploring alternative algorithms to eliminate this quirk.

they would have been increased even more in manufacturing (by 141.8 percent, or more than double the actual profits which accrued to capitalists there). If the reinvestment rate out of nonagricultural profits was relatively high, as most of us believe, then the elimination of factor market distortions would have resulted in a significant rise in saving and accumulation, especially so in manufacturing. Of course, the elimination of the capital market distortions would also have made accessible to all potential savers the high rates of return in industry, and if saving was responsive to the rate of return, then economy-wide accumulation would have gotten an even bigger boost.

As we pointed out, Table 11 assumes capital to be immobile, so only the impact of labor market failure can be assessed there. The influence of these distortions are much smaller than in Table 10 where capital is allowed to chase after labor. I prefer the longer run assessment implied by Table 10 where imperfect and distorted capital markets are at least allowed some success in seeking out higher returns. Nonetheless, even under capital immobility assumptions, wage gaps still have a significant influence. Elimination of the wage gap would have raised GNP by 0.6 percent (the deadweight loss), nonagricultural employment by 11.7 percent, and non-agricultural output by 5.5 percent.

IX. Why didn't manufacturing capital migrate to the countryside to exploit rural labor surplus in the South?

Those large wage gaps in the South of England certainly pose a puzzle.

One can, of course, offer plausible explanations for the inability of rural emigration to eliminate the labor market disequilibrium between London and the southern countryside. The rate of emigration of the rural workforce *was* impressive, but it was restricted to young adults (Williamson, 1985b). For whatever the reason, those in their thirties and above rarely migrated. Even though those in their teens and twenties were very responsive to employment opportunities in London, that age cohort was, after all, a small share of the total rural labor force. Thus, the ability of rural emigration to accommodate the labor market disequilibrium was limited.

But surely there were no such constraints on the migration of manufacturing capital. Why didn't Ipswich, Great Yarmouth or Southampton become the Prestons, Oldhams, and Huddersfields of the South? Certainly factories migrated to labor surplus areas up North. And certainly they did so in New England early in America's ante bellum development, as they did in Japan early in the Meiji industrialization effort. Why didn't factories migrate to rural surplus areas in the South of England? Was power (e.g., coal) so much more expensive there that the advantage of cheap labor was offset? Were transport costs of intermediate inputs and finished manufactures so much higher? Were the agglomeration economies in key sectors, like textiles, so overwhelming that migration of factories away from the booming North was cost-inefficient even in the face of cheap southern labor? Or, is this another example of factor market failure?

This paper does not offer an answer to these questions, but they certainly need attention.

X. Implications

Factor markets *did* fail during the First Industrial Revolution, and it had important quantitative implications for employment growth in the cities, for the structural transformation of the economy, and perhaps even for accumulation. In a world where capital and labor were mobile but only imperfectly so, the following tentative implications seem warranted.

Economists almost always find deadweight losses associated with market failure to be modest. Industrial revolutions may be an exception. Labor market failure around 1831 may have cost England about 3 percent of GNP, a significant amount for an economy whose per capita income was growing at only about 0.5 percent per annum (Crafts, 1985, p. 45). When capital market failure is added, however, the figure rises to 7 percent. Factor market failure *did* matter in an aggregate sense, although the really significant failure was in capital markets.

In spite of high rates of emigration (Williamson, 1985b) and an "early release" of farm labor in England (Crafts, 1985), there were far too many farmers and laborers in agriculture. Wage gaps between city and countryside starved industry for labor and glutted the countryside. As a result, the agricultural labor force in 1831 may have been too big by 39 percent. In addition, rate of return differentials imply that industry was starved for and agriculture was glutted with capital. Too much capital in agriculture meant too many farmers working with that capital. The combined influence of labor and capital market failure may have made the agricultural labor force too big by as much as 58 percent in 1831. These figures are very large, so it is no wonder that English agriculture underwent such dramatic relative decline across the nineteenth century.

Industrial output and employment growth was certainly dramatic after the French Wars, but, nonetheless, that growth was seriously constrained by factor market distortions. Around 1831, nonagricultural employment would have been about 23 percent higher had factor market distortions been absent. The rate of industrialization was retarded on that score, and labor market failure contributed a good share to that result.

Recent work suggests that the rate of accumulation was slow in England during the French Wars *and* after (Crafts, 1985; Williamson, 1985a). One likely explanation among others is that capital markets failed to accommodate adequately investment demands in industry, and that industrial accumulation was, therefore, constrained by profits. The results reported here suggest that labor market distortions contributed to low profits by making labor too expensive in the cities and towns. Capital markets contributed to low profits, of course, by starving industry for capital. Nonagricultural profits might have been about 78 percent higher in 1831 had these factor market distortions been absent. In addition, we have that puzzling finding that manufacturing capital was reluctant to move out into the countryside in the South of England so as to exploit surplus labor there. If these findings are even close to the mark, they offer a promising explanation for slow rates of accumulation in England.

What remains to be seen, of course, is whether these tentative findings will hold up under more detailed scrutiny. There are two avenues that might be pursued, both of which would serve to deflate, but not destroy, the significance of these findings. First, the assumptions employed here might well be challenged. The most important of these is probably that the prices of tradables—manufactures and agricultural commodities—are taken as exogenous. To the extent that the decline of agriculture and the expansion of manufacturing would have raised agriculture's terms of trade, then the impact of factor market failure was smaller than estimated. How much smaller hinges on alternative assumptions about price elasticities of foreign supply of agricultural goods and foreign demand for manufactures. Second, the view that wage and rate of return gaps reflect disequilibrium and factor market distortion may also be challenged. If, for example, the rate of return gaps reflect risk, then we have overstated the influence of capital market failure. If, for example the wage gaps can be partially explained by moving costs, differences in efficiency embodied in labor, or any of the other forces listed in Section VI, then we have overstated the influence of labor market failure. Indeed, some might wonder how labor or capital market disequilibria could persist so long. After all, measured wage and rate of return gaps remain an attribute of English factor markets throughout the 19th century, although they never seem to get larger than in the middle of the century where we have made the factor market failure assessment. We need two ingredients to make the persistence of factor market disequilibria plausible—unbalanced factor demand expansion and constraints on mobility. The former has always been an attribute of industrial revolutions. The latter can be explained in a world where both physical and human capital are putty-clay, that is, only new capital and young adult labor migrate. Even though the rate of rural emigration of young adults was very rapid, those who migrated were almost never in their thirties and above. For one reason or another, older rural laborers simply did not leave. Thus, the labor market disequilibrium between city and countryside could not be accommodated by even the responsive migration of an age cohort which, after all, was only a small share of the total rural labor force.

What also remains to be seen is whether factor market failure was more serious in early nineteenth century England than it was in the followers who were about to mimic the First Industrial Revolution. Is it possible that the more rapid growth of the followers can be explained by more efficient factor markets? The answer awaits a careful comparative assessment of the magnitude of labor and capital market failure during industrial revolutions in England, France, Germany, America, Japan and even the Third World.

Harvard University

APPENDIX: MODELLING THE GENERAL EQUILIBRIUM EFFECTS OF FACTOR MARKET FAILURE

The general equilibrium model used in Section VIII has two versions, one where capital is mobile between sectors but with a wedge driving a gap between rates of return in agriculture and elsewhere, and one where capital is completely immobile between agriculture and elsewhere. The second is only an extension of the first, and thus this Appendix will dwell only on the first. Both are variants of a parent model that has been used elsewhere to analyse the impact of the French Wars (Williamson, 1984), the determinants of inequality across the British Kuznets Curve (Williamson, 1985a), and the impact of the Irish on British labor markets (Williamson, 1986b).

The model has five domestic factors of production:

farm land (J), excluding improvements other than initial clearing for cultivation and pasture;
capital (K), consisting of all reproducible capital in the private and public sectors, excluding dwellings;
unskilled labor (L), or total manhours compensated at the unskilled wage rate, including family labor time utilized on farms and in nonfarm proprietorships;
skills (S), or all attributes of labor inputs generating earnings in excess of the unskilled wage; and
intermediate resource inputs (B), used directly in the manufacturing sector or indirectly in the urban sectors facilitating manufacturing production.

In addition, the model introduces one imported intermediate input:

imported raw material inputs (F), processed by manufacturing and unavailable at home.

As with all comparative static models, factor endowments are given, so the first four in the list are determined exogenously. Intermediate inputs (F and B), however, are determined endogenously in response to supply and demand, domestic and foreign.

These factor inputs are used in the production of four sectoral outputs:

agriculture (A), or all national income originating in agriculture, forestry, and fisheries;
manufacturing (M), or all national income originating in manufacturing, building, and construction;
the tertiary sector (C), or all national income originating in finance, trade, gas, electricity and water, private services, local and national government, transport and communications; and
intermediate resources (B), or all national income originating in mining and quarrying.

The model is open to trade, and it conforms to the reality that Britain was a net importer of agricultural goods and a net exporter of manufactured goods. The small-country assumption has prices of all tradables determined exogenously by commercial policy (the Corn Laws) and by world markets. That is, demands for exportables and supplies of importables are taken to be highly price elastic. The home-produced intermediate good B cannot be traded internationally (for example, coal) while the foreign-produced intermediate good F cannot be produced at home (for example, cotton). Tertiary outputs (home services) cannot be traded.

Production relationships can be summarized as follows:

$$A = A(L, K, J),$$
$$M = M(L, K, S, B, F),$$
$$C = C(L, K, S, B),$$
$$B = B(L, K).$$

Capital and unskilled labor are assumed to move freely among all sectors, *except* that a gap is driven between wages and rates of return in agriculture and elsewhere, thus accommodating the labor and capital market failure discussed in the text; skilled labor is mobile between the tertiary and manufacturing sectors to which its use is restricted; land is specific to agricultural production; the imported intermediate resource (cotton) is an input to manufacturing only; and the home-produced intermediate resource (coal) is used in manufacturing and the service sector.

By the small-country assumption, P_A, P_M, and P_F are taken as exogenous. The remaining eight prices are determined endogenously:

d = rent earned on an acre of cleared farm land under crop or pasturage;
r_A = rent (or rate of return) earned on reproducible capital in agriculture;
r_I = rent (or rate of return) earned on reproducible capital in all nonagricultural sectors, and where the ratio of nonagricultural to agricultural rates of return is determined exogenously;
w_A = the wage rate (or annual earnings) for unskilled farm labor;
w_I = the wage rate (or annual earnings) for common labor in all nonagricultural sectors, and where the ratio of nonagricultural to agricultural unskilled wages is determined exogenously;
q = the wage (or annual earnings) for skills;
P_C = the price of tertiary services; and
P_B = the price of home-produced resources.

The first six of these prices are factor rents. Thus, the distribution of income can be explored by the behavior of farm rents and profits ($dJ + r_A K_A$), profits in nonagriculture ($r_I K_I$), the earnings of skills (qS), and the wages of unskilled labor ($w_A L_A + w_I L_I$).

The model also predicts the following seven quantities:

A = home-produced agricultural goods;
M = home-produced manufactured goods;
C = home-produced tertiary services;
B = home-produced resources;
A_M = imported agricultural goods;
M_X = exported manufactured goods;
F = imported intermediate goods.

Final product demands are endogenous, where demands are a function of per capita income, relative prices and population. National income is defined as:

$$Y = P_A A + P_M M + P_C C + D$$

where resource output, $P_B B$, is excluded since it is an intermediate good, and D is the net trade deficit in nominal terms. A final equation insures that the trade account is in balance:

$$P_A A_M + P_F F = P_M M_X + D.$$

The model can easily be converted into rates of change, and the experiments reported in the text exploit that fact.

In private correspondence and discussion, Peter Solar and Miles Kimball have pointed out some inconsistencies among the parameters used in earlier versions of this model. The listing which follows gives (c1821) empirical content to the model used here, and it includes a revision of those values which troubled Solar and Kimball:

Technology. Elasticities of substitution in production (σ_{ij}^k) are revised from my book (Williamson, 1985a, p. 242), in part to make them consistent at the value added level, but still retaining capital-skill relative complementarity:

$$\sigma_{KL}^A = \sigma_{KS}^A = \sigma_{JK}^A = \sigma_{LJ}^A = 1 \qquad \text{(Cobb-Douglas)}$$

$$\sigma_{KL}^M = \sigma_{LS}^M = 1.4059, \ \sigma_{KS}^M = 0.7029 \qquad \text{(CES)}$$

$$\sigma_{KL}^C = \sigma_{LS}^C = 1.0102, \ \sigma_{KS}^C = 0.5051 \qquad \text{(CES)}$$

$$\sigma_{KL}^B = 1 \qquad \text{(Cobb-Douglas)}$$

Demand. Based on "stylized facts of demand", the price elasticity of demand (ε_j) for manufactures is assumed elastic, for agriculture inelastic, and for services unit elastic, with no changes from my book (Williamson, 1985a, p. 242). In addition, Engel Effects are captured by assumptions on income elasticities (η_j)—high for manufactures and low for agriculture, with only little change from my book. Thus:

$$\varepsilon_A = -0.6, \ \varepsilon_M = -1.3, \ \varepsilon_c = -1.0$$

$$n_A = 0.6, \ n_M = 1.35, \ n_c = 1.11$$

The cross-price elasticities (ε_{ij}) are implied by adding-up conditions (Williamson, 1985a, p. 242):

$$\varepsilon_{AM} = 0.0896, \ \varepsilon_{AC} = -0.0896, \ \varepsilon_{MC} = 0.1080$$

$$\varepsilon_{MA} = -0.1580, \ \varepsilon_{CA} = -0.2712, \ \varepsilon_{CM} = 0.1612$$

Input Mix in 1821. The initial sectoral distribution of labor, capital, skills and intermediates are unchanged from my book (Williamson, 1985a, pp. 243–244), and thus they are not repeated here.

Demand and Output Mix in 1821. The distribution of output and final demand by sector are revised only slightly from my book (Williamson, 1985a, pp. 243–244) so they are not repeated here.

Factor Shares in 1821. The share of factor payments in total value added by sector (θ_{ij}) have been revised from my book (Williamson, 1985a, p. 241), primarily to reflect wage and rate of return differentials now introduced in the model as factor market distortions. Thus:

$$\theta_{JA} = 0.32559 \quad \theta_{KM} = 0.26206 \quad \theta_{KC} = 0.40571 \quad \theta_{KB} = 0.31520$$

$$\theta_{KA} = 0.35778 \quad \theta_{LM} = 0.36456 \quad \theta_{LC} = 0.36943 \quad \theta_{LB} = 0.68480$$

$$\theta_{LA} = 0.31663 \quad \theta_{SM} = 0.10551 \quad \theta_{SC} = 0.21474$$

$$\theta_{BM} = 0.03899 \quad \theta_{BC} = 0.01011$$

$$\theta_{FM} = 0.22888$$

REFERENCES

BARNSBY, G. J. (1971), "The Standard of Living in the Black Country During the Nineteenth Century," *Economic History Review* 24(2), 220–239.

BELLERBY, J. R. (1953), "Distribution of Farm Income in the United Kingdom 1867–1938," *Journal of the Proceedings of the Agricultural Economics Society* 10(2), 127–138.

BELLERBY, J. R. (1956), *Agriculture and Industry Relative Income*, London: Macmillan.

BERRY, A. and R. H. SABOT (1978), "Labour Market Performance in Developing Countries: A Survey," *World Development* 6(9/10), 1199–1242.

BOWLEY, A. L. (1900a), *Wages in the U.K. in the Nineteenth Century,* Cambridge: Cambridge University Press.

BOWLEY, A. L. (1900b), "The Statistics of Wages in the United Kingdom During the Last Hundred Years: Part VI: Wages in the Building Trades—English Towns," *Journal of the Royal Statistical Society* 63, 297–314.

BOYER, G. R. (1985), "The Old Poor Law and the Agricultural Labor Market in Southern England: An Empirical Analysis," *Journal of Economic History* 46(1), 113–135.

CAIRD, J. (1967), *English Agriculture in* 1850–51, New York: Augustus Kelley.

CAIRNCROSS, A. K. (1949), "Internal Migration in Victorian England," *Manchester School of Economics and Social Studies* 17(1), 67–85.

CAIRNCROSS, A. K. (1953), *Home and Foreign Investment* 1870–1913, Cambridge: Cambridge University Press.

CAPIE, F. (1983), "Tariff Protection and Economic Performance in the Nineteenth Century," in: J. Black and L. A. Winters (eds.), *Policy and Performance in International Trade,* London: Macmillan.

CHENERY, H. and M. SYRQUIN (1975), *Patterns of Development,* 1950–1970, Oxford: The Clarendon Press.

CLARK, C. (1957), *The Conditions of Economic Progress,* London: Macmillan (3rd edition).

COMMITTEE OF THE STATISTICAL SOCIETY OF LONDON (1840), "Report on the State of the Working Classes in the Parishes of St. Margaret and St. John, Westminister," *Journal of the Statistical Society of London* 3, 14–24.

COMMITTEE OF THE STATISTICAL SOCIETY OF LONDON (1848), "Investigation into the State of the Poorer Classes in St. George's in the East," *Quarterly Journal of the Statistical Society of London* 2, 193–249.

CRAFTS, N. F. R. (1982), "Regional Price Variations in England in 1843: An Aspect of the Standard-of-Living Debate," *Explorations in Economic History* 19(1), 51–70.

CRAFTS, N. F. R. (1985), *British Economic Growth During the Industrial Revolution,* Oxford: Clarendon Press.

CROUZET, F. (1965), "Capital Formation in Great Britain During the Industrial Revolution," in: *The Proceedings of the Second Conference of Economic History,* The Hague, 1965. Reprinted in F. Crouzet (ed.), *Capital Formation in the Industrial Revolution,* London: 1972.

DAVID, P. A. (1975), *Technical Choice, Innovation and Economic Growth,* Cambridge, Cambridge University Press.

DEANE, P. and W. A. COLE (1962), *British Economic Growth* 1688–1959, Cambridge: Cambridge University Press.

DENISON, E. F. (1967), *Why Growth Rates Differ: Postwar Experience in Nine Western Countries,* Washington, D.C.: The Brookings Institution.

DENISON, E. F. (1974), *Accounting for United States Economic Growth,* 1929–1969, Washington, D.C.: The Brookings Institution.

DENISON, E. F. and W. K. CHUNG (1976), *How Japan's Economy Grew So Fast,* Washington, D.C.: The Brookings Institution.

DOUGHERTY, C. and M. SELOWSKY (1973), "Measuring the Effects of the Misallocation of Labour," *Review of Economics and Statistics* 55(3), 386–390.

FAIRLEE, S. (1969), "The Corn Laws and British Wheat Production, 1829–1876," *Economic History Review* 22(1), 88–116.

FISHLOW, A. and P. A. DAVID (1961), "Optimal Resource Allocation in an Imperfect Market Setting," *Journal of Political Economy* 69(6), 529–546.

GREENWOOD, M. J. and L. B. THOMAS (1973), "Geographic Labor Mobility in Nineteenth Century England and Wales," *Annals of Regional Science* 7(2), 90–105.

GREG, W. R. (1839), "Report on the State of the Working Classes in Part of Rutlandshire," *British Association for the Advancement of Science* 9, 112–114.

HAMMERMESH, D. S., and J. GRANT (1979), "Econometric Studies of Labor-Labor Substitution and Their Implications for Policy," *Journal of Human Resources* 14(4), 518–542.

HARLEY, C. K. (1982), "British Industrialization Before 1841: Evidence of Slower Growth During the Industrial Revolution," *Journal of Economic History* 42(2), 267–289.

HARRIS, J. R., and M. TODARO (1970), "Migration, Unemployment, and Development: A Two-Sector Analysis," *American Economic Review* 60(1), 126–142.

HOUSE OF COMMONS (1843), *Parliamentary Papers* 22.

HOUSE OF COMMONS (1843), *Parliamentary Papers* 45.

HUNT, E. H. (1973), *Regional Wage Variations in Britain* 1850–1914, Oxford: Clarendon Press.

JAMES, J. A. and J. S. SKINNER (1985), "The Resolution of the Labor-Scarcity Paradox," *Journal of Economic History* 45(3), 513–540.

JONES, E. L. (1964), "The Agricultural Labour Market in England, 1793–1872," *Economic History Review* 17(2), 322–338.

JONES, G. S. (1971), *Outcast London*, Oxford: Oxford University Press.

KELLEY A. C. and J. G. WILLIAMSON (1984), *What Drives Third World City Growth*?, Princeton, N.J.: Princeton University Press.

KNIGHT, J. B. (1972), "Rural-Urban Income Comparisons and Migration in Ghana," *Bulletin of Oxford University Institute of Economics and Statistics* 34(2), 199–228.

KOFFSKY, N. (1949), "Farm and Urban Purchasing Power," *Studies in Income and Wealth* vol. 11, New York: National Bureau of Economic Research.

KUZNETS, S. (1966), *Modern Economic Growth*, New Haven: Yale University Press.

KUZNETS, S. (1971), *Economic Growth of Nations*, Cambridge, Mass.: Belknap.

LEIBENSTEIN, H. (1957), "The Theory of Underemployment in Backward Economies," *Journal of Political Economy* 65, 91–103.

LEWIS, W. A. (1954), "Development with Unlimited Supplies of Labour," *Manchester School of Economics and Social Studies* 22, 139–191.

LINDERT, P. H. and J. G. WILLIAMSON (1983), "English Workers' Living Standards During the Industrial Revolution: A New Look," *Economic History Review* 36(1), 1–25.

MARGLIN, S. A. (1984), *Growth, Distribution and Prices*, Cambridge, Mass: Harvard University Press.

MATTHEWS, R. C. O., C. H. FEINSTEIN, and J. C. ODLING-SMEE (1982), *British Economic Growth* 1856–1973, Stanford, Calif.: Stanford University Press.

MAYHEW, H. (1861), *London Labour and the London Poor*, London: Griffin Bohn.

MAZUMDAR, D. (1973), "Labour Supply in Early Industrialization: The Case of the Bombay Textile Industry," *Economic History Review* 26(3), 477–496.

MCCLOSKEY, D. N. (1980), "Magnamimous Albion: Free Trade and British National Income, 1841–1881," *Explorations in Economic History* 17(3), 303–320.

MCCLOSKEY, D. N. (1981), "The Industrial Revolution 1780–1860: A Survey," in: R. Floud and D. McCloskey (eds.), *The Economic History of Britain Since* 1700, *Volume I*: 1700–1860, Cambridge: Cambridge University Press.

MCKINNON, R. (1973), *Money and Capital in Economic Development*, Washington, D.C.: Brookings Institution.

MITCHELL, B. R., and P. DEANE (1962), *Abstract of British Historical Statistics*, Cambridge: Cambridge University Press.

MOKYR, J. (1985), "The Industrial Revolution and the New Economic History," in: J. Mokyr (ed.), *The Economics of the Industrial Revolution*, Totowa, N. J.: Rowman and Allanhead.

NICHOLAS, S. and P. R. SHERGOLD (1985a), "Internal Migration in England, 1817–1839," Working Paper No. 39, The Australian National University: Canberra, Australia.

NICHOLAS, S. and P. R. SHERGOLD (1985b), "Intercounty Labour Mobility During the Industrial Revolution," Working Paper No. 43, The Australian National University: Canberra, Australia.

POLLARD, S. (1978), "Labour in Great Britain," in: P. Mathias and M. M. Postan (ed.), *The Cambridge Economic History of Europe*: *Volume VII*: *The Industrial Economies*: *Capital, Labour, and Enterprise*, Part I, Cambridge: Cambridge University Press.

POLLARD, S. (1981), "Sheffield and Sweet Auburn—Amenities and Living Standards in the British Industrial Revolution: A Comment," *Journal of Economic History* 41(4), 902–904.

POLYANI, K. (1944), *The Great Transformation,* New York.

POOR LAW COMMISSION (1842), *Local Reports on the Sanitary Condition of the Labouring Population of England.*

POSTAN, M. M. (1935), "Recent Trends in the Accumulation of Capital," *Economic History Review* 6(1). Reprinted in: F. Crouzet (ed.), *Capital Formation in the Industrial Revolution,* London: 1972.

RAVENSTEIN, E. G. (1885), "The Laws of Migration," *Journal of the Statistical Society* 48, 167–227.

RAVENSTEIN, E. G. (1889), "The Laws of Migration," *Journal of the Statistical Society* 52, 214–301.

REDFORD, A. (1926), *Labour Migration in England,* 1800–1850, Manchester: Manchester University Press.

RIMMER, W. G. (1960), "Working Men's Cottages in Leeds, 1770–1840," *Publications of the Thoresby Society* 46(108), pt. 2, 165–199.

SHOVEN, J. B. and J. WHALLEY (1984), "Applied General-Equilibrium Models of Taxation and International Trade," *Journal of Economic Literature* 22(3), 1007–1051.

STATISTICAL COMMITTEE OF THE TOWN COUNCIL (1840), "Report upon the Condition of the Town of Leeds and of its Inhabitants," *Journal of the Statistical Society of London* 2, 397–424.

SQUIRE, L. (1981), *Employment Policy in Developing Countries,* Oxford: Oxford University Press.

THOMAS, V. (1980), "Spatial Differences in the Cost of Living," *Journal of Urban Economics* 8, 108–122.

THOMPSON, F. M. L. (1963), *English Landed Society in the Nineteenth Century,* London: Routledge and Kegan Paul.

TODARO, M. P. (1969), "A Model of Labor Migration and Urban Unemployment in Less Developed Countries," *American Economic Review* 59(1), 138–148.

VEDDER, R. and D. COOPER (1974), "Nineteenth Century English and Welsh Geographic Labor Mobility: Some Further Evidence," *Annals of Regional Science* 8.

WELD, C. R. (1843), "On the Condition of the Working Classes in the Inner Ward of St. George's Parish, Hanover Square," *Journal of the Statistical Society of London* 6, 17–23.

WILLIAMSON, J. G. (1981), "Urban Disamenities, Dark Satanic Mills, and the British Standard of Living Debate," *Journal of Economic History* 41(1), 75–83.

WILLIAMSON, J. G. (1982), "Was the Industrial Revolution Worth It? Disamenities and Death in 19th Century British Towns," *Explorations in Economic History* 19(3), 221–245.

WILLIAMSON, J. G. (1984), "Why Was British Growth So Slow During the Industrial Revolution?," *Journal of Economic History* 44(3), 687–712.

WILLIAMSON, J. G. (1985a), *Did British Capitalism Breed Inequality?*, London: Allen and Unwin.

WILLIAMSON, J. G. (1985b), "The Urban Transition in England, 1776–1871: A Demographic Reconstruction," HIER Discussion Paper No. 1146, Harvard University.

WILLIAMSON, J. G. (1985c), "Migrant Earnings in Britain's Cities in 1851: Testing Competing Views of Urban Labor Market Absorption," HIER Discussion Paper No. 1176, Harvard University.

WILLIAMSON, J. G. (1986a), "Did British Labor Markets Fail During the Industrial Revolution," HIER Discussion Paper No. 1209, Harvard University.

WILLIAMSON, J. G. (1986b), "The Impact of the Irish on British Labor Markets During the Industrial Revolution," *Journal of Economic History* 46 (3), 693–720.

Oxford Economic Papers 39 (1987), 679–698

SLIDING SCALES AND CONCILIATION BOARDS: RISK-SHARING IN THE LATE 19th CENTURY BRITISH COAL INDUSTRY*

By JOHN G. TREBLE

I. Introduction

A RECENT topic of discussion among labour economists and in the political arena has been the idea that wages should be calculated not as a fixed weekly or monthly quantity, but on a profit sharing basis. One major proponent of such a scheme is Weitzman (1984) who argues in favour of share systems on the ground that they would produce chronic excess demand for labour and hence eliminate unemployment.

In his book, Weitzman queries why we do not observe more share contracts in labour markets. After all, if they were Pareto superior to our current arrangements, we would expect to see them implemented. He also points out that certain late nineteenth century British wage payment methods (the so-called 'sliding scales') are crude share contracts. The principle of the sliding scales was that the wage rate was pegged to the price of output. To the extent that profits (in an accounting sense) are correlated with the price of output, such a scheme would have the effect desired by Weitzman. When output demand falls, the price of labour would fall with a tendency to stabilise the demand for labour.

Weitzman's question as to why we do not observe more share contracts in labour markets is made even more poignant by the fact that such contracts have existed in the past and have fallen into disuse. If, as Weitzman claims, they are desirable in ameliorating employment fluctuations, there must have been some countervailing undesirable features that caused them to fade from the scene. There are several candidates for these undesirable features, chief among which is the extent to which such schemes expose workers to a risky income stream.

Our focus in this paper is on wage payment mechanisms in the British coal industry and in particular in the transition from sliding scales to the conciliation boards that replaced them. The overt purpose of this transition was to allow additional freedom in bargaining; to allow factors other than the price of coal to bear on the determination of the wage rate. The first goal of this paper is to ask whether this purpose was served by the

* Thanks are due to Eric Evans, Joyce Bellamy, the staff of the archives listed in the Appendix and of various branches of the National Union of Mineworkers. The paper has benefitted from comments of participants in the ESRC Quantitative Economic History conference, Birkbeck College, London, September 1986, the Unemployment Seminar at the Centre for Labour Economics, London School of Economics, and two anonymous referees. The final revision was ably assisted by Gary Tennant. The research on which this paper is based was financed by the British Academy and the ESRC (Contract No. F00232162).

conciliation boards. In particular, to what extent were conciliation boards different from sliding scales? To what extent did conciliation boards limit the variation in wage rates, and thus alter the extent to which risk was shared in the industry?

Our conclusion is that the main institutional difference was not the form of the collective bargaining rules, but the imposition of limits on the extent to which wages could vary. These limits were incorporated into the conciliation board agreements. Between them the wage rate varied in much the same way under the conciliation boards as it had done under the sliding scales.

In examining these questions we use the extensive records that were maintained by the Conciliation Boards. Their negotiations were recorded verbatim, and we are thus able to judge on the basis not only of their recorded decisions but also on the basis of the arguments on both sides which led to those decisions.

There have, of course, been previous studies of these institutions. Ashley (1903) discusses at length the virtues and vices of sliding scales and concludes: "On all the Conciliation Boards the representatives of the miners now insist on discussing all the circumstances of the trade, and not prices only, and their claim is practically allowed." As we shall see below, although there were indeed discussions, these had very little impact on the outcomes, which followed closely a sliding scale pattern. Rowe (1923) states: ". . . as a matter of fact, economic necessity and the lingering influence of the sliding scale principles, have resulted in wages following prices very closely. The greater steadiness of wages in the Federated Area is not due to the Conciliation Board system, but merely to the fact that home prices fluctuate less than export prices." Rowe produces no direct statistical evidence to support this view, and as we shall see, his last remark is not quite right. The conciliation board system was accompanied by effective limits on the variation of wage rates. Evans (1961) argues as follows: "Except that the wage rate was less sensitive to changes in coal prices, conditions were virtually the same as under the sliding scale. Indeed, the conciliation board agreement was inferior to the later sliding scale in periods of high prices, for the maximum wage clause set a ceiling to the wage rate, as the miners found to their cost during 1908." This statement is open to objections on several fronts. The lower sensitivity of wage rates to coal prices was caused not by a change in the sliding scale arrangement, but by the fact that changes in wage rates were made less frequently under the conciliation boards than under the sliding scale regime. Whether the implied smoothing of the workers' income stream was to their advantage or disadvantage is a question whose answer depends *inter alia* on their attitude to risk. Similarly, if the maximum and minimum rates were set with the purpose of diminishing income risk, and perceptions of that risk were accurate when the agreements were negotiated, it seems strange to argue that lower wages experienced at the top end of the range of price variation are in some sense unfair.

A similar criticism can be levelled at the work of Porter (1970): "The fixing of a minimum rate had the further disadvantage that it was usually accompanied by a maximum rate demanded by the employers for the concession of a minimum." It is undeniable that from the union point of view, a sliding scale with a minimum but no maximum would be the best arrangement, since it would give them the best of both worlds with an opportunity to share in high profits when markets were buoyant, with protection against low wage rates (if not low wages) when markets were slack. But this does not imply that an arrangement with a maximum and a minimum is not better than an arrangement with no minimum at all. Porter continues: "These reasons go far in explaining the dissatisfaction with, and eventual breakdown of, selling-price sliding scales in the coal industry." We will show in the rest of this paper that conciliation boards can be interpreted as a continuation of sliding scales under another name, so that what is frequently claimed in the literature to be the demise of the sliding-scales in the coal industry is an illusion.

Finally, Church (1986): "One of the aims of the miners in rejecting sliding scales lay in the abolition of the maxima and minima." It is a matter of fact that the only sliding scale in the coal industry before 1914 to have maxima and minima was the earliest South Wales sliding scale agreement. These limits were dropped in 1880. We show below that the major distinguishing feature of the conciliation board was the incorporation of maximum and minimum limits in the agreements.

The main innovation of this paper is the argument that the history of sliding scales and conciliation boards in the coal industry can be viewed as a part of a process by which the burden of the risk induced by shifts in the demand function for the output was shifted from the employees to the employers. This is in contrast to the approach of previous writers (particularly Evans and Porter) whose evaluations are in terms of ex post wage rate levels rather than in terms of ex ante expected rates and an associated measure of risk. We take the view that it is not only the level of the wage rate (or wages) generated by a contract that is of importance to the signatories, but also the extent to which the wage rate (or wages) vary. Assessment of sliding scales, conciliation boards (or, indeed, any wage-fixing arrangement) should, we claim be based on what the agents involved expect those outcomes to be, rather than on the outcomes observed with the benefit of hindsight.

The task of assessing anticipated risk is for many types of wage contract close to impossible. In the context of sliding scales and the closely related conciliation boards, we construct a meaningful measure of the degree of wage rate risk to which the workers were exposed by these contracts. The measure used, as far as the author knows, has not been previously used in the study of risk inherent in a contract. It can be justified in two different ways, and is used in the later part of the paper to assess the extent to which the risk-sharing properties of the contracts were changed by the changes in institutional structure. It should be stressed at this stage that our measure should be treated with some caution. In the first place, it is only an approximation to the true extent of risk-sharing. The full evaluation of risk-sharing requires more information, particularly about hours of work, than we currently have at our disposal. We comment briefly on approaches to this problem at the end of this paper. Second, it is important that the measures of risk-sharing computed in this paper are not misinterpreted. They can be thought of as measures of risk-sharing, or, indeed, as measures of wage rate risk, but they should not be confused with measures of the risk which workers faced in their consumption decisions. In order to assess that risk, an evaluation of anticipated consumption price risk and its correlation with wage rate risk would need to be undertaken. This is beyond the scope of the present paper.

The paper is organised as follows: In Section II we show that the conciliation boards retained the principle of the sliding scale, despite having formally rejected it and demonstrates the importance of the wage rate limits imposed by the conciliation board agreements. Section III develops a measure of exposure to risk, and applies it to sliding scale and conciliation board data. Section IV contains a summary of our conclusions, discusses some unresolved issues and gives a necessary condition for further investigation.

II. Quantitative analysis

In the 1870's the main technique for achieving an alteration in the wage rate in British coalmines was for deputations of men and masters to meet informally without the benefit of rules of procedure and to make their demands. Sometimes this worked satisfactorily, but sometimes negotiations would break down, in which case there might be a strike or a lockout, or alternatively, the parties might agree to put the matter before an arbitrator. These informal proceedings led in many coalfields to the setting up of automatic "sliding scales", under which wage rates would move up and down by predetermined amounts in response to changes in the average selling price of coal. A sliding scale agreement had three major elements: i) a method by which the average selling price of coal was to be determined. This varied from coalfield to coalfield, but was usually carried out by an independent firm of accountants according to an agreed methodology; ii) a step size by which wages would rise relatively to the price of coal. This might be something of the order of $1\frac{1}{4}\%$ on the 'standard' for every 1d increase in the price of coal; and iii) a price band equivalent to a given rate of wages. Negotiations over sliding scale agreements would typically include discussion of all three aspects of the sliding scale.[1]

The sliding scales were scrapped at various dates between 1893 and 1903, and were replaced by the conciliation boards. The overt purpose of the

[1] For a detailed discussion of the operation of the South Wales sliding scale see Evans (1961).

change was to escape from the rigidity of the sliding scales, and to permit factors other than selling prices to be taken into account in the determination of the wage rate. The function of both sliding scales and conciliation boards was to determine the absolute rate of wages within the area of their jurisdiction. Relative wage rates were determined either at the local level by discussions between the local union branch and the management of individual pits, or by a Joint Committee of miners and owners, which acted as a court of appeal in local disputes and also made general changes in the relative wage rates from time to time.[2] These relative wage rates were referred to collectively as the "standard" or "basis", and changes in absolute wage rates were always expressed in terms of a percentage of the standard. Even though the structure of wage rates set by the standard was not absolutely immutable, it was always given a base date. Thus, for instance, negotiators in Scotland referred to "the standard (or basis) of 1888", even though relative wage rates may have been changed since that date.

Changes in the absolute level of wages were expressed in terms of a percentage on the standard, rather than as a percentage on the current wage level. Thus an increase of 10% on the standard would represent the same number of pennies whatever the current wage rate may have been. This can (and did) lead to some confusion because a given percentage on the standard will represent a different rate of increase depending on what the current wage rate might be. For instance, if the wage rate stood at the standard, an increase of 10% on the standard would also be an increase of 10% on the current wage rate, but if the wage rate stood at 100% above the standard, an increase of 10% on the standard would represent only a 5% increase on the current wage rate.

A further peculiarity of late nineteenth century wage negotiations that is worth pointing out is that wage increases were always expressed in units which made it easy for the men to check that they were being paid correctly. These units were usually 3d per shift, or 3d in the pound. Because of this, the data generated by the wage negotiations in the conciliation boards is discrete. The unit in percentage terms varied from board to board because they each had different standards, and consequently 3d per shift represented a different percentage of the standard in each conciliation board. Thus wage changes in Scotland were always made in multiples of $6\frac{1}{4}\%$ on the standard, while in South Wales they were always in multiples of $2\frac{1}{2}\%$ on the standard.[3]

Evaluation of these wage fixing contracts by measuring their effect on the expected wage rate has been attempted by several writers.[4] The major

[2] In the North–East the cavilling system implied that actual wages were stochastic. Individual teams of workers drew lots to determine their place in the structure of relative wages. For a discussion of cavilling see Daunton (1983).

[3] For a detailed description of wage setting in the coal industry at this time, see Rowe (1923).

[4] A summary of and a further contribution to this literature can be found in Church (1986) appendix 7.1.

problem lies in the measurement of the basis wage rates. The issue of whether the miners did better under the conciliation boards than they did under the sliding scales remains unresolved and is probably not a well formulated question. We take the view that any evaluation of the contracts is impossible without taking into account their implications for the variation in wages, as well as their expected value. We see the assessment of these implications as the main contribution of the current paper.

The main problem confronting us in measuring the degree of wage variation is that the variability in the system is not exogenous. If we could believe a model where the two parties shared between them some exogenous risk (a kind of "divide-the-random-dollar" game) we could measure the risk faced by the workers relative to the size of the exogenous risk. In the systems with which we are dealing here, though, there are moral hazard problems that enable the employers and the employees to vary the degree of risk to which the whole system is subject. The mechanism by which income variation could be altered independently of the wage rate was, of course by varying hours, and both parties engaged in autonomous hours variation from time to time: mineowners by closing the pits for a few days, miners by absenting themselves from work. We can, however, measure the extent to which workers were exposed to risk, assuming that these endogenous effects are not present, and this is the approach that we adopt below. The measure that we use is independent of the basis wage rate and we therefore do not need to consider the problem of local negotiations.

The purpose of this section is to show the main difference between the conciliation boards and the sliding scales was the presence of limits placed on variation of wage rates in the conciliation boards. We show by means of some statistical analysis that these limits were effective, and by means of some simple graphical presentations that similar limits were not present in the sliding scale regimes.

Estimation is by piecewise linear regression, achieved by incorporating slope and intercept dummies into linear regressions, in order to capture the effects of the limits. The results also yield estimates of the parameters of the sliding scales implicit in the behaviour of the conciliation boards, which are used in the next section in our assessment of risk-sharing.

A sliding scale is an arrangement in which wage rates are determined by the price of output. Three parameters were determined by a sliding scale contract.

i) $\bar{w}$, a "basis wage rate" expressed in constant units (e.g. South Wales expressed the basis wage in 1879 pounds),
ii) $\bar{p}$, a "basis price", expressed in current units. This is the price at which the current wage rate would be equal to w.
iii) $\bar{r}$, a ratio according to which current wage rates would be increased or decreased relative to w, in response to fluctuations in the output price.

Denoting the current wage rate by w and the current output price by p, we can express the sliding scale as

$$w(p) = \frac{\bar{w}}{100}[100 + \bar{r}(p - \bar{p})] \tag{1}$$

Our data are drawn from various sources which are listed in Appendix B. The main data source is the verbatim minutes of the conciliation boards. From these we extracted the ascertained prices as reported to the boards, and the agreed percentage addition to basis wages. The data therefore relate decisions to information available to the boards at the time of the decision. For convenience we have modified equation (1) slightly by multiplying through by $100/\bar{w}$. This gives

$$100\frac{w}{\bar{w}} = [100 + \bar{r}(p - \bar{p})] \tag{2}$$

In all the regressions reported below, the dependent variable is the agreed percentage multiple, and the main independent variable is ascertained output price. The key relationship is thus:

$$100\frac{w}{\bar{w}} = \alpha + \beta p \tag{3}$$

Equating parameters in (3) and (2) implies that estimates of $\bar{r}$ and $\bar{p}$ can be derived from estimates of α and β by using equation (4)

$$\begin{aligned} \bar{r} &= \beta \\ \bar{p} &= (100 - \alpha)/\beta \end{aligned} \tag{4}$$

The equations used as estimating equations are modified versions of equation (3). The modifications involve the addition of an error term and the inclusion in the equation for each coalfield of a set of intercept dummies and a slope dummy designed to capture the effects of the limits placed on the range of variation of wage rates.

The maintained hypothesis is that there was an implicit sliding scale underlying the conciliation boards' decisions.[5] This sliding scale we assume was fixed throughout their currency but was subject to limits (explicitly laid down in the constitutions) on its range of applicability. The model is illustrated in Fig. 1.

This system was modelled by fitting equation (3a)

$$100\frac{w}{\bar{w}} = \alpha + \beta p + \sum_i \gamma_{1i}\,\mathrm{d}_{ui} + \sum_i \gamma_{2i}\,\mathrm{d}_{Li} + \delta_S + \varepsilon \tag{3a}$$

[5] This hypothesis has been formulated in the light of the verbatim record, which contains frequent references to precedents and to defunct sliding scale agreements. There was also a lot of discussion of the weight that variables other than the output price should have on the wage rate. An earlier version of this paper contained a description of these deliberations that have been removed from the present version for reasons of space.

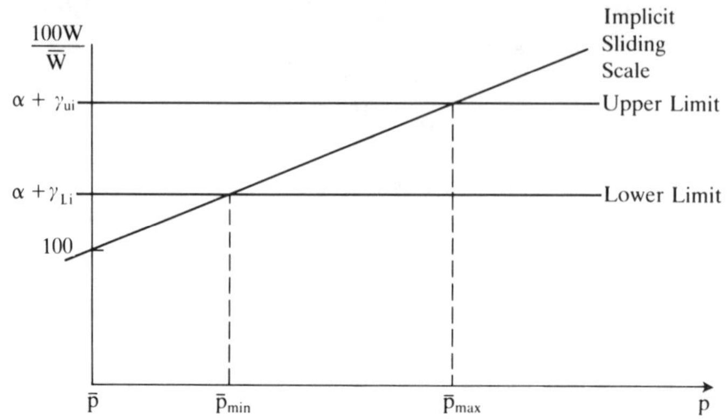

FIG. 1

This equation is derived from equation (3) by the addition of three extra terms. The d_u terms are dummies set to 1 when the price of coal is greater than p_{max} and zero elsewhere. If more than one upper limit was imposed during the life of a board, then d_u was entered as a vector of dummies, one for each separate value of p_{max}. The d_L terms are defined similarly, except that it applies to lower limits. The slope dummy S was defined as

$$S = \left(\sum_i d_{Li} + \sum_i d_{ui}\right)p$$

Our maintained hypothesis is that outside the limits p_{min} and p_{max}, the slope of the relationship between w and p should be zero. This implies

$$\beta = -\delta$$

The results are tabulated in Table 1.

In each case $\beta + \delta$ is less than one standard error different from zero. The estimated intercepts of the horizontal portions of the piecewise linear specification are also close to the values laid down in the constitutions, being again less than one standard error different in each case.

These results therefore strongly support the view that the wage limits were rigorously adhered to, and that the piecewise linear structure is an accurate representation of the way in which actual wage rates were generated under the conciliation board regime. In the next section we use these estimated parameters to calculate measures of the wage rate risk generated by the conciliation board and we compare these with measures calculated from the sliding scale regimes.

The foregoing discussion raises the question of whether the sliding scale regimes were adhered to, or whether there were implicit limits in their operation that were not laid down in clauses of the contracts. The data that we have at our disposal to address this question are rather limited but the

TABLE 1

	Constant	Price	Intercept Dummies 1	2	3	4	Slope Dummy	n	$\bar{R}^2$	DW
Durham	76.4	0.680	—	—	—	—	—	63	0.95	0.69
	(1.98)	(0.021)								
Northumber-land	56.81	0.801	—	—	—	—	—	57	0.98	0.47
	(1.25)	(0.014)								
Federated Area	61.5	0.978	95.6	109.2	118.3	102.3	−1.111	39	0.75	1.17
	(11.06)	(0.130)	(15.94)	(16.85)	(17.58)	(16.94)	(0.174)			
South Wales	70.3	0.466	71.2	47.1	—	—	−0.0375	47	0.90	0.65
	(6.89)	(0.042)	(16.79)	(13.12)			(0.090)			

Notes: (a) Figures in brackets are standard errors.

(b) Intercept dummies are set to one when the ascertained price of coal is greater (less) than the minimum (maximum) price at which the wage rate was at its maximum (minimum), and to zero otherwise. The list below shows the wage rate appropriate for each dummy and indicates whether the limit is a maximum or a minimum.

	Dummy Number	Equals one if
Federated Area	1	$p > \bar{p}_{\max}$ equivalent to $w = 145$
	2	$p > \bar{p}_{\max}$ equivalent to $w = 160$
	3	$p > \bar{p}_{\max}$ equivalent to $w = 165$
	4	$p < \bar{p}_{\min}$ equivalent to $w = 150$
South Wales	1	$p > \bar{p}_{\max}$ equivalent to $w = 160$
	2	$p < \bar{p}_{\min}$ equivalent to $w = 130$

(c) Price data are quarterly (monthly in Scotland) ascertained prices; wages data are agreed percentage additions to wages.

(d) No results are reported for Scotland because of the presence there of pseudo-sliding scales or "Wages Agreements".

data that we do have provide no support for the view (expressed by an anonymous referee) that "the explicitly stated maxima and minima in the conciliation boards wage-price relationship were tacit in the sliding scale relationship." If this were the case we would expect to see a similar piecewise linear pattern generated by sliding scale data as has been shown to be present in the conciliation board data. In order to see where we might set the limits on variations in the wage rate, we began by plotting wages against prices for the sliding scale data. These plots showed no evidence whatsoever of any flattening of the relationship at the extremes for any of the coalfields for which we have data. There was sometimes evidence of slight deviations from the sliding scales in the middle of the range of variation, but the plots gave no support for the idea of implicit limits.[6]

[6] Once again, considerations of space prohibit displaying this evidence. Full details can be obtained from the author.

In this section we have sought to show that the main difference between the sliding scale regimes and the conciliation board regimes was the imposition of limits on the variation of wage rates under the conciliation board regimes. Our conclusion, in a nutshell, was that sliding scales imposed a linear relationship on wages and output prices, while the conciliation boards generally imposed a piecewise linear relationship, with the implicit sliding scale relationship being flattened at the upper and lower limits. However, not all the conciliation boards were subject to these limits.

When limits were present in a conciliation board agreement, they were rigorously adhered to. The sliding scale agreements also seem to have been rigorously adhered to. From simple plots of wages against prices we can find no evidence of flattening of the relationship at the ends.

III. Wage rate risk

In this section we use the parameter estimates of the previous section, and the agreed parameters of sliding scales to try to assess the impact of the sliding scales on the degree of ex ante wage rate risk to which miners were exposed by the agreements. As we pointed out in the introduction, previous studies have ignored this aspect of these arrangements. We show here that the limits on the variation of wage rates specified in the conciliation board agreements were generally very effective in limiting wage rate variation. In fact in the years immediately before the first world war the limits were almost equivalent to a fixed wage contract.

In order to do this we need first to construct a measure of the risk to which workers were exposed. In particular, given equation (1), we can ask what the extent of wage rate risk would be for a given degree of output price risk. Two natural measures of this spring to mind: First, an economist's first response to a question about responsiveness is usually to calculate some sort of elasticity. Second, we might think of comparing variance-based measures of wage rate variability and output price variability such as the relevant coefficients of variation. We shall see that these two ideas are closely related.

Using equation (1) we can calculate the first two central moments of the wage rate:

$$Ew = \frac{\bar{w}}{100}[100 + \bar{r}(Ep - \bar{p})]$$

and

$$\text{Var}\, w = \sigma_w^2 = \left(\frac{\bar{w}}{100}\right)^2 \bar{r}^2\, \text{Var}\, p.$$

The coefficient of variation of w is thus:

$$CV_w = \frac{\bar{r}\sigma_p}{1 + \bar{r}(E_p - \bar{p})}$$

This is not in itself an appropriate measure of the extent to which the sliding-scale contract exposed workers to wage-rate risk because it is dependent on the distribution of the exogenous risk. In order to allow for this we normalise by dividing by the coefficient of variation of p.

This yields:

$$R_u = \frac{CV_w}{CV_p} = \frac{\bar{r}E_p}{1 + \bar{r}(E_p - \bar{p})} \tag{5}$$

which will be our measure of the extent which workers were exposed to risk by a sliding-scale regime.

This measure can be derived by an alternative route. From equation (1) calculate the elasticity of the wage rate with respect to output price

$$\frac{\mathrm{d}w}{\mathrm{d}p} \cdot \frac{p}{w} = \frac{\bar{r}p}{1 + \bar{r}(p - \bar{p})} \tag{6}$$

and (5) is revealed to be this elasticity evaluated at the expected output price.

Equation (5) needs careful interpretation. It is not a measure of the total risk to which workers were exposed. For it to be this we would have to assume both consumption prices and hours of work to be constant. If consumption prices were to vary (as no doubt they did during this period) and real wage rates were included in the numerator of equation (5), the value of (5) could either rise or fall dependent on the correlation coefficient between consumer prices and wage rates. We have not tried to address this problem in this paper for the following reason. We think we can assume that the wage rate paid to miners and its variation were probably minor determinants of the price of the consumer goods that they bought and its variation. The main purpose of this paper is to say something about the relative variability in wage rates in two regimes. This question of relative variability does not hinge on the question of consumer prices if the latter can be treated as exogenous.

This is not to say that the overall riskiness of the miners' consumption stream is an unimportant question. It is simply not the question that we attempt to answer here.

The question of hours variation is more difficult to address, since we cannot argue that hours of work are exogenous. We have been unable to find in the literature any suggestion that the determinants of hours of work changed as a consequence of the conciliation boards, and we take this silence as evidence of a concensus that there was no such change. We intend in future work to pursue this issue further. (See conclusion.)

Finally, it should be noted that the locally negotiated wage rates are irrelevant to the measure. This is because the coefficient of variation is independent of the mean. Under the wage payment arrangements outlined earlier, local negotiations affected the mean wage only. Hence considerations of wage drift due to local negotiations do not arise.

To understand what the measure is trying to capture think of a firm whose output price varies from time to time. In a world of perfect information, the firm would want to vary labour demand and in general, the wage rate in order to track these changes in the output price. If information is imperfect, however, there may be reason for the firm to want to fix the wage rate and bear a greater proportion of the risk in the system itself.

This is the idea that is captured by the measure in equation (5). The system is subject to exogenous risk. How much of that risk is passed on to the workers?

One more twist is necessary before we apply (5) to the data. We intend to apply the measure not only to explicit sliding scales but also to the implicit sliding scales that were operated under the conciliation board agreements. Many of these, (and some explicit scales) were subject to limits on their domain[7] of operation so that maximum and minimum prices ($p_{\max}$ and $p_{\min}$) were set, and equation (1) modified to:

$$w(p)=\begin{cases}\dfrac{\bar{w}}{100}[100-\bar{r}(\bar{p}_{\min}-\bar{p})] & p\leqslant\bar{p}_{\min}\\[2ex] \dfrac{\bar{w}}{100}[100-\bar{r}(p-\bar{p})] & \bar{p}_{\min}<p<\bar{p}_{\max}\\[2ex] \dfrac{\bar{w}}{100}[100-\bar{r}(\bar{p}_{\max}-\bar{p})] & p\geqslant\bar{p}_{\max}\end{cases} \tag{1a}$$

This means that $w(p)$ is a mixed discrete and continuous random variable. Indeed, if we assume that p has a Normal distribution then $w(p)$ has a doubly-truncated Normal distribution mixed with mass-points at the truncations. The formulae for the moments of $w(p)$ are rather complicated and we do not reproduce them here,[8] although we use them later in the paper to calculate a constrained version of measure (5), i.e.

$$R_c=\frac{CV_w}{CV_p} \tag{5a}$$

where CV_w is calculated using the moments of the constrained distribution of wage rates in place of the unconstrained moments used in (5).

In order to compute the measures in equations (5) and (5a) it is necessary to make some assumptions about the distribution of output prices. This is not simply a question of thinking up some numbers for the mean and variance, and then comparing institutional arrangements, because the institutional arrangements will have been influenced by and will reflect the expectations of the parties as to what prices might be during the period of

[7] Formally, these limits were usually expressed as limits on the range of $r(p-\bar{p})$. It is convenient for us to think of them as limits on p.

[8] Patel and Read (1982), p. 35 give formulae for the moments of the truncated distribution without mass points. The necessary modification is straightforward.

the proposed arrangement. These expectations would be different for different coalfields.

The issue of expected prices is important because it bears upon the risk limiting properties of the wage-rate limits. Suppose that the distribution of wage rates produced by the unlimited sliding scale were to have mean μ and variance σ^2, then limits placed at $\mu \pm 2\sigma$ would have little effect on the coefficient of variation of actual wage rates. If the limits were placed at $\mu - 4\sigma$ and μ the coefficient of variation of actual wage rates would be heavily reduced.

Expected price distributions should therefore be allowed for in the assessment of risk. We tried to do this in several ways, and in Tables 2A–2E we report the results of two different formulations of expectations.

We use means and variances of ascertained prices:

i) for a period of three years prior to the date we are considering,

TABLE 2A
Durham

		Expectations			*Institutional Parameters*				*Risk Measures*	
		n	μ	σ	$\bar{r}$	$\bar{p}$	*U*	*L*	*Unconstrained*	*Constrained*
1st S.S. April 1877	i)	7	92.5	30.3	0.625	72	—	—	51.2	—
	ii)	6	58.5	3.8					39.9	—
2nd S.S. December 1879	i)	8	58.3	4.6	0.625*	54	—	—	35.5	—
	ii)	6	54.7	1.5					34.0	—
3rd/4th S.S. April 1882	i)	9	54.5	1.7	0.625**	48	—	—	32.7	—
	ii)	12	57.3	1.9					33.8	—
End of 4th S.S. March 1889	i)	12	53.4	1.1	0.625	48	—	—	32.3	—
	ii)	12	79.4	10.0					41.4	—
End 4th S.S. March 1889	i)	12	53.4	1.1	0.680	34.71	—	—	32.2	—
	ii)	12	79.4	10.0					41.4	—
1st C.B. January 1895	i)	12	68.7	5.0	0.680	34.71	—	—	37.9	—
	ii)	6	61.1	0.8					35.2	—
2nd C.B. October 1899	i)	12	68.8	5.5	0.680	34.71	—	—	38.0	—
	ii)	12	105.0	17.3					48.3	—

* Except between 70d and 74d when $\bar{r} = 1.25$.
** Except between 68d and 72d when $\bar{r} = 1.25$.

TABLE 2B
Northumberland

		Expectations			Institutional Parameters				Risk Measures	
		n	μ	σ	$\bar{r}$	$\bar{p}$	U	L	Unconstrained	Constrained
1st S.S. 1879	i)	6	76.1	15.5	0.781*	61.28	—	—	53.3	—
	ii)	12	58.6	2.5					46.7	—
2nd S.S. 1883	i)	12	58.6	2.5	0.75*	56	—	—	43.1	—
	ii)	12	60.4	2.5					43.9	—
3rd S.S. 1887	i)	12	57.8	3.0	1.25**	65	—	—	79.4	—
	ii)	2	55.2	0.7					78.6	—
1st C.B. July 1894	i)	12	78.9	8.6	0.801***	53.9***	—	—	52.7	—
	ii)	10	68.2	6.7					49.0	—
2nd C.B. January 1900	i)	12	74.3	9.7	0.801***	53.9***	—	—	51.1	—
	ii)	12	106.0	16.3					59.9	—
End of 2nd C.B. July 1911	i)	12	90.3	5.8	0.801***	53.9***	—	—	56.0	—
	ii)	n.a.	n.a.	n.a.					n.a.	—
4th S.S. March 1914	i)	n.a.	n.a.	n.a.	1	63	65	25	n.a.	n.a.
	ii)	3	112.44	1.5					75.2	75.2

* These scales incorporated "double jumps" at regular intervals. This ratio is an average.
** The scale allowed for smaller ratio at prices above 65d. Prices this high were not experienced, either three years before the agreement, or during its currency.
*** Computed from regression reported in Table 1.

TABLE 2C
Federated area

		Expectations			Institutional Parameters				Risk Measures	
		n	μ	σ	$\bar{r}$	$\bar{p}$	U	L	Unconstrained	Constrained
2nd C.B. 1899	i)	n.a.	n.a.	n.a.	0.978	39.4	45	30	n.a.	n.a.
	ii)	12	102.9	18.3					62.1	14.4
1900	i)	7	76.9	6.9	0.978	39.4	60	30	55.0	47.4
	ii)	12	106.6	14.0					62.9	28.8
1904	i)	9	99.5	11.7	0.978	39.4	60	35	61.3	37.4
	ii)	8	80.2	1.5					56.1	56.0
1907	i)	8	80.2	1.5	0.978	39.4	60	$37\frac{1}{2}$	56.1	53.5
	ii)	7	96.9	6.4					60.7	47.1
1909	i)	10	91.8	9.6	0.978	39.4	65	50	59.4	31.8
	ii)	n.a.	n.a.	n.a.					n.a.	n.a.

TABLE 2D
Scotland

		Expectations			Institutional Parameters				Risk Measures	
		n	μ	σ	$\bar{r}$	$\bar{p}$	U	L	*Uncon-strained*	*Con-strained*
C.B. January 1899	i)	n.a.	n.a.	n.a.	1.27*	16.9*	75	31.25	n.a.	n.a.
	ii)	24	89.1 #	12.0 #					59.0	15.4
C.B. January 1900	i)	24	89.1 #	12.0 #	1.27*	86.2	100	37.5	109.1	4.5
	ii)	25	113.6 #	26.8 #					107.0	50.3
1st Wages Agreement May 1902	i)	34	109.0 #	22.6 #	1.39	86.2	100	37.5	115.0	51.4
	ii)	29	75.4	3.4					123.3	0.0†
2nd Wages Agreement November 1904	i)	30	75.2	3.4	1.56	89.45	100	37.5	150.8	0.0†
	ii)	32	75.8	8.4					150.2	0.0
C.B. May 1907	i)	36	75.0	8.1	1.56	89.45	100	37.5	151.0	0.0
	ii)	27	93.9	12.0					137.0	13.3
3rd Wages Agreement July 1909	i)	36	92.0	11.9	1.56	93.45	100	50	146.8	1.9
	ii)	35	83.4	6.8					154.3	0.0
C.B. June 1912	i)	35	83.4	6.8	1.27*	93.45	100	50	121.4	n.a.†
	ii)	22	109.6	5.4					115.5	0.0

* Computed by author by fitting linear regression to the observations of wages and prices during period when no wages agreement was current.

Data suspect.

† Constrained too far out in the tail for computation to be possible.

ii) for a period of three years following the date we are considering or until the end of the current agreement (whichever is shorter).

The first of these formulations assumes that expectations are based on fairly recent past experience, the second can be interpreted as forward-looking (and accurate) expectations. A comparison of these two sets of results can be interpreted as yielding information about the outcome relative to expectations. The qualitative nature of all the results including those reported in Tables 2A to 2E is fairly robust to the alternative specifications.

The results reported in the tables once again should be interpreted carefully. What we have attempted to do is to measure the extent to which workers' wage contracts exposed them to a share of the risk faced by the enterprise in which they were employed. Given our data we are able to make comparisons through time and across jurisdictions or regimes.

TABLE 2E
South Wales

		Expectations			Institutional Parameters				Risk Measures	
		n	μ	σ	$\bar{r}$	$\bar{p}$	U	L	Unconstrained	Constrained
1st S.S. 1875	i)	n.a.	n.a.	n.a.	0.625	144	67.5	0	n.a.	n.a.
	ii)	5	117.8	7.0					88.0	0.2
2nd S.S. 1880	i)	3	107.7	4.9	0.625	102	—	—	65.0	—
	ii)	7	104.1	4.9					64.2	—
3rd S.S. 1882	i)	7	104.1	4.9	0.625	96	—	—	61.9	—
	ii)	9	116.5	2.0					64.5	—
1887	i)	9	105.3	7.5	0.625	96	—	—	62.2	—
	ii)	7	110.4	14.0					63.3	—
4th S.S. 1890	i)	9	107.3	13.6	0.833	96	—	—	81.7	—
	ii)	9	156.4	7.4					86.7	—
5th S.S. 1892	i)	12	148.7	15.2	0.73	96	—	0	78.4	78.4
	ii)	17	124.4	15.5					75.2	72.9
C.B. 1903	i)	17	180.1	15.4	0.466*	63.7*	—	30	54.4	54.0
	ii)	12	148.5	6.3					49.6	49.4
C.B. 1905	i)	12	176.7	11.3	0.466*	63.7*	60	30	53.9	50.2
	ii)	12	180.3	4.3					54.4	54.3
C.B. 1910	i)	12	176.7	11.3	0.466*	63.7*	60	35	53.9	50.2
	ii)	12	180.1	4.1					54.4	54.3

* Computed from regression reported in Table 1.

In principle there are two ways in which the degree of risk exposure can be reduced in a sliding scale type contract. The first is by reducing the value of $\bar{r}$ (*ceteris paribus*), which reduces the elasticity in equation (6). The second is by the imposition of limits on the range of variation of wages.

The first of these effects is captured by the unconstrained measure (5), the second by the constrained measure (5a). These measures are reported for all the various regimes for which we have data and for all five jurisdictions (except Durham and Northumberland where there were no limits. Therefore the constraint measure does not apply.).

The first finding is that the unconstrained measures of risk exposure do not vary much over time. There is no evidence that the values of the implicit sliding scale parameters were used to much effect, although there was considerable time and effort spent negotiating these from time to time. Such efforts would have had an impact on the mean wage rate, but there is no evidence to suggest their use as a tool to limit exposure to risk. If anything risk exposure according to the unconstrained measure tends to rise towards the beginning of the First World War.

Secondly, the unconstrained measures vary substantially from jurisdiction to jurisdiction. Durham has a risk exposure that is quite low at around 35%.

Northumberland's is rather higher in the mid-40's. For both of these areas, the measure tends to rise at the start of the 20th century. The Federated Area is fairly similar, while both Scotland and South Wales show very high rates of risk exposure on the unconstrained measure.

Turning now to the constrained measures. These are irrelevant in Durham and Northumberland where no constraints were imposed. In the remaining jurisdictions it is evident from the Tables that the limits on the movement of wage rates were extremely effective in reducing wage rate exposure. Indeed, in the Federated Area, South Wales and Scotland the upper limit is the most important determinant of actual wage rates.

The results document the dangers involved in interpreting the constitutions of these bargaining units. The coalfield that *prima facie* exposed its workers to most wage rate risk (Scotland) is revealed as one of the more successful in limiting the degree to which wage rates varied.

The Durham and Northumberland miners accepted a higher degree of wage rate risk than miners in other areas, although in all areas the tendency was towards less wage rate risk as the institutions developed.

Perhaps the most striking fact to be shown by the tables, though, is the importance of maximum and minimum constraints on wage rates, as compared to the importance of scrapping of the sliding scales. In those areas where conciliation boards were introduced without maxima or minima the change in the institutional structure does not seem to have affected the degree of wage rate risk much at all. However, those areas that had constraints on the movement of wage rates, seem to have set those constraints at effective levels, and succeeded in reducing the degree of wage rate risk considerably. This lesson is learned most clearly in the case of South Wales where the constrained sliding scale of 1875 was abandoned in 1880. The increase in wage rate risk at this time is apparent from Table 2D. A similar *reduction* in wage rate risk was not achieved by the introduction of the ineffective minimum in 1892 but by the conciliation board (with wage rate constraints) in 1903. The conciliation board's constraints only really began to bite, though, with the increase in output prices after 1905.

IV. Conclusion

There are several reasons for studying the extent to which wage contracts expose workers to risk. i) Recent developments in labour economics (the "implicit contract" theories) have stressed the role of the firm in supplying to workers a form of insurance against income risk as well as providing them with income. ii) The interpretation of the historical record concerning trade union development and the history of collective bargaining may be altered if we take account of risk. iii) Recent policy developments involve a deliberate attempt to increase the extent to which workers are exposed to risk.

In general, it is not possible to measure the risk to which workers believe themselves to be exposed. But in the case of the sliding scales and the conciliation boards it has proved possible to do this because the wage rate risk can be inferred directly from the structure of the wage contracts.

The main conclusion of this paper is that the importance of the change from sliding scale to conciliation board lay mainly in the inclusion of wage rate maxima and minima as part of the conciliation board constitutions.[9] Of the two bargaining units not to have such limits in their agreements, one (Northumberland) ultimately abandoned the conciliation board without limits, in favour of a sliding scale with limits.

These conclusions, strong as they are, beg several questions that seem at the moment to be intractable. The main difficulty inhibiting further investigation of the nature of these wage-setting mechanisms is the paucity of available information about actual hours of work. Many researchers have attempted to make progress in this direction (a summary can be found in Church [1986], pp. 234–259), but due to the apparently frequent use of temporary pit closures by employers and the propensity of miners to work fewer shifts than were available, no satisfactory data series exists. This hampers any attempt to assess income risk, or, viewing the system from the employers' side, wage bill risk. An attempt to use a profit maximizing model of the firm to simulate hours distributions is reported in an earlier version of this paper (Treble [1986]). The results were far from satisfactory, and we are now investigating the possibility of constructing actual hours of work series from extant wages books.

We began this paper with a reference to the work of Weitzman, and his claim that share contracts have certain desirable properties. In the coal industry, the share contracts died as a consequence of an extended sequence of negotiations, proceeding at a different pace in each coalfield and resulting in the imposition of progressively tighter limits on the movement of wage rates. This suggests that the variability of wage rates may have been an undesirable feature of these contracts from the union's point of view, but it also begs a number of questions that could be tackled, if better information on hours were available.

i) Did the income or wage bill risk in the contracts decline in the same fashion as the wage rate risk, or did steadiness in wage rates engender greater variation in hours and employment?

ii) If wage bill risk was diminished what changes in the industry enabled it to do so? It is not difficult to understand why the union would want to reduce risk, but why should firms be prepared to bear a greater degree of risk than previously? Implicit contract theory (Hart [1980]) suggests that a shift of this kind could be connected with the increase in the extent of limited liability in the ownership of firms.[10]

iii) Finally, the sliding scales continued in the iron industry for several years after they were formally abandoned in the coal industry. It seems

[9] This justifies Arnot's concentration on the history of these limits in various works.
[10] This has been documented for the period 1895–1913 by Church (1986) p. 141.

possible that a comparison of the two industries would enable hypotheses concerning these contracts to be tested.

Further progress does, however, seem to be dependent on the construction of satisfactory data on hours.

University of Hull

APPENDIX. SOURCES

1. Scotland. The only surviving records of the Scottish wage negotiations seem to be a series of printed verbatim reports of the conciliation board proceedings. There are at least two extant copies of them. One is held by the National Library of Scotland (DEP 227/1-8), the other by the Mitchell Library, Glasgow (338.272 Sco).
2. Northumberland. The records of the Northumberland wage negotiations are the most complete of all the conciliation board records. They are held in the Northumberland Record Office, and consist of minute books in duplicate (NRO 759/33-4 and NRO 263), verbatim reports of proceedings (NRO 759/35-37, NCB/C2/3-7), accountant's certificates (NCB/C1/21-23), printed verbatim reports and proceedings of arbitration tribunals from 1875–1877 (NRO 759/A2/1-3, NRO 759/A1/28-31), abbreviated printed conciliation board proceedings (NRO 759/68), a document entitled "Changes in Wages since 1879" (printed in 1905 or 1906), a book of tables showing advances and reductions in wages for Northumberland and Durham (NCB/C5/3) (printed about 1887 and updated by hand to 1908) and a book of draft minutes of the Northumberland Miners' Mutual Confident Association's Wages Committee. (This contains reports of the union's discussions immediately prior to the conciliation board meetings.) (NRO/759/31-32).
3. Durham. County Durham's records are mostly housed at the County Record Office. The main sources for the work reported in this paper are the minutes and proceedings of the conciliation boards (D/DCOMPA/135, 137; D/EBF 37; NCB/I/CO 67, 73; and D/DMA 81). In addition, there are verbatim reports of arbitration proceedings, 1874–1881 (D/DMA 83-86), accountant's certificates (NCB/I/CO 81, 82), and a useful booklet published by the Durham Miners' Association entitled "Changes in Wages in the Durham Coal Trade 1871–1924" (D/DMA 250).
4. Federated Area. The original documents relating to the conciliation board for the Federated Area do not appear to have survived. However, the minutes of MFGB contain printed verbatim reports of the proceedings. Internal evidence indicates that not all the meetings of the board were printed and circulated but the meetings where wage changes were made appear always to have been circulated. The largest gap, however, is the lack of reports of negotiations setting up conciliation boards.

   The MFGB minutes (bound in annual volumes) are fairly widely available, although it proved difficult to put together a complete run partly because some of the bound volumes have some sets of minutes missing. The work reported in this paper is based on volumes held at the Mitchell Library, Glasgow, the National Library of Scotland, the University College of Swansea's Library and the headquarters of the National Union of Mineworkers at Sheffield.

   In addition, the Clwyd County Record Office at Hawarden holds a volume by Thomas Ashton giving brief details of the meetings of the Federated Area's conciliation board from 1894 to 1913 (D/NM/312).
5. South Wales. Documents relating to the South Wales miners were the subject of an emergency rescue operation carried out by the University College of Swansea when the NUM's South Wales branch moved its office from Cardiff to Pontypridd. They are now held at the University College's Library.

   There are some gaps in the verbatim reports (specifically, August and November 1910, February and November 1911 and February 1913). The Collection consists of verbatim reports and minutes of the meetings of the conciliation board together with original agreements. (H1-121, Hubert Jenkins 2-4). In addition, there is a bound volume containing all the sliding scales and subsequent agreements (F6).

6. Cumberland. Few records of the Cumberland board have survived. The documents held at the Cumbria County Record Office at Carlisle at concerned only with arbitrated decisions. They are for the most part formal verbatim minutes of the proceedings (T/NCB/1-8, 18, 19).

REFERENCES

ARNOT, R. PAGE (1949) *The Miners: A History of the Miners' Federation of Great Britain, 1889–1910,* G. Allen & Unwin, London.

ARNOT, R. PAGE (1967) *South Wales Miners, Glowyr De Cymru: A History of the South Wales Miners' Federation 1898–1914,* G. Allen & Unwin, London.

ASHLEY, W. J. (1903) *The Adjustment of Wages,* Longmans, Green & Co., London.

CHURCH, R. (1986) *The History of the British Coal Industry Vol. 3: 1830–1913 Victorian Pre-eminence,* Clarendon Press, Oxford.

DAUNTON, M. J. (1983) "Down the Pit: Work in the Great Northern and South Wales Coalfields, 1870–1916." *Economic History Review.*

EVANS, E. W. (1961) *The Miners of South Wales,* University of Wales Press, Cardiff.

HART, O. (1983) "Optimal Labour Contracts under Asymmetric Information: An Introduction." *Review of Economic Studies,* v.L, pp. 3–35.

PATEL, J. K. and READ, C. B. (1982) *Handbook of the Normal Distribution,* New York, M. Dekker.

PORTER, J. H. (1970) "Wage Bargaining Under Conciliation Agreements, 1860–1914." *Economic History Review,* 2nd Series, v XXIII, pp. 460–475.

ROWE, J. W. F. (1923) *Wages in the Coal Industry,* P. S. King & Son, London.

TREBLE, J. (1986) "Sliding Scales and Conciliation Boards: A Quantitative Analysis." University of Hull Department of Economics Discussion Paper, August.

WEITZMAN, M. L. (1984) *The Share Economy,* Harvard.

Oxford Economic Papers 39 (1987), 699–718

NATURAL MONOPOLY AND RAILWAY POLICY IN THE NINETEENTH CENTURY*

By J. S. FOREMAN-PECK

AMONG nineteenth century industries that impressed contemporaries and later historians as the embodiment of mid-Victorian efficiency and technical precocity, railways are preeminent. Yet the equally mid-Victorian ethic of competition seemed to many observers incompatible with the satisfactory operation of the railway network. They judged that once the great boom of 1845–47 was over, bursts of competition which created excessively high costs alternated with the formation of local or regional monopolies that charged the public inordinately high prices. By the late 1860s an active political debate ensued as to whether more railway competition should be encouraged or instead tighter regulation or nationalisation would offer a better solution. The results of analyses of three data sets in this paper are consistent with a less than efficient mid-Victorian industry organisation, both in comparison with those of other countries and measured against a plausible theoretical optimum. The evidence appears to favour the view that a more vigorous state railway planning policy could have increased the gains to the British economy, and that at least in the nineteenth century such a policy was certainly possible, judging by the experience of other European nations.

1. The decline of competition

British railway policy, in contrast to those policies of continental Europe, may be said to have operated a market test for natural monopoly; if one firm was more efficient than two, then only one would survive in the market. In the early days the only British restraint upon the play of market forces was imposed by the private act procedure of Parliament which required that if the railway companies were to obtain limited liability, each new project must pass the examination of committees of both Houses. Critics were quick to point out that British construction costs were higher than in the rest of Western Europe but their claims were ignored, at least in part because of the strong representation of the railway interests in Parliament. Fear of monopoly did lead to the creation of a supervisory body, the Railway Department of the Board of Trade in 1840, to little avail however because the Department lacked effective powers (Parris 1965).

* An earlier version of this paper was read at the 1986 ESRC Quantitative Economic History Conference and at the University of Southampton. The present form has been improved by comments of participants in these meetings and by anonymous referees. I am grateful for research assistance from Phillip Robinson.

Until then Parliament had been guided by a belief in the efficacy of competition; entry into railway transport was intended to be open in the same way as to canal transport, with the lines being used by independent contractors. For reasons of safety this policy was abandoned during the 1840s and thereafter competitive pressures were confined to points between which there was more than one railway, or sea freight offered an alternative transport mode. Sea competition helped to keep down London-Southampton and London-Liverpool rates and on the London-Birmingham route, competitive railway lines reduced rates between the 1840s and the 1860s.

New railway entry could also lower charges, if the industry was not a sustainable natural monopoly. The greatest period of new entry to the industry was the 1840s (BPP 1872) when the following new lines or alterations of existing lines were projected. Such was the excessive optimism of these years that 1560 miles of line proposed in the acts between 1845 and 1847 were subsequently not built.

TABLE 1
New Railways Projected 1844–7

Year	*Acts*	*miles of line*	*Capital authorised* £m
1840	47	805	20.5
1845	120	2700	59.5
1846	270	4538	132.6
1847	190	1354	39.128

Source: BPP 1867 pt 1 p. xvii.

Soon afterwards the amalgamation movement began. In 1843 70 railway companies controlled 2100 miles of track in Great Britain, the largest operating 118 miles. The London to Liverpool and Bristol to Leeds routes were each owned by three separate companies. Twenty two years later, through growth and amalgamation, 11,451 miles of line were worked by 78 companies, the largest system consisting of 1274 miles (BBP 1867 pt 1, p. lxxxii).

Operation of such a large interconnecting network required some cooperation in traffic management and to this end the Railway Clearing House was established in 1847. Conveyance of through traffic encouraged combination because lines had to be managed as if they belonged to one company. But refusal or obstruction of interconnection remained a competitive weapon that could operate against the public interest. Recognition of this potential divergence of private from public benefits underlay the Railway Gauge Act of 1846 which standardized the network on Stephenson's 4 ft $8\frac{1}{2}$ in gauge, at the expense of Brunel's broad gauge Great Western.

A more interventionist role for the state was permitted by the 1844 Railway Act. As well as requiring the famous daily Parliamentary trains, the Act gave the government an option to buy out in 1869 all private railway companies established since 1844. The late 1860s therefore saw a public debate on the benefits and costs of state ownership and control of the railway system. Nationalisation of the telegraph network at the same time, gave further impetus to the discussion. Jevons (1867) spelt out the conditions under which state ownership might be as successful as the Post Office of the time was judged to be, rather than as wasteful as the dockyards.

Though Jevons concluded railways were not a suitable candidate for state enterprise, elsewhere (Jevons 1874) he conceded that some form of railway regulation was desirable and a number of influential men continued to advocate state ownership (see Biddulph Martin (1873) and the debate on his paper). Others, such as the majority of the 1867 committee, contended that the existing regulatory framework, weak though it was, rather than competition, was responsible for defects of the system; Parliamentary consideration of schemes "on their own merits" had led to inconsistent decisions and for example sometimes had required two stations serving a town when one would have been adequate.

Where companies did not amalgamate, agreements to eliminate competition by other means became increasingly common. Pooling arrangements dividing up the country's traffic were noted in 1853 and two decades later, normal price competition by established railways had disappeared. New entry could still lower rates temporarily, as the 1889 opening of the Barry Railway did for South Wales coal, but even this effect was attenuated as early as 1863 by agreements between companies concerning new lines. By 1911 new entry was improbable because no competitive schemes in the preceding twenty years were likely to have achieved an adequate return on capital. Between 1872 and 1907 when the total railway mileage in England had increased from 11,136 to 15,897, concentration continued to rise from 16 companies owning 85% of the mileage to 13 companies owning 88%, (BPP 1911, App. 1). The market test seemed to be indicating that the industry was a regional natural monopoly at least.

Official opinion had hardened against railway competition by the 1870s. The 1872 Committee reported (BPP 1872, p. xviii) 'Committees and commissions have for the last 30 years clung to one form of competition after another yet it has become more and more evident that . . . competition must fail to do for railways what it does for ordinary trade.' In the face of increasing railway concentration and cartelization, the British solution was more regulation, which became effective and substantial with the Act of 1868. Thereafter state control of rates and schedules, as well as safety regulations, (which under the 1889 Act were costly) increased. Labour costs were raised by the limitation of working hours in the interests of safety by an Act of 1893.

2. Regulatory policy and railway performance

If railways were a natural monopoly then the market may have proved an inefficient regulator both while monopoly was emerging from the process of competition and when dominant firms established sole control. In the second case the excessive prices charged by profit maximisers might have been avoided by repeated franchise bidding.

Chadwick (1859) proposed this solution of 'competition for the field' as a response to what he saw as the failure of British policy towards natural monopoly. French railway policy, Chadwick maintained, entailed franchise bidding (though in fact for very long leases) and not only were operating and construction costs lower in France, despite more expensive coal, iron and steel, but accident rates were also less severe. Rowland Hill, no doubt impressed by the nationalised Post Office system, supported Chadwick, but the majority of his colleagues on the 1867 Royal Commission remained unconvinced, citing a French report of 1863 as to the unsuitability of the leasing scheme in an English context (BPP 1867, pp. xxxv–vii). Closely related is the recommendation of contestable market theorists (Baumol 1982) that policy should be directed to minimising sunk costs so as to encourage the threat of 'hit and run' entry. The threat of competition then encourages cost minimisation and competitive prices without the expensive duplication of plant that actual competition would require. As we have seen in Section 1 this strategy did not prove possible. Even had the sunk costs of the railway track been removed as an entry barrier by allowing contractors to run trains on railways owned by a 'common carrier', the problem of regulation of the common carrier would have remained, as it did for canals before the railway age. Instead by the end of the nineteenth century most of Europe had opted to 'internalise' regulation by at least some degree of state ownership and the United Kingdom chose increasingly detailed arms-length regulation.

Property rights theorists emphasize the inefficiency of state-owned enterprise which they claim must ensue from the inability of tax payers to monitor enterprise performance as efficiently as private stockholders may through capital markets (Millward and Parker 1983). For a natural monopoly which has evolved through the market test there may be more than offsetting inefficiencies in a regulated privately owned industry. Duplicated plant built during the competitive era may be capitalised into industry costs by amalgamation to form regional monopolies. Regulation which seeks to ensure such amalgamated companies earn a reasonable return on their capital then makes permanent this over-capitalisation.

There is a considerable literature which supports such a view of nineteenth century railway competition and British policy. At first (before 1850) high British construction costs were usually blamed on the land prices demanded by avaricious landowners. In fact it was often competition between companies that allowed landowners to hold out for high prices but in any event land costs were generally less than one fifth of company capital outlays before the mid-century (Pollins 1952). Some portion of the high construction costs can be attributed to the disadvantages of being first (Pollins 1971, pp. 31–33) and during the 1850s and early 1860s, consistent with this explanation, the ratio of railway company capital to railway mileage tended to fall. From the 1870s until the outbreak of the First World War the railway system was expanded by virtually 50% in terms of rail miles, but capital per mile almost doubled. While Aldcroft (1968) emphasized managerial incompetence as an explanation for rising capital costs, Cain (1972) argued that competition on the basis of quality rather than price was responsible, and Irving (1978) pointed out that political pressures became inimical to efficient management until 1899. The 1872 Parliamentary Joint Select Committee accused companies of pursuing competitive projects, duplicating lines and stations while deliberately undercosting their adventures to secure the approval of their shareholders (BPP 1872, p. 12). Examples of such behaviour included the London extension of the Midland railway in the 1860s after the end of the common purse agreement in 1857 with the London and North Western (Channon 1972) and the war between the London Chatham and Dover, and the South Eastern Railways from the 1860s to the 1890s (Pollins 1971, p. 110). Much money and energy was absorbed in attempts to frustrate the Parliamentary maneouvres of rival companies. The costs of the safety regulations of the 1889 Act, nominal additions to capital, and the debiting of capital account with expenditure which could have been paid out of revenue also raised costs, as did the widespread provision of tracks and sidings and the general enlarging of the capacity of the system. Yet railway systems elsewhere in the world also had to respond to the demands of expanding traffic and seem to have done so at lower costs.

In one sense at least railway competition seemed to work. Britain achieved a dense network of railway lines relatively early in the nineteenth century. In view of the concentrated population and high wages, construction of such a system was bound to be fairly expensive, though equally the utilization and profitability of the network could be expected to be substantial. The building of the extension to Waterloo station serves as an illustration both of how urbanisation drove up railway costs, and of how the market ensured rapid, if not cheap, development. During the railway boom of the 1840s, the original terminus of the London and South Western Railway at Nine Elms Vauxhall proved an inconvenient distance from central London. The Railway therefore extended their line to Waterloo station (opened in 1848) at a cost of £800,000 for a distance of little more than two miles. The cost was in large measure due to the six bridges needed and the speed at which they were built. The skew arch crossing Miles Street, South Lambeth was very difficult to build, being 48 feet wide on one side and only 38 feet on the other, forming a curve of 54 feet span. 90,000 bricks were required yet this great arch was completed in 45 hours (Clunn 1932).

Belgian railway construction was just as rapid but Belgium adopted a more interventionist policy which some contemporaries judged responsible for her more favourable railway rates. The Belgian government constructed the principal trunk lines on the basis of a proposal of 1833 to link the major towns with the sea and with the French and Prussian frontiers. By August 1838 159 miles of the four branches centred on Malines were open. Construction costs and the accuracy of their estimates compared favourably with those for English lines, even taking topography into account. Consequently Belgian rail fares on the Brussels-Antwerp lines were less than a half of those on the comparable Liverpool-Manchester line and more traffic was generated as a proportion of the population (Rawson 1839).

Throughout the remainder of the nineteenth century, Belgium's railway network continued to be the system most comparable with Britain's, and one that consistently charged lower freight and passenger rates. In 1856 Belgian third class fares per mile were one quarter lower than the British fares, (Chadwick 1859, p. 382) and in 1883 they were 40% less, while freight was similarly cheaper (Mulhall 1892, p. 498). Baxter noted in 1866 that Belgian fares had always been much below those on English lines, but he did not allow this observation to qualify his panegyric on the British system. He maintained that the distribution of the Belgian population conferred an advantage.

"A system which will pay admirably between large cities at short distances from each other and on lines which cost little to construct might break down completely on lines of expensive construction in more thinly inhabited districts." (Baxter 1866, p. 583).

One of the points at issue is of course precisely whether the more expensive construction was justified or whether the alternative systems offered different incentives to supply efficiently the desired quantity of railway services. Similar considerations apply to the claim that national construction costs were not comparable with each other because Britain had a higher proportion of double, treble and quadruple track than, say, America. The only social justification for more multiple tracks is a correspondingly greater volume of traffic, although in fact competition between railways for business may lead to unnecessary duplication or underutilisation of track.

3. Natural monopoly theory and railways

More systematic appraisal of the nineteenth century railway industry's performance is possible. Recent research has elaborated the industry cost conditions which can, at least within a static model, allow one firm to supply an industry demand more cheaply than two or more. Earlier analysts focussed upon economies of scale; J. S. Mill (1965, pp. 141–2) had remarked upon the futility of a multiplicity of producers in the London gas and water industries in the middle of the nineteenth century. The modern concept of a subadditive cost function is more general (Baumol 1977). A cost function is subadditive if

$$C\left(\sum_{k=1}^{n} Q_k\right) < \sum_{k=1}^{n} C(Q_k) \tag{1}$$

where the Q_k may be different quantities of the same output (economies of scale) or quantities of different outputs. For a railway cost function the Q_k may be traffic of different regions, or branch and main line traffic, or goods and passenger traffic, or different volumes of, say, goods traffic. Shared track, a common cost, may make the operation of freight and passenger services together cheaper than operating them on different networks. The ability to feed branch traffic directly on to trunk routes, or from region to region, without changing trains may lower costs. High volumes of traffic may permit greater utilisation of fixed costs such as stations and station staff.

Under any of the above specifications of Q_k railway outputs are multidimensional. The basic units of work performed by railway systems are ton/miles (Q_{TM}) and passenger/miles (Q_{PM}). The exact combination of distance travelled and volume moved may however influence railway costs. For that reason Caves, Christensen and Swanson (1981) include in their cost function a second output variable, average haul length (Q_H). Costs may increase because the distance moved has increased or because the quantity shifted (Q_G) has risen. Because of our interest in system planning and integration it is desirable to disaggregate ton or passenger miles, further distinguishing the number of hauls (Q_N) or trains run.

$$Q_{TM} = Q_G \times Q_N \times Q_H \tag{2}$$

If ton miles (Q_{TM}) increase, holding constant the haul length (Q_H), then either more goods (Q_G) are moved or the number of hauls increases. The average goods load (Q_L) may be defined as Q_G/Q_N. If the average load rises, maintaining train miles and haul length constant, then rearrangement of (2) shows that number of hauls must fall. Passenger traffic is analogous. The following restrictions are therefore expected to hold.

$$C = c(\overset{+}{Q}_{TM}\overset{-}{Q}_L, \overset{-}{Q}_H, \overset{+}{Q}_{PM}, \overset{-}{Q}_{PL}, \overset{-}{Q}_{PH}, \overset{+}{w}, \overset{-}{T}) \tag{3}$$

where Q_{PM}, Q_{PL}, Q_{PH} are passenger miles, passenger load and average passenger haul, w is a vector of factor prices and T an index of technology.

The scale elasticity RTS, measures overall scale economies generated by specific internal economies such as cost complementarity and output specific economies of scale. Summing over outputs

$$RTS = \left(\sum (\partial \ln c/\partial \ln Q_k)\right)^{-1} \tag{4}$$

A sufficient condition for subadditivity is cost complementarity, where an increase in the production of Q_k lowers the incremental cost of producing

Q_l. More readily obtainable from econometric estimates is local cost complementarity defined as

$$CC_{kl} = \partial^2 C / \partial Q_k \, \partial Q_l < 0 \tag{5}$$

Substantial negative load or haul elasticities may be indicative of cost complementarities between the outputs of different railway networks which the data cannot isolate. Whether cost complementarities can be distinguished also depends in part upon the form of the cost function adopted.

Common flexible functional forms which can identify these effects include the translog (TL) and the generalized translog (GTL) functions. Both result from a second order Taylor series approximation to the general form of (3). Both contain the natural logs of w and C but the GTL substitutes the Box–Cox transformation for the natural log of the Q_k and T in the TL. The Box–Cox transformation of output Q_k is $Q_k^* = (Q_k^{\lambda_k} - 1)/\lambda_k$. As λ_k approaches zero the Box–Cox expression reduces to the logarithmic transformation of Q_k. The full GTL function is:

$$\begin{aligned}\log C = \alpha_0 + \sum^{m} \alpha_i \log w_i + \sum^{n} \alpha_{Q_k} Q_k^* + \beta T^* + \tfrac{1}{2}\beta_T T^{*2} \\ + \tfrac{1}{2}\sum_i^m \sum_j^m \gamma_{ij} \log w_i w_j + \tfrac{1}{2}\sum_k^n \sum_l^n \delta_{kl} Q_k^* Q_l^* \\ + \sum_i^m \sum_k^n \rho_{ik} Q_k^* \log w_i + \sum_i^m \beta_i T^* \log w_i + \sum_k^n \beta_{Q_k} Q_k^* T^*\end{aligned} \tag{6}$$

In the GTL model local cost complementarity is:

$$CC_{kl} = \frac{C}{Q_k Q_l}\left[\frac{\partial \log C}{\partial \log Q_k}\frac{\partial \log C}{\partial \log Q_l} + \delta_{kl} Q_k^{\lambda_k} Q_l^{\lambda_l}\right] \tag{7}$$

Statistical precision of parameter estimates may be improved, when the firm chooses cost minimising inputs to produce exogenously determined volumes of output, by estimating cost share equations simultaneously with the cost function (e.g. Fuss and Waverman 1981).

If cost function parameter estimates show that economies of scale or load factors are unexhausted then it is possible that industrial organisation was inefficient and other arrangements of railway networks might have reduced costs. However identifying these forms of subadditivity for a cross section of railways within a geographical area does not necessarily imply a suboptimal national railway organisation (although it is consistent with that state of affairs) because outputs may be demand constrained. Transport between A and B is not necessarily a perfect substitute for transport between C and D but in the long run the mobility of economic location increases substitutability.

Whereas comparisons within a country allow the estimation of a company cost function, comparisons between aggregate national systems permit industry cost functions to be estimated. Even when national company cost functions are identical, different national configurations of firms could generate different industry cost functions. If in one national industry some companies are so small because of 'business stealing' (Mankiw and Whinston 1986) that they are operating at ranges of output over which scale economies are unexhausted, or lack of network integration raises each company's costs, then that industry's costs will be higher than those of other comparable industries. For similar reasons crosshauling could raise train miles or volume miles and create a potential source of cost reduction. A failure to integrate networks may require more trips or hauls than necessary because of the need to change trains; in either case loads per train will be suboptimal and national railways costs will be higher than necessary.

4. Testing the efficiency of the railway regime

(i) *The British cross-section sample*

Our first test of the appropriateness of the reliance on competition then is to estimate a railway cost function from cross-section data in the Railway Returns for 1865 (BPP 1866). This year was chosen as one of the latest before substantial regulation was introduced and for comparability with Hawke's (1970) classic study. Forty-six railways in Great Britain with ten miles of railway or more were found to have reasonably complete data. The returns provide working expenditure figures, capital costs (calculated from each railway's debenture rate times the sum of paid up capital and debenture loans) and three output measures for each of the two types of traffic, passenger and freight. These are numbers of trains, volume carried and train miles.

From the three output measures we can infer the average load per train and the average distance travelled per train but because passengers and freight did not travel the whole distance, we cannot deduce ton miles and passenger miles. The closest approximation to these variables are the rather large numbers obtained by assuming no intermediate loading or unloading of freight or passengers which we call "maximum passenger miles" and "maximum ton miles". For our purposes the critical assumption is that there are no major differences between systems in intermediate loading and unloading.

Factor prices in the cross section are largely embodied in the constant term of the cost function. Regional variation in railwaymen's pay was very limited, reduced in part by agreements between employers (Hunt 1973, pp. 57, 351). Coal prices must have varied as much from one section of a railway to another as between railways, in view of the key role of transport costs in coal price determination. Consequently no attempt was made to measure either factor price for individual railways and estimation of the cost function simultaneously with cost shares was impossible.

TABLE 2
British Railway Systems' Mean Outputs in 1865

Goods train load	104.8 tons
Passenger train load	111.78 passengers
Goods train haul	32.73 miles
Passenger train haul	35.43 miles
"Maximum ton miles"	91.04 million
"Maximum passenger miles"	258.99 million

Source: 46 Railways in the Railway Returns of 1865 (BPP 1866).

The mean values of the output measures in our sample are presented in Table 2.[1]

In order to capture the variety of possible forms of subadditivity we test down from a generalized translog cost function to a more specific functional form with relatively well-defined coefficients. With six output variables, no factor prices and no technology terms there are twenty eight parameters to estimate. Following Caves, Christensen and Swanson (1981) we set the Box–Cox parameters $\lambda = 0.1$. To avoid unnecessary detail we do not report the full results here but note that only four coefficients (those on maximum passenger miles, on the interaction between the average loads of goods and of passenger trains, on the interaction between passenger load and goods load, all positive, and on the square of passenger miles) were significant at the 5% level on a one-tailed test. When $\lambda = 0$ the fit of the equation was improved. The sum of squared residuals fell from 3.8424 to 3.0208. Six parameters passed the significance test above and were all included in a more specific equation (1 in Table 3) based upon the first order terms. Computation of the cost complementarity statistic (7) showed it to be positive for all values of the significant coefficients and first order terms. The sum of squared residuals rose to 6.326 for the restricted translog equation but an F test suggested that the restriction was not rejected at the 5% level. A comparison of this functional form with a more restricted cost function containing only first order variables (equation 2 in Table 3) implied that in the interests of more precise coefficient estimates the interaction terms could be dropped without a significant reduction in the sum of squared residuals of the equations.

Typically the profit maximising firm chooses outputs and costs simultaneously. Consequently the error term in a stochastic cost function is not independent of the output variables and coefficient estimates may be

[1] For comparative purposes, Hawke (1970) thought an average goods haul of 33 miles and average goods train loads of 55.7–58.3 tons were reasonable. He noted that, except for the problems of returns and express fares, average fares per mile and receipts by passenger class allowed the computation of passenger miles in total from the Railway Returns. At the individual company level insufficient average fare data was available to justify including the variable in our sample, and also for comparison with the train mile figure, the 'maximum' measure was adopted.

biased. We employ the Hausman (1978) test to judge whether railway outputs were endogenous. The test that the output vector Q is not correlated with the random error (u) is equivalent to the test of the hypothesis that $A = B$ in the equation

$$C = \hat{Q}A + (Q - \hat{Q})B + u \tag{8}$$

where $\hat{Q}$ is a matrix of predicted values from the regression of Q on an instrumental variable set. We use 1860 values of Q as instruments, which reduces the sample size from 46 to 34. The test involves comparing the likelihoods of the OLS cost function (2) (on the smaller sample) and equation 3 in Table 3. The likelihood ratio is:

$$LR = -2 \log \lambda = 2(\log L(\bar{\psi}) - \log L(\bar{\psi}_0)) = 2(-17.3652 + 21.0591) = 7.3876$$

which compares with a critical value of $\chi^2_{.05}(6) = 12.6$. The hypothesis that the Q vector is not exogenous is rejected. Similar findings were obtained when only the goods output vector was treated as potentially endogenous.

These econometric results might have been generated by small railways being constrained by their local demands from achieving better haul and load characteristics, whereas large railways, those in environments which allowed expansion, might have been able to arrange traffic more conveniently to themselves. Dividing the sample into railways with more than 100 miles of line and those with less, did not produce coefficient estimates that were markedly different on an F test of the addition of the large railway data to the small railway data structure (equations 4 and 5). The data are consistent with scope for improvement being common to large and small railways.

Equation 2 shows very small unexploited overall economies of scale (including cost complementarities) for maximum passenger and freight ton miles together, with RTS = 1.05 and the sum of the two coefficients not differing significantly from unity (standard error 0.051). The average passenger train haul does show substantial cost reductions could have been obtained from longer hauls, by reducing the number of trains run. With a smaller number of trains the magnitude of multiple tracking could have been reduced and with it the capital costs per rail mile. Higher freight and passenger loads per train would also have lowered costs, consistent with Irving's (1978) view that better traffic management, perhaps through system integration could have been beneficial.

(ii) *International time-series/cross-section samples*

If there were unexploited opportunities for system integration at the national level then comparisons with other countries, where the state almost invariably took a greater hand in positive railway planning, can be expected to show higher costs for the British regime. The empirical question is how to

TABLE 3
Total Cost Functions for British Railways in 1865

	(1) Restricted Translog	(2) Log–Log	(3) Hausman Test	(4) Log–Log Railways under 100 miles	(5) Log–Log Railways over 99 miles
SSR	6.326	9.1221	5.5287	3.9739	2.9438
n	46	46	34	25	21
$\bar{R}^2$	0.9519	0.9395	0.9264	0.8427	0.8296
constant	1.6656*	0.3473	—	−1.1310	0.5001
	(0.66)	(0.47)		(−0.98)	(0.26)
Goods train load	−1.8950*	−0.4587*	[−0.7727]	−0.1403	0.6741*
	(−3.61)	(3.53)	[(−1.23)]	(−0.70)	(3.05)
Passenger train load	−1.8222*	−0.2761*	[0.2851]	−0.6266*	−0.1412
	(−1.73)	(−1.92)	[(0.14)]	(−2.28)	(0.60)
Goods train haul	−0.0990	0.0472	[−0.1246]	−0.2497	0.1335
	(−0.7223)	(0.35)	[(−0.42)]	(−1.15)	(0.50)
Passenger train haul	−0.0011	−0.3948*	[−0.7215]*	0.0774	−0.6361*
	(−0.0011)	(3.67)	[(2.62)]	(0.34)	(3.32)
Max. ton miles	0.7710*	0.3475*	[0.4930]*	0.2724*	0.3151*
	(4.57)	(5.34)	[(2.5)]	(3.14)	(2.89)
Max. pass. miles	0.7428*	0.6094*	[0.1069]	0.7533*	0.6713*
	(9.27)	(7.95)	[(0.08)]	(5.71)	(3.80)

(Passenger load)^2	−0.1883	—	—	—	—
	(−1.50)				
Ton miles × passenger load	(0.3318)	—	—	—	—
	(1.64)				
Passenger haul × goods load	0.750	—	—	—	—
	(0.45)				
Passenger haul × ton miles	−0.1779*	—	—	—	—
	(−2.88)				
Passenger haul × passenger load	0.5242*	—	—	—	—
	(2.8891)				
┼Passenger miles	—	—	0.9679*	—	—
			(3.01)		
┼Passenger load	—	—	−0.2193	—	—
			(−0.96)		
┼Ton miles	—	—	0.4102	—	—
			(1.31)		
┼Goods load	—	—	−0.5168	—	—
			(1.75)		
┼Passenger haul	—	—	1.4538	—	—
			(0.25)		
┼Goods haul	—	—	−0.7319	—	—
			(−0.23)		

Notes: * indicates significance at 5% level, t statistics in parentheses. All variables in logs. [ ] = predicted values, ┼ = residuals.

distinguish such avoidable industry costs from those arising from national economic and topographical conditions.

The first data set we employ to confront this issue is a pooled cross-section/time-series sample of countries with observations at generally decadal intervals from 1840 to 1910. The data are much poorer than the British cross-section but do permit a focus upon railway capital costs, the bone of contention in the British regime. The dependent variable is the capital outlay on railways. Given the integration of the nineteenth century world capital markets, the costs of borrowing did not vary greatly between national railways, but Britain's systems generally had access to among the lowest costs of capital. British capital costs relative to other nations will therefore be understated and the results of the test biased against the hypothesis of excessive capitalization.

Competition between companies may be expected to change costs with the expansion of systems, but the impact of national economic conditions should be stable. A country with a concentrated population needing expensive multiple tracking in one decade will have had similar requirements relative to more sparsely populated countries in earlier decades. Because of the absence of matching factor prices and system utilisation data, the capital cost function estimated from this sample is in a simplified form with rail mileage as the long run output variable. The form adopted is:

$$\log(\text{capital costs})_{it} = a_0 + a_1 \log(\text{rail mileage})_{it} + a_2\,\text{time} + a_3 \log(\text{capital cost})_{it-1} + a_4 \log(\text{rail mileage})_{it-1} + a_5 D$$

where i indexes the country, the subscript $t-1$ refers to the previous decade and D is a vector of country dummies. The time variable captures the cost impact of quality enhancement, of safety regulations and with the opposite sign, of learning effects.

The regression equation in Table 4 suggests that a more parsimonious form may be adopted in which capital costs per rail mile depend, with an elasticity of 0.7, on the previous decade's capital costs per rail-mile. Even then the United Kingdom is the only country with a significant positive country dummy; costs per rail mile in each decade grew proportionately more in the United Kingdom, independently of general improvements accruing to all national rail networks. Belgium is taken as the comparison country for the sample—all other countries with significant country effects have lower capital costs per mile than Belgium and of course than the United Kingdom. The capital cost economies of scale coefficient is about the same as the scale estimate obtained from the British cross-section sample, and capital costs rose on average at about $\frac{1}{2}$% p.a. because of improvements to the systems.

Railway systems such as the United Kingdom's that ran more train miles per mile of track than average necessarily required more expensive constructions. However Table 5 shows that, around 1906, whereas the

TABLE 4
Cross-National Comparison of Railway Capital Costs 1840–1910

Constant	−4.7045*
	(1.1490)
log rail mileage$_t$	0.9486*
	(0.0389)
Time	0.0046*
	(0.0013)
log capital cost$_{t-1}$	0.7013*
	(0.0908)
log rail mileage$_{t-1}$	−0.7090*
	(0.0873)
United Kingdom	0.3007*
	(0.0777)
France	0.1080
	(0.06322)
Germany	0.422
	(0.0750)
Switzerland	−0.1278*
	(0.0549)
Sweden	−0.4081*
	(0.1443)
United States	0.0147
	(0.1386)
Canada	−0.1887*
	(0.0910)
India	−0.2629*
	(0.1170)
Australia	−0.2943*
	(0.1129)
Russia	−0.0256
	(0.745)
Austria	−0.0299
	(0.0622)
Italy	−0.0439
	(0.0596)
$\bar{R}^2$	0.9974
SSR	0.3667

* indicates significant at the 5% level.

Data sources: U.K. Statistical Abstract for Foreign Countries (various), M. Mulhall *Dictionary of Statistics* (1882), A. Webb *New Dictionary of Statistics* (1911).

United Kingdom's construction costs were two thirds greater than those of the Belgian railways, United Kingdom train miles per mile were only 12% higher. From Table 5 the United Kingdom can be seen to be almost alone among the industrial nations in abjuring the at least partial state ownership that went along with state planning of the railway system. Only the United

TABLE 5
National Railway Systems c. 1906

	Construction costs per mile of railway c. 1906 £	*Length of line open to traffic 1906*	*Train miles per mile of line, av. 1902–1906*	*Percentage of lines owned by the State, 1906*	*Gross per mile expenses, annual averages c. 1902–06 £*	*Gross receipts per mile, annual averages 1902–06 £*
United Kingdom	56,000	23,060	17,729	0	2,928	4,617
France	28,600	29,270	8,728	5.9	1,341	2,531
Belgium	34,000*	2,880	15,808	87.8	2,315	3,728
Holland	13,700*	2,180	11,807	53.2	1,691	2,022
Germany	21,400	34,480	11,212	92.8	2,123	3,415
Sweden	6,570	8,100	3,405	32.2	503	742
Norway	7,660	1,580	3,236	85.4	474	623
Denmark	9,900*	2,080	n.a.	56.2	1,371	1,684
Switzerland	23,900	2,675	9,304	56.0	1,656	2,574
Spain	20,350	9,195	n.a.	0	654	1,341
Portugal	n.a.	1,420	n.a.	39.4	n.a.	n.a.
Italy	21,000	10,110	5,178	77.1	1,240	1,588
Austria-Hungary	18,360	24,479	6,449	64.1	1,138	1,803
Russia in Europe	18,800	32,740	6,392	60.3	1,398	2,144
Bulgaria	8,570	970	n.a.	76.3	n.a.	n.a.
Serbia	12,700	440	n.a.	88.6	n.a.	n.a.
Romania	18,064	1,975	4,221	100	740	1,305
Greece	n.a.	845	n.a.	0	n.a.	n.a.
United States	14,200	222,635	4,885	0	1,341	2,011
Argentina	10,800	14,550	2,042	11.8	562	1,034
Japan	9,100	5,010	7,359	35.3	689	1,383
India	8,800	29,100	3,934	74.6	504	1,011
Canada	12,700	22,170	3,281	7.7	808	1,162

Source: A. D. Webb, *The New Dictionary of Statistics*, London, Routledge 1911 citing principally U.K. *Annual Abstract of Foreign Countries*. Also U.K. *Annual Abstract of the British Empire*.

Note: * = state owned lines only.

States, Greece and Spain in this sample pursued similar policies. Utilisation data is lacking for Greece and Spain leaving only the United States in a similar position to Britain, and Lardner writing in 1850 thought American regulation was more effective than British (Parris 1965, p. 9). Table 5 suggests US performance compares favourably with Romania's and Italy's but unfavourably with India's. Obviously such comparisons are far less convincing than that with Belgium, given the greater differences between national economic environments.

The second cross-national data set, Table 5 pooled with similar observations for 1895, offers an alternative means of controlling for the influence of economic conditions on the capital costs of railways. Train miles run provides a measure of traffic carried (though as discussed above, a less than perfect one). Urbanisation, for instance, could raise construction costs but it would also enhance the demand for transport as measured by train miles. Less densely populated countries require more rail miles for given train miles, thereby incurring different construction costs. Both length of line and train miles are therefore included as arguments of the capital cost function below. If having allowed for the effects of these variables, differing national costs are identified, then these may be attributed to the organisation of the industry, rather than to the economic environment. Variable costs and revenues equally may be expected to differ between countries with traffic conditions and network configurations. In turn variations in industry organisation could create different relations between train miles run and these variables; a regulated or state operated industry could generate less revenue per train mile than a private monopoly, working expenditure could be raised by competitive 'business stealing' in the same way as with fixed costs or by labour costs enhanced by measures such as the 1893 Act. By the late nineteenth century, as we have suggested, British regulation was probably sufficiently close to prevent monopolistic revenues or excessive variable costs. The effects of the competitive origin of the railway system should be observable only in the capital costs.

Table 6 shows that for the United Kingdom there was a significant national effect on capital costs that could be attributed to industry organisation, but no comparable influence was at work on the revenue account.[2] Regulation seems to have encouraged behaviour comparable to nationalised enterprises for working costs and earnings, but not for past decisions. The construction cost equation predicts that if the UK had had a regime similar to other countries', construction costs per mile in 1902–06 would have been £37,750 instead of £56,000, about 32% lower, and railway usage and social savings would have been accordingly greater.

In contrast to the Averch–Johnson model, state regulation in the UK exerted direct pressure on prices and services, rather than on rates of

[2] A number of specifications were tried in formulating these regression equations for the 1906 sample including polynomials in train miles, and proxies for factor prices—income per head for wages and export or import average values of coal prices.

TABLE 6

OLS Analysis of Pooled Cross-National Railway Cost and Revenue Data for c. 1895 and c. 1906

Dependent Variable	*Constant*	*Train Miles per Rail Mile*	*D × Train Miles per Mile*	*SSR*	$\bar{R}^2$
Construction Cost	5190.57*	1.8361*	1.1015*	0.6309×10^9	0.828
per Mile	(1959.7)	(0.2566)	(0.2596)		
Working Expenses	160.347	0.1436*	0.0112	0.1717×10^7	0.854
per Mile	(102.24)	(0.0134)	(0.0135)		
Revenue	274.233	0.2238*	0.0265	0.4351×10^7	0.865
per Mile	(162.74)	(0.0213)	(0.0215)		

Notes: The restrictions imposed in the above equations were tested and found consistent with the data. * indicates significance at the 5% level. 32 observations for each equation. D is the United Kingdom dummy variable.

return, lowering the return on railway capital and restricting railway expansion. Given that the companies had to pay for the expensive system and could generate the revenue if permitted to do so by government, the alternative policy was to permit a higher UK rate of return. A higher return would also have restricted the use of railways, unless the capital values were written down, an outcome that amalgamations into territorial monopolies were intended to prevent. UK gross working expenses in 1906 were £2,928 per mile and the railways were allowed to earn £4,617 per mile. As a return on previous investment—the £56,000 construction costs per mile—that left £1,689, amounting to a 3% return. Had construction costs been lowered to the levels predicted by the equation of Table 6 when the UK dummy took a zero value, this return would have risen to 4.47% (compared with 4.16% for France).

UK construction costs were a considerable proportion of total railway costs. At 4%, construction costs amounted to 43% of the sum of working expenses and payments on construction outlays, at 5% they were 48.9%. Thus a reduction of UK construction costs to levels predicted for the continental regimes would probably have lowered total rail costs by between $0.43–0.49 \times 0.32$ or 14–16 per cent. Applying the static social saving approach to this figure suggests an increase in GNP of the order of 3/4%. As a static benefit this is a downward biased figure; increased sales encouraged by lower prices and costs would probably have enhanced the figure.

Conclusion

Competition in the railway system had burnt itself out by the end of the nineteenth century because both suppliers and customers found it incompatible with the technical conditions of the industry. Regression estimates of a cost function based on Railway Returns data suggests that, at the level of the individual railway in 1865, before the onset of substantial regulation, there were unexploited economies of system integration or economies of scope. National economic and topographical conditions alternatively may have been entirely responsible for high British railway capital costs but two other experiments do not support that explanation. Even allowing for general expensive improvements in service between 1840 and 1910, and recognising that country characteristics could raise the *level* of capital costs, Britain still showed the greatest *increases* in capital costs per rail mile. Around the turn of the century British capital costs per train mile were far more expensive than most other countries', though revenues and variable costs were comparable to those of other national systems.

The most credible inference is that the largely unregulated free enterprise system of railway investment probably raised construction costs by 50% and lowered national income per head by at least $\frac{3}{4}$% in static terms around 1906. The counterfactual is a more interventionist, but competent regime in the early years of railway development that planned a national trunk layout and prevented wasteful competition, either by state ownership (the conventional solution) or by effective regulation. Such a regime is not perhaps a historically plausible alternative but it is one that places the liberal order in perspective.

REFERENCES

ALDCROFT, D. H. (1968) 'The Efficiency and Enterprise of British Railways 1870–1914' *Explorations in Entrepreneurial History*, 5.

BAUMOL, W. J. (1977) 'On the Proper Cost Test for Natural Monopoly in a Multiproduct Industry' *American Economic Review*, 67, 809–822.

BAUMOL, W. J. (1982) 'Contestable Markets: An Uprising in the Theory of Industry Structure' *American Economic Review*, 72, 1–15.

BAXTER, R. D. (1866), 'Railway Extension and its Results' *Journal of the Statistical Society of London*, 29, 549–595.

British Parliamentary Papers
(1852) *Select Committee on Amalgamation of Railways and Canals* xxxviii; (1866) *Railway Traffic Returns* lxiii; (1867) *Royal Commission on Railways* xxxviii; (1872) *Report from the Joint Select Committee of the House of Lords and the House of Commons on Railway Amalgamation*; (1911) *Departmental Committee on Railway Agreements and Amalgamations* Cmnd 5927.

CAIN, P. J. (1972) 'Railway Combination and Government, 1900–1914' *Economic History Review*, 25, 623–6.

CAVES, D. W., CHRISTENSEN, L. R. and SWANSON, J. A. (1981), 'Productivity Growth, Scale Economies and Capacity Utilization in US Railroads 1955–74' *American Economic Review*, 71, 994–1002.

CHADWICK, E. (1859), 'Results of Different Principles of Legislation and Administration in Europe; of Competition for the Field as Compared with Competition Within the Field of Service' *Journal of the Statistical Society of London*, 22, 381–420.

CHANNON, G. (1972) 'A Nineteenth Century Investment Decision: The Midland Railway's London Extension', *Economic History Review*, 25, 448–470.

CLUNN, H. (1932) *The Face of London: The Record of a Century's Changes and Development*, London: Simpkin Marshall.

FUSS, M. A. and WAVERMAN, L. (1981) 'Regulation and the Multi-Product Firm: The Case of Telecommunications in Canada' in G. Fromm (ed.) *Studies in Public Regulation*, M.I.T.

HAUSMAN, J. A. (1978) 'Specification Tests in Econometrics' *Econometrica,* 46, 1251–71.

HAWKE, G. R. (1970) *Railways and Economic Growth in England and Wales 1840–1870,* London: Oxford University Press.

HUNT, E. H. (1973) *Regional Wage Variations in Britain 1850–1914,* London: Oxford University Press.

IRVING, R. J. (1978) 'The Profitability and Performance of British Railways 1870–1914', *Economic History Review,* 31, 46–66.

JEVONS, W. S. (1867) 'On the Analogy between the Post Office, Telegraphs and other Systems of Conveyance of the United Kingdom as regards Government Control' *Manchester Statistical Society,* 91–104.

JEVONS, W. S. (1874) 'The Railways and the State' in *Essays and Addresses of the Owens College Manchester,* London, Macmillan.

MANKIW, N. G. and WHINSTON, M. D. (1986) 'Free Entry and Social Inefficiency' *Rand Journal of Economics,* 17, 48–58.

MARTIN, R. BIDDULPH (1873) 'Notes on the Purchase of the Railways by the State' *Journal of the Statistical Society (of London)* 36, 177–202.

MILL, J. S. (1965) *Principles of Political Economy,* University of Toronto Press, London: Routledge Kegan Paul.

MILLWARD, R. and PARKER, D. 'Public and Private Enterprise: Comparative Behaviour and Relative Efficiency' in R. Millward *et al. Public Sector Economics* London: Longman.

MULHALL, M. G. (1892), *Dictionary of Statistics,* London: Routledge.

PARRIS, H. (1965) *Government and the Railways in Nineteenth Century Britain,* London: Routledge & Kegan Paul.

POLLINS, H. (1952) 'A Note on Railway Constructional Costs 1825–1850'. *Economica,* n.s. 19, 395–407.

POLLINS, H. (1971) *Britain's Railways: An Industrial History,* Newton Abbot: David and Charles.

RAWSON, R. W. (1839) 'On Railways in Belgium' *Journal of the Statistical Society of London,* 2, 47–62.

WEBB, A. D. (1911) *A New Dictionary of Statistics,* London: Routledge.

Oxford Economic Papers 39 (1987), 719–737

THE COSTS OF PUBLIC AND PRIVATE GAS ENTERPRISES IN LATE 19th CENTURY BRITAIN*

By ROBERT MILLWARD *and* ROBERT WARD

Introduction

Debates on the efficiency of publicly owned firms are only occasionally enriched by detailed statistical comparisons with private firms existing in the same country in the same industry. Public utilities in Britain before the Second World War provide one such opportunity, contrasting with the post-1945 experience where whole sectors have been either public or private, rendering comparisons of productivity, unit costs and price policy relatively meaningless. In gas, water, electricity and tramways at the end of the 19th century municipally owned enterprises coexisted with private companies, each enterprise usually having a local monopoly, or at least not facing competition "in the field". In this respect the setting has some similarities with modern USA whose institutional variety has proved a rich data base for public and private comparisons.

In the light of the likely set of incentives in different institutional settings those economists drawn to theorise on the role of "ownership" have tended to conclude that public firms would be less efficient in achieving the objectives of the owners than would private firms.[1] The argument is not concerned particularly with the level of profitability which will be a more important objective in private firms. Rather it is argued that public firms suffer first from the inability of their owners, except at prohibitive cost, to sell their rights in the enterprise, which reduces pressure on management. Secondly the control frameworks developed to promote cost effectiveness are most successful, so the argument goes, when designed and executed by those with a direct economic interest. At the same time the accumulation of evidence on the performance of public and private enterprises is still in its infancy and at this stage no clear superiority of private companies, in terms of cost effectiveness, has appeared.[2]

The issue was a live concern by the end of the 19th century in Britain and in USA where the experience of municipalisation in Britain was watched with great interest. There was much concern by British observers about the rise in local authority debt and the efficiency of municipal enterprises even

* Thanks are due for comments on this paper from participants of the ESRC Quantitative Economic History Study Group Conference, Birkbeck College, London, September 1986.

[1] See Alchian (1965) and more generally Millward (1982).

[2] Comparisons of public and private enterprises, which make due allowance for output, factor prices and cover all cost categories, are still limited. In the cost function studies of railroads, airlines, electricity supply, water supply, mainly in North America, no clear cost superiority for private enterprise exists. Distinct differences are apparent in comparisons of fares and tariffs where the link between prices and costs is much closer in private firms. See Millward (1982) and (1983), Chapter 5.

though their arguments were not couched in the above terms. The American R. P. Porter felt that "...with the exception of two or three exceptionally well managed municipal gas plants, the British Corporation plants are neither so well nor so economically managed as the private plants, nor do they serve the public so advantageously".[3] Statistical support for the arguments was enhanced by the growing body of Board of Trade returns on the public utilities. The debate was in part about prices and profits, but also about costs, where, however, the focus became average unit costs so that there were no serious attempts to examine how costs varied systematically with output, factor prices or plant vintages.

Since then, interest in statistical comparisons seems to have waned. Indeed Herman Finer in his authoritative 1941 study of municipal trading avoided "...comparisons of the *success* of municipal and private enterprises ... for the reason that they are practically impossible. Comparisons between one municipal utility and another are also practically impossible..." said Finer (p. 35n) resting his case on Pigou's dictum "...that attempts to conduct a comparison by reference to statistics are foredoomed to failure". There is a more up-to-date secondary literature in economic history books and journals on municipal performance related to gas. Little of this literature is concerned with detailed determinants of costs or prices nor with looking systematically at significant samples of undertakings so that the observations on performance are either guesses or are closely qualified.[4]

A pioneering study in this area is that by Foreman-Peck and Waterson (1985) for the 1930s, which found a slight cost superiority for private firms. The study was concerned with electricity but they did encounter significant data problems which meant the results have to be interpreted with caution. They did have data on capital costs, but their main results related to operating costs and can be extended to apply to total costs only if the production function can be shown to be homothetic, and for some coefficients Cobb–Douglas. Homotheticity was however rejected in their results (p. 93) and by extension a Cobb–Douglas function cannot be presumed. It was not possible to impose cost homogeneity. Finally they had no measure of technical progress so that some of the important sources of cost differences could not be explored. The present study did use data on

[3] p. 111. For the debate more generally see Ashley, Avebury, Howe, Maltbie and the National Civic Federation.

[4] Waller (1983) ch. 7 has a good coverage of the issues including some of the difficulties of interpreting statistics for activities meshed in with municipal accounts. He suggests on p. 308 that the municipal undertakings fell into bad ways later in the century when competition from private enterprises was eliminated but gives no statistical backing for this conclusion. Chatterton (1972) provides a useful review of government influence on the London gas companies, confirming Falkus' earlier position (1967). Their view that the changing structure of the industry can be explained by increasing government control has recently been challenged in Matthews' examination (1986), of the role of economic forces, and especially the secular decline in unit costs, for the London gas companies. Matthews does in addition look at costs and prices in a sample of public and private but, as we note later, does not provide a systematic analysis of their determinants.

capital costs and incorporates an estimate of technical progress. However one should not claim any significant data superiority to that of Foreman-Peck and Waterson. It is really complementary to their study in this respect.

The basic data relates to a sample of 35 gas undertakings for the year 1898, with the data covering various dimensions of output, factor prices, labour, other operating costs and capital costs as well as a proxy measure, albeit crude, for technical progress. The basic purpose is to evaluate the comparative performance of public and private undertakings. As a by-product it is also possible to report several results relating to features of the costs of gas production in this period: factor demand elasticities, scale economies and technical change, factor substitution elasticities and the importance of population density for transmission costs.

The gas industry and municipalisation at the end of the 19th century

The gas industry was born in the early years of the 19th century. Private enterprise dominated what was then a speculative venture. Even by 1845, when all towns with 2,500 or more inhabitants had a gas supply, there were only 6 municipal gas corporations.[5] From about that period competition "in the field" had virtually disappeared outside London, though the gas undertakings were never granted exclusive franchises and the threat of entry remained. The legal powers of government to regulate tariffs, dividends and supply obligations were strengthened. Local authorities never acquired the power to compulsorily purchase private gas companies but public ownership did increase. The reasons for this are beyond the scope of this paper but the relative ineffectiveness of regulation was a contributory factor. [cf. Millward 1986]. In 1875 there were 66 municipial corporations and a total of 148 publicly owned gas enterprises accounting for some 30% of the total of authorised undertakings and a slightly larger proportion of total sales. By the 1890s the average size of municipal and private plants in terms of gas production was about the same and of the 661 authorised undertakings in 1898, 222 were publicly owned accounting for about a third of total sales, a figure which had risen to about 40% on the eve of the 1st World War (Falkus 1977 Table III, Maltbie pp. 538/9, Balfour Committee pp. 311–12, 324–5).

At the turn of the century the relative performance of public and private undertakings was a matter of keen debate. By this stage the Board of Trade were producing comprehensive returns for all authorised undertakings and in 1905 a large team of officials and experts from the USA investigated, on behalf of the National Civic Federation, several undertakings in great detail producing a three volume report in 1907. The broad approach in all these

[5] The term "municipal gas corporation" refers to publicly owned undertakings in towns which had the status of corporate boroughs. The early development of the gas industry is discussed in Johnes and Clegg (1847), Livesey (1894), Falkus (1967), (1982). For its development during the 19th century see also Maltbie (1900), Robson (1935), Falkus (1977), Williams (1981), Millward (1986).

studies was to look at average values for certain performance indicators for samples of public and private firms making informal allowances for other factors which were at work. Thus in the years between 1895 and 1905 gross profits as a proportion of capital employed were for many gas undertakings in the range 4%–9%. Calculations using all the Board of Trade data as well as samples of the larger undertakings suggested municipal and private rates of return were broadly similar with, if anything, the private company rate of return slightly higher (Donald p. 72, Howe p. 35, 40, Maltbie p. 563). These profit rates will be reflecting both price and cost factors. For seven large towns in 1905 the National Civic Federation study (p. 212) found that prices were higher in the municipal firms, as had Porter (p. 111) for 1901, but much of the other evidence, including the comprehensive data of the Board of Trade, suggested that prices per cubic foot of gas were lower in the publicly owned sector, the importance of which was recognised in the larger average number of consumers in public enterprises. (Donald p. 72, Howe p. 35, Maltbie p. 556, Balfour Committee p. 312). Of course lower prices may be offset by poor quality. One measure of the illuminating power of gas is its candlepower. Whilst available figures suggested this was higher in the municipal firms, there was considerable dispute concerning the accuracy of the data.[6] Lower prices can also be offset by high meter rents but in this case there seems less dispute that these were lower in the municipal firms: in 1898 for example 12% of the customers supplied by private companies got their meters free whilst for the municipals the figure was 62% (Donald p. 72, Maltbie p. 553).

Prices and profits may of course be simply reflecting costs, which can clearly vary with output levels, the prices of materials and other inputs, the geographical setting as well as with institutional factors. Most of the existing studies concentrated on identifying differences in unit costs, and hence implicitly allowed only for the level of output. Again the National Civic Federation's study for seven large towns suggested (p. 207) unit labour costs and unit material costs were higher in the municipals, but the other studies tended to point the other way. Donald (p. 72) found unit operating costs for 1897 lower in Manchester than Liverpool (private). The comprehensive Board of Trade data for 1898 suggested that unit operating costs were lower in municipals, whilst for 1903/4 the same source showed municipal operating costs 10% lower than private, matching the 10% lower figure for the average level of prices (Maltbie p. 569, Howe p. 35). The precise source of all these cost differences was not, however, analysed systematically and the figures do not include capital costs.

Data sources and the broad features of the sample of gas undertakings

The efficiency of the gas undertakings is unlikely to be reflected in the level of profits since each enterprise had an element of monopoly power in

[6] See the contrasting evaluation of candlepower in two of the sections of the National Civic Federation study, one written by M. R. Maltbie (pp. 214–19) and the other written by C. L. Edgar and W. Clark (pp. 314–22). The candlepower data quoted later in this paper relates only to figures confirmed by Board of Trade inspectors.

being the sole supplier for its area. Moreover gas prices were regulated and the uneven strength of that regulation meant that the margin between price and cost was not under the complete control of management. There are good reasons then for concentrating more on the costs of the gas undertakings. The level and quality of output together with the range and number of consumers are therefore treated as data. So also are the prices paid for inputs, though the case of capital is not straightforward. We deduce how costs vary with all these variables by examining a cross-section of gas undertakings in 1898; and inquire whether, after allowing for differences in the variables in different geographical and institutional settings, private companies were more cost effective than the public firms. In this section we set out in broad terms how output and factor prices are likely to affect the costs of a gas undertaking. Then we describe the data sources and set out the broad economic features of the sample.

The total costs of a gas undertaking are likely, first, to be affected by the total quantity of gas produced. Given the nature of gas retorts, economies of scale may be expected over some ranges of output. The quality of the gas may also influence costs and here we include candlepower as a reflection of its illuminating properties. Other things being equal technical progress would lower the costs of producing any given quantity and in this study an attempt is made to reflect this in measures of the age of plant or the number of years since renovation and expansion had taken place. Turning now to distribution costs, each consumer will occasion a certain amount of costs associated with pipes, connections and repairs. Thus plants of the same vintage and same output may nevertheless be associated with different total costs for the undertakings, if the number of consumers varies. The location of consumers will also affect the size of the distribution network and the costs of servicing that network. The mileage of the distribution mains of a gas undertaking will be some reflection of the dispersal of consumers. However undertakings with the same number of consumers and the same mileage of distribution mains may nevertheless have different distribution costs when the mains cover a large geographical area rather than being concentrated on two sides of a number of adjacent streets. In addition to the number of consumers a relevant variable would therefore be the distribution mains mileage per square mileage of the towns served or alternatively a population density variable. Finally costs will vary with the prices paid for inputs. The level of wage rates, coal prices and interest rates paid on loans are taken as the key factor prices likely to influence costs.

Thus in a very general form the annual costs of a gas enterprise may be represented as:

$$C = f(Y, N, CP, M, I, P_w, P_t, P_k, D) \tag{1}$$

where Y is gas made in cubic feet, N is the number of consumers, CP is the candlepower of the gas, M is population density, I is the age of the plant, P_w the wage rate, P_t the price of coal, P_k the interest rate on loans and D is a dummy variable which takes a value of 1 for public firms and 0 for private.

Data is therefore required on all cost categories, on the various dimensions of output and on factor prices. The best source proved to be the Analyses of Gas Accounts in the weekly "Gas World". For 1897/8 there is detailed financial and operating data on 3 London companies, 13 other private companies and 19 Local Authority-owned undertakings. Details are given in Annex 1. It was possible to calculate the annual cost of each of these enterprises and the mean values are shown in Table 1. Measured by their total annual cost the size of the average London gas company, at nearly £2 million, was some 10 times that of the average provincial private gas company which was of roughly the same size as the average publicly owned enterprise. The raw data on wages and salaries in manufacture, in distribution and for management and directors was combined to yield the figures for labour costs which were only one eighth of total costs. Outlays on coal were substantial and accounted for a further third of total costs. Other operating costs included repair and maintenance of plant and the distribution network, servicing public lamps, rents, rates, other taxes, etc.

Capital costs are a traditionally difficult area. The Gas World source included an estimate of the book capital value of the works though we have no way of assessing how far this corresponded to a market valuation of the assets. An annual capital cost figure should ideally incorporate a measure of the annual decline in the market value of assets plus a rate of interest or profit on that used up capital. In Table 1 a rough proxy to this is taken as 10% of the capital value. An alternative is to allow for the differing rate of interest paid by the undertakings for their loan capital and the cost function is estimated later in these two alternative forms. The figure of 10% happens to be double the highest loan rate of interest in the sample and so a crude

TABLE 1
Costs of a Gas Enterprise in 1898 (Mean Values in £)

	London Companies		*Other Private*		*Public*	
1. Labour costs		249,009		24,389		22,062
(Wages and Salaries)		(12.6%)		(13.9%)		(13.7%)
2. Other Operating Costs						
a) Coal	615,865		55,899		54,184	
b) Other	426,290		35,162		32,484	
Total		1,042,155		91,061		86,668
		(52.8%)		(51.9%)		(54.0%)
3. Capital Costs						
Capital Value	6,815,595		599,468		517,194	
Annual Capital						
Cost = 10% Value		681,559		59,947		51,719
		(34.6%)		(34.2%)		(32.2%)
Total Cost		1,972,723		175,397		160,449
		(100%)		(100%)		(100%)

Source: See text.

allowance for the varying interest rates might be to take each undertaking's annual capital costs as $2rk$ where k is the capital value of works and r is the interest rate. This estimate of capital costs improved the statistical fit, so even though the effect was slight this version of the result is quoted in the later sections of the paper. Either way the mean shares of the three cost categories do not vary greatly between the different categories of enterprises identified in Table 1.

The Gas World data also includes various dimensions of the output of the gas undertakings and the mean values are shown in Table 2. In the sample the average public firm, though similar to the provincial private company in the quantity of gas produced and in its total cost, has almost twice the number of consumers, a feature well established in the contemporaneous literature and deemed to reflect the lower average prices charged by the public firms. The annual cost of gas per consumer in the public firms, at £4.3, is therefore well below the figure for provincial gas companies and also below the average for the London companies. The consumer receiving supplies from the private companies on average however acquired considerably larger quantities. Even so, cost per million cubic feet of gas for the private companies, at £169:00, was some 15% higher than for the public firms and the quality of gas as measured by candlepower, or the spread of consumers as indicated by the population density data, do not detract from that.

It is clear from Table 2 that some of the reasons for that difference may lie simply in the level of input prices. The Gas World figures include estimates for each enterprise of expenditure on coal and tonnage used, from which was deduced a figure for the average coal price per ton for each enterprise and this was used as the factor price corresponding to non-labour operating costs. The price of capital in Table 2 refers to the interest rate paid on loans. The Board of Trade returns include figures on various categories of loans outstanding and the interest rate on each. A weighted average was calculated for each enterprise. Wage rates for each enterprise, that is on a town basis, proved the most difficult data problem. The weekly Gas World did not include relevant data. From 1893, Board of Trade wage data included figures for "rates of wages paid to workers in and about gas works". Unfortunately the regions identified were too large for this study of town gas works. However the regional variation in these wages is highly correlated with the Board of Trade engineering wage data for fitters and turners which is available at a more local level. The data for turners was therefore used in this study as a proxy for gas works wage rates. Full details are given in Annex 1.

The northern industrial cities were often served by municipally owned enterprises. Table 2 suggests that the average publicly owned gas undertaking was faced with lower wage rates than the average private company. The public firms were also favoured, in this sense, in terms of the average price they paid for coal and the average interest rate on loans. The precise

TABLE 2
Gas Unit Costs and Factor Prices in 1898

	London Companies	*Other Private*	*All Private*	*Public*	*All Pooled*
Annual Cost of a Gas Enterprise in £ million	1.972	0.175	0.512	0.160	0.321
Number of Consumers	165,704	19,651	47,036	36,712	41,432
Cost per Consumer in £	11.9	8.9	10.9	4.3	7.7
Gas Made in Million cubic feet	11,602	1,048	3,027	1,093	1,977
Gas Made per Consumer in thousand cu. ft.	70	53	64	29	48
Cost per Million cubic feet in £	170	167	169	147	162
Candlepower	16	15.9	15.9	19.4	17.8
Length of Distribution Mains in miles	1052	218	375	176	267
Population Density (inhabitants per acre)	60.6	19.5	26.9	20.3	23.3
Wage Rate (shillings per week)	38.0	36.4	36.7	33.6	35.0
Price of Coal in £ per ton	0.56	0.65	0.63	0.49	0.55
Price of Capital (% interest rate on loans)	4.11	4.02	4.04	3.44	3.71
Technology Vintage of Plant (age in years)	33	26.2	27.5	20.9	23.9

Source: See text.

effect on costs will be examined in the econometric analysis. Similarly another source of the unit cost differences between public and private may be the vintage of plant used. Precise data on this was not available but the proxy measure whose mean values are shown in Table 2 is an estimate for each undertaking of the weighted average age of its loan stock. Needless to say this is very rough data indeed. The cost figures in Table 1 and 2 are consistent with those quoted by Matthews (1986) for 1883 and 1914 for samples of local authorities and private gas undertakings. On their own, however, such data can tell us little about performance unless one controls as precisely as possible for variables, other than ownership, which affect costs. We now do this by estimating the cost function.

Cost shares, factor prices and factor demand

In estimating equation (1) a translog. form was taken since this prejudges very little about the nature of production. See Annex 2 for a full specification. It allows each variable to have a direct effect on costs, plus indirect effects which depend on the levels of each of the other variables. There is likely to be a high correlation between the independent variables of equation (1). Estimation therefore proceeded in two stages. The proportionate change in costs in response to a change in factor price, $\partial \log C/\partial \log P_W$ for example, is equal, whatever the form of the cost function, to that factor's share of total cost. The data available allows costs to be divided into labour, other operating costs (henceforth called the coal share) and capital costs. Data on each share can therefore be used in preliminary regressions to obtain some of the coefficients. In the second stage of estimation the results for these coefficients are fed back into the cost function and a second regression run to estimate the remaining coefficients. This procedure is not without its problems specifically because of the interrelationship between the equations for factor shares. This matter is referred to later and dealt with in detail in Annex 2.

We start with the equation for labour's share which is:

$$S_w = a_w + a_{yw} \log Y + a_{cpw} \log CP + a_{nw} \log N + a_{mw} \log M + a_{ww} \log P_w + a_{wt} \log P_t + a_{wk} \log P_k + a_{wi} \log I + a_{wd} D + u_w \quad (2)$$

where u_w is the error term and a_w, a_{yw}, etc. are constant coefficients from the translog cost function.

For the cost function to correspond to a well-behaved production function, it is required that a uniform proportionate rise in all factor prices leads, with output constant, to an equivalent rise in total cost leaving the relative share of each factor unchanged. In the above this implies $a_{wk} = (-)(a_{ww} + a_{wt})$ and the F statistic for this one restriction was 1.340 so that given 25 degrees of freedom, it could not be rejected. Similar procedures were used for the coal share equation, S_t, but this contains a coefficient a_{wt} which symmetry requires should be the same as a_{wt} estimated in (2). There are thus two restrictions in this case but the F statistic was 0.024 so that again the restriction seems valid. Since the three shares must add up to unity, the coefficients for capital's share S_k may be derived, as we show shortly, from the coefficients already estimated for S_w and S_t.

A characteristic of some production functions is homotheticity which would mean that the proportionate effects of factor prices and output on costs are independent of each other. Thus the proportionate effect of a change in the wage rate on costs would be independent of the level of output implying that in the labour share equation $a_{yw} = 0 = a_{cpw} = a_{nw} = a_{mw}$. Equation (2) was therefore estimated with these four additional restrictions and the F test statistic was 2.444 in a comparison with the regression involving only the factor price homogeneity restriction. Thus production homotheticity seems a valid restriction and the results for this regression were, with t ratios in brackets and with R^2 adjusted for degrees of freedom:

$$\begin{aligned} S_w = {} & \underset{(0.86)}{0.094} + \underset{(1.35)}{0.0481} \log (P_w/P_k) - \underset{(-3.11)^*}{0.0616} \log (P_t/P_k) - \underset{(-4.16)^*}{0.0525} \log I - \underset{(-2.92)^*}{0.0289} D \\ & R^2 = 0.36 \qquad a_{wk} = 0.0135 \qquad \text{* Significant at 0.05 level.} \end{aligned} \quad (3)$$

The only *a priori* expectation we have with respect to the sign of the coefficients is that the demand for labour varies inversely with the wage rate. The price elasticity of the demand for labour, with output constant, can be deduced from the above equation [cf. Christensen and Greene 1976, Pescatrice and Trapani 1980] though the key coefficient is not statistically significant. The sample mean labour share, $\bar{S}_w$, is 14% so the elasticity is:

$$\varepsilon_{ww} = \frac{a_{ww}}{\bar{S}_w} - (1 - \bar{S}_w) = (-)0.52 \tag{4}$$

With more than two inputs the signs of the cross elasticities involve no clear expectations in economic theory and the results will be discussed later as will be those for technical progress and the ownership dummies. In the meantime we may note that with a translog cost function the coal share equation is

$$\begin{aligned} S_t = a_t + a_{yt} \log Y + a_{cpt} \log CP + a_{nt} \log N + a_{mt} \log M \\ + a_{wt} \log P_w + a_{tt} \log P_t + a_{tk} \log P_k + a_{ti} \log I + a_{td} D + u_t \end{aligned} \tag{5}$$

As already noted factor price homogeneity, that is $a_{tk} = (-)(a_{wt} + a_{tt})$, has been found to be a valid restriction of this equation in conjunction with the symmetry restriction that $a_{wt} = a_{wt}$ from the labour share equation. Production homotheticity would require that the output coefficients in (5) are zero. Comparisons with the regression without these four restrictions yielded an F statistic of 2.480 so that homotheticity cannot be rejected and the final form is therefore:

$$\begin{aligned} S_t - a_{wt} \log (P_w/P_k) = \underset{(5.55)}{0.753} + \underset{(0.99)}{0.0508} \log (P_t/P_k) + \underset{(0.29)}{0.0104} \log I + \underset{(-0.20)}{0.0053} D \\ R^2 = 0.0 \\ a_{wt} = (-)0.0616 \qquad a_{tk} = 0.0108 \end{aligned} \tag{6}$$

With the low R^2 and t values the coal share varies mainly with the wage rate and is equal to $0.75–0.06 \log P_w$. Since the coal share can also be interpreted as measuring the elasticity of total cost with respect to the coal price, then the results imply that a 10% rise in coal prices would increase total costs by 7.5% less an amount that gets bigger with the level of wage rates. The mean elasticity is equal to the mean coal share, 0.55. At that share value the own-price elasticity of demand for coal is (−)0.36; it has the right sign but the key coefficient is statistically insignificant. Note that the data on the share of coal in total costs strictly refers to non-labour operating costs so that the above elasticities exaggerate the effects of changes in coal prices.

Finally, the capital share equation in general form is:

$$\begin{aligned} S_k = a_k + a_{yk} \log Y + a_{cpk} \log CP + a_{nk} \log N + a_{mk} \log M + a_{wk} \log P_w \\ + a_{tk} \log P_t + a_{kk} \log P_k + a_{ki} \log I + a_{kd} D + u_k \end{aligned} \tag{7}$$

One approach to estimating the coefficients in (7) is to recognise that the three share equations must add up to unity. Symmetry with the coefficients of the other equations in conjunction with factor price homogeneity implies:

$$a_{kk} = (-)(a_{wk} + a_{tk}) = (-)0.0243 \tag{8}$$

The last result implies an own-price elasticity of demand for capital of (−)0.77 but again the constituent coefficients are not statistically significant. Factor price homogeneity also means that for each independent variable, the three coefficients across the three equations must sum to zero.[7] Hence all the output coefficients in the capital share equation must equal zero. Also:

$$a_k = 1 - a_w - a_t = 0.153 \tag{9}$$

The results for the technical progress variable and the dummy will be considered later. This procedure for deducing the coefficients of the third equation may not be invariant to which equation is chosen as third. This issue is discussed in Annex 2.

Substitution between factors

The degree of substitutability in the gas technology may be indicated by the partial elasticity of substitution. This measures the percentage rise in the ratio of, say, labour to capital in response to a given percentage rise in the relative price of capital, with output constant. It can be shown [cf. Christensen and Greene 1976, Pescatrice and Trapani 1980] that at the sample mean this substitution elasticity is measured as

$$\delta_{wk} = 1 + \frac{a_{wk}}{\bar{S}_w \bar{S}_k} \tag{10}$$

and the cross price elasticities as:

$$\varepsilon_{wk} = \bar{S}_k \delta_{wk}; \qquad \varepsilon_{kw} = \bar{S}_w \delta_{wk} \tag{11}$$

As may be seen in Annex 2 the results are such that a fall in the price of capital reduces the demand for labour and the ratio of labour to capital; it also reduces the demand for coal and the ratio of coal to capital. But the precise sizes of these effects are not statistically significant. For labour and coal we have the following statistically significant results:

$$\delta_{wt} = 0.12 \qquad \varepsilon_{wt} = 0.06 \qquad \varepsilon_{tw} = 0.02 \tag{12}$$

Thus a rise of 10% in the wage rate leads to an increase of 0.2% in the demand for coal and a 10% rise in the relative wage rate is associated with a rise of 1.2% in the ratio of coal to labour. As labour becomes relatively more costly there is substitution towards technologies which are more

[7] Cf. Christensen and Greene p. 660.

capital intensive and more coal intensive though the latter effect is small and the former is not statistically significant. The same applies when the price of coal rises and leads to substitution towards technologies involving a lower ratio of coal to capital and a lower ratio of coal to labour.

Finally the deduced results for the capital share equation imply:

$$a_{ki} = (-)(a_{wi} + a_{ti}) = 0.0421$$
$$a_{kd} = (-)(a_{wd} + a_{td}) = 0.0236 \quad (13)$$

The result for a_{kd} suggests that municipal enterprises have a higher capital share than private firms and, from equations (3) and (6), a lower labour share. Finally, we can note that the lower is I the more modern is the capital equipment assumed to be. The result for a_{ki} suggests that the more modern vintages reduce the share of capital costs in total costs and largely at the expense of a higher labour share. Technical progress appears to be Hicks-type capital saving.

Scale economies, technical progress and the role of ownership

The share equations capture the effect of changes in factor prices on costs, including any indirect effects, if they exist, through output and technical change. It remains to estimate from the main translog. cost function the direct effect of output and technical progress on costs and this is achieved by treating as the dependent variable an element, G, which is $\log C$ net of the parameters and variables already estimated. As may be seen from Annex 2 the translog. function allows that the effect of output (in all its dimensions) on costs, might vary with the level of output and also with the vintage of plants. In fact, the latter effect was found to be insignificant, and given very high correlations between the independent variables this indirect effect of technical progress was eliminated. For similar reasons candlepower and all the dummy slope variables were eliminated. There were problems in capturing the role of consumer numbers and location. As well as the number of consumers, and population density, other variables like the mileage of distribution mains and the area of the territory, were tested. In the end it was found that the effects on costs of output in all its dimensions were best portrayed by the quantity of gas made and population density. The general form of the model is therefore:

$$G = A + a_y \log Y + \tfrac{1}{2}a_{yy}(\log Y)^2 + a_m \log M + \tfrac{1}{2}a_{mm}(\log M)^2$$
$$+ a_i \log I + a_d D \quad (14)$$

where the coefficients carry the same interpretation as they have in the full translog. function. The output coefficients reflect the elasticity of total cost and if the production function is homogeneous the elasticities are constants implying that the two squared terms in (14) can be eliminated. The F statistic for these two restrictions was 3.44 so there is a high probability that such a restriction would not be valid. The underlying production function is therefore homothetic but not homogeneous. The results for (14) were:

$$\begin{aligned} G = {} & 1.22 + 0.437 \log Y + (0.0406)\tfrac{1}{2}(\log Y)^2 + 0.146 \log M \\ & (0.77)\ (1.83)^* \qquad (2.33)^* \qquad\qquad (1.67)^* \\ & - (0.0803)\tfrac{1}{2}(\log M)^2 + 0.136 \log I + 0.0292D \qquad (15) \\ & (-2.23)^* \qquad\qquad (2.62)^* \qquad (0.74) \end{aligned}$$

$R^2 = 0.99$ * Significant at 0.05 level

In terms of the quantity of gas made there are initially sizeable scale economies with total costs rising at only $\frac{2}{5}$ the rate of output. However the elasticity with respect to gas made is $0.44 + 0.04 \log Y$ so that decreasing returns to scale set in at an annual gas production of 1.3 million cubic feet, which is above the sample mean of one million for the provincial gas undertakings. The proportional effect of population density on costs is $0.14–0.08 \log M$ so that increases in population density reduce costs once inhabitants per acre are 5.75 or more. Since the sample mean density was 23.34 and all but three companies had densities greater than 5.5 then effectively this variable is one which lowers the level of costs. At any given population density the average cost curve is U shaped with the base corresponding to a production value greater than the average for the provincial gas undertakings. The lower is population density the higher is the level of that cost curve. The expansion of an undertaking involving equal percentage increases in gas production and in the size of territory served, but with total consumer numbers fixed, would cause average costs to rise if $0.34 + 0.04 \log Y + 0.08 \log M$ exceeded unity. Even at the sample mean for the provincial undertakings this condition is met. The London companies were therefore clearly operating at a point where expansion of this kind would raise average costs.

Finally it would appear that ownership does not play much part, at least in comparing situations where population density and the total quantity produced is the same. Excluding the plant vintage variable I from (14) put the coefficient on the dummy term at $(-)0.01$ implying that costs were some 1% lower in municipal enterprises and that part of the source of the municipals' superiority lies in having more modern capacity. But none of these results was statistically significant. The municipal firms do not have higher costs than private firms but neither do they have statistically significantly lower costs.

Conclusions

The evidence from the cost function estimates suggests that the demand for each factor of production is inversely related to its price though the effects are not statistically significant. The technology of gas production at the end of the 19th century was such that labour costs were less than 15% of total costs. Coal was a very important item and the elasticity of total cost with respect to coal prices was upwards of 0.3. The evidence also suggests an element of substitutability between all factors of production. Economies of scale exist and are initially sizeable; but beyond the sample mean size of the provincial undertakings, unit costs tend to rise. The U shaped cost curve is however lower the greater the population density.

Although the share of capital in total costs was, on average, less in municipally owned enterprises, when account is taken of the level of factor prices, including interest rates, the share is at a statistically significant higher level. Costs per cubic foot of gas were some 15% lower in municipal enterprises but after standardising for factor prices, and population density, as well as quantity of gas, the municipal enterprises had total costs only 1% lower than private companies. An important element of this appears to be the use of plants of more modern vintage; such plants have a significant impact in lowering total costs and the bias is towards capital saving. The difference in costs between municipal and private is however small and was not in fact statistically significant. The evidence for this industry in this period is therefore that public firms were just as cost effective as private companies.

University of Salford, U.K.

ANNEX 1

Gas works data sources

1. The main source was the weekly "Gas World" (GW). For the broad period under consideration it was found that the best data coverage for both public and private undertakings was the year 1898. The accounts for the private companies were generally for the year ended June 1898 and for municipal enterprises it was March. Further data on the sample were obtained from the return published by the Board of Trade (BoT 1899).
2. Data definitions were as follows:
   a) Measures of Output
   Gas made: thousand cubic feet of gas made (i.e. gas sold, gas used on works and gas unaccounted for) (GW).
   Candle power: illuminating power of gas produced, as confirmed by Board of Trade inspectors (GW and BoT).
   Number of consumers: total number of private customers (GW and BoT).
   Mains mileage: total recorded mains mileage (GW and BoT).
   Population density: inhabitants per acre (1901 Census of Population: England and Wales Summary Table II and Census of Scotland Table 1).
   b) Factor Shares and Total Cost.
   C: total cost measured as the gross cost of gas manufacture plus 10%, or alternative percentages, of the capital value of the works (GW).
   S_w: the total of all payments to labour (wages, salaries and directors' fees) for manufacture, distribution, payment collection and management, as a proportion of total cost (GW).
   S_k: 10%, or alternative percentages, of the capital value of the works as a proportion of total cost (GW).
   S_t: the total of all remaining cost headings as a proportion of total cost (GW).

c) Factor Prices

P_w: price of labour. See para. 3 below.

P_k: price of capital. The Board of Trade returns give details of all issued loan stock and the rates of interest payable on each. Weighted averages of these rates were taken, the amounts of each issue being used as the weights (BoT).

P_t: price of other inputs. As the principal other input was coal, the total amount spent on coal was divided by the tonnage of coal carbonised to arrive at an average cost per ton of coal used (GW).

d) Index of Technology (I): In the absence of any other measure, an attempt was made to estimate the average age of plant by using the issue date of loan stock. A weighted average date was constructed which was then subtracted from 1898 to give an average estimated age of capital.

3. A major data problem was wage rates since though Gas World included figures on outlays on wages and salaries it did not include employment data. In 1892 BoT published "Return of Rates of Wages paid by Local Authorities and Private Companies to police and workpeople employed on roads, etc. and at gas and water works". The regions identified were too large to be useful for a study of town gas undertakings. In 1893 the BoT started publishing its annual "Report on Standard Time Rates of Wages". This included data on fitters' and turners' wages at a local level which was closely correlated with the gas wages figures. Comparing 1885 gas wage data and 1886 engineering wage data over regions the following results emerged:

	R	Rank R	t
Gas workers to Fitters	0.800	0.467	1.49
Gas workers to Turners	0.877	0.697	2.75

Critical R (difference from zero, at 0.01 significance level, $8df$) = 0.765
Critical t (0.05 significance level, $8df$) = 2.31

There does therefore appear to be a statistically significant correlation and rank correlation between the regional wage distribution of gas workers and engineering turners. The use of time rate of wages data for engineering turners in 1898 as a proxy for the unavailable data on the rate of wages of gas workers in 1898 seems justifiable.

4. The undertakings, the exact financial accounting year in question and the source of wages data were as follows:

Municipal	*Year ended*	*Wages Town*
Blackburn Corporation	25.3.98	Bolton
Bolton Corporation	31.3.98	Bolton
Bradford Corporation	31.3.98	Bradford
Carlisle Corporation	30.6.98	Preston
Darwen Corporation	31.3.98	Bolton
Dundee Gas Commissioners	30.4.98	Dundee
Dunfermline Corporation	15.5.98	Edinburgh
Edinburgh and Leith Corporation	15.5.98	Edinburgh
Glasgow Corporation	31.5.98	Glasgow
Lancaster Corporation	25.3.98	Preston
Manchester Corporation	31.3.98	Manchester
Nottingham Corporation	31.3.98	Nottingham
Oldham Corporation	25.3.98	Oldham
Salford Corporation	31.3.98	Manchester
Stafford Corporation	31.3.98	Derby
Stoke-on-Trent Corporation	31.3.98	Derby
West Bromwich Corporation	31.3.98	Wolverhampton
Widnes Corporation	31.3.98	Liverpool
Wigan Corporation	31.3.98	Wigan

Private	*Year ended*	*Wages Town*
Alliance & Dublin Consumers Gas Co.	30.6.98	Dublin
Barnet District Gas and Water Co.	30.6.98	London
Brighton and Hove General Gas Co.	30.6.98	Brighton
Brentford Gas Co.	30.6.98	London
Bristol Gas Co.	30.6.98	Bristol
Bromley Gas Consumers' Co.	30.6.98	London
Commercial Gas Co.	30.6.98	London
Croydon Commercial Gas and Coke Co.	30.6.98	London
Crystal Palace District Gas Co.	30.6.98	London
Gas Light and Coke Co.	30.6.98	London
Harrow and Stanmore Gas Co.	30.6.98	London
Hastings and St. Leonards Gas VCo.	30.6.98	Brighton
Newcastle-upon-Tyne & Gateshead Gas Co.	31.12.97	Newcastle
Sheffield United Gas Light Co.	30.6.98	Sheffield
South Metropolitan Gas Co.	30.6.98	London
Tottenham & Edmonton Gas Light Coke Co.	30.6.98	London

ANNEX 2

The full model

1. The full unrestricted translog. cost function is:

$$\begin{aligned}\log C = {} & A + a_y \log Y + a_{cp} \log CP + a_n \log N + a_m \log M + a_i \log I + a_d D \\ & + a_w \log P_w + a_t \log P_t + a_k \log P_k + \log I[\tfrac{1}{2}a_{ii} \log I + a_{id} D] \\ & + \log Y[\tfrac{1}{2}a_{yy} \log Y + a_{yw} \log P_w + a_{yt} \log P_t + a_{yk} \log P_k + a_{yi} \log I + a_{yd} D] \\ & + \log CP[\tfrac{1}{2}a_{cpp} \log CP + a_{cpw} \log P_w + a_{cpt} \log P_t + a_{cpk} \log P_k + a_{cpi} \log I + a_{cpd} D] \\ & + \log N[\tfrac{1}{2}a_{nn} \log N + a_{nw} \log P_w + a_{nt} \log P_t + a_{nk} \log P_k + a_{ni} \log I + a_{nd} D] \\ & + \log M[\tfrac{1}{2}a_{mm} \log M + a_{mw} \log P_w + a_{mt} \log P_t + a_{mk} \log P_k + a_{mt} \log I + a_{md} D] \\ & + \log P_w[\tfrac{1}{2}a_{ww} \log P_w + a_{wt} \log P_t + a_{wk} \log P_k + a_{wi} \log I + a_{wd} D] \\ & + \log P_t[\tfrac{1}{2}a_{tt} \log P_t + a_{tk} \log P_k + a_{ti} \log I + a_{td} D] \\ & + \log P_k[\tfrac{1}{2}a_{kk} \log P_k + a_{ki} \log I + a_{kd} D] \qquad \text{(A1)}\end{aligned}$$

Differentiating this with respect to $\log P_w$ yields the labour share equation (2) in the text. Similarly $\partial \log C/\partial \log P_t$ yields the coal share equation (5) in the text whilst equation (7) involves the same procedure with the price of capital.

2. The unconstrained estimates of the share equations are not reported here. Across the three equations it was found that the three coefficients corresponding to any given independent variable added up to zero whilst $a_w + a_t + a_k = 1$. This is to be expected since the three shares must add up to unity irrespective of whether some or none of the independent variables are statistically significant. Factor price homogeneity implies in addition that in any given share equation the coefficients associated with the three price variables should also sum to zero and the F statistic quoted in the text showed that it is a valid restriction on the labour and coal equations. Analogously symmetry requires that coefficients like a_{wt} as estimated in the labour share equation should be the same when estimated in the coal equation. Again this is shown in the text to be a valid restriction as is production homotheticity. Proceeding in this way yields the results reported in equations (3) and (6). Symmetry and factor price homogeneity imply all the coefficients in the capital share equation can now be deduced from the coefficients already estimated.

3. The full results for the elasticities were as follows:

	Labour	*Coal*	*Capital*
ε_{wi}	(−)0.52	0.06*	0.41
δ_{wi}	—	0.12*	1.31
ε_{ti}	0.02*	(−)0.36	0.32
δ_{ti}	0.12*	—	1.06
ε_{ki}	0.18	0.58	(−)0.77
δ_{ki}	1.31	1.06	—

* Significant at 0.05 level

4. The results so calculated may be sensitive to which equation is taken as the residual third. Ideally the three share equations should be estimated simultaneously, with the various constraints imposed, so that the estimation of the set of coefficients would take into account the error sum of squares of all three equations. This has been done with the use of a computer programme involving Gauss-Newton simultaneous non-linear constrained step-wise iterative least squares. The results were as follows:

		Simultaneous	*Original*
$aw =$		0.077 (0.34)	0.094 (0.86)
$at =$		0.723 (4.51)	0.753 (5.55)
$ak =$		0.200 (1.08)	0.153
$aww =$		0.059 (0.81)	0.0481 (1.35)
$att =$		0.043 (1.05)	0.0508 (0.99)
$akk =$		−0.004 (0.062)	−0.0243
$awt =$		−0.053 (1.35)	−0.0616 (3.11)
$awk =$		−0.006 (0.10)	0.0135
$atk =$		0.010 (0.273)	0.0108
$awi =$		−0.0504 (1.91)	−0.0525 (4.16)
$ati =$		0.00965 (0.36)	0.104 (0.29)
$aki =$		0.0408 (1.53)	0.0419
$awd =$		−0.0284 (1.36)	−0.0289 (2.92)
$atd =$		0.004 (0.02)	−0.0053 (0.02)
$akd =$		0.0244 (1.20)	0.0342
$\bar{R}^2$:	S_w	0.313	0.3234
	S_t	−0.034	−0.192
	S_k	0.212	

As this method is iterative and requires an initial set of parameter estimates, it is possible that any set of final estimates could in fact represent only a locally optimal solution. To test for this, various different sets of initial values were tried. These included a "neutral" set of initial parameter values (0.33 for the intercepts and zeros for all the slopes) and also the set of values reported in the paper. All these runs yielded the same results. These new results are sufficiently close to the originals for the initial conclusions, in particular the acceptance of the constraints of factor price homogeneity and production homotheticity, still to be accepted. The main differences come in the significance of the coefficients estimated initially in the labour share equation (especially *awt, awi* and *awd*).

5. The share equations are the basis for estimating all coefficients involving factor prices. These can therefore be removed to the left hand side of the above translog. function to define a new variable.

$$G = \log C - \log P_w(S_w - \tfrac{1}{2}a_{ww} \log P_w) - \log P_t(S_t - \tfrac{1}{2}a_{tt} \log P_t) - \log P_k(S_k - \tfrac{1}{2}a_{kk} \log P_k) \quad \text{(A2)}$$

where a_{ww}, a_{tt}, a_{kk} are the estimated coefficients from the share equations. The variable G now becomes the dependent variable in the regression as follows:

$$G = A + \log Y(a_y + \tfrac{1}{2}a_{yy} \log Y + a_{yi} \log I) + \log CP(a_{cp} + \tfrac{1}{2}a_{cpp} \log CP + a_{cpi} \log I)$$
$$+ \log N(a_n + \tfrac{1}{2}a_{nn} \log N + a_{ni} \log I) + \log M(a_m + \tfrac{1}{2}a_{mm} \log M + a_{mi} \log I)$$
$$+ \log I(a_i + a_{ii}\tfrac{1}{2} \log I) + D(a_d + a_{yd} \log Y + a_{cpd} \log CP + a_{nd} \log N$$
$$+ a_{md} \log M + a_{id} \log I) \quad \text{(A3)}$$

The terms involving candlepower were found to be insignificant as were the squared terms involving $\log I$ and the dummy slope variables. Given high multicollinearity on the first run these terms were omitted. Testing for production homogeneity involves testing whether the omission of the squared terms involving Y, M and N is a valid restriction. As reported in the text, this hypothesis could not be accepted so that the relevant estimating equation is no. 15 in the text. The coefficients in this equation have also been re-estimated by the use of a G variable calculated with the use of the new a_{ww}, a_{tt}, a_{kk} estimates from the simultaneous method. The results were very similar, as follows:

	Re-estimates		*Original*
A	1.29 (0.67)	1.82 (0.89)	1.22 (0.77)
ay	0.47 (1.62)	0.46 (1.47)	0.44 (1.83)
ayy	0.04 (1.76)	0.04 (1.71)	0.04 (2.33)
am	0.10 (0.99)	0.10 (0.90)	0.15 (1.67)
amm	−0.06 (1.45)	−0.06 (1.37)	−0.08 (2.23)
ai	0.14 (2.30)	—	0.14 (2.62)
ad	0.08 (1.67)	0.04 (0.79)	0.03 (0.74)
R-bar^2	0.993	0.992	0.995

The coefficient on the dummy in the middle column is therefore still small and statistically insignificant. The broad conclusion remains therefore that the costs of public and private firms were similar. The plant vintage variable again indicates that the equipment of private firms was not as modern as that of the public firms and, if it had been, their costs would have been lower. On this new estimate they would have been lower by an amount which is still small, though now statistically more significant.

REFERENCES

ALCHIAN, A. A. (1965), "Some Economics of Property Rights", *Il Politico,* reproduced in A. A. Alchian, *Economic Forces at Work,* Liberty Press 1977.

ASHLEY, P. C. (1901), "Municipal Trading in Great Britain", *Quarterly Journal of Economics,* vol. XV, pp. 458–464.

AVEBURY, Lord (1900), "Municipal Trading", *Contemporary Review,* vol. 78, July, pp. 28–37.

Balfour Committee on Industry and Trade (1928), *Further Factors in Industrial and Commercial Efficiency.*

CHATTERTON, D. A. (1972), "State Control of Public Utilities in Nineteenth Century: The London Gas Industry", *Business History,* vol. 14, pt. 2, pp. 166–178.

CHRISTENSEN, L. R. and GREENE, W. H. (1976), "Economies of scale in US Electricity Power Generation", *Journal of Political Economy,* 84, pp. 655–76.

DONALD, R. (1903), "Success of Municipal Ownership in Great Britain", *Street Railway Journal,* vol. 21, pp. 30–34, 72–76.

FALKUS, M. E. (1967), "The British Gas Industry before 1850", *Economic History Review,* December, pp. 494–508.

FALKUS, M. E. (1977), "The Development of Municipal Trading in the 19th Century", *Business History,* vol. XIX, no. 2, pp. 134–161.

FALKUS, M. E. (1982), "The Early Development of the British Gas Industry 1790–1815", *Economic History Review,* 35, pp. 217–234.

FINER, H. (1941), *Municipal Trading,* Allen and Unwin.

FOREMAN-PECK, J. and WATERSON, M. (1985), "The Comparative Efficiency of Public and Private Enterprise in Britain: Electricity Generation between the World Wars", Supplement to VM.95, *Economic Journal.*

JOHNES and CLEGG (1847), "Observations or general Report on the Existing System of Lighting Towns with Gas, by Messrs. Johnes and Clegg, Surveying Officers", *Parliamentary Papers,* XXII.

HOWE, F. C. (1906), "Municipal Ownership in Great Britain", *Bulletin of the Bureau of Labour,* no. 62, pp. 1–123.

LIVESEY, G. (1894), "The Inception and Development of Gas Lighting", *Journal of Gas Lighting and Water Supply,* Oct. 2.

MALTBIE, M. R. (1900), "Gas Lighting in Great Britain", *Municipal Affairs,* vol. IV, pp. 538–73.

MATTHEWS, D. (1986), "Laissez-faire and the London Gas Industry in the Nineteenth Century: Another Look", *Economic History Review,* vol. XXXIX, no. 2, May pp. 244–263.

MILLWARD, R. (1982), "The Comparative Performance of Public and Private Ownership", ch. 4 in Lord Roll of Ipsden (ed.) *The Mixed Economy,* Macmillan.

MILLWARD, R. *et al.* (1983), *Public Sector Economics,* Longmans.

MILLWARD, R. (1986), "The Emergence of Gas and Water Monopolies in 19th Century Britain: Why Public Ownership?", *Salford Papers in Economics,* 86–4.

National Civic Federation (1907), *Municipal and Private Ownership of Public Utilities,* USA.

PESCATRICE, D. R. and TRAPANI, J. M. III (1980), "The Performance and Objectives of Public Utilities Operating in the United States", *Journal of Public Economics,* 13, pp. 259–76.

PORTER, R. P. (1902), "The Failure of Municipal Ownership in England", *Street Railway Journal,* Aug. & Sept., pp. 109–114 & 216–70.

ROBSON, W. A. (1935), "The Public Utility Services", in H. J. Laski, W. I. Jennings and W. A. Robson (eds.) *A Century of Municipal Progress: The Last Hundred Years,* Allen and Unwin.

WALLER, P. J. (1983), *Town, City and Nation: England 1850–1914,* OUP.

WILLIAMS, T. I. (1981), *A History of the British Gas Industry,* OUP.

Oxford Economic Papers 39 (1987), 738–759

TECHNOLOGY, PRODUCTIVITY, AND PROFITS: BRITISH–AMERICAN WHALING COMPETITION IN THE NORTH ATLANTIC, 1816–1842*

By L. E. DAVIS, R. E. GALLMAN, *and* T. D. HUTCHINS

Introduction

WHALING brings to mind Captain Ahab struggling with Moby-Dick or a rapacious captain of a gargantuan mothership prepared to drive the world's largest mammal to extinction for nothing more than a few cent's profit or to meet the plan's target. There is however, another—less colourful and emotional—side to the industry. The history of whaling provides an opportunity to observe the effects of technical change and government policy on the shifting fortunes of the world's maritime nations and on the process of economic change itself.

One or two nations have typically had a near monopoly of whaling, but with the passage of time there has been a continual turnover among the industry's leaders. In the seventeenth century the Dutch displaced the British; in the eighteenth century the British displaced the Dutch; in the nineteenth century American whalers drove the British from the seas, only to find themselves pushed out by the Norwegians; and in the present century the Norwegians, in turn, found their dominance undercut by the Japanese and Russians.

Competitive turbulence is a characteristic of the industry that makes it ideal for the study of international differences in productivity, but it is not the only such characteristic. Other industries, such as agriculture and mining, draw on a stock of national resources, and it is almost impossible to disentangle the effects of differences in natural endowment from differences in productivity. In whaling the natural resource (the stock of whales) is owned by no one, and all nations are normally free to exploit it.

If the economic world operated as a simple general equilibrium model, without political intervention, the whaling industry of the early nineteenth century might have become truly international, gathering inputs from the most favorable markets and applying techniques generally known to exploit a natural resource hunted through international waters. To ask whether the fleet of one nation was more or less productive or profitable than the fleet of

* Evidence from the Joseph Dias manuscript is published with the permission of the Baker Library of the Harvard University Graduate School of Business. The research has been supported in part by NSF grants BNSD-8011494, SES-8121026, and by the National Bureau of Economic Research projects (1) Productivity and Industrial Changes in the World Economy and (2) the Development of the American Economy; and by the Center for Advanced Study in the Behavioral Sciences. Davis and Gallman are Associates of the NBER and Davis was a Fellow at CASBS when the paper was written.

another would be meaningless, because it would be impossible to distinguish them. If an artificial discrimination were made—on the basis of ownership, for example—there would be no observable systematic differences in productivity or profitability.

The history of nineteenth-century whaling, however, exhibits both international and purely national elements. The resources did, in fact, travel international waters and were thus open to the whalers of all nations. Sailors and whaling experts were drawn from a variety of labour markets. The composition of the crew of the *Pequod* no doubt reflects literary imperatives, but Herman Melville did not distort the whaling world when he set it down. Melville had sailed in American and Australian whalers in the 1840s and knew that whaling crews were recruited from many nations and races. Moreover, for at least the past hundred years the same store of technical knowledge had been generally available to entrepreneurs of all nations. The *Truelove,* for example, one of the most successful British whalers, was built in America in 1764. Captured by the British during the Revolution, it was sold to private owners in 1780. Between then and 1868 it completed seventy-two whaling voyages.[1]

In spite of these elements of internationalism, the British and American nineteenth-century fleets differed in several important respects that had significant consequences for both productivity and profits. While crews of American vessels were sought in all markets, officers were usually nationals. In Britain, where the government viewed the fishery as a training ground for the navy, both officers and crew members were usually British. In both countries the agents and owners—the men who selected the vessel types, fitted out the fleet with rigging and implements, and set the destinations and durations of their voyages—were residents, if not always citizens. As a result, neither capital nor labour was completely mobile, and agents in the two countries faced different relative prices. At the same time, there were international differences in vessel design and the skill composition of crews. Thus, international differences in productivity could and did appear, and these differences are worthy of careful analysis. Pure productivity effects—including effects embodied in the capital stock, the human resources employed, and the institutional structure that regulated and constrained economic activity—seem easier to sort out in whaling than in most other industries.

This study focuses on the competition between the British Northern fleet and the American Atlantic fleet in the period 1816 through 1842. The prize sought by both fleets was the baleen whale, which yielded both whale oil and whalebone (also called "baleen," a strong, flexible material put to uses

[1] J. T. Jenkins, *A History of the Whale Fisheries from the Basque Fisheries of the Tenth Century to the Hunting of the Finner Whale at the Present Date* (London: H. F. and G. Witherby, 1921), pp. 205–206. William Scoresby, *An Account of the Arctic Regions with a History and Description of the Northern Whale-Fishery,* Volume 2: *The Whale Fishery* (Archibald Constable, 1820, reprinted 1969 by David and Charles), p. 100.

now met by plastics or speciality steels), although the American fleet reported the capture of sperm whales as well. The territory hunted by the British consisted of Hudson's Bay, Davis Strait, Baffin Bay, Greenland, and the North Atlantic; the American fleet exploited all of those grounds, but its vessels also sailed into the South Atlantic.[2] At the outset the British fleet dominated world whaling. In 1816 British owners sent 150 vessels to the northern fishery; in contrast their American counterparts sent two. Twenty-seven years later, the entire British fleet (both its northern and southern components) had shrunk to fewer than thirty vessels, while the Americans could count almost 700 ships, barks, brigs, sloops, and schooners searching for whales over six of the seven seas; of that total, more than a quarter operated in the Atlantic, Hudson's Bay, and Davis Strait.

To understand the dynamics of the competition it is necessary to analyze the activities of the two fleets in the area of sharpest competition—the North Atlantic. Data on the British fleet hunting in the northern fishery have been taken from Parliamentary Papers, and from Jenkins, Jackson, and McCulloch.[3] The American data refer only to vessels from New Bedford (a leading whaling port) hunting in the Atlantic and its northern reaches. They were drawn from Dias's comprehensive compilation of whaling voyages augmented by a variety of other sources.[4] In order to calculate the relative productivities and profitabilities, both data sets were extended by estimation. Some of the problems of estimation are discussed in the text and notes, but others have had to be left untreated here. The final results are clearly subject to error, but the major conclusions appear secure.

Historical background

British whaling dates from 1607 when Henry Hudson, while searching for a northern trade route to Russia, stumbled on the rich grounds off

[2] We would have preferred to study fleets hunting over identical grounds. While both fleets could have operated in the north and the south Atlantic, the British agents did not choose to send their vessels south when winter drove them from their northern grounds (see below). The sperm whales appearing in the American records were probably taken chiefly in the South Atlantic.

[3] J. T. Jenkins, op. cit.,; Gordon Jackson, *The British Whaling Trade* (London: Adam and Charles Black, 1978); and J. R. McCulloch, *A Dictionary of Commerce and Commercial Navigation* (London: Longman, Brown, Green, and Longman, 1842).

[4] Joseph Dias, *MSS, The New Bedford Whaling Fleet, 1790–1906,* on deposit at Baker Library, Harvard Business School. The only mention of this manuscript that we have seen in print is: Anonymous, "The New Bedford Whaling Fleet, 1790–1906," Bulletin of the Business History Society 6 (December 1931), pp. 9–14. For further information on the Dias data see L. E. Davis, R. E. Gallman, and T. D. Hutchins, "The Structure of the Capital Stock in Economic Growth and Decline: The New Bedford Whaling Fleet in the Nineteenth Century," in Peter Kilby (ed.), *Quantity and Quiddity*: *Essays in U.S. Economic History in Honor of Stanley Lebergott* (Middletown, Connecticut; Wesleyan University Press, 1987). See, also, the same authors, "Productivity in American Whaling: The New Bedford Fleet in the Nineteenth Century," manuscript.

Spitzbergen.[5] His reports touched off a multi-national wave of entry as whalers from most of the maritime nations of Europe rushed to compete with the English-based Muscovy Company.[6] Competition proved costly, and in 1619 the principal whaling nations agreed to divide the ground amongst themselves. The British and Dutch were the chief beneficiaries of the division, but the Dutch made more of their advantage and succeeded in dominating the industry for the next 130 years.[7] Dutch dominance depended on their 1619 locational allocation, on their lower cost structure, and on their greater willingness to search aggressively for new hunting grounds.[8]

In the middle of the eighteenth century, however, the British industry's prospects brightened. On the one hand, domestic demand for whale oil rose as textile manufacturers began to use more of it and as increasing urbanization led to a greater demand for lighting in the cities. On the other hand, the government, concerned with the training of seamen, moved to encourage the trade. For the previous twenty-five years His Majesty's Government had paid a bounty of twenty shillings a measured ton for each voyage to the northern fishery. In 1750 the bounty was doubled. For a series of reasons, some political and some economic—troubles between England and the continental countries and changes in the profitability of competing maritime pursuits—the Dutch industry began to contract; and the English benefitted from higher prices and larger catches. During the American Revolution, the Royal Navy drove colonial whalers from the seas; and at the war's end, a prohibitive protective tariff proved as effective as the navy at keeping colonial imports out of the British market. Although the numbers fluctuated, on average more than 125 British vessels returned from the northern ground each year between 1785 and 1818.[9]

A part of the British industry until 1776, nonexistent between then and 1783, and pushed off the seas again during the War of 1812, the American fleet provided no competitive threat during the period of British growth and prosperity. After the Treaty of Ghent, however, the American industry entered into a period of such rapid and sustained expansion that the four decades between 1820 and 1860 have become known as the "Golden Age" of American whaling. It was in the first two of those four decades that Anglo-American competition was at its height. By the third there were few British whalers left to compete. (See Table II, Panel B.)

Styles of whaling

A contemporary observer, Charles Enderby of Britain's greatest family of whaling merchants, attributed the British loss in the competition with the

[5] W. Martin Conway (ed), *The Early Dutch and English Voyages to Spitzbergen in the Seventeenth Century,* reproduced by Commission of the Hakluyt Society from the Edition Originally Published by the Society in 1904 (Lichtenstein: Kraus Reprint Ltd., 1967), p. 1.
[6] *Ibid.,* p. 5.
[7] Scoresby, *The Whale Fishery,* p. 56.
[8] Jackson, *British Whaling,* p. 26.
[9] Jackson, *British Whaling,* p. 82, 119.

Americans to three factors: failure of vessel design, failure of seamen, and the high cost of vessels.[10] To these should be added a fourth: changes in government policy. For almost a century British whaling was the recipient of a stream of direct and indirect government subsidies.[11] A subsidy of twenty shillings a vessel ton (it had been forty until 1813) inflated the returns from a typical voyage by $1302, while very high tariffs protected British whalers from foreign competition.[12] In 1843, for example, when the price of whale oil in the United States stood at $0.41 a gallon, the British *tariff* was $0.72 a gallon.[13] It is the purpose of this study to compare trends in British and American productivity and to attempt to assess the relative importance of each of these four factors (vessel design and cost, the quality of seamen, and government policy) in the demise of the British whaling enterprise.

Despite the fact that shipowners on both sides of the Atlantic had access to the same technology, there were important differences between the technical configurations of the British and American fleets. The British used larger vessels and adopted a configuration that displayed a much higher labour-capital ratio than did the Americans. In terms of institutional technology, British owners recalled their vessels after each hunting season. Most American vessels, on the other hand, remained at sea for two seasons; and their owners adopted a very different method for paying their seamen.

At the end of the War of 1812, a typical British vessel was about 325 tons; its American counterpart, at 265 tons, was only four-fifths as large. Over time, however, the size of an average vessel fell in the U.K. but rose in New England, and by the early 1840s the difference between the two was a mere three percent. The British average was just over 300 tons, the American ten less. The changes in U.K. vessel size can probably be explained in part by the nature of the bounty payment. As long as the government tied the payment to size of a vessel, there was an economic incentive to use larger ships. When the bounty was cut off that incentive disappeared.

British vessels proved much more costly to build, and the margin widened with the passage of time: costs in America edged downward and those in Britain rose. Although the data are not as good as one might like, it appears that, on average, a British vessel cost between 1.3 and 2.3 as much per ton as a vessel built in the United States. Higher construction costs were, however, partly offset by lower interest charges. For the entire period 1816–1842 the long-term government interest rate averaged 3.8 percent in Britain and 7.7 percent in the U.S.

[10] William Armstrong Fairburn, *Merchant Sail* (Fairburn Marine Educational Foundation Center: Lovell, Maine, 1945–55), Vol. II, pp. 1007–1008.

[11] The maritime historian William Fairburn has argued that "the whaling industry was not a success in Britain except during the years that the government supported it with bounties and warships." *op. cit.*, p. 1007.

[12] For simplicity all cost and revenue figures are denominated in United States dollars of 1880.

[13] The tariff figure is from Gordon Jackson, *The British Whaling Trade* (London: Adam and Charles Black, 1978), p. 127.

The typical British northern whaler was rigged as a ship, carried six small boats, and employed close to fifty men (the average was forty-six in 1816–25 and forty-eight in 1836-42). The American fleet was much more diverse: in addition to ships, it included barks, brigs, sloops, and schooners. A vessel usually carried only four small boats, and the crew most often totaled fewer than twenty-five. In the first decade three-quarters of the vessels were ships; and one in ten was a bark. By the end of the period, however, the proportion of ships had fallen to just over one in two and barks had come to represent a quarter of the total. Over the same period, average crew size had risen from fewer then twenty to almost twenty-five.

Differences in vessels and crew sizes meant very different labour-capital ratios in the two fleets. On average an American vessel used 0.08 men per ton and a British vessel 0.14 during the period of active hunting. It appears that the two fleets were moving toward a single optimal vessel size, but there is little evidence of movement toward a single labour-capital ratio. The British used 1.9 times as much labour per ton in the first decade, 1816–25, and the figure for 1836–42 was still 1.7. The British taste for larger crews may have been a holdover from an earlier period when the government required the owner to carry two *extra* apprentices for each one hundred tons to qualify for the tonnage bounty.[14]

Weather in the North Atlantic and Davis Strait is foul. Between storms and the icepack it was impossible to hunt for more than a few months in late spring and summer. British owners sent their vessels north each hunting season, and the whalers returned to port when the season was over. Except in emergencies, no major repairs were done at sea. British vessels returned to their home ports after each hunting season for refitting and repairs, and when they returned the blubber was unloaded and transported to a shore-based refinery. For the Americans, however, the journey south did not always mean a journey home. Instead of steering for New Bedford or Nantucket, the vessels often headed for the Central or South Atlantic and continued the search for whales. American owners often kept their vessels at sea for two (and sometimes more) seasons. Repairs, including many major repairs, were carried out while the vessels were at sea or weathering in some inlet far from home. Unlike their British counterparts, American crews included a number of skilled artisans (carpenters, blacksmiths, sailmakers, etc.). Moreover, the Americans tried-out (the whalemen's term for rendering) the blubber by boiling it over a fire build in the brick tryworks that was constructed on the deck of almost every vessel. Both repairs and trying-out were done while the search for whales continued.

The average voyage length for the U.K. fleet was 5.5 months, and there is little evidence of any trend. For American vessels, however, the average was 14.5 months, and the figure rose from just over 12 months during the first two decades to 20.6 in the last seven years. Although it might appear

[14] Jackson, *British Whaling*, p. 72.

that the British and American industries drew from different pools of institutional technologies, such was not the case. Both technologies (one season and then home for repairs and refining; multi seasons with some repairs and refining effected aboard) were known and available in both countries. Like the choice of different production technologies in high-wage low-interest and low-wage high-interest countries, the decisions about the appropriate institutions were made by businessmen on the spot. Theory would suggest that their choices were dictated by relative prices; however, it is also possible that those choices may have been influenced by the British method of bounty payment. A British ship owner was paid for each voyage to the north; and, although the evidence is unclear, it may have been that the government counted each voyage as one trip. Such a policy would certainly induce captains to return to Britain at the end of each season.

It may be true that the relative voyage lengths explain the differences in the structure of labour payments. Whether that theory is correct or not, the institutions that evolved in the two countries were very different.[15] In the United States, in addition to subsistence, each crew member was paid a specified fraction of the total revenues earned on the voyage. These payments averaged $20.54 per vessel ton per year (thirty-four percent of total revenues). In the U.K., payment was a mix of monthly wages, bonuses that were "catch" dependent, and, until 1824, some fraction of the government tonnage subsidy. Despite the higher labour-capital ratio that prevailed, annual payments to labour were lower because the larger British crew size was more than offset by the shorter voyage length. Thus labour costs in British vessels averaged $11.51 a ton per voyage of five and half months, a figure that represents only twenty-three percent of all revenues.

For twelve months's work both an American and a British seaman generated about $750 in revenues, but the cost of a British seaman was 1.2 times the cost of his American peer. That comparison may, however, underestimate the true relative cost of British seamen. An examination of American and British crew lists indicates that there was, on average, a much higher concentration of artisans on American vessels. Moreover, the British government continued to try to entice American seamen to relocate in the U.K., and despite a lay of forty-four percent, British owners in the southern fishery found themselves unable to attract skilled seaman. A quality-adjusted comparison may thus indicate that the true relative wage in Britain was even higher than the 1 to 1.2 ratio.

Productivity differentials

The measurement of total factor productivity has benefitted in recent years from important theoretical developments and empirical tests. Perhaps

[15] In the southern fishery where voyages were longer, the British used a system very similar to the American except that labour's share of the lay was forty-four percent in the British fleet, compared with about thirty-four percent in the American. See Jackson, *British Whaling Trade*, p. 100; and Davis, Gallman, and Hutchins, "Productivity . . . ," *op. cit*.

the most interesting and valuable development was the discovery that well known index numbers can be used to measure intertemporal and interspatial productivity differences accurately, without the need to fit econometric functions. The implicit aggregator involved is the translog, which Heien describes as "a reasonably good second order approximation to any arbitrary production function."[16] These indexes—called superlative indexes—handle multiproduct firms and industries of the type dealt with here. They are transitive (no base reversal problems), and they can be readily computed from input and output quantities and prices. In short they are nearly ideal for a study of international differences in productivity.

The index used in this paper—drawn from Caves, Christensen, and Diewert (1982b)—was devised precisely to permit international comparisons. It rests on two important assumptions: that perfect competition and constant returns to scale prevail in each of the industries to be compared. The first condition never holds, literally, but in the present instance it comes much closer than is usually the case. There is no evidence that any single owner ever controlled more than three or four vessels, and most owned only one. Moreover, there were some seven hundred American and two hundred British whalers that could have hunted the North Atlantic had they chosen, and these figures do not include the merchant marine—vessels that could easily have been converted to whaling. Over one-half of American whalers did, in fact, enter the whaling fleet from some other maritime activity.

As to the second assumption—constant returns to scale—exploration of the U.S. data set has shown that whaling productivity increased modestly, but significantly, with vessel size when all other relevant considerations (e.g., vessel type, hunting ground, time), are held constant.[17] This increase was probably not a true scale phenomenon, but rather a matter of differences in factor proportions.[18] Even should this conclusion prove incorrect, the breach of the constant returns condition is unlikely to prove important. Productivity rose only modestly with vessel size and not at all once a capacity of four hundred tons had been reached.

[16] Dale M. Heien, "Productivity in U.S. Food Processing and Distribution," *American Journal of Agricultural Economics,* 65 (1983), 297–302. See, also: D. W. Caves, L. R. Christensen, and W. E. Diewert, "Multilateral Comparisons of Output, Input, and Productivity Using Superlative Index Numbers," *Economic Journal,* 92 (1982), 73–86 (hereafter, 1982a); "The Economic Theory of Index Numbers and the Measurement of Input, Output and Productivity," *Econometrica,* 50 (1982), 1393–1414 (hereafter 1982b); W. E. Diewert, "Exact and Superlative Index Numbers," *Journal of Econometrics,* 4 (1974), 115–145; Mieko Nishimizu and Sherman Robinson, "Trade Policies and Productivity Change in Semi-Industrialized Countries," *Journal of Development Economics,* 16 (1984), 177–206; William A. Barnet, Edward K. Offenbacker, and Paul A. Spindt, "The New Divisia Monetary Aggregates," *Journal of Political Economy,* 92 (1984), 1049–1085; Michael Denny and Melvyn Fuss, "A General Approach to Intertemporal and Interspatial Productivity Comparisons," *Journal of Econometrics,* 23 (1983), 315–330.

[17] See Davis, Gallman, and Hutchins, "Productivity in American Whaling," *op. cit.*

[18] See Scoresby, *op. cit.*, pp. 506–507.

Denny and Fuss have tested a superlative index by comparing productivities estimated from the index with productivity estimates obtained by fitting appropriate functions econometrically.[19] In their first test, across regions of Canada, the two techniques yielded virtually identical results. Denny and Fuss concluded that the more involved, cumbersome, and difficult procedure—econometric fitting—yielded no better results than did the index number procedure. Their second test—a comparison of aggregate productivity in Japan and in the U.S. from 1952 to 1973—proved less supportive. The index number procedure overstated relative U.S. productivity in every year by from five to twenty percent. In two years the econometric procedures showed that Japan was more productive, but the index number estimates indicated the reverse.

The Japan–U.S. results, however, do not bring the use of the index number procedure into serious question. Denny and Fuss were comparing entire economies, economies with quite different structures and resource endowments. The present paper compares the same industry in two countries—an industry characterized by natural resources held in common and technical information that moved easily across national borders. The index number procedure is much better adapted to this problem than to either of the two treated by Denny and Fuss. In any case even in the comparison of Japan and the U.S., the index number procedure let Denny and Fuss identify the more productive economy in twenty out of twenty-two years. In the two years in which the procedure failed, the measured levels of productivity in the two countries—by both techniques—are so close that no reasonable analyst would regard the difference as meaningful. Thus, even in the Japan–U.S. case, the index number procedure yielded good nonparametric results.

The mathematical specification of the form of the index employed is:

$$\ln \lambda = \tfrac{1}{2} \sum_i (R_i^k + \bar{R}_1)(\ln Y_i^k - \overline{\ln Y_n}) - \tfrac{1}{2} \sum_n (W_n^k + \bar{W}_n)(\ln X_n^k - \overline{\ln X_n}),$$

where the R's are the shares of total revenue earned by the two individual outputs; the Y's are quantities of individual outputs; the W's are factor shares of income; the X's are quantities of factor inputs; the $\bar{R}$'s, $\bar{Y}$'s, $\bar{W}$'s and $\bar{X}$'s are average values across both sets of observations (i.e., Britain and U.S.).

We have distinguished two outputs (the Y's of the formula): whale oil, and baleen (whalebone). These are the only outputs reported by the British Northern fleet. The New Bedford whalers also reported some sperm oil. For present purposes, we have combined New Bedford whale and sperm oil quantities and values (the R's of the formula). On the input side we have included only vessels that returned to port. The issues involved in

[19] Michael Denny and Melvyn Fuss, "A General Approach to Intertemporal and Interspatial Productivity Comparisons," *Journal of Econometrics,* 23 (1983), 315–330.

incorporating lost vessels (and men) in the calculation are complex, and we chose to avoid them at this time. Since loss rates seem to have been virtually identical for both fleets, this decision is unlikely to bias the results.

Labour was measured in terms of man-months; capital, in terms of ton-months, the tons referring to measured vessel capacities. The British and American formulae for estimating vessel capacity were similar, but not identical. The British rule was: "length taken", minus 3/5 "breadth", the result multiplied by breadth, that result multiplied by one-half breadth (to represent depth), the whole expression divided by 94.[20] The American rule was the same, except that the divisor was 95.[21] Thus, if all measurements were made in the same way, the U.S. rule would result in measured tonnages just over one percent smaller than those produced by the British rule.

Measurements, however, were not made in the same way. For both countries breadth was to be measured at the widest place: "outside and outside, immediately above or below the main wale." According to the British rule, however, deductions were to be made for "doubling, sheathing, or any extraordinary thick stuff worked thereon"; the American rules make no mention of such deductions.[22] Since northern whalers were often doubled and sheathed, the American system probably produced wider breadths than did the British. Both countries called for measures of length from stem post to stern post, but in the American case, the measurement was to be made above the main deck, in the British case, along the keel, with an allowance made for the overhang of the prow, but not the stern. Once again the American dimension was probably very slightly larger than the British. In all likelihood, the differences between the measurements of breadths and lengths compensate for the difference between the denominators in the British and American formulae. Thus we assumed that the tonnage measures were identical. The British rule changed in 1836, but vessels built before that date were apparently allowed to retain their original measurements. We assumed that all British whalers were built before 1836 and kept their pre-1835 measurements.

Three separate sets of productivity indexes are contained in Table I, the three differing in their measurement of the two inputs: man-months and vessel ton-months. In Variant A, the months are months at sea. Clearly, these indexes understate the true volumes of inputs consumed by the whaling industry, since they do not take into account down time for refitting between voyages. In the case of the British fleet, since vessels were kept at home for extended periods between hunting seasons, down time was considerable.

Variant B was constructed on the assumption that only vessels figured in

[20] Scoresby, *op. cit.*, p. 512, has an abstract of the rules.
[21] Fifth Congress, 3rd Session, Chapter 22, 1799, Statues at Large, Vol. I., pp. 675–676. The rule refers to all double-decked vessels. Virtually all whaling vessels were double-decked.
[22] Scoresby, *op. cit.*, p. 512.

TABLE I

Indexes of relative total factor productivity in whaling, British Northern fleet, U.S. (New Bedford) Atlantic (incl. Hudson's Bay and Davis Strait) fleet, 1817–1842, *base** = 100.

	Variant A+		*Variant B*+		*Variant C*+	
	Brit.	*U.S.*	*Brit.*	*U.S.*	*Brit.*	*U.S.*
1817	79	127	67	149	55	182
1818	91	110	74	136	63	160
1819	86	117	71	140	60	167
1820	93	107	77	130	66	153
1821	88	114	74	135	63	159
1822	91	110	76	132	64	157
1823	219	46	177	56	153	65
1824	98	102	83	121	71	141
1825	62	162	54	187	46	215
1817–1825(1)	101	111	84	132	71	157
(2)	[95]	[106]	[79]	[127]	[67]	[149]
1826	118	85	101	99	90	111
1827	124	80	102	98	92	109
1828	153	65	127	79	113	89
1829	116	86	98	102	87	114
1830	49	204	43	233	36	274
1831	63	158	54	185	48	210
1832	145	69	120	83	107	94
1833	133	75	113	88	101	99
1834	123	82	104	96	91	109
1826–1834(1)	114	100	96	118	85	134
(2)	[108]	[93]	[91]	[110]	[80]	[124]
1835	71	141	62	161	52	193
1836	40	249	37	271	29	347
1837	53	187	47	213	37	267
1838	247	41	192	52	163	61
1839	78	128	66	152	52	194
1840	64	156	58	172	44	227
1841	143	70	120	83	97	103
1842	178	56	143	70	117	85
1835–1842(1)	109	129	91	147	74	185
(2)	[91]	[110]	[78]	[129]	[63]	[160]

* The base in each year is average total factor productivity in that year for the two fleets. + For the definitions of these variants, see text.

(1) Simple averages of the index number.

(2) Antilogs of the means of the natural logs of the annual indexes.

Sources: See text and appendix.

the activities of the fleet during these refitting and waiting periods; the men are assumed to have found alternative employment. Variant C, on the other hand, rests on the assumption that both men and vessels were held out of other gainful activity. If a part of the down time imputed to the British vessels had been spent in some alternative productive activity (the coasting trade, for example), Variant C would overstate British productive inferiority. The overstatement, if it exists, is unlikely to be large. The alternative occupations open to British vessels would have been second best activities (why else would anyone have risked life, limb, or vessel while whaling in the waters off Greenland and in the Davis Straight) in which productivity was less than that attained in whaling. Furthermore, no remotely plausible second activity could have made use of a crew of fifty. A substantial part of the whaler's crew would almost certainly have suffered unemployment, or been forced to take much less remunerative jobs ashore.

Finally the indexes incorporate three biases, and all three lead to understatements of American superiority. First, the British brought back unprocessed blubber. The Americans, on the other hand, tryed-out the blubber aboard ship and returned with oil. Thus a correct productivity comparison would require that some additional labour and capital be assigned to British production to adjust for the resources used in the first stage of the refining process. Second, the inclusion of skilled craftsmen in the American crews meant that a great deal of refitting and repair could be done at sea. Conversely, the British employed shore-based dockyard workers for those tasks. Neither Variant A nor B picks up any of those workers, and Variant C captures only a part of the shore based labour.[23] Third, the British brought back only whale oil while the Americans returned with a mix of whale and sperm oil. To the extent that, in the long run, prices reflect real costs, sperm whales must have been more costly to catch than baleens (between 1816 and 1845 sperm oil, on average, cost 2.3 times as much as whale oil). Thus the resources required to catch a sperm whale were almost certainly greater than those needed to capture a baleen; but, in the productivity calculations, sperm oil has been treated as if it were whale oil. Thus all three indexes are biased against the Americans.

Each pair of indexes expresses a comparison for a single year. The comparison was computed originally in natural logs, but antilogs have been taken to give the indexes clearer intuitive meaning. Each index number expresses American and British productivity relative to the average productivity of both fleets for the year in question. It should be understood that the indexes do not permit intertemporal comparisons of absolute levels.

The most striking feature of the table lies in the extreme variability of the index numbers. For example, regardless of the variant used, the U.S. fleet is shown to have been substantially more productive than the British fleet in

[23] The Variant C measures rests on the assumption that the crew stayed with the vessel while it was in port. The British crewmen were, however, seamen not artisans and could not have effected all the necessary repairs.

1822, and substantially less so in 1823. This variability reflects a very real and important characteristic of whaling. Productivity could and did vary widely from one year to the next, depending upon the fortunes of the hunt. The year 1823 was, in fact, a very bad year for the Americans, but not so for the British. The explanation for the variation in the relative measure of success probably rests on the fact that the two fleets did not hunt exactly the same grounds. Both ranged Davis Strait, Hudson's Bay, Baffin Bay, and the Greenland waters, but the British Northern fleet devoted all its efforts to these grounds, while the Americans also hunted other parts of the Atlantic during the off season. Thus, a bad year in the rest of the Atlantic would affect the Americans but not the British.

A similar consideration may explain the relative success of the British in the last two years of the period. By that time the British fleet had shrunk to a shadow of its former self. With many fewer vessels hunting, greater success may have been achieved by each. It is also likely, however, that given the maleability of the capital stock, the strong end-of-period performance reflects, at least in part, the Darwinian characteristics of the last survivors of the competitive struggle.

Because of the year to year variability in the index number, it is necessary to look at the broad patterns and the averages, rather than at individual observations, if the relative degree of success of the two fleets is to be understood. No matter which index is used, those broad measures under-

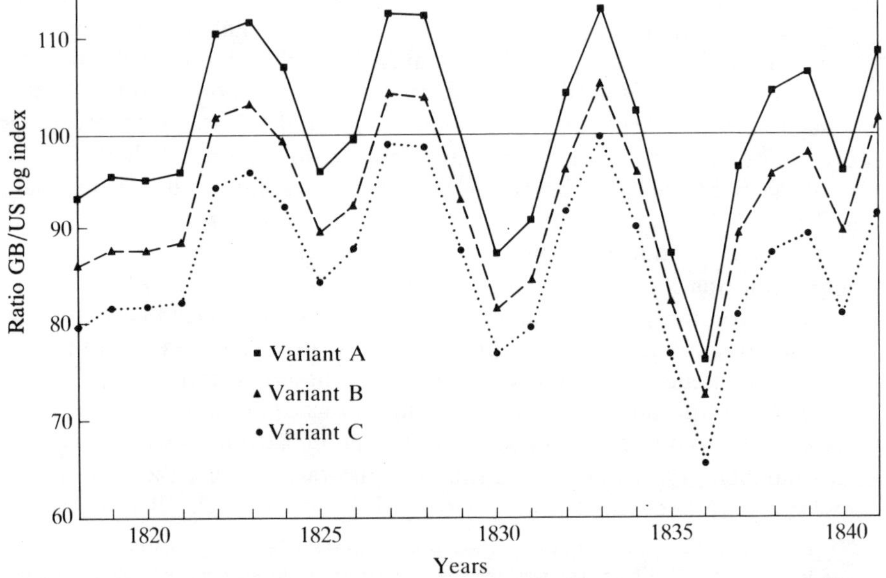

FIG. 1. Three year moving average, log form

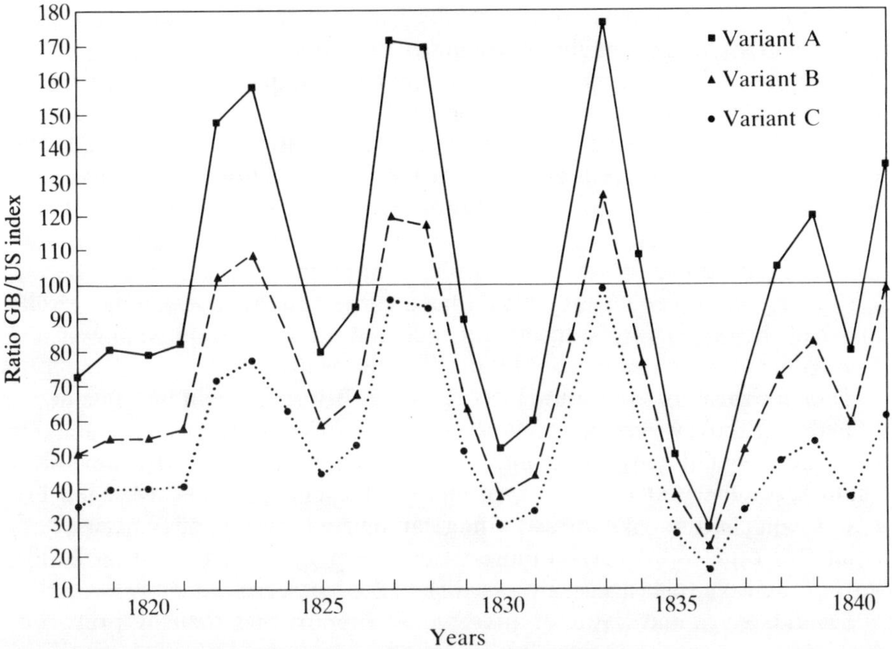

FIG. 2. Three year moving average, anti-log form

score the superior productivity of the Americans. Even the Variant A indexes—indexes that are heavily biased against American productivity—show that in fifteen out of twenty-six years, and two out of three major sub-periods, American productivity exceeded British. In the case of the Variant C indexes, American superiority is exhibited in twenty out of twenty-six years, and all three sub-periods. Moreover, in two additional years (1832 and 1833), British superiority was very slight. The case for higher American productivity during the period 1817–1842 seems to be overwhelming.

Differential profitability

The productivity indexes indicate that resources devoted to whaling in the United States produced more oil and bone than the same quantities of labour and capital did in Great Britain. It is, however, profit not productivity that induces businessmen to organize economic activity, capitalists to provide the savings that produce the capital stock, and workers to leave the farm for a life before the mast. The data gathered in the course of this study make it possible to estimate American and British profit rates.[24] The profit rates in

[24] The U.S. profit figures are voyage figures from the New Bedford fleet averaged by year. The rates calculated for the period 1816 to 1845 may appear high, but they are consistent with contemporary estimates. Revenues were calculated by multiplying the catch (whale oil, sperm

turn provide some indication of why the British chose to put their resources to work in such a seemingly unproductive enterprise.

Panel D of Table II provides a number of alternative estimates of the profits that were (or might have been) earned by a British entrepreneur, as well as the rates received by his American competitor.[25] Costs C1, C2, and C3 embody three different estimates of the price of a ton of shipping, but it is the two estimates of revenues that are of most interest.[26] R1 reflects the total revenues actually received by British shipowners (it includes earnings from the subsidy as well as the tariff-inflated prices of whale oil and bone); R2 reflects the revenues they would have earned had there been no subsidy and had they been forced to market their output at prices prevailing in the U.S. (i.e., at prices unaffected by the British tariff).

Two conclusions stand out. First, had the British government pursued a "hands off" policy (i.e., no bounties and no tariffs), it seems highly unlikely that there would have been *any* British whaling industry. By the lowest estimate of the cost of vessels, profits for the entire period averaged less than seven percent. In contrast, American owners (owners of firms in a very competitive industry) earned more than forty percent. The yield on British government consols (a safe alternative) was 3.8 percent.

Second, given the levels of government support that actually prevailed,

footnote 24 (*contd.*)

oil, and whale bone) by average prices. Costs recognized include: (1) depreciation, (2) value of vessels lost at sea, (3) foregone interest, (4) wages (calculated at 34 percent—the average total lay—of revenue), (5) crew maintenance, and (6) ship supplies. The costs that have not been included are those incurred in refitting the vessel in port between voyages. To that extent the profit figures are overstated; however, the same costs have been omitted from the U.K. calculation, and they are almost certainly larger. The G.B. profits have been calculated in a similar fashion, except that the sources employed were studies or reports on part or all of the nation's whaling fleet. Those sources include: J. T. Jenkins, op. cit.; W. Scoresby, op. cit.; O. G. Jackson, op. cit.; J. R. McCulloch, op. cit.; and British Parliamentary papers, 1845 (504), XLVII, 515. Crew maintenance was assumed to be equal to the U.S. figure for each month at sea. All other estimates were drawn from the sources cited.

[25] The American profit calculations are based on the assumption that vessels remained in port for refitting for an average of 2.5 months between voyages. We believe that 2.5 months represents an upper bound. Although there are some problems with outliers, an analysis of all New Bedford vessels hunting in the Atlantic grounds between 1817 and 1843 indicates that both the median and modal stay in port was 2.0 months. If, on the assumption that vessels "in port" for more than ten months were actually engaged in some non-whaling activity, the distribution of "port time" is truncated at that figure, the mean of all voyages 1817 to 1843 is 2.36 months. Of the 211 observations, 119 show a port time of two months or less and another twenty indicate a port time of less than three months.

[26] C1 was derived from an examination of secondary sources. These sources are primarily literary, and quantification was not the authors' major interest. They show a gradual increase in the relative cost from 1.76 in the first decade, to 2.65 in the second, and to 2.94 in the third. Over all the difference averages 2.31. C2 is based on the frequently cited "fact" that on average British vessels cost 1.5 times as much as American. C3 is from U.S. Government, *Report of the Commissioner of Navigation to the Secretary of the Treasury, 1886* (Washington D.C.: GPO, 1886), pp. 22–27. The adjustment is 1.34, the average of the estimates for 1821, 1825, 1826, 1829, 1830, 1832, 1835, 1840, and 1845 reported in the table on page 25. Unfortunately, the report centres on the loss of the American position in the iron shipbuilding industry, and there is no source reported for the price of wooden vessels.

TABLE II
Comparative G.B. and U.S. (New Bedford) Atlantic whaling data

Panel A

Years	*Average tonnage* G.B.	*Average tonnage* U.S.A.	*% Tons lost* G.B.	*% Tons lost* U.S.A.	*Months at sea* G.B.	*Months at sea* U.S.A.	*Men/ton/voyage* G.B.	*Men/ton/voyage* U.S.A.
1816–25	319	265	0.0336	0.0751	5.2	12.2	0.1409	0.0741
1826–35	323	286	0.0659	0.0440	5.9	12.4	0.1409	0.0794
1836–42	310	292	0.0241	0.0226	5.3	20.6	0.1526	0.0911
All years	318	279	0.0425	0.0424	5.5	14.5	0.1439	0.0805

Panel B

Years	*Men/ton (adj)* G.B.	*Men/ton (adj)* U.S.A.	*Employment* G.B. *(man years)*	*Employment* U.S.A. *(man years)*	*Labour cost/ton/yr* G.B. c$'s	*Labour cost/ton/yr* U.S.A. c$'s	*Crewfood/ton/yr* G.B. c$'s	*Crewfood/ton/yr* U.S.A. c$'s
1816–25	0.0611	0.0595	2592	442	11.61	20.95	5.08	6.25
1826–35	0.0692	0.0639	1782	1372	13.41	22.09	5.72	6.81
1836–42	0.0669	0.0795	770	1466	8.64	17.76	5.57	12.98
All years	0.0656	0.0667	1820	1051	11.51	20.54	5.45	8.82

Panel C

	Total revenue per ton G.B.R1 c$'s	*Total revenue per ton* G.B.R2 c$'s	*Total revenue per ton* G.B.R3 c$'s	*Vessel cost per ton* U.S.A. c$'s	G.B.C1 c$'s	G.B.C2 c$'s	G.B.C3 c$'s	U.S.A. c$'s
1816–25	42.54	39.27	32.58	61.61	123.24	105.00	93.80	70.00
1826–35	68.65	68.65	40.62	64.97	145.80	82.50	73.70	55.00
1836–42	23.51	23.51	16.39	52.23	175.25	90.00	80.40	60.00
All years	47.28	46.06	31.36	60.42	143.00	92.78	82.88	61.85

Panel D

Years	*G.B.* R1C1	*G.B.* R1C2	*G.B.* R1C3	*G.B.* R2C1	*G.B.* R2C2	*G.B.* R2C3	*U.S.A.*
1816–25	10.4	14.2	17.2	2.1	4.7	6.6	31.6
1826–35	21.3	46.9	54.1	1.8	12.9	16.1	57.8
1836–42	−3.1	1.6	2.8	−7.4	−6.3	−6.0	36.9
All years	10.9	23.1	27.1	−0.3	4.9	6.8	42.7

C1 G.B. vessel costs from literary sources.
C2 G.B. vessel costs at 1.5 times U.K.
C3 G.B. vessel costs at 1.34 times U.K.
R1 G.B. revenues at British prices and bounty.
R2 G.B. revenues at British prices but no bounty.
R3 G.B. revenues at U.S. prices and no bounty.

profits in Britain appear to have been sufficient to command continued investment until the mid 1830s. Although the profits of British whalers were seldom equal to those earned by their American counterparts, alternative investments in G.B. were also less rewarding than those in the United States. British earnings in the first decade after the Treaty of Ghent appear to have been in the ten to seventeen percent range, at a time when 4.5 percent was available to those risk-averse investors who chose government bonds. The industry was even more attractive during the next decade. Returns were almost certainly above twenty (and perhaps more than fifty) percent, at a time when the consol rate had fallen to 3.5. In the United States, profit rates were over thirty percent in the first and nearly sixty percent in the second decade.

After 1835, however, despite the protective tariff on whale oil, there is little evidence that the British industry remained economically viable. Independent of the measure of vessel cost chosen, profits were negative more often than they were positive. Although a businessman might earn only 3.3 percent on his portfolio of government bonds, his whaling earnings would have been no more then that amount, and he might have suffered a loss of three percent. The return was small for so risky an enterprise. The three profit measures based on G.B. revenues (R1C1, R1C2, and R1C3) yield average values of 10.9, 23.1, and 27.1, but the standard deviations are 18.4, 30.8, and 34.3, respectively. In contrast the standard deviation of the consol series (average 3.7) was 0.4.

The causes of the failure of British productivity and profits are unexplained. The high cost of G.B. vessels is not entirely to blame, although costs certainly adversely affected profits. To protect the British shipbuilding industry the government prohibited the importation of foreign vessels from 1786 to 1849; potential shipowners were required to "buy British."[27] Even if they had been able to use American vessels, and if the domestic market for whale oil had continued to benefit from the tariff, it does not appear that

[27] The prohibition was contained in 26 Geo. III c. 60, an extension of the navigation laws dealing with the registration of vessels to the free American colonies. The law was repealed in 1849. See John G. B. Hutchins, *The American Maritime Industries and Public Policy, 1784–1914: An Economic History,* Harvard Economic Studies, Vol. LXXI (Cambridge, MA: Harvard University Press, 1941), p. 175. The restrictions on foreign vessels did not apply to British colonies; and, if whaling had been able to survive in the U.K. for only a few more years, it would have been able to draw on Canadian shipyards for its capital equipment. During the years in question, however, the Canadian shipbuilding industry was still in its infancy. Its "vessels, which in model resembled the American cargo ships, were generally constructed at first of relatively poor hardwoods, and later of Canadian spruce, which timbers were often used unseasoned, were frequently of light scantling, and were commonly poorly fitted and fastened." The Canadian vessels were, however, inexpensive. In 1840 they sold for about three-fourths of the price of their American competitors. The industry was not large, exporting in total only about one hundred vessels to the U.K. each year. Within twenty years, however, the industry had expanded (quality had gone up and relative prices had fallen); and by 1860 the Canadian shipyards had become a force to be reckoned with in the world shipbuilding industry. John G. B. Hutchins, *The American Maritime Industries and Public Policy, 1789–1941: An Economic History,* (Cambridge, Mass.: Harvard University Press, 1941), pp. 300–301.

the industry would have remained viable after the mid 1830s. Using American shipping would have increased first-decade profits to more than twenty-five and second-decade earnings to a very substantial seventy-five percent, but over the last seven years, even with American ships and barks, British profits would likely have been less than seven percent. Moreover, even if British whaleman had used American built vessels, had they been forced to sell at American output prices, the industry might have been marginally profitable in the first decade and fairly profitable in the second; but annual losses would likely have averaged more than five percent over the last period.[28]

It appears that Fairburn was correct: British whaling was a creature of war and other governmental policies. Before the Boston Tea Party had escalated into a full-scale conflict, the New England colonies had supplied three-quarters of the whale oil sold in the British market. Soon after Cornwallis's surrender, British merchants were faced by Yankee whalers in the Thames "with full cargoes of oil of excellent quality, which was offered below the prevailing London price."[29] The official British response to their intrusion was the imposition of a high protective tariff on whale oil and yet one more attempt to induce Nantucket whalers to shift their base of operations to Great Britain.

For an industry so long dependent on the good offices of His Majesty's Government, it is not surprising that the causes of the absolute and relative decline in whaling profitability can be traced in part to changes in government policy. Policy changes, however, are not the only explanation: there were also structural differences in the two economies that had implications for the profits of the whaling fleets—at least in the short term. But government policy certainly did change. In 1824 the government refused to renew the tonnage bounty, and, although one historian has argued that its value was "so slight . . . that its passing was hardly noticed," the bounty had accounted for between a fourth and a fifth of the profits earned in the nine preceding years.[30] Similarly, while the tariff on whale oil remained high until 1843, the rate on whale oil substitutes was cut sharply. For example, the duty on rape seed (a substitute for whale oil in textile

[28] The estimates of British profitability (R1 refers to total revenues including bounties and British prices, R2 to American prices and no bounties) based on American vessel prices are as follows:

YEARS	R1 CUSA	R2 CUSA
1816–25	26.5	12.3
1826–35	76.9	26.0
1836–42	6.8	−5.1
All years	40.1	12.9

Under the most favorable assumptions, the ratios of British to American profits in the three periods were 0.54, 0.94, 0.08.

[29] Jackson, op. cit., p. 91; Fairburn, op, cit., II, p. 996.

[30] Jackson, op. cit., p. 118. Depending on the cost measure the difference in profits is twenty-seven, twenty-four, or twenty-two percent (3.0 on 11.1, 3.5 on 14.7, or 3.9 on 17.5).

production) was cut from £1 to 1 shilling (from $4.54 to $0.24) a quarter between 1822 and 1827. In that period imports of seed rose by 650 percent.[31]

At a more fundamental level, however, all of the industry's problems cannot be blamed on changes in government policy. In the United States demand for whale oil plummeted after coal oil and, to a lesser extent, manufactured gas became available, but those products did not reach the American market until mid-century. In Great Britain, on the other hand, both coal oil and coal gas appeared shortly after the end of the Napoleonic Wars. By the 1820s, cities like London had substituted first coal oil and then gas for whale oil in their street lamps. Although the question is beyond the scope of the present inquiry, it is interesting to speculate about the causes of the American lag in the innovation of whale oil substitutes. How much of the lag was the product of differences in the structures of the two economies, and how much was the result of differences in relative prices—differences that reflect the high British tariff on whale oil?

Saddled with a cost structure that made the British noncompetitive in the international market, no tariff and no bounty within reason could have supported the industry in the face of an almost complete dearth of domestic demand. It is not surprising, therefore, that when in 1843 the British government reduced the tariff on whale oil from $0.72 to $0.16 a gallon, the effect was felt by fewer than twenty shipowners and fewer than one thousand seamen.

Conclusions

At the end of the Napoleonic Wars, British whalers enjoyed a near monopoly of the world's whale fishery. In the third quarter of the eighteenth century, government subsidies and improvement in crew quality had combined to make that fleet a lower cost producer, the Dutch had turned to other maritime pursuits, and the navy had eliminated colonial competition. After Yorktown, tariffs replaced the fleet as a barrier to foreign competition in the British domestic market, and as the new century dawned, the Royal Navy, charged with isolating Napoleonic Europe, provided *de facto* protection in most of the rest of the markets of the developed world. The year 1814 saw almost two hundred British whalers hunting the northern and southern fisheries, while only two American vessels were active.

Three decades later the American fleet had grown to almost seven hundred and the British had shrunk to twenty-seven. Given equal access to the stock of natural resources and to the menu of alternative technologies, the two fleets—British and American—had met in head-to-head competition in the waters off Greenland and in the Davis Strait. From the point of view of a study of the relationships among productivity, policy, and

[31] *Ibid.*, p. 122.

economic change, the microcosm that was the northern fishery provides a nearly ideal historical laboratory. What factors explain the shift in industrial leadership from the old to the new world? Was the shift rooted in emerging differences in underlying productivity, to differences in input or output prices, or to changes in the economic environment?

The evidence indicates that all three contributed. On average, American productivity was high, but probably not high enough to account fully for the observed difference in profitability. It should be kept in mind that the measured relative British productivity figures are biased upward by the equality of treatment given in the estimating procedure both to British blubber and American oil, and to sperm and whale oil, and by the failure to adjust American productivity for repairs and refitting carried out during the course of a voyage. It is comforting to note that both the productivity and the profit estimates yield similar results. The British were less productive and they were substantially less profitable. In the middle period (1826 to 1834), however, the productivity difference narrowed, and the British whalers proved themselves to be almost as profitable as their American competitors. Moreover, it appears that if, in that period, the British had been able to continue to operate in the protected domestic market and had the government permitted them to use American-built vessels, as well, they would have earned even more than their Nantucket and New Bedford peers. If, in fact, that happy state had persisted for the entire twenty-six year period, the profit rate in the two countries would have been nearly equal. The "it might have been" estimates suggest that despite the profits that could have been earned, if only the world had been different, low British productivity had important implications for the industry's long-term survival. Even American-built vessels would not have saved the British fleet had the owners faced American competition in the British market for whale oil and baleen.

Higher wage and vessel costs depressed British profits, but they do not account for the measured "productivity gap." The question still remains: Why, if larger crews and shorter voyages were both unproductive and unprofitable, didn't the British owners and captains adjust to the superior American technology? Although the question is far from settled, the answer may lie in the quality of British crews. The literature is replete with horror stories about the sailors who manned those vessels. Jackson, writing about the northern fishery during the period of its most rapid growth, has little good to say about the British decision

> . . . to recruit "Greenmen," a term which had nothing to do with Greenland, but indicated that they were new to the job—and therefore cheaper. Such moves are perhaps best illustrated by the *Robert* of Peterhead . . . which in 1795 had only two "sailors" among its crew of twenty-three. The final stage . . . came when the cheapest native crews were swelled by half-starved wretches picked up for a song in the Shetlands . . .[32]

[32] *Ibid.*, pp. 72–73.

Nor does the quality of the crews appear to have improved over time. Although the subject of the inquiry was the southern not the northern fishery, an owner appearing before a Parliamentary select committee in 1844 testified that British seamen, who has been "the best sailors in the world" in 1801 were by 1844 "the worst description."[33] It should be noted that it was in 1801 that the crews had been "swelled by half starved wretches." At the same time that the British owners were lamenting the sad state of domestic seamen, they argued that American "crews, bred in the trade and enthusiastic in their pursuit of it," were better whalemen than the British.[34]

Although it is difficult to sort out cause and effect, crew quality may have affected productivity not only directly but indirectly through voyage length as well. American crews included a number of skilled artisans. It appears that they were able to carry out a substantial amount of maintenance during the voyage itself. The British, on the other hand, depended on shore-based workmen for the bulk of their refitting and repair. A British vessel usually carried a carpenter and his mate but few other artisans.[35] American vessels included among their crews not only carpenters but sailmakers, blacksmiths, riggers, and even coopers. Maintenance and repair were primary activities on American vessels during the winter months when weather and ice pushed the vessels and their crews southward.

There may have been yet another reason for the apparant intransigence displayed by British business in their refusal to choose long voyages. If, in fact, the bounty payment was tied to voyages rather than trips to the north, adoption of the American institutional technology could have proved costly. The bounty did disappear in the mid 1820's, but given the relatively long lags inherent in any structural innovation, the British may have been out of business before they had a change to exploit the American institutional technology.

The economic evidence indicates that, by American standards, British whalers were neither productive nor profitable. The historical records show that it was bounties and warships that gave the British their initial dominance over the Dutch, and it was the same ships of the line, this time supported by a series of protective tariffs, that maintained that monopoly in the fact of incipient American competition. Taken together the conclusion appears obvious: the British monopoly was rooted, not in economic superiority, but in governmental policy.

Such policies are not immutable. To the extent that they are effected through a distortion of relative prices, they tend to induce substitution against the protected commodities. Coal oil may well have been an inferior substitute for whale oil in a technical sense, but in an economic sense it was a superior substitute at the tariff-inflated price of whale oil. Government policy is frequently rooted in some noneconomic argument in a

[33] *Ibid.*, p. 135.
[34] *Ibid.*, p. 141.
[35] Jenkins, *op. cit.*, p. 189.

government's objective function; and the weights assigned to the argument can change with social and political conditions. As long as a continental war was a serious threat, the British government was prepared to pay, and pay handsomely, for a ready supply of ships and seamen. As the threat of war receded, the political revenues attached to the policy waned as well; but the costs in terms of taxes, foregone alternatives, and consumer discontent remained high. The policy became politically unprofitable. Finally, the distribution of political influence is not a constant. Whalers and oil merchants were a force to be reckoned with in the eighteenth century, but fifty years later it was the textile manufacturers and merchants who commanded the government's attention. Although this study began as an exercise in economics, it has become increasingly apparent that the final chapter can be written only if the focus is shifted from economics to political science.

California Institute of Technology
University of North Carolina, Chapel Hill
University of North Carolina, Chapel Hill

Oxford Economic Papers 40 (1988), 695–718

FEMALE LABOUR FORCE PARTICIPATION IN INTERWAR BRITAIN*

By T. J. HATTON and R. E. BAILEY

ONE of the most prominent changes in the labour market in the last century was the rise in female participation. The proportion of females in the total labour force rose from 27 per cent to 39 per cent between 1881 and 1981. This rise began in the interwar period. The crude participation rates from the census are somewhat misleading because of changes in the school leaving age (which determines the minimum age used in calculating the participation rate) and retirements from the labour force in the upper age groups. For the age range 15–59 the female participation rate was constant at 38 per cent for census years from 1901 to 1931, rising to 43 per cent in 1951, 47 per cent in 1961 and 55 per cent in 1971 (Hakim, 1980, p. 559). Thus the revolution in female participation, as reflected in the census, is mostly a product of the last 50 years. The participation rate for married women was approximately 10 per cent in 1911 and 1931, rose dramatically to 21.7 per cent in 1951, and then doubled again to 42.9 per cent in 1971.

This paper studies female participation in the interwar years, when this transformation was just beginning. We analyse two cross sections, one based on household data from the New Survey of London Life and Labour and the other from the 1931 census. Empirical studies of cross sections for the 1970's and 1980's typically associate participation with a range of demographic and household variables and focus particularly on the behaviour of married women; their findings are generally consistent with standard models of labour supply.[1] But there has been little analysis of female participation in the era before the second World War when conditions presumably differed. We wish to know whether such models would receive support for the earlier period and how the results might differ.

The growing literature on the history of women's work stresses the importance, extent and variety of women's contribution to both the market and non-market economy.[2] Where participation is discussed, the role of women as wage earners is typically linked to household needs, labour market forces and institutional variables. These factors include the need to augment family income, the burden of domestic responsibilities, employers' willingness to use female labour, the degree of occupational segregation, industrial structure and organisation and prevailing social attitudes. An

* We are grateful to Nicholas Crafts, Nicholas Dimsdale, Peter Sinclair and an anonymous referee for advice and suggestions in revising the paper. Any remaining errors are our own.

[1] For recent surveys see Killingsworth (1983), Killingsworth and Heckman (1986) and Pencavel (1986).

[2] For recent surveys of this literature see Lewis (1984), Roberts (1988).

empirical analysis of female participation may shed light on some of these issues.

The Female Labour Market in Interwar Britain

The pattern of women's employment in the interwar period retained many of the features which had become established in the late nineteenth century. Despite a gradual change in attitudes towards women's work from the turn of the century, the statistics on female participation display little change: female employment was still largely concentrated among single women, and in a narrow range of occupations.

It is odd that such low participation rates persisted, given the experience of the First World War. Between 1914 and 1918 an estimated two million women replaced men in the labour force. The proportion of females in total employment rose from 24 percent in July 1914 to 37 percent in November 1918. Women were drawn into occupations previously reserved for men. Though "dilution" involved some deskilling, this showed than women in large numbers were willing and able to take on a wide range of industrial employment. To many contemporaries, the war had marked a permanent breakthrough in the position of women in the labour market (see Andrews 1981, p. 176). Yet the 1921 census indicates that the lasting effects of the war on participation were marginal. In contrast, the Second World War is often thought to have precipitated the revolution in female participation which took place after 1945.[3]

During the First World War formal collective agreements which opened industrial jobs to women explicitly stated that this was to be for the duration of the War only. The Restoration of Pre-War Practices Act of 1918, though only enforceable for one year, echoed earlier agreements, was widely accepted and strictly interpreted by employers and unions (McCalman 1971, p. 39). The disappearance of females in these trades in the boom years immediately after the war suggests that it was largely the reversion to pre-war practice rather than the ensuing slump which reduced the opportunities for industrial participation (Lewis, 1984, p. 180; c.f. Pigou, 1947, p. 20). After the Second World War, however, attitudes had changed: an official compaign was staged to retain women, particularly married women, in the labour force. By contrast, following 1918, the ban on employing women after marriage was re-imposed in many occupations (Braybon, 1981, ch 7; Riley, 1981, pp 75–80).

In the late nineteenth century the three major sectors outside agriculture where women worked were domestic service, the clothing trade and the textile manufacturing industries. In the 1901 census these accounted for just over 60 percent of females who were recorded as occupied (with over 30 percent in domestic service alone). By 1931 these three occupations

[3] For recent accounts of women's work in the First and Second World Wars and immediate postwar developments see Braybon (1981) and Summerfield (1984) respectively.

accounted for 41 percent of the total while the growing areas of female employment—clerks and typists, shop assistants and managers—accounted for another 21 percent (Gales and Marks, 1974, p. 64). Though the census evidence suggests a decline in the proportion of all females working in occupations where there was very high ratio of females to males, various measures of occupational segregation do not indicate a dramatic fall in concentration overall (Hakim, 1978, p. 1265). The falls in domestic service and the textile trades were offset by the rise of new female occupations with a relatively small effect on the demand for female labour overall. Despite some evidence of a gradual rise in the proportion of females in a range of trades during the interwar period (Home Office, cmd. 3508, 1930, Leser, 1952, p. 330) it appears that much of the growth in female employment in the 1930s was in the newer and faster growing industries located in the South of England (Heim, 1984).

The occupational structure of women's employment is largely reflected in the spatial variations in rates of participation across towns and counties (which are examined in more detail below). Female participation was much higher in areas where female employing industries were strongly represented, and in the larger towns where there was a wider range of opportunities for female employment. Simple correlations show that in 1931 high female participation was most strongly correlated with the share of occupied females in the traditional sectors of domestic service, textiles and clothing. The 1931 pattern of participation rates across towns resembles the 1911 pattern closely, more so than in 1951.[4] Different traditions in the employment of females were established in different industrial areas, depending on their industrial and occupational structure. This remained very marked during the interwar period and only broke down after the Second World War as areas of traditionally low participation levelled upwards.

These variations were most marked among married women. Large scale employment of married women focussed mainly on Lancashire and the surrounding area, the Midlands and in certain parts of London. Married women were most affected. But these areas also recorded higher participation among single, widowed and divorced women. In 1921, in the Lancashire region, the overall participation rate was 40 per cent and the share of married women among those occupied was 19 per cent; in South Wales the percentages were 20 and 9 respectively. As Gittins (1982, chs 3, 4) has shown, variations in the level of female employment, and in occupational structure, gave rise to differences in the demographic structure and in patterns of marriage and fertility. Due to migration, areas of low female participation generally had below-average ratios of women to men in the population. In areas with little female employment, women married younger and employment after marriage was unusual. Where factory work

[4] These findings are discussed in more detail in a precursor to the present paper (Hatton, 1986, pp 13–16).

was common fertility was low, except where the occupation could be carried on part-time or in the home. Such findings remind one that demographic variables often included in models of participation may partially reflect labour market conditions.

The proportion of women occupied in different areas depended partly on the level and composition of demand for female labour. But supply side factors also played a role. The age structure of the population, the demographic structure of the household, rates of marriage, levels of dependency and household income and needs varied across regions for various reasons, some of them independent of immediate labour market conditions. The degree to which these factors contributed directly to the structure of participation, and the relative importance of different effects, have not previously been explored in the interwar context. This is done in a later section of this paper.

Such effects might be seen more clearly if the participation behaviour of individuals is studied in one particular labour market. Participation varied widely across different household types. Those noting this usually attribute it to a combination of institutional and economic factors, often stressing the role of household needs (see Roberts 1982). Females were paid less than males, and could not contribute as much to household income. But female earnings might provide the margin over a subsistence income and thus induce greater participation. In the absence of a male bread-winner, and other forms of income, there was no alternative to market work (Lewis, 1984, pp. 145, 151). Married women's prospects might be limited by lack of opportunities for employment or the presence of children or other dependents. So it was often unmarried daughters of working age who adopted the role of primary or secondary earners. Clearly the responses depended on the capacity of other earners in the household, and the size, composition and age structure of the individual family. We address this and other issues in detail in our analysis of individuals from the New Survey of London Life and Labour.

One such issue is the impact of unemployment for which the interwar period is notorious. Some contemporaries in Britain and the United States thought that high unemployment among males forced some females to seek work who would not otherwise have done so (see Strachey, 1934, Woytinsky, 1940). One might expect such effects to depend on the household role of the female concerned and on which other household members were unemployed. Evidence recently adduced for the U.S. supports the presence of an "added worker" effect for married women but suggests this was attenuated by the provision of relief schemes (Margo, 1988, p. 347). On the other hand, the climate of high unemployment reinforced attitudes against married women working. Though the overall unemployment rate for women was lower than that for men, the rate for married women was substantially higher. The relatively poor prospects of employment (particularly for those with little labour market experience) may have reduced participation at a time of high unemployment generally—the "discouraged worker" effect. If this were found to dominate, it might help to explain why female participation stayed low between the wars despite the presence of trends (such as smaller family sizes) which could have raised it.

Several postwar studies have examined how female participation responds to changes in wage rates. Rising real wage rates, particularly for females, are seen as contributing to the postwar rise in participation. In a household context the effect of changes in the wage would depend on the flexibility of household roles, the availability of part-time work and the nature of household technology. This leads one to ask whether a positive link between participation and wage rates can be identified for an earlier era. Handled carefully, cross-sectional results can offer some clues to whether the labour supply function for females has changed over the last 50 years and, if so, how.

Data from the New Survey of London Life and Labour

The New Survey of London Life and Labour (NSLLL) provides a unique opportunity to examine female participation at the individual level before the Second World War. The survey was undertaken at the London School of Economics under the direction of Hubert Lewellyn-Smith between 1929 and 1931. It was designed to shed light on social and economic conditions among working class households on a basis comparable with Charles Booth's pioneering inquiry of 40 years earlier. The resulting nine volume work gives a comprehensive picture of London life ranging from work and wages to housing conditions and poverty to travel and leisure activities, often with detailed comparisons across boroughs. The investigation involved a street survey similar to Booth's and also a detailed enquiry into the domestic circumstances of 28,100 households. This represents an average sampling factor of one in 60 households for the survey area (higher in some small boroughs to provide at least 500 households from each). The surviving record cards have been used in an examination of the incidence of unemployment by Eichengreen (1987) but have not so far been used to analyse labour force participation.

The data set used in this paper is derived from information on 1356 households, a random sample of one in every twenty of the original record cards. The data were collected and processed by Colin Linsley for his Ph.D. thesis (Linsley, 1986) on housing and poverty in interwar London.[5]

Two obvious but important qualifications concern the coverage of the Survey. First, it is confined to London. The area covered extended beyond the county of London (the area examined by Booth) to reflect the expansion of London in the intervening years and to provide an area broadly similar in

[5] We are grateful to Colin Linsley for permission to use the data set and, in particular, for providing it in a form which made its analysis straightforward.

character to that in the earlier study. Nine districts were added to the County of London to make a total of 38 boroughs.[6] The survey area covered 5.7 million persons, some 72.5 per cent of the Greater London area and 14.4 per cent of the population of England and Wales in 1928. The second limitation is that, since the main objective was to examine poverty and overcrowding, the House Sample enquiry covered only working class households as defined by the occupation of the head of the household or in cases such as the self employed, if the head's annual income fell below £250. The excluded middle class families comprise 28 per cent of families in the survey area.

If conditions in London differed from those in other areas, or the working and middle classes behaved differently, the Survey would not be representative of the country as a whole. However, the Survey offers detailed information on individual households, virtually unparalleled among prewar sources and superior in some ways to many postwar surveys. Furthermore working class households in the capital are sufficiently important to deserve separate analysis. We attempt to gain a broader perspective for England and Wales as a whole by examining evidence from the census in later sections of the paper.

The Survey was carefully conducted. Serious efforts were made to ensure that the households were randomly selected and the information obtained was as complete as possible. The houses to be visited were selected for each Borough from the Parliamentary Registers or from School Attendance Officer's lists to ensure that the houses were spread uniformly across the Borough and every house had an equal chance of inclusion. Substitutions were made only when no one normally slept at the address. If information could not be obtained at one visit, repeat visits were made.[7]

Three types of information were included on the cards: demographic data and family structure; income, earnings, hours of work and work expenses; and housing details including rent paid. Family relationships were defined relative to the head of the household, normally the husband if the household contained a married couple or, if not, the senior adult or main breadwinner. The ages of each member were recorded, children being defined as those under 14. Family members were classified as earners or non-earners. Earners' work expenses and hours were recorded for both "last week" and a "full week". From this (and any other income entered separately) each household's income was calculated for last week and a full week. Full week income was calculated as that which would have obtained in the absence of irregular or short-time employment, unemployment or

[6] These external boroughs are in the East: Barking, East Ham, Leyton, Tottenham, Walthamstow and West Ham; in the West, Acton Hornsey and Willesden. A full list of the boroughs included in the survey is given in the note to the appendix. The record cards appear to have survived in their entirety with the exception of those for Walthamstow which are now missing.

[7] The instructions given to investigators and the definitions used are outlined in Llewellyn-Smith ed, (1932), Vol 3, Appendix 1.

TABLE 1
Averages from sample of NSLLL (Females aged 14 and above)

	All Females	*Household Heads*	*Wives*	*Other Members*
Number	1788	236	1012	540
Average Age	38.0	56.3	41.3	24.0
Participation Rate (percentage)	30.6	44.5	6.0	70.6
Hourly Wage (pence) (Participants only)	6.53	8.20	7.13	5.98
Number in Family:				
Adults	3.15	1.95	2.78	4.35
Children	0.97	0.36	1.15	0.88
Gross Household Income (shillings in Full Week)	92.9	51.8	86.6	122.4
Minimum Income plus Rent (shillings)	45.0	29.8	43.4	54.8

illness.[8] The demographic information on the card was used to calculate the minimum household income (exclusive of rent) for a basic dietary standard.

From our sample of the record cards we identified 1788 females aged 14 or over and, in the light of differing household responsibilities, we further subdivided these into household heads, the wives of heads and other family members. Participation status is defined by whether the individual was recorded as an earner. This only proved ambiguous in a few cases, mainly among household heads, who though entered as earners had no earnings either last week or in a full week. These were appropriately re-classified. The omission of age was almost entirely confined to individuals who could be identified as being adults. In such cases age was inferred, where possible, from the age of other related family members, chiefly children or spouses.

To obtain an hourly wage rate we divided full-week earnings by full-week work-hours, if recorded; for others, we substituted the average wage in factories, workshops and dressmaking for the relevant age group.[9] The remaining variables were taken as reported on the record card. Only four households had to omitted for lack of information.

Some of the averages emerging from our sample are given in Table 1. There are rather few household heads in comparison with wives and other family members. The high average age of household heads reflects the preponderance of widows and single women living alone. The other household members are relatively young, reflecting the large numbers of daughters in that group. Participation rates also vary dramatically across the

[8] See Llewellyn-Smith (ed.) Vol. 3 (1932), p. 61.
[9] Llewellyn-Smith (ed.) Vol. 6, (1934) p. 83. The imputation of wage rates was necessary in only 29 cases of the 547 earners in the sample.

groups, very high for 'others'—not surprisingly in the light of their youth, and very low for wives. Overall participation rates are significantly lower than those for the same Boroughs recorded in the census of 1931, probably reflecting the paucity of domestic servants (who, if living-in, would have been found in middle class households) and the fact that the survey counts earners as participants rather than those returning an occupation as in the census.

The computed hourly wage for participants also reflects the differing age and experience of the sub-groups. Since the wage rate profile rose sharply up to the mid-20s age group, the wage for other household members is low relative to heads of households and wives. The high participation rate of other household members tends to pull down the average. The table shows that family size also differs quite sharply. Female heads tended to have small families with few children present while other household members (typically from families with working age sons and daughters) came from the largest families. Not surprisingly, gross household income also rises across the three groups the number of adults in the household. In each group average household income is considerably above the minimum. The minimum itself, however, is a bare dietary standard (plus fuel) which was intended to be comparable with Booth's standard of the early 1890s to which rent paid was added but with no allowance being made for other types of expenditure.[10] Household heads are poorest, with less than double the minimum; other household members are above twice the subsistence standard.

The three groups clearly differ in family structure, needs, and their relation to the labour market. It is therefore worth examining their participation behaviour separately. In the following section we specify and estimate participation functions for the various groups.

Participation Functions from the NSLLL

The standard utility maximising household labour supply model is used to analyse the participation decision. Given the tastes and behaviour of other family members, household utility depends on the labour-leisure choice of each individual member. Utility maximising hours of work, therefore, depends on the household's characteristics (including income), the individual's characteristics and the wage rate she faces. The reservation wage is defined as the highest rate which would leave the individual's utility maximising hours of work at zero, and depends on the same factors.

$$W_i^* = F(Z_i) + \varepsilon_i \qquad (1)$$

where $F(\cdot)$ is a functional form to be specified.

[10] The minimum standard and its comparability with the line of division between Booth's classes C, D and E, F are discussed in Llewellyn Smith (ed), Vol 3 (1932), Appendix 2. For a standard family (Man, Wife, Three children) minimum needs were defined by the survey as 34s to which 6s 6d would be added as an allowance for clothing and cleansing and light (p. 435).

Household member i will participate in market work if the utility from so doing exceeds that from remaining out of the labour market. Equivalently she will participate if the actual wage exceeds the reservation wage, namely, if

$$W_i > W_i^* \quad \text{or} \quad W_i > F(Z_i) + \varepsilon_i \tag{2}$$

Let P_i indicate participation status, $P_i = 1$ denoting participation and $P_i = 0$ denoting non-participation.

The probability that the individual will be observed to participate ($P_i = 1$) is, therefore,

$$\Pr(P_i = 1) = \Pr(W_i - F(Z_i)) > \varepsilon_i \tag{3}$$

It is usual to assume that ε_i obeys a normal distribution. The probit technique is appropriate if this is so, and is employed in our empirical work.

A number of variables are included to reflect factors determining the reservation wage. Age is clearly a major determinant of participation. Since the age profile of participation status does not follow a simple relationship we include age as a set of dummy variables distinguishing narrow age cohorts at the lower end of the spectrum and aggregating those over 65 into one group at the upper end. For the small group for which age was not recorded and for which there was no basis for imputation a separate dummy variable was used. As the survey is relatively rich in information on family structure we are able to include several variables which might reflect the balance of household income needs and household responsibilities. This includes the number of children in the household, which we split into three age groups, each of the three variables measuring the number in the relevant group. One would expect these to lower participation, particularly for married women and especially where the children are relatively young. We also include the total number of adults in the household and the number of labour market participants (exclusive of the individual concerned). The former would presumably raise participation by increasing household needs, but the number of earners in the household should reduce it, by raising household responsibilities and reducing the need to earn.

As we have noted, interest surrounds the possible effect of unemployment of other household members on female participation. We attempt to measure this effect through two variables, a dummy for whether the household head, is unemployed, and a variable for the number of other earners unemployed. Where the individual concerned is a household head, the head unemployed variable is naturally set to zero. If unemployment of other family members affects participation through the negative income effect, then it should raise the probability of participation. We should also observe the effect on participation of family income as a whole. Net family income is defined as earnings minus work expenses and state insurance deductions plus other income, excluding the income of the female concerned. Its influence can, therefore, be interpreted as a pure income effect. The net family income variable used is for a full week and is intended to reflect the permanent income of the family. This had the advantage of recognising the long term nature of the participation decision. In addition, since the unemployment of other family members will not affect income in a full week, the effect of such unemployment is not included in the income term. If leisure is a normal good, the income of other family members should depress the probability of participating.

Other variables were included to capture specific effects of interest. Female participation might be high in households for which the absence of the woman's earnings would result in severe poverty for the family. We therefore define a dummy variable for whether the net income of other family members was less than the minimum income needs of the family for food, fuel and rent. In addition a dummy variable was defined to denote whether or not the household paid rent. This is to capture unmeasured elements of permanent income and wealth not fully reflected in the income term. The sign of this is ambiguous since it may also reflect past participation and earning capacity.

Finally, we include a variable for the hourly wage. We observe the wage only for participants and need to impute a wage for non-participants. We obtained this from a first stage regression for the hourly wage, the predicted values from which were included in the participation equation. Unfortunately the data set does not contain all the variables which should ideally be included in a wage equation. In particular, the data set lacks information on years and type of education and training, and years of labour market experience. The estimated wage equation is based upon the age dummies and a sequence of location dummy variables (defined by groups of the London boroughs). The individual's age is clearly a major determinant of the wage rate and the location dummies are intended to capture differences in the occupational structure of different local labour markets. The inclusion of the location dummies also enables us to identify the effect of the predicted wage rate in the participation equation.

Given that positive wage rates are observed only for females who are participants, the ordinary least squares estimators of the wage equation will suffer from sample selection bias as will the predicted wage rates computed using these estimators. We therefore estimated a wage equation using the sample selection correction method of Heckman (1979). The supplementary equation used to generate the selection adjustment required for the Heckman procedure is a reduced form version of the participation equation. This reduced form participation equation and the resulting wage equation (both estimated for the whole sample) are reported in the appendix. We use the predicted wage generated by this method in the final structural version of the participation equation.[11]

[11] The use of these techniques is discussed in Madalla (1983) Ch. 6. This three stage method has recently been used in the context of female participation by Sprague (1988). It should be noted that, because of the use of the predicted wage rate in the participation equation, the standard errors reported in Table 2 are not asymptotic standard errors but those computed in the final stage probit equation.

The results for the whole sample and the three sub-samples are presented in Table 2. The results for the whole sample in equation (1) indicate an age profile of participation rising to the 18–19 age group and then declining to age 25–34 (the omitted group) with further decline in the probability of participation setting in from age 45 onwards. As to the presence of children, the coefficients plausibly suggest negative effects on the probability of participating which diminish as the age of children rises. However, the effects are modest and even the presence of infants reduces the participation probability by only 6 percentage points. The number of adults in the household, and the number of participants among other household members, are quite well determined and have the expected signs. From this it appears that the presence of additional adults encourages participation by increasing income needs while the presence of additional participants in the household reduces it, perhaps by raising the individual's household responsibilities.

Turning to the effects of the unemployment of other family members, there is some evidence of a positive effect both for unemployment of the household head, and other members, which the point estimate suggests raises the probability of participation by about 10 per cent. This is consistent with the household income effect which is negative and well determined. Thus a drop of 27s 6d per week would induce an increase in the probability of participating by 10 percentage points. There is also some evidence of a rise in the participation probability if the household's income would otherwise be below minimum needs but this result will be further qualified. The effect of the wage is poorly determined and gives an elasticity of participation (calculated at the means) of 0.79.

We tested whether the three subgroups should be pooled. The results showed significant differences among the three groups.[12] This is not surprising given the differences in their participation rates. Differences are evident in the age profiles even though observations are lacking for household heads and wives in some of the younger age groups. Participation by household heads peaks in the 45–54 age group. For wives and other family members, it peaks in the late teenage group and then declines steeply especially for other family members.

One might have expected major differences to arise from the presence of children but the effects are relatively small for all three groups. In particular they are surprisingly small for wives. It appears that wives were typically not earners largely irrespective of presence of children. The positive effect of the number of adults and the negative effect of the number of participants

[12] The likelihood ratio test for the pooled sample (which included the two dummies for household status) as compared with the three separate equations gives a χ^2 value of 69.6 as compared with the critical 5% value of 40. It should be noted that the equations for household heads and wives used in this test are not those in the table, where age groups have been pooled due to the fewness of observations (see note to Table 2). We also performed tests to see if any two of the three groups could be combined. The likelihood ratio test gave χ^2 values of 51.2 for heads and wives combined, 35.9 for heads and others combined and 42.8 for others and wives combined. The critical 5% χ^2 level (18 degrees of freedom) for these tests is 28.9.

TABLE 2

Probit Equations for Female Participation

	All Females		*Household Heads*		*Wives*		*Others*	
	Coeff	dP/dx	*Coeff*	dP/dx	*Coeff*	dP/dx	*Coeff*	dP/dx
Constant	−0.47	−0.13	−1.86	−0.79	−0.49	−0.04	−0.61	−0.20
	(0.75)		(2.12)		(0.85)		(1.13)	
Age 14–15	0.49	0.14	—				0.67	0.22
	(0.51)		—				(0.76)	
Age 16–17	0.86	0.24	—				1.01	0.33
	(0.38)		—				(0.54)	
Age 18–19	1.04	0.29	—		0.63	0.05	1.09	0.35
	(0.29)		—		(0.85)		(0.39)	
Age 20–24	0.56	0.16	*		−0.20	−0.02	0.77	0.25
	(0.17)		—		(0.35)		(0.23)	
Age 35–44	−0.09	−0.02	0.17	0.07	−0.08	−0.01	0.17	0.05
	(0.15)		(0.55)		(0.20)		(0.48)	
Age 45–54	−0.14	−0.04	0.47	0.18	−0.44	−0.04	−0.67	−0.22
	(0.21)		(0.64)		(0.27)		(0.52)	
Age 55–64	−0.46	−0.13	−0.19	−0.07	−0.77	−0.06	−1.51	−0.49
	(0.28)		(0.74)		(0.34)		(0.60)	
Age 65+	−1.69	−0.47	−1.48	−0.58	*		−2.28	−0.74
	(0.21)		(0.53)				(0.42)	
Age not known	0.01	0.00	1.15	0.45	−0.47	−0.04	−0.21	−0.07
	(0.23)		(0.80)		(0.46)		(0.35)	
Children 0–4	−0.20	−0.05	−0.04	−0.01	−0.28	−0.02	0.09	0.03
	(0.09)		(0.30)		(0.13)		(0.16)	
Children 5–9	−0.08	−0.02	−0.26	−0.10	−0.09	−0.01	−0.06	−0.02
	(0.07)		(0.24)		(0.10)		(0.10)	
Children 10–13	0.02	−0.01	−0.04	−0.02	0.04	0.00	−0.08	−0.03
	(0.08)		(0.25)		(0.13)		(0.11)	
No. of Adults	0.31	0.09	0.14	0.06	0.16	0.01	0.32	0.10
	(0.07)		(0.18)		(0.16)		(0.09)	
No. of Participants	−0.23	−0.07	0.31	0.12	0.14	0.02	−0.49	−0.16
	(0.09)		(0.25)		(0.20)		(0.12)	
Head Unemployed	0.34	0.10			0.71	0.06	0.01	0.00
	(0.26)				(0.43)		(0.40)	
Others Unemployed	0.39	0.11	1.05	0.41	0.24	0.02	0.16	0.05
	(0.18)		(0.42)		(0.38)		(0.24)	
Other Household Income	−0.26	−0.07	−0.62	−0.24	−0.33	−0.03	−0.20	−0.07
(£ in a Full Week)	(0.04)		(0.16)		(0.08)		(0.05)	
Income below	0.23	0.06	0.35	0.14	−0.08	−0.01	−0.35	−0.11
Minimum	(0.14)		(0.30)		(0.29)		(0.25)	
Non-rent paying	0.24	0.07	0.45	0.18	0.16	0.01	0.38	0.12
	(0.18)		(0.46)		(0.35)		(0.24)	
Predicted Wage	0.15	0.04	0.25	0.10	−0.08	−0.01	0.20	0.06
(shillings)	(0.09)		(0.22)		(0.12)		(0.14)	
Household Head	−0.53	−0.15						
	(0.21)							
Wife of Head	−1.59	−0.45						
	(0.21)							
Log likelihood	−578.3		−103.6		−199.6		−244.8	
% Classified Correctly	87.4		81.4		94.1		80.7	

* For household heads aged 20–24 and Wives and 65+ there were relatively few observations. When these terms were included the standard errors became very large and convergence proved difficult. We have therefore combined heads aged 20–24 with those aged 25–34 (the omitted group), and wives aged 65+ with the 55–64 age group.

can be traced mainly to the responses of other family members rather than the heads or wives. This shows that the role of others, as earners or nonearners, depended largely on whether the remaining family members were in the work force. In particular, it seems likely that their earning capacity was called on when there were few other earners in the family such as parents or siblings.

As regards income effects on participation, the added worker effect appears strongest for household heads. Similarly, although the negative effect of family income is well determined for all groups the numerical effect on participation for household heads is much larger than for the others. Responsibility for maintaining family income was apparently felt most strongly by household heads though it is present for all females. Although the coefficients are not well determined, participation by household heads appears higher if the family would otherwise be in poverty, but this is not so for the two other groups. Although the coefficients on wages are positive for heads and others, that for wives is negative. However, all the wage coefficients are poorly determined, suggesting for this time period at least that other factors (such as the availability of jobs) may have been important.

How do our results compare with those obtained from micro data for the 1970's and 1980's (which have concentrated mainly on married women)? Studies by Layard et al. (1980) and Zabalza (1983) point to declining participation rates for ages above 25–34 which are steeper than those estimated here for married women but not as steep as the profile for 'others'.[13] They also find rather stronger effects than we observe from the presence of children particularly if under the age of 5. This lowers the probability of participation by about 0.5 (Zabalza 1983, see also Joshi 1986). It appears to be more the fact of marriage than the presence of children which explains low participation rates in the interwar years.

Our results for wage and income elasticities can be summarised as follows:

	All Females	*Heads*	*Wives*	*Others*
Income	−0.96	−1.02	−1.88	−0.46
Wage	0.79	1.87	−0.59	0.52

These can be compared with results of a recent study by Joshi (1986). For married and non-married women respectively, she found income elasticities of −0.32 and −0.10 and wage elasticities of 0.45 and 0.35. Compared with this (and other studies cited by Joshi), our wage elasticities for non-married women appear higher and married women lower though in view of their insignificance we cannot place much weight on the point estimates. By contrast, our income elasticities are much larger and, in view of their

[13] In static cross sections these age profiles will be affected by cohort effects when participation rates have been rising and will, therefore, be steeper than otherwise—a factor which should be absent in the 1930s.

apparent significance, should be taken more seriously. In part this may reflect our specification of other family income for a full week but, even so, it suggests powerful negative income effects. Consistent with this we find some evidence of an added worker effect especially for wives, a result which contrasts with the negative effect of the husband's unemployment found in recent studies (e.g. Layard *et al.* and Joshi).

Data from the 1931 Census

To shed further light on female participation in the interwar period we study a cross section from the 1931 census. The analysis of labour supply decisions in London provides insight into differences in individual behaviour in the country's largest labour market. But participation patterns vary widely between different areas. Table 3 gives the proportion of females aged 14 and over who returned an occupation in twelve regions of England and Wales. Participation rates ranged from less than one in five in South Wales to over two in five in Lancashire and Cheshire. Greater London was second only to the North West, and far above the average of 34.2 for England and Wales as a whole.

This pattern of participation is much as it was throughout the second half of the nineteenth century. It was gradually eroded from 1931 onwards so that by 1971 (on different regional definitions) the range was from 35.7 per cent in Wales to 45.4 per cent in the West Midlands. These variations are usually associated with the industrial and occupational structure of the region. To some extent they reflect the divide between urban and rural areas with higher participation rates in the former. But between towns the range of variation is even greater.[14]

In 1931 participation rates ranged between 11 percent in the Rhondda and 62 per cent in Blackburn. Clearly the contrast between mining areas and textile areas is stark and underlines the importance of differing industrial structures. But even among towns not based on textiles or mining there are substantial variations which can also be associated with the prominence of certain industries. Though our analysis of participation in London showed that household characteristics, demographic factors and economic variables such as income were key determinants of participation, variations in these could hardly account for the enormous regional variations observed. We therefore seek to take account of the occupational structure as well as the demographic and household circumstances of the female population.

The census aggregates the population in several different ways but for the purposes of cross-sectional analysis the choice is between counties or towns. We focus on towns both because this provides more observations and

[14] Across the twelve regions the standard deviation in percentage points is 6.9 while across 144 towns it is 9.3.

TABLE 3
Regional Female Participation Rates from the 1931 Census (percentages)

North 1 (Northumberland and Durham)	23.1	Midland 1 (West)	36.0	Greater London	39.9
North 2 (North Yorks and Cumberland)	27.5	Midland 2 (East)	34.9	South West	27.4
North 3 (East and West Ridings)	35.4	East	26.4	Wales 1 (South)	19.5
North 4 (Lancashire and Cheshire)	41.9	South East	36.1	Wales 2 (North)	28.8

because the distinction between participation and non-participation would be rather more clear cut than in rural areas. The unit of observation is a County Borough or any other urban area (Metropolitan Borough or Urban District) with a population exceeding 50,000. This gives 144 observations in all. 29 of these are London boroughs and a number of others, mainly in Essex and Middlesex, are in the London area.

Similar census based studies of female participation have been undertaken for the post-war period. Those by Greenhalgh (1977) and McNabb (1977) use the 1971 census. Since the available data are slightly more limited for 1931 we cannot provide directly comparable estimates. One important limitation is that, for 1931, across towns, we cannot separate married women from others reported as occupied (though they are reported separately for the population as a whole). But the regional classification from the 1921 census shows that in areas where there was a high aggregate participation rate, the rate was higher among all groups, married, single, and widowed and divorced. Differing regional conditions appear to have affected all groups.

The dependent variable used in the logit regression analysis reported below is the proportion of women aged 14 and over who were reported as occupied. Three types of variables are used to explain the cross-sectional variation. First, there are variables reflecting differences in demographic composition including age, dependency and marital status, all of which might influence willingness to participate. Next come variables relating to wages and income. Here we are forced to develop crude proxies in the absence of suitable supplementary data which can be linked to the census. Last, we include broad measures of industrial composition, in the light of the obvious cross-sectional relationships between industrial structure and female participation. These may be taken to represent the availability of female jobs and to reflect attitudes arising from different industrial traditions. Because we are dealing with averages, not individuals, and because we have relatively few degrees of freedom, the variables are of necessity aggregated more coarsely than for the NSLLL data.

Various demographic measures can be obtained from the county tables of the census. Two marital status variables were used: the proportion married; and the proportion widowed and divorced, taken as one category because of the very small number of divorcees observed. From the data on ages we distinguish three age groups, 15–24, 25–44 and 45–64 omitting the group with ages of 65 and over.[15] From the tables on ages, the number of children aged 0–4 and 5–9 are distinguished. The ratios of these to the adult female population gives a measure of dependency. A slightly different dimension of household structure is given by the average size of private family (obtained from the housing tables).

Though wage rates and income are variables of interest for the analysis of labour supply no direct measures of these are available from the census and there are almost no alternative sources for regional or local cross sections. The only wage variable which could be matched to the set of towns was for the collectively agreed wage for building labourers in October 1929. While this may be a reasonable measure of the unskilled wage for males it is probably a poor proxy for female wages across individual towns. It does capture the regional wage gradient from London to the major conurbations then down to the small urban areas but, of course, there is no variation within the London area. The unemployment rate used is the census rate for males to avoid the simultaneity arising from use of the female unemployment rate. Given the total absence of variables on family income, we assume that housing standards are closely related to income and resort to crude proxies from the housing tables. The number of persons per room in private families gives an inverse measure of living standards while the percentage of the population living more than two to a room gives a crude measure of poverty.

From the occupation tables a number of variables were obtained to capture differences in occupational structure. It would be inappropriate to use the share of females in different occupations since these are part of the dependent variable. Instead, we focus on males' occupations. The number of males in an occupational class relative to the total number of adult females in the population was calculated for twelve groups and each was entered as a separate variable. It the coefficients on each of these variables reflected the female/male proportions in each occupation, taken together they would provide a measure of the number of female jobs relative to the female population. Insofar as they reflect the broad characteristics of the industrial ethos of different towns which developed during the nineteenth century, they may be thought of as reflecting supply side forces as well. Six of the occupational categories are those in which females were concentrated, accounting for 82 per cent of occupied females in England and Wales.

[15] Since the age groups are quinary it is not possible to take the youngest age group from 14 upwards.

A further five are major male employing occupations (accounting for 38 per cent of males) leaving one residual category.[16]

Empirical Results from the 1931 Census

The female labour force participation rate is a limited dependent variable. Hence we use the logistic transformation so that in estimation it is taken as $\ln(P/(1-P))$ where P is the participation rate. Although the towns vary greatly in populations, serious heteroscedasticity was not found.[17] The equations were therefore estimated by ordinary least squares and the results in Table 4 give the estimated coefficients with standard errors and the implied slope coefficients for P with respect to each variable, evaluated at the mean of P. Initial experiments showed that some of the variables contributed little to the explanation. These were dropped to gain more precise estimates for the remainder. The upper age group 45–64 was eliminated so that the excluded group is now 45 and above and the two variables for children 0–4 and 5–9 were combined into one. Similarly the proportion widowed and divorced was combined with single females, the excluded group, and (in the light of the correlation with the number of children and the housing density variables) the variable for family size was excluded.

The first equation in the table is restricted to those supply side variables typically used to explain participation. Most of the coefficients have the expected sign, and some are significant. Together, the variables explain nearly 60 per cent of the variation. As expected, the age variables indicate a large positive effect for the younger age group and a smaller effect for the 25–44 age group but surprisingly, neither coefficient is significant. The proportion married and the ratio of children 0–9 to adult women both have strong negative effects. Furthermore, the marginal effects are very large and, particularly for the latter, larger than suggested by the micro data results. The number of persons per room in private families and the proportion more than two per room also come in strongly with opposite signs. Given that these are rough proxies for income, the results are hard to interpret quantitatively. As an inverse proxy for income, the positive coefficient on persons per room suggests a strong negative income effect, a result consistent with our earlier findings. But the proportion living in over crowded conditions appears to lower participation in contrast to the earlier result for the poverty variable. In part this may reflect the failure to distinguish clearly between poverty and the demographic structure of the

[16] The major female employing orders are XIII (Textiles), XIII (Clothing and Dress), XXIII (Commerce, Finance and Insurance) XXV (Professionals), XXVII (Personal Service), and XXVIII (Clerks, Draughtsmen and Typists). The five major orders of male employment are III (Mining and Quarrying), XI (Metals and Engineering), XV (Wood and Furniture), XVIII (Builders and Bricklayers) and XXIII (Transport and Communication).

[17] The test adopted as that suggested in Koenker (1981) using total female population in each town as the criterion for potential differences in error variances across towns.

TABLE 4
Logit Equation for Female Participation

	Equation (1)		*Equation* (2)			*Equation* (2) *continued*	
	Coeff	dP/dX	*Coeff*	dP/dX	*Males in:*	*Coeff*	dP/dX
Constant	−0.98	−0.23	−1.33	−0.31	Textiles	2.99	0.70
	(0.51)		(0.46)			(0.66)	
Age 15–24	1.906	0.44	7.04	1.64	Clothing	0.03	0.01
	(1.44)		(1.28)			(0.67)	
Age 25–44	0.87	0.20	0.52	0.12	Commerce	−2.05	−0.48
	(0.68)		(0.48)			(1.53)	
Married	−3.13	−0.73	−1.55	−0.36	Professional	−8.66	−2.02
	(0.63)		(0.69)			(2.63)	
Children 0–9	−2.32	−0.54	−0.61	−0.14	Personal Service	2.43	0.57
	(0.42)		(0.35)			(0.75)	
Persons per Room	2.54	0.59	0.72	0.17	Clerks + Typists	−1.43	−0.33
	(0.44)		(0.38)			(1.09)	
% More than 2 per Room	−4.56	−1.06	−1.35	−0.32	Mining	−2.39	−0.56
	(1.07)		(0.82)			(0.41)	
Male Unemployment Rate	0.43	0.10	−0.29	−0.07	Metals	−1.47	−0.34
	(0.46)		(0.39)			(0.49)	
Wage Rate	0.40	0.09	1.47	0.34	Wood + Furniture	−2.28	−0.53
	(0.74)		(0.65)			(1.12)	
					Building	−1.45	−0.34
						(1.63)	
					Transport	−2.70	−0.63
						(0.62)	
					Other	−1.29	−0.30
						(0.44)	
R^2	0.59					0.84	
Residual Sum of Squares	9.43					3.37	
Heteroscedasticity	0.003					0.62	

family. The results for the unemployment rate and for the wage rate correspond to our earlier findings. Both yield positive coefficients, but neither is significant.

Given that participation rates varied so widely across towns, it is perhaps surprising that so much of the variation can be explained by this set of variables. Furthermore, some of the coefficients are rather large and, for reasons given earlier, one might suspect that the household and demographic structure was influenced by labour market conditions faced by women in different towns and industrial regions. This view appears to be broadly confirmed by the results in equation (2) where the set of variables representing the occupational structure are included. Nearly 85 per cent of the variation is explained by the two sets of variables together and, when the occupational variables alone were used, the results (not shown) explained 65 per cent of the variation.

When the occupational variables are included, the coefficients on the labour supply variables change, in some cases dramatically. The most surprising result is the rise in the size and significance of the coefficient on the proportion of females aged 15–24. This coefficient is now implausibly large: the marginal probability derived from it now exceeds one. Though this result is fairly robust to the inclusion of other available variables, we think that it may be capturing the effects of omitted variables which we cannot measure. By contrast the remaining household variables now yield lower coefficients most of which are more consistent with the results from micro data. In particular, the proportion married, and especially the ratio of children to adult females, now have a smaller impact on the probability of participation. In addition, the effects of housing density and the degree of overcrowding are reduced, suggesting that these variables are correlated with the industrial structure of different towns.

The only variable to change sign is unemployment but this should not be too surprising since the incidence of unemployment was related to industrial and occupational structure. Though equation (2) suggests a net discouraged worker effect, the coefficient is small and insignificant. To the extent that it captures the balance of added and discouraged worker effects, unemployment does not appear to have affected participation strongly in either direction. More notable is the increase in the size and significance of the coefficient on the wage rate. This now implies a wage-elasticity of participation of 0.54. This result must be treated with caution since these are male wage rates, an imperfect proxy for female rates. If any weight can be attached to this finding, it points to an upward sloping labour supply curve provided the constraints and behaviour associated with different structures of demand for female labour are taken into account.[18]

Turning to the occupational categories, it is not surprising to find strongly significant positive coefficients for occupations such as textiles and personal service. The substantial lowering effects on participation of the white collar occupations, commerce, professional and clerks and typists is unexpected but could reflect differences in class composition across towns. The male-dominated occupations all appear with negative signs. The low participation rates in areas of heavy industry are reflected in the coefficients on mining, metals and transport. The coefficients may be interpreted by calculating the effect of transferring one male worker from one occupation to another. Thus, shifting one male from textiles to mining would lower participation by 1.26 females. Though the variables are coarsely aggregated occupational groups, they have significant and in some cases dramatic effects on the participation rates among towns.

Greenhalgh (1977) and McNabb (1977) analysed participation of married women across towns and sub-regions, respectively, based on the 1971

[18] An alternative interpretation would be that the male/female wage differential is determined by the occupational structure and that this is therefore captured by the occupational variables.

census. Both obtained positive coefficients for the female wage and found that the effect of a rise in all wage rates (male and females) increased participation. Their elasticities exceed those we obtained for 1931. The net effect of an overall rise in unemployment was found to be positive by Greenhalgh and negative by McNabb but only the latter controlled for industrial structure as reflected in the proportion in female intensive industries. Both obtained modest negative and insignificant coefficients for the presence of children. Overall, the results for 1931 seem broadly comparable with those of 1971 once the effects of occupational structure are allowed for. While there is some evidence of such effects in 1971, they are clearly larger in 1931 and the range of variation in participation rates was accordingly greater.

Conclusion

This paper has examined two sets of cross-section data on female participation: micro data for London, and aggregate data for towns in England and Wales. The aim was to shed new light on the factors affecting participation in the period before the recent growth in female activity rates.

Our analysis of the NSLLL underlined the importance of age and household status. It also confirmed the emphasis of the historical literature that it was marriage rather than the presence of children which led to low participation rates among wives relative to other groups. The added worker effect was identified for wives and household heads but was probably attenuated due to the existence of unemployment benefits. Wage elasticities were similar to those obtained on more recent cross sections but income effects were considerably larger. Overall the results are broadly consistent with other findings and suggest that the basic determinants of participation have not changed greatly though the relative impact of different variables has altered.

Our analysis of the census addresses the question: why do we observe such large variations in participation rates across towns? An explanation which relies on the typical supply side variables alone is inadequate. Our results support the views of historians who have stressed the importance of geographical differences in occupational and industrial structure. While these reflect differences in the strength of demand for female labour they probably also reflect different attitudes and behaviour arising from diverse industrial traditions. Once these effects are taken into account the effects of demographic and household variables are broadly similar to that obtained on postwar samples.

Static cross-section results may be a poor guide to understanding changes over time. We can only speculate on the issue of why female participation remained relatively low up to the 1930s. First, the results do not suggest on balance that participation was held down by the direct effects of high unemployment though such effects might have operated indirectly. Second, the effect of rising real wages would not have had such strong positive effects as during the postwar period because of the large negative household income effect. Third, changing attitudes towards married women working, and not changing rates of dependency, were critical to the expansion of labour market activity in this group. Finally, in some areas participation was as high as in the postwar era and it was the expansion of employment opportunities together with the breaking down of regional traditions in the other areas which contributed significantly to raising the national average. This feature has been largely overlooked and merits further attention.

University of Essex

APPENDIX

TABLE 1
Selection Equation and Wage Equation

	Selection Equation	*Wage Equation*
Constant	0.61	78.40
	(0.30)	(7.57)
Age 14–15	−0.24	−61.3
	(0.20)	(7.21)
Age 16–17	0.34	−42.2
	(0.21)	(6.44)
Age 18–19	0.72	−27.00
	(0.21)	(5.79)
Age 20–24	0.48	−6.92
	(0.16)	(5.26)
Age 35–44	0.01	4.33
	(0.15)	(7.63)
Age 45–54	−0.33	−15.95
	(0.17)	(8.78)
Age 55–64	−0.80	−27.73
	(0.19)	(10.45)
Age 65+	−1.76	−0.58
	(0.21)	(17.14)
Age not known	−0.04	1.32
	(0.23)	(8.72)
East Outer North	−0.23	2.91
	(0.19)	(7.02)
East Outer South	−0.37	5.84
	(0.19)	(6.86)
East External	−0.64	2.65
	(0.17)	(6.53)
West Inner	−0.19	7.16
	(0.17)	(6.04)
West Outer North (1)	−0.17	8.18
	(0.15)	(5.14)
West Outer North (2)	0.19	12.00
	(0.18)	(6.57)
West Outer South	−0.25	14.70
	(0.15)	(5.38)

TABLE 1
(continued)

	Selection Equation	*Wage Equation*
West External	− 0.05	16.96
	(0.20)	(7.15)
Head born in South East England	0.42	4.60
	(0.14)	(5.38)
Head of Houshold	−0.39	14.48
	(0.18)	(6.22)
Spouse of Head	−1.91	−20.68
	(0.15)	(12.82)
Children 0–4	−0.20	
	(0.09)	
Children 5–9	−0.10	
	(0.07)	
Children 10–13	−0.04	
	(0.08)	
No. of Adults	0.33	
	(0.07)	
No. of Participants	−0.26	
	(0.09)	
Head Unemployed	0.40	
	(0.26)	
Others Unemployed	0.34	
	(0.18)	
Household Income	−0.26	
(£ in a Full Week)	(0.04)	
Income below Minimum	0.21	
	(0.15)	
Non-Rent paying	0.12	
	(0.18)	
Selection correction		8.44
		(7.71)
log likelihood	−563.9	
Standard Error of Estimate		29.3

Notes

The additional variables used for identification are the borough dummies and "Head born in South East England" i.e., birth place of the household head, 1 if London or the South East and 0 if elsewhere.
Following the NSLLL classification the boroughs are grouped as follows:
East Inner (the excluded group): Bethnal Green, Shoreditch, Stepney, Bermondsey;
East Outer North: Hackney Poplar, Stoke Newington;
East Outer South: Deptford, Greenwich, Lewisham, Woolwich;
East External: Barking, East Ham, Leyton, Tottenham, West Ham;
West Inner: City, Finsbury, Holborn, Westminster, Southwark;
West Outer North (1): Fulham, Hammersmith, Islington, St. Pancras,
West Outer North (2): Chelsea, Hampstead, Kensington, Paddington, St. Marylebone,
West Outer South: Battersea, Camberwell, Lambeth, Wandsworth;
West External: Acton, Hornsey, Willesden.

REFERENCES

Andrews, I. O. (1918), *The Economic Effects of the War Upon Women and Children in Great Britain,* New York: Oxford University Press.

Braybon, G. (1981), *Women Workers in the First World War,* London: Croom Helm.

Eichengreen, B. (1987), "Unemployment in Interwar Britain: Dole or Doldrums" *Oxford Economic Papers,* 39, 597–623.

Eichengreen, B. and Freiwald, S. (1985), "From Survey to Sample: Labour Market Data for Interwar Britain", *Historical Methods,* 18, 125–136.

Gales, K. E. and Marks, P. H. (1974), "Twentieth Century Trends in the Work of Women in England and Wales", *Journal of the Royal Statistical Society,* Series A, 137, 60–74.

Gittins, D. (1982). *Fair Sex: Family Size and Structure 1900–39,* London: Hutchinson.

Greenhalgh, C. (1977), "A Labour Supply Function for Married Women in Great Britain", *Eonomica,* 44, 249–265.

Hakim, C. (1978), "Sexual Divisions within the Labour Force: Occupational Segregation", *Department of Employment Gazette,* 92, 1264–1278.

Hakim, C. (1980), "Census Reports as Documentary Evidence: The Census Commentaries, 1801–1951", *Sociological Review,* 28, 551–580.

Hatton, T. J. (1986), "Female Labour Force Participation: The Enigma of the Interwar Period", Essex Discussion Paper, 285.

Heckman, J. (1979) "Sample Selection Bias as a Specification Error" *Econometrica,* 47, 153–161.

Heim, C. (1984), "Structural Transformation, the Demand for New Labour and Uneven Development in Advanced Economies: The Case of Interwar Britain" *Journal of Economic History,* 44, 585–595.

Home Office Memorandum Cmd 3508 (1930), *A Study of the Factors which have Operated in the past and those which are operating now to Determine the Distribution of Women in Industry,* London: HMSO.

Joshi, H. (1986), "Participation in Paid Work: Evidence from the Women and Employment Survey" in R. Blundell and I. Walker (eds.) *Unemployment, Search and Labour Supply,* Cambridge: University Press.

Killingsworth, M. R. (1983), *Labour Supply,* Cambridge: University Press.

Killingsworth, M. R. and Heckman, J. J. (1986), "Female Labour Supply" in O. Ashenfelter and R. Layard (eds.) *Handbook of Labour Economics,* Vol 1, Amsterdam, North Holland.

Koenker, R. (1981) "A Note on Studentizing a Test for Heteroscedasticity", *Journal of Econometrics,* 17, 107–112.

Layard, R., Barton, M. and Zabalza, A. (1980), "Married Women's Participation and Hours", *Economica,* 47, 51–73.

Leser, C. E. V., (1952), Men and Women in Industry *Economic Journal,* 34, 438–452.

Lewis, J. (1984), *Women in England,* Brighton: Wheatsheaf.

Linsley, C. A. (1986), *The Housing Market, Deprivation and Household Behaviour in Interwar Britain: A Microeconometric Analysis of the New Survey of London Life and Labour,* Ph.D. Thesis, University of Essex.

Llewellyn-Smith, H. (ed.), (1930–5) *The New Survey of London Life and Labour,* Vols 1–9, London: P. S. King.

Madalla, G. S. (1983), *Limited-Dependent and Qualitative Variables in Econometrics,* Cambridge: University Press.

Margo, R. (1988), "Interwar Unemployment in the United States: Evidence from the 1940 Census Sample" in B. Eichengreen and T. J. Hatton (eds.), *Interwar Unemployment in International Perspective,* Dordrecht: Kluwer.

McCalman, J. (1971), "The Impact of the First World War on Female Employment in England", *Labour History,* 21, 36–47.

McNabb, R. (1977), "The Labour Force Participation of Married Women", *Manchester School,* 45, 221–235.

PENCAVEL, J. (1986), "Labour Supply of Men: A Survey" in O. Ashenfelter and R. Layard (eds.) *Handbook of Labour Economics,* Vol. 1, Amsterdam: North Holland.
PIGOU, A. C. (1947), *Aspects of British Economic History 1918–45,* London: Macmillan.
RILEY, D. (1981), "The Free Mothers; Pronatalism and Working Women in Industry at the End of the Last War in Britain", *History Workshop,* 11, 59–118.
ROBERTS, E. (1982), "Working Wives and their Families", in T. Barker and M. Drake (eds.) *Population and Society in Britain 1850–1980,* London: Batsford.
ROBERTS, E. (1988), *Women's Work 1840–1940,* London: Macmillan.
SPRAGUE, A. (1988), "Work Experience Earnings and Participation: Evidence from the Women and Employment Survey" Oxford Institute of Economics and Statistics Discussion Paper 43.
STRACHEY, R. (1934), "Current Social Statistics: The Census: Occupations of Women", *Political Quarterly,* 5, 549–561.
SUMMERFIELD, P. (1984), *Women Working in the Second World War,* London: Croom Helm.
WOYTINSKY, W. S. (1940), "Additional Workers and the Labour Market during Depressions: A Reply to Mr. Humphrey" *Journal of Political Economy,* 48, 735–740.
ZABALZA, A. (1983), "The CES Utility Function, Non-Linear Budget Constraints and Labour Supply. Results on Female Participation and Hours", *Economic Journal,* 93, 312–330.

Oxford Economic Papers 40 (1988), 719–750

PRICE AND EXCHANGE RATE DETERMINATION DURING THE GREENBACK SUSPENSION

By CHARLES W. CALOMIRIS*

I. Introduction

DURING the suspension of convertibility of greenbacks into gold from 1862 through 1878 the greenback price of the gold dollar ranged from par to 2.5 (see Fig. 1). The monetarist explanation for these exchange rate movements espoused by Friedman and Schwartz (1963) views the supply of greenbacks and the growing real demand for money as the sources of domestic price movements and, through them, the depreciation and subsequent appreciation of the currency. A different explanation provided by Mitchell (1903, 1908) and Studenski and Krooss (1963) argues that expectations regarding government fiscal policy and fiscal shocks (e.g., battle reports), which affected the probability and expected timing of resumption of specie convertibility, caused changes in current exchange rates and prices.

Recent theoretical contributions by Sargent and Wallace (1981), among others, have demonstrated the potential importance of fiscal expectations for determining the current level of prices and exchange rates. For example, an expectation of fiscal profligacy may imply future money supply growth and inflation which causes the current level of real money demanded to decline; thus for a given level of current money supplied, the price level rises and the currency depreciates. Assuming the market in which currencies are traded operates efficiently, movements in the exchange rate properly track news of changes in expected government policy.

Evidence from currency and securities markets (discussed below) indicates that mid-nineteenth-century American financial markets responded to expectations of government policy changes in a manner consistent with market efficiency. In applying the Sargent–Wallace approach to the history of greenback exchange rate determination, however, one must take account of institutional peculiarities of the period. First, for most of the period of suspension the supply of paper high-powered money was not held fixed by the government; national banks were authorized to supply a perfect substitute for greenbacks in the form of national bank notes. From mid-1870 on bank notes rather than greenbacks were the marginal component of the paper high-powered money supply. Second, the potential for a return to promised gold dollar parity meant that expectations of fiscal

* I would like to thank Moses Abramovitz, Michael Bordo, Lou Cain, Paul David, Paul Evans, Glenn Hubbard, Jonathan Hughes, Joel Mokyr, Larry Neal, Cormac O'Grada, Bruce D. Smith, Peter Temin, Elmus Wicker, Gavin Wright, and seminar participants at Stanford University, Northwestern University, the University of Chicago, and Indiana University for comments on preliminary versions of this paper.

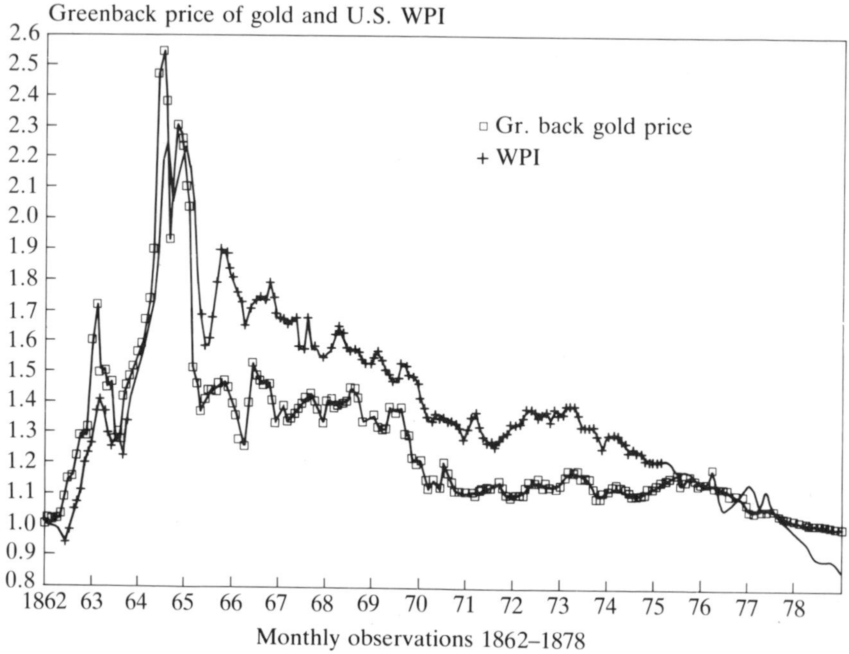

FIG. 1. Greenback price of gold and U.S. WPI

policy influenced exchange rates primarily through their effect on the perceived probability and timing of resumption.

Section II presents a model of financial markets for the post-Civil War years in which the institutional peculiarities of the money supply process and the potential for resumption play important roles in exchange rate determination. The results of the model lend support to the historical accounts of Mitchell and Studenski and Krooss. Current or expected marginal changes in the supply of greenbacks have no effect on prices or exchange rates, while resumption expectations play a central role in determining the current exchange rate and price level. Resumption expectations imply expected future values of the exchange rate and price level. Government money-supply policy effectively pegs the nominal rate of interest and the equilibrium rate of expected inflation. The nominal money stock adjusts endogenously to the level demanded (through the issue of national bank notes, the creation of bank deposits, and gold flows) given the predetermined nominal interest rate and price level.

Section III provides evidence to support the assumptions and conclusions of the model, including evidence of the importance of fiscal policy news in short- and long-run exchange rate and price determination for the period of greenback suspension.

II. A model of price determination

Defining the money stock

In order to discuss the role of money in price determination one must first define the relevant monetary aggregate. Defining the money stock is always a delicate task—all the more so for the Greenback Era. Potential candidates for inclusion are gold, greenbacks, national bank notes, and the deposits at state and national banks. The uses of these various components of money differed. National bank notes and greenbacks passed as currency; gold was used as a transacting medium primarily in California or, more generally, for foreign transactions; deposits became increasingly popular relative to currency during the period as urbanization and the development of clearing houses facilitated check clearing and consumer familiarity (see Cagan (1965)). Each component of money was introduced through a different supply process. Gold was produced in the U.S., and exported or imported to meet demand; deposits were issued by state and national banks; notes were issued by national banks under strict government regulations, and greenbacks were issued directly by the government.

Before proceeding to the issue of how the aggregate supply of notes and greenbacks was determined, it is important to discuss their substitutability. National bank notes and greenbacks traded at par even when their respective supplies varied independently. This indicates, *de facto,* that they were perfect substitutes. Furthermore, note issues were printed by the government and backed 111 percent by government bonds held on deposit at the Treasury. Thus notes were essentially indirect obligations of the government, no different—from the standpoint of the public—from greenbacks. There was one segment of the market, however, for whom greenbacks and notes were not perfect substitutes: the national banks. National banks were required to hold between 6 percent and 25 percent reserves in lawful money (gold or greenbacks)[1] on all note issues, until 1874 when this requirement was reduced to a uniform 5 percent. Because gold was trading at a premium relative to greenbacks throughout the suspension, greenbacks were a superior reserve asset for banks relative to gold. Banks were always inframarginal holders of greenbacks (the public always held both notes and greenbacks); therefore, banks' preference for holding greenbacks over bank notes did not influence the relative value of greenbacks and banknotes.

Consumers' money demand

The question of whether the nominal money supply was controlled by government policy is central to the discussion of exchange rate determination. In order to show that money—however defined—was not fixed by

[1] There were interest-bearing legal tender notes as well. Greenbacks were always the marginal reserve asset, as discussed in footnote 4 below.

TABLE 1
Selected Monetary Statistics

	Total Greenbacks G	Bank Holdings of Greenbacks G^P	Public Holdings of Greenbacks G^P	Public Holdings of National Bank Notes N^P	Total Bills $(G^P + N^P)$ B	Wholesale Prices P	Real Bills (B/P)	Real Income y	$\frac{B/P}{y}$	Commercial Paper Rate
	(1)	(2)	(3)	(4)	(5)	(6)	(7)	(8)	(9)	(10)
1868	328,572	100,166	228,406	294,369	522,775	158	3,308.7	7,927	0.417	6.69
1869	314,767	80,934	233,833	291,750	525,583	147	3,575.4	8,712	0.410	9.43
1870	324,963	94,573	230,390	288,648	519,038	135	3,844.7	9,627	0.399	6.52
1871	343,069	122,138	220,931	311,406	532,337	127	4,191.6	10,290	0.407	5.55
1872	346,169	122,994	223,225	329,037	552,262	137	4,031.1	11,000	0.366	7.17
1873	348,464	106,381	242,083	338,962	581,045	132	4,401.9	11,740	0.375	7.97
1874	371,421	103,108	268,313	340,266	608,579	124	4,907.9	11,970	0.410	5.70
1875	349,686	87,493	262,193	340,547	602,740	117	5,151.6	12,070	0.427	4.76
1876	331,447	90,837	240,610	316,121	556,731	106	5,252.2	12,470	0.421	4.54
1877	337,899	78,004	259,895	301,289	561,184	106	5,294.2	13,010	0.407	4.44
1878	320,906	71,643	249,263	311,724	560,987	88	6,374.9	14,770	0.432	4.22

Sources: Greenbacks and bank notes are expressed in thousands of nominal dollars. Data on total greenbacks, bank notes in the hands of the public and price are from *Historical Statistics of the United States*, first edition, series x433, x434, and app. 24, respectively. Data are for June. Real output is from Officer (1981) and commercial paper rates are from Macaulay (1938). Column (10) is a five-month average of commercial paper rates centered in June. Bank holdings of greenbacks are from the *Report of the Comptroller of the Currency*, 1879.

government policy, it is sufficient to establish that the narrowest monetary aggregate which includes the component supplied by the government was not fixed by government policy. Thus in order to demonstrate money supply endogeneity, *a fortiori,* I assume that the demand for real paper "bills" (greenbacks plus national bank notes) is separable from the demands for deposits and gold.[2] For simplicity I develop the model without deposit and gold demands initially and include them subsequently.

Consumers' demand for real paper bills takes the general form:

$$\left(\frac{B}{P}\right)^D = h(y, i_{pb}); \qquad h_1 > 0, \qquad h_2 < 0; \tag{1}$$

where B is nominal bills, P is the price level, y is real income, and i_{pb} is the nominal yield on private bonds.

By definition,

$$B \equiv N^p + G^p, \tag{2}$$

where N^p is public holdings of national bank notes and G^p is public holdings of greenbacks. The supply of total greenbacks is assumed fixed by the government.[3] By definition:

$$G \equiv G^p + G^b; \tag{3}$$

where G^b is the banking sector's holdings of greenback reserves.[4]

[2] Table 1 provides some empirical evidence for the stability of the demand for paper bills. The ratio of real bills to real income (shown in column (9)) is nearly constant, and its variation over time is negatively correlated with that of interest rates (column (10)).

[3] Our assumption of greenback supply exogeneity requires some qualification. Under the formula stipulated from January 1875 to May 1878 by Congress, total greenback supply responded to bank note supply such that greenbacks were reduced by \$0.8 for every \$1 of new bank notes. The supply of greenbacks, however, could not fall below \$300 million. Secretary Bristow interpreted this law to permit reductions in greenbacks as *gross*, rather than net, note issues rose. This regulation had no effect on the equilibrium supply of bills, since bank notes still could rise to adjust as needed. Thus this law does not affect the solution for equilibrium discussed below.

[4] State bank holdings of greenbacks or national bank notes as reserves against deposits are ignored in equations (2) and (3) because their inclusion would complicate, but not alter, any of our conclusions. State bank deposits were a small fraction of total deposits—\$143 million out of \$796 million total deposits in 1878 (see Studenski and Krooss (1963), p. 177). National bank holdings of bank notes or greenbacks as reserves against deposits are also excluded from equations (2) and (3) for simplicity; moreover, since national banks which issued notes as well as deposits enjoyed economies of scope in reserve holdings it is unclear what the true marginal reserve cost of deposit supply would be. Thus the deposit reserve cost was less for national than for state banks, and similarly, the effective required reserves on notes were less than the legal reserve requirement τ.

Greenbacks were not the only legal reserve for note issue; gold and interest-bearing legal tender notes were other options. From the standpoint of the model's solution, it is necessary to verify that greenbacks were the *marginal* reserve asset. To discover whether greenbacks were the marginal reservable asset one must check to see that: (1) required reserves for total notes issued exceeded the available supply of interest-bearing legal tender notes; and (2) required reserves for outstanding notes did not exceed the available supply of greenbacks plus interest-bearing legal tender. These are sufficient conditions because the order of opportunity

Banks' note supply

The supply of national bank notes depended on the expected profitability of bank note issues. Banks which devoted a unit of capital to purchasing bonds as backing for notes earned dividends from government bonds purchased, less the cost of holding zero-interest greenback reserves and paying a 1 percent tax on notes outstanding. The supply function for national bank notes, given free entry, takes the form of a zero-economic-profit condition. The profit condition, derived in the Appendix, may be written:

$$s = L(i_b - (0.9\tau)i_l - 0.009) - \pi^e, \quad (4)$$

where s is the real expected marginal profit rate banks earn from devoting capital to purchasing bonds in order to issue zero-interest bank notes, π^e is expected inflation, τ is the proportion of greenback reserves required relative to notes issued, and i_l is the expected return to bank loans.[5] s is given exogeneously by alternative uses of bank capital. The profit rate reflects (the inverse of) the amount of capital one must devote to the purchase of bonds (L), the yield earned on government bonds (i_b), the opportunity cost of holding greenback reserves on bank notes [$(0.9\tau)i_l$], and the federal tax on bank note issues [0.009]. The coefficient 0.9 on the greenback reserve cost term reflects a 111 percent bond reserve requirement, and the 0.009 tax cost reflects a 1 percent federal tax on national bank notes, again multiplied by the note-to-bond reserve ratio.

Footnote 4 (*continued*)

cost from highest to lowest was gold, then greenbacks, then interest-bearing reserves. These conditions are verified easily. As shown in Table 1, the total supply of notes from 1868 to 1878 varied between \$300 million and \$340 million, while total outstanding greenbacks varied between \$314 million and \$348 million because they exclude issues not in circulation. During this period, interest-bearing legal tender notes were not sufficient to provide required reserves for all bank notes. Interest-bearing legal tender consisted of the one- and two-year notes of 1863 and the compound interest notes of 1863 and 1864. By 1867, only the compound-interest notes circulated. National bank holdings of these notes reached a peak of \$84 million in 1867. (*The Report of the Comptroller of the Currency*, 1879). The compound interest notes were exchanged for the 3 percent certificates of 1867. By the end of 1868, interest-bearing legal tender had practically disappeared from the economy. Even in 1867, bank holdings of legal tender currency always exceeded holdings of compound interest notes. This means that greenbacks were needed over and above interest-bearing reserves. The supply of greenbacks was sufficient to keep banks from resorting to gold. Therefore, greenbacks were clearly the relevant reservable asset for notes for 1868–1878.

[5] The relevant i_l is the lowest i_l among banks eligible to issue notes, since banks competed nationally in supplying notes. Legal requirements ranged between 5 percent and 25 percent depending on the date and location of the bank. Initially, only New York banks were required to keep the full 25 percent reserves; other cities' banks had a small effective reserve requirement of 12.5 percent; country banks had an even smaller requirement of 6 percent. In June 1874 reserve requirements were lowered for all banks to 5 percent. Presumably the true costs of holding greenback reserves were less than that indicated in equation (4), since superfluous reserves on bank notes would allow national banks to reduce reserves they would otherwise hold against deposits.

Steady-state equilibrium

We solve for the steady state where prices adjust fully and real output is predetermined in factor markets ($y = \bar{y}$).[6] Let the real rate of interest in the private bond market be determined exogeneously by international productive opportunities and time preference $r_{pb} = \bar{r}_{pb}$.[7]

For simplicity, assume that the real return on bank loans r_l equals the real rate on bonds, due to arbitrage between bank and bond finance. Abstracting from risk differentials, $r_l = \bar{r}_{pb}$.

Banks were not the sole holders of reservable bonds. As Cagan (1965) and Friedman and Schwartz (1963) point out, this holds throughout the period of greenback suspension. In this case, the real rate of return on bonds used as reserves for bank notes is governed by arbitrage across bond markets and is exogeneous to the supply and demand of bank notes. Thus, abstracting once again from risk differentials, $r_b = \bar{r}_{pb}$.

Rewrite equation (4) under our assumption of common real expected rates of return across financial markets ($r_{pb} = r_b = r_l$):

$$\pi^e = \frac{s - L(1 - 0.9\tau)r_{pb} + 0.009L}{L(1 - 0.9\tau) - 1}, \qquad (5)$$

where $[L(1 - 0.9\tau) - 1]$ is positive (see the derivation in the Appendix). Equation (5) determines the equilibrium rate of expected inflation, and hence, the equilibrium nominal interest rate ($\bar{r}_{pb} + \pi^e$). Under the assumptions that banks earn a competitive return on capital devoted to note creation, and that the cost of a government "license" to issue currency is described in equation (4), equation (5) solves for the level of inflation (or deflation) which is consistent with zero economic profits to marginal note-issuing banks. Intuitively, the potential profitability of issuing national bank notes limits the equilibrium rate of seigniorage (or inflation tax). Note that for identical non-negative values of r_{pb} and s equation (5) implies a positive nominal interest rate, since $\pi^e > -r_{pb}$.

Even under such simplifying assumptions, with many variables determined exogenously to monetary policy, N and P remain indeterminate in equations (1) through (4) in the absence of a description of the process by which price *level* expectations are formed. Rewrite equation (1) substituting $\bar{r}_{pb}$, $\bar{y}$, and π^e from equation (5):[8]

$$\left(\frac{B}{P}\right)^* = h\{\bar{y}, \bar{r}_{pb} + \pi^e\}. \qquad (6)$$

[6] For evidence to support the assumption of relatively short-run price flexibility for this period see Sachs (1980), Calomiris (1985), Calomiris and Hubbard (1986, 1987), and Delong and Summers (1984), as well as the discussion in Section III.

[7] Real interest rate parity equations which equate pound-dollar forward premia with the London–New York commerical paper rate differential (using monthly data) support this assumption. (See Calomiris and Hubbard (1987)).

[8] Note how different the solution would be under maintained specie parity. If a credible government return to fixed gold parity were accomplished, π^e would be exogenous. At the same time, the supply of greenbacks would be determined by redemption at the Treasury, in order to bring supply and demand into equilibrium.

Equation (6) solves for real bills $(B/P)^*$ but not for N, B, or P. From equations (2) and (3) we have:

$$\frac{G - G^b + N}{P} = \left(\frac{B}{P}\right)^*, \tag{7}$$

or

$$\frac{G + (1-\tau)N}{P} = \left(\frac{B}{P}\right)^*. \tag{8}$$

Given G and $(B/P)^*$ there is no unique solution for B^*, N^*, and P^*.

A unique solution for nominal bills, notes and the price level can be obtained if one adds to these equations an expectation of a particular greenback price of gold (ε) at some fixed point in the future due, say, to certain resumption at par at time x:

$$E\varepsilon_x = 1. \tag{9}$$

Assume the gold price of commodities (P^s) is given on world markets:

$$\bar{P}^s = \frac{\varepsilon}{P}. \tag{10}$$

This assumption is defended in Section III, below. Setting $\bar{P}^s = 1$ we have:

$$EP_x = 1. \tag{11}$$

This terminal condition for the price level, together with the equilibrium rate of inflation from (5), determines a unique price path P_t recursively. Given τ, G, $(B/P)^*$, and P_t we can solve for B_t and N_t as well.

Thus expectations are crucial for determining the levels of nominal variables. Note that *changes in G have no effect on the equilibrium time path of price or the exchange rate.* The time paths of the price level and the exchange rate instead depend crucially on the probability of parity resumption and its timing. As the likelihood of parity resumption rises or as events occur which lead people to anticipate that resumption will happen sooner than they had previously expected, the price level will fall. Political news of changes in resumption policy, or changes in fiscal policy which affect the ability or the costliness of the government's resuming would influence the current exchange rate and price level.[9]

[9] In order to verify that our equilibrium solution is appropriate we must make sure that the equilibrium values we derive do not lead to contradictions of our assumptions. The first condition to verify is the bondholder arbitrage condition. This is only relevant if the public is holding some of the bonds used by banks as reserves—that is, if banks are not holding all government bonds as required backing for bank notes. Implicitly we have assumed that:

$$RB^s > (1.1)N^*,$$

where RB^s is the exogenous supply of "reservable" bonds. If this condition were violated, equation (5) would no longer hold. In this equilibrium case, N^* would be directly constrained

The intuition for the result that the price level is independent of greenback supply is that so long as an endogenous perfect substitute (bank notes) exists for nominal greenbacks on the *margin,* the nominal supply of greenbacks will have no effect on the nominal equilibrium supply of total bills, and hence will have no effect on the time path of the price level. This is illustrated in Fig. 4. The current price level is given by world gold prices and resumption expectations. The real supply function for bills has two components: the exogenous (vertical) supply of greenbacks and the (horizontal) supply function for national bank notes. Marginal changes in the supply of greenbacks (shifts to the right or left in the supply function) are offset by changes in national bank note supply; real money, the price level, nominal bills, and expected inflation remain the same.[10]

Footnote 9 (*continued*)

by the scarcity of reservable bonds:

$$N^* = (0.9)RB^s.$$

Starting at time x we would solve recursively for the expected inflation rate using this path of N^* and the condition $EP_x = 1$, in order to satisfy the demand function for real bills. In this case, the time path of price would be influenced by the supply of greenbacks, because an increase in the supply of greenbacks would not be offset by a reduction in the supply of notes. Of course, this would only be true for a limited range of increases in G, since large increases in G would eventually cause a relaxation of the bond supply constraint. These ruminations are, from the standpoint of history, quite beside the point, since the assumed condition was never violated during the period of greenback suspension (see Friedman and Schwartz (1963), p. 23).

Another counterfactual caveat to our equilibrium arises from the potentially binding constraint that the total supply of greenbacks poses for the supply of national bank notes. In other words, our solution implicitly requires that, at each point in time,

$$N^* < \frac{G}{\tau}.$$

Otherwise, the public holds no greenbacks and the requirement that banks redeem bank notes in greenbacks on request implies only a one-sided arbitrage condition: The price level denominated in greenbacks (P^g) must be greater than or equal to the price level denominated in bank notes (P^n):

$$P^g \geqslant P^n.$$

In this case,

$$B^* = \frac{G}{\tau}.$$

Now the equilibrium rate of expected inflation, the time path of B^* and the condition $EP^g = 1$ would be used to solve recursively for P^n in order to satisfy the real demand for bills. As before, this caveat is irrelevant to the history of greenback suspension, because the public always held greenbacks as well as bank notes (see Table 1).

A final counterfactual caveat involves the non-negativity constraint on national bank notes. If $N^* = 0$ then $B^* = G$. In this case, one would solve recursively for the time path of price and inflation given EP_x and the demand function for real bills.

[10] In principle, changes in the supply of greenbacks could influence expectations of government resumption policy (and hence, the current exchange rate) by altering the potential gain to the government from default. Empirical evidence reported below, however, does not support such a connection between greenback issues and exchange rates.

Adding the demands for gold and deposits to the model

In addition to bills, the public held deposits and used gold for foreign transactions, domestic transactions (especially in California), and potentially for portfolio diversification. Write the demand for gold as:

$$\left(\frac{C\varepsilon}{P}\right)^D = \gamma(y, i_{pb}, i_d, f); \qquad \gamma_1, \gamma_4 > 0, \qquad \gamma_2, \gamma_3 < 0, \tag{12}$$

where C is the gold holdings of the public, i_d is the interest rate earned on deposits, and f is the expected rate of greenback depreciation relative to gold. The demand functions for bills and deposits Q take the form:

$$\left(\frac{B}{P}\right)^D = h(y, i_{pb}, i_d, f); \qquad h_1 > 0, \qquad h_2, h_3, h_4 < 0, \tag{13}$$

and

$$\left(\frac{Q}{P}\right)^D = \delta(y, i_{pb}, i_d, f); \qquad \delta_1, \delta_3 > 0, \qquad \delta_2, \delta_4 < 0. \tag{14}$$

Given (10), expected inflation and currency depreciation are equal:

$$\pi^e = f. \tag{15}$$

Abstracting from the spread between bank loan and deposit rates of return, we may rewrite equations (12) through (14) to solve for equilibrium values of real bills, deposits, and gold:

$$\left(\frac{B}{P}\right)^* = h\{\bar{y}, \bar{r}_{pb} + \pi^e, (\bar{r}_{pb} + \pi^e), \pi^e\}, \tag{16}$$

$$\left(\frac{Q}{P}\right)^* = \delta\{\bar{y}, \bar{r}_{pb} + \pi^e, (\bar{r}_{pb} + \pi^e), \pi^e\}, \tag{17}$$

$$(C\bar{P}^s)^* = \gamma\{\bar{y}, \bar{r}_{pb} + \pi^e, (\bar{r}_{pb} + \pi^e), \pi^e\}. \tag{18}$$

As before, in order to solve for B^*, N^*, and P^* one must incorporate price expectations from equation (11). C^* and Q^* are derived solely from the demand equations and the assumption of perfectly elastic gold and deposit supplies (i.e., exogenous real interest rates).

Forming price expectations under uncertainty

When resumption is uncertain agents update their beliefs about the timing and likelihood of resumption as news emerges of changes in the government's ability or willingness to resume convertibility.

What would have determined the value of greenbacks if the government had announced a credible policy of never returning to any maintained parity? To the extent that this event had a positive probability, the potential purely fiduciary value of greenbacks was relevant for their current value. In the context of our model, without an expectation of a future price level, the current price level is indeterminate, because the total supply of bills is endogenous. Additional assumptions regarding the behavior of the government under a fiduciary regime are necessary to solve this indeterminacy problem.

A simple solution to this probelm is to posit a target price path under the potential fiduciary regime, to which all other government policy instruments would adjust. For simplicity, assume the fiduciary target path would be $P_t = \hat{P}$ for all time. As long as $\hat{P} > 1$, expectations of a quicker or more likely return to maintained parity would lead today to currency appreciation and price deflation. Assuming resumption is expected to occur, or not to occur, at time x, the expectation at time t of the price level at time x is the probability weighted sum of par value and the fiduciary price level:

$$E_t P_x = \tilde{a}_t(1) + (1 - \tilde{a}_t)\hat{P}, \tag{19}$$

where $\tilde{a}$ is the probability of resumption, and $\hat{P} > EP_x > 1$. Under risk neutrality, to arrive at the current price level P_0 one solves for the price path recursively from $E_0 P_x$ using the value of π^e derived from equation (5):

$$P_0 = (E_0 P_x) \exp(-\pi^e x). \tag{20}$$

"News" which implies quicker expected resumption (a reduction in x), a higher probability of resumption, or a lower expected fiduciary price level, all reduce the price level today:[11]

$$P_0 = Z(\tilde{a}, x, \hat{P}); \qquad Z_1 < 0,\ Z_2,\ Z_3 > 0. \tag{21}$$

III. Empirical evidence

My empirical efforts to verify the applicability of the model presented in Section II to the period of greenback suspension divide in two: first, to evaluate some of the assumptions which underlie the model; second, to provide evidence in support of the connection between expectations of appreciation and the perceived long-run backing of the currency.

Verifying the assumptions of the model

Among the important assumptions of the model in Section II are: (1) free entry in bank note supply (2) the efficiency of asset markets; and (3) the

[11] An extension of the model would be to consider the behavior of risk-averse agents, for whom higher moments of probability distributions would be relevant. If agents were risk-averse, for example, mean-preserving increases in the variance of density functions for the timing of resumption and the fiduciary equilibrium price would reduce the current value of greenbacks relative to gold (and commodities). Risk aversion is potentially important for understanding the portfolio demand for gold in an equilibrium with expected deflation. The findings of Roll (1972) and those discussed below suggest that deflation was expected, and we know gold was held by many agents, though one might argue that foreign transactions and California regulations, rather than risk-aversion, were at the heart of the demand for gold. Gold was required to pay interest on coin-paying bonds, to pay duties, for foreign trade, and for transactions in California (see Lester (1939)).

international determination of commodity gold prices. I discuss each in turn.

A free-entry caveat: the nominal ceiling on national bank notes, 1867–1870

Our model assumes an endogenous, competitively supplied level of national bank notes; yet national banks did not come into existence until 1863 and a nominal ceiling of $300 million was placed on bank note supply initially. Once that amount had been subscribed, no more notes could be issued. As Dewey (1903) shows, the aggregate note ceiling was a binding constraint through 1870, though legislated regional distribution guidelines were never enforced.[12] The raising of the note ceiling constraint in July 1870 to $354 million rendered the ceiling irrelevant until it was eliminated altogether in January 1875. Still, from 1867 until 1870 the $300 million ceiling on notes, together with the supply of greenbacks, fixed the supply of nominal bills (see Fig. 2). The effective ceiling on notes until July 1870 made greenbacks supply a binding constraint on total bills. Potentially, this could have exerted an important influence on nominal variables.

Analyzing the effect of the supply of greenbacks on the price level and exchange rate for the period 1862–1866 is difficult because the supply function for state bank notes and their substitutability with greenbacks would have to be specified, as well as the peculiarities of the initial period of adjustment in national bank note supply from 1864 to 1867. Instead I focus on the period from 1867 on.

How does the $300 million national bank note ceiling change the solution for the equilibrium time path of price for 1867 to 1870? The solution depends on whether agents anticipate the relaxation of the note supply constraint. Suppose first that they do. Then from the time the constraint is relaxed, t_1 to time x, the equilibrium is as before. From the initial moment to t_1, one solves for the time path of price recursively using the price level at t_1 as the starting point. π^e at t_1 is the (higher) rate of expected inflation consistent with $\bar{N}$ (the note ceiling), the price level at t_1, and the real bills demand function.

Note that equation (6) no longer determines π^e; in the presence of the note ceiling, competition among banks for providing notes does not occur. Instead equation (6) solves for the new higher level of equilibrium seigniorage rent, s, given the solution for π^e.[13] If prior to its removal the

[12] See Dewey (1903), pp. 385–387.

[13] The rate of seigniorage on note issues is difficult to measure directly. First, the calculation depends crucially on the measured opportunity cost to banks in the loan market, which James (1976) argues varied greatly across regions. Second, the extent of leveraging of bank capital in bond purchasing by banks is crucial and unclear. Third, there may be invisible costs or benefits to banks from issuing notes. Finally, effective reserve requirements varied depending on the location of the bank and its reserve-to-deposit ratio. These issues are discussed in the Appendix.

Calomiris (1985) reports measures of nominal seigniorage. Though these estimates provide only a very rough indication of nominal profitability, perhaps with greater confidence one can discuss the estimated changes in note profitability through time. The removal of the nominal

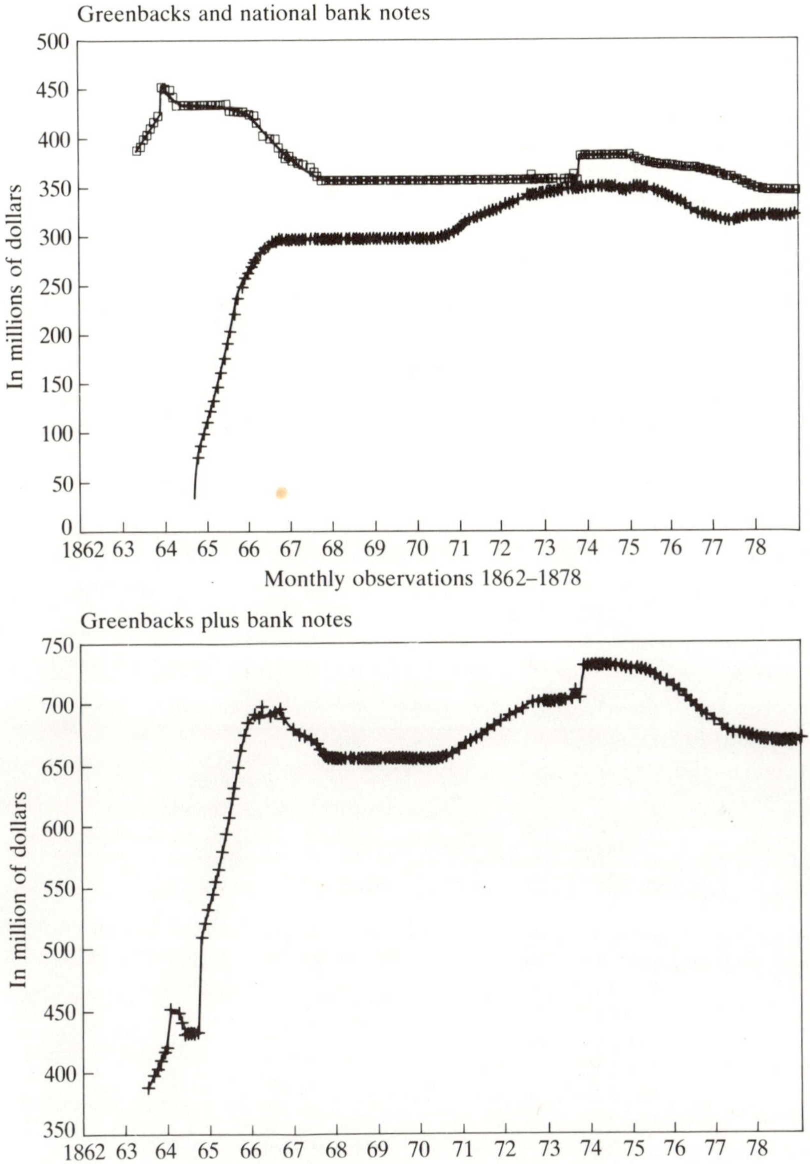

FIG. 2. Greenbacks and National Bank Notes

Footnote 13 (*continued*)
ceiling on notes does not seem to have had a large impact on nominal profits, though by all measures there is a slight decline in profit from the end of 1870 to the end of 1871. At the same time there was a 0.5 percent decrease in estimated long-run expected deflation, therefore, the small nominal decline in seigniorage may have been associated with a slightly greater real decline. For 1874–78, however, nominal and real profitability rise to higher levels. This confirms the view that profits from note issue were not significantly higher during the period the ceiling acted as an effective constraint, and that the ceiling offered little liquidity rent to note issuers.

ceiling were expected to persist, then one would solve in the same manner for the time path of price recursively from P_x rather than P_1.

Under the binding note ceiling expectations of resumption remain an essential component of the solution for the price level and exchange rate through their effect on ε_x and P_x, but the price and exchange rate paths from time zero to the time the ceiling is relaxed also will depend on the inital exogenous level of bills supplied. The level of nominal notes initially supplied, along with P_x, determine the equilibrium rate of seigniorage, and therefore, the rate of inflation.

One way to measure the importance of the ceiling's effect on the time path of price from 1867 to 1870 is to compare short-run expected rates of inflation before 1870 with those afterward. If the ceiling was important, expected rates of inflation should have been higher before 1870 than after.

No comparable short-term yields on gold- and greenback-denominated securities exist from which to derive inflation expectations. Actual annual inflation and greenback depreciation for 1867 through 1878 are provided in Table 2. Though *ex post* data may be poor indicators of the relevant *ex ante* series, to the extent that annual inflation and depreciation were foreseen, Table 2 suggests that expected inflation or greenback depreciation was not

TABLE 2
Annual Rates of Inflation and Greenback Depreciation

	Percent Inflation	*Percent Greenback Depreciation*
July 1867–July 1868	−2.47	2.43
July 1868–July 1869	−5.33	−4.18
July 1869–July 1870	−9.78	−15.21
July 1870–July 1871	−6.24	−3.26
July 1871–July 1872	7.68	1.06
July 1872–July 1873	−2.94	1.40
July 1873–July 1874	−5.83	−4.85
July 1874–July 1875	−5.63	4.37
July 1875–July 1876	−9.38	−2.88
July 1876–July 1877	−0.94	−5.83
July 1877–July 1878	−15.48	−4.19

Sources: Inflation is defined using the Warren-Pearson monthly wholesale price index, *Historical Statistics of the United States,* first edition, series app. 24, Greenback depreciation relative to gold is measured using end-of-month exchange rates reported in *Hunt's Merchants' Magazine* and *The Commercial and Finanical Chronicle.* Inflation and depreciation are measured as rates of change in the three-month averages of the price index and exchange rate, centered in July.

reduced after July 1870. If one compares the three years before July 1870 with the three following years, inflation and currency depreciation actually were greater on average in the later period.

These considerations suggest that from 1867 to 1870 the nominal ceiling on bank notes was not an important influence on the value of greenbacks. That is, the constrained and (counterfactual) unconstrained levels of nominal bank note supply were not very different from 1867 to 1870.

Market efficiency: tests and implications

Is it appropriate to assume that exchange rates and prices reflected informed expectations of fiscal policy and the long-run backing of the currency? What evidence can one muster to show that markets responded efficiently to news and that fiscal policy was an important component of news?

Market efficiency is separate from the issue of what constitutes news; but if gold market efficiency can be defended empirically, this may shed light on the question of what variables the market reacts to as news. For example, if exchange rates follow a random walk, then short-run innovations in exchange rates have a permanent effect. It follows that the "random" component of the exchange rate series reflects "fundamentals" of short- and long-run exchange rate determination. Variables which reflect important news of long-run interest should be correlated with these unpredictable short-run changes in exchange rates.

Roll (1972) shows that partial autocorrelations among innovations in weekly and monthly gold/greenback exchange rates provide evidence in favor of a random walk, and therefore, market efficiency. In order further to test market efficiency I regress—using end-of-month data—the natural log of the exchange rate on its lagged value and test the residuals of the regression for autocorrelation. The random walk specification is a more restrictive one, because it constrains the coefficient on the lagged term to be unity.

ARIMA identification procedures suggest either an AR(1) process or a random walk. As Table 3 shows, the estimated coefficients for the AR(1) specification are very close to unity. Furthermore, differencing does not produce strong negative first order serial correlation of errors. Together, these results indicate that the series is probably best described as a random walk. Results are reported for both specifications in Tables 3 and 4. The regression equations and significance levels for partial autocorrelation tests of the residuals are described in Table 3. These tests confirm the efficiency hypothesis. No significant seasonality or moving average process is evident in monthly exchange rate movements. Partial autocorrelations are given in Table 4, for the whole period and for three subperiods divided by the end of the Civil War and the Resumption Act of 1875. Furthermore, changes in sign and magnitude of the partial autocorrelation coefficients from

TABLE 3
Modeling Exchange Rate Movements

Sample	*Lag Coefficient**	*Constant**	*Standard Error*	*Q Statistic†*	*Q Significance Level*
			AR(1) Equations		
1862, 1–1865,4	0.904 (16.02)	0.0499 (1.78)	0.094	$Q(18) = 10.7$	0.91
1865,5–1875,1	0.964 (42.6)	0.0058 (1.04)	0.027	$Q(30) = 39.9$	0.11
1875,2–1878,12	0.978 (25.05)	−0.0009 (−0.25)	0.015	$Q(18) = 16.2$	0.58
1862,1–1878,12	0.976 (53.7)	0.0075 (1.43)	0.047	$Q(42) = 49.2$	0.21
			Random Walk Equations		
1862,1–1865,4	N/A	0.010 (0.63)	0.0965	$Q(18) = 10.1$	0.93
1865,5–1875,1	N/A	−0.002 (−0.89)	0.0268	$Q(30) = 40.5$	0.09
1875,2–1878,12	N/A	−0.003 (−1.25)	0.0144	$Q(18) = 17.0$	0.52
1862,1–1878,12	N/A	0.000 (0.00)	0.0473	$Q(42) = 51.4$	0.15

**t*-statistics are in parentheses.

† The Q statistic measures the joint significance of the partial autocorrelation coefficients, adjusting for increases in the standard errors of estimated coefficients as the lag length increases. See Box and Jenkins (1976), p. 394.

subperiod to subperiod suggest that trading rules derived from previous observations would not have been profitable out of sample.[14]

International determination of commodity gold prices

For our steady-state model to be applied to short-run price movements two strong assumptions regarding commodity price determination must be satisfied: first, that prices adjust *quickly* to shocks which alter the equilibrium price level; and second, that world gold prices are homogenous

[14] Friedman and Schwartz recognize the influence of expectations on bond prices. Furthermore, they realize that given the high gold yields on bonds, there is evidence that bond dealers expected a rise in the gold value of greenbacks (pp. 72–74). Why then did they not include these expectations in their analysis of greenback valuation? On this point, Friedman and Schwartz are silent except for the comment that "the purchasers of government securities were a much more mixed and broader group than the speculators in foreign exchange were, so we are dealing with the expectations of two very different groups" (Friedman and Schwartz, p. 73, footnote 82). Roll (1972) and Russel (1976) note the inconsistency of the position taken here by Friedman and Schwartz.

TABLE 4
Partial Autocorrelation Functions of Residuals

	Log Levels AR(1)				*Random Walk*			
Lag	1862,1–1865,4	1865,5–1875,1	1875,2–1878,12	1862,1–1878,12	1862,1–1865,4	1865,5–1875,1	1875,2–1878,12	1862–1878,12
1	0.186	0.105	−0.165	0.176	0.171	0.088	−0.180	0.162
2	−0.112	−0.172	−0.212	−0.065	−0.121	−0.187	−0.235	−0.077
3	−0.066	−0.024	−0.221	−0.062	−0.067	−0.043	−0.255	−0.075
4	0.170	−0.077	0.032	0.164	0.180	0.096	−0.011	0.152
5	−0.177	−0.129	−0.015	−0.124	−0.166	−0.154	−0.055	−0.135
6	0.112	−0.124	0.210	0.084	0.125	−0.155	0.177	0.072
7	0.038	−0.129	0.120	0.031	0.059	−0.170	0.100	0.022
8	−0.121	0.021	−0.047	0.013	−0.105	−0.027	−0.064	0.002
9	−0.147	−0.015	0.313	0.090	−0.135	−0.066	0.307	−0.101
11	−0.203	0.001	−0.064	−0.100	−0.187	−0.053	−0.060	−0.113
10	−0.168	0.283	−0.126	−0.022	−0.158	0.237	−0.129	−0.037
12	−0.109	0.055	−0.164	−0.003	−0.118	0.023	−0.174	−0.022
13	−0.022	0.025	0.114	0.051	0.020	0.000	0.105	0.033
14	0.012	0.146	0.056	−0.018	0.028	0.132	0.056	−0.034
15	−0.160	0.040	−0.147	−0.153	−0.153	0.031	−0.148	−0.173
16	0.219	0.091	0.029	0.179	0.252	0.088	0.026	0.162
17	0.065	−0.125	0.012	0.032	0.097	−0.126	0.015	0.018
18	−0.085	0.034	−0.083	0.050	−0.036	0.031	−0.084	0.039
19	−0.098	−0.055	−0.130	0.000	−0.035	−0.057	−0.135	−0.008
20	−0.098	0.003	−0.034	−0.015	−0.066	0.000	−0.042	−0.027

across countries within narrow bandwidths of autonomous domestic variation which result from information and transaction costs. The bandwidths must be narrow in the sense that most price variation—especially persistent large price changes—is governed by common international factors.

Before summarizing the evidence which supports these assumptions it is worth emphasizing that neither short-run price flexibility nor common international commodity gold prices is a crucial assumption for the main conclusion of our model—that long-run price level movements are determined by policy expectations rather than by exogenous money supply innovations. If we relax these two assumptions—allow prices to adjust sluggishly and assume an exogenously-determined domestic supply of gold, instead of international price arbitrage to which the supply of gold is endogenous—our long-run equilibrium would be different only in the role played by the fixed supply of gold. Fiscal news still would fix exchange rates, while the price level would be influenced by exchange rate changes as well as the level of gold supply.

In support of the assumption of rapid price adjustment, one can appeal to the relative homogeneity of commodities in the nineteenth century and the relative absence of labor market contracting. Using monthly data for 1879 through 1914, Calomiris and Hubbard (1986) find evidence of rapid adjustment of prices, relative to output, to shocks which affect both price and output over the course of the business cycle—the reverse of the standard result for post-World War II data. These results confirm those in Sachs (1980) and DeLong and Summers (1984).

Calomiris and Hubbard (1987) present evidence of two kinds in favor of elastic gold flows and common short-run international determination of commodity gold prices for the period 1879 to 1914. ARIMA models and event studies indicate that perturbations in the demand for gold are resolved within approximately three months. Tariff-adjusted price ratios for sugar, wheat and cotton yield estimated transaction-cost bandwidths of approximately 10 percent of traded goods prices in both the short and long runs. These results indicate that short-run variations in commodity prices mainly reflect rapid, common international adjustment and that full adjustment occurs rapidly.[15]

[15] For convenience, the model of Section II carries the assumption of common international gold prices a step farther to the assumption of common gold-price levels, or "purchasing power parity (PPP)." In the real world, of course, changes in the composition of consumption and investment goods will alter the price deflator relevant for asset demand equations even when individual commodity prices are constant. Moreover, nontraded goods may not bear as close a relation to one another across countries as traded goods, though McCloskey and Zecker (1985) argue nontraded goods prices should be linked by common factor costs. The upshot of these considerations is that in empirical work one would expect to find persistent deviations, or drift over time, in a PPP index, which reflects the changing composition of goods, and the bandwidths of autonomous domestic variation. This qualification of the model in Section II implicitly is included in the empirical model reported below. The domestic price equation is estimated in log first-differences with foreign price terms on the right-hand side. In addition, several lagged domestic price terms which appear on the right-hand side could approximate an MA(1) process in domestic price change, which would allow drift over time in the PPP index.

Evidence from reduced-form vector autoregressive (VAR) models confirms that unpredictable changes in price indexes are highly correlated between the U.S. and Britain, and that full adjustment of U.S. or British price levels to simulated shocks originating in the other country's prices essentially takes place within six months. Calomiris (1985, chapter 3) finds, for the period 1867 through 1878, that the correlation between monthly unpredictable wholesale price inflation in Britian and the U.S. ranges from 0.3 to 0.4 depending on the variables included in the forecasting equations.

Testing the predictions of the model

The model of Section II implies that news relevant for movements in exchange rates and prices primarily involves expectations of future government policy. Here I present evidence of three kinds in support of the importance of fiscal news: first, evidence from securities markets that changing perceptions of the long-run specie value of greenbacks were linked to expectations of resumption; second, exchange rate data on the value of greenbacks relative to government money with different backing (the old demand notes); third, evidence from a vector autoregressive model which shows that government bond "funding" policy was an important element of news in exchange rate determination.

Expected appreciation: evidence from bond-market yields

According to equation (4), the equilibrium expected rate of deflation and currency appreciation is given by expected real rates of return in financial markets, marginal reserve requirements, the tax on bank note issues, and the degree of capital leveraging in note issuing. This suggests that the long-run pattern of exchange-rate appreciation and price deflation should have been largely anticipated, and that forecast errors in long-run expected inflation should be related to news about the timing and likelihood of resumption, since actual appreciation is the sum of predictable smooth changes in the exchange rate and unpredictable leaps related to news.

Evidence in support of deflationary expectations comes from comparisons of yields on greenback- and gold-denominated securities. Interest differentials between bonds which paid in greenbacks and those which paid in gold were negative, which implies an expected capital gain on greenback-denominated principal. Roll (1972) reports this result for the Civil War years, using government securities of similar maturity denominated in greenbacks and coin for comparison.[16]

[16] There is some question regarding the extent to which Roll is able to attribute differences in interest rates to differences in the numeraire of the securities. Whether before 1869 government bonds were seen as gold-denominated *ex ante* is a subject of debate. Roll claims that his observed yield differentials provide evidence for a perceived difference in numeraire. He recognizes, however, that there are alternative interpretations of his results and that, therefore, interest rate differences may reflect other factors in addition to expectations of exchange rate changes (e.g., a premium related to the relative riskiness of greenback-denominated securities).

TABLE 5
Bond Yield Differentials and Long-Run Appreciation

	(1) *Average Differential Between Gold and Greenbacks Yield**	(2) *Expected Appreciation (Current Differential Less Differential for July-December* 1878)	(3) *Average Actual Rate of Greenbacks Appreciation to* 1881†	(4) *Appreciation Forecast Error* (2)–(3)
January–June 1869	1.33	3.53	2.00	1.53
July–December 1869	0.49	2.69	1.85	0.84
January–June 1870	−0.52	1.68	0.93	0.75
July–December 1870	−0.42	1.78	0.93	0.85
January–June 1871	−1.01	1.19	1.09	0.10
July–December 1871	−0.95	1.25	1.10	0.15
January–June 1872	−0.02	2.18	1.26	0.92
July–December 1872	0.01	2.21	1.40	0.81
January–June 1873	−0.09	2.11	1.90	0.21
July–December 1873	−0.26	1.94	1.39	0.55
January–June 1874	−0.65	1.55	1.60	−0.05
July–December 1874	−0.45	1.75	1.50	0.25
January–June 1875	0.07	2.27	2.36	−0.09
July–December 1875	0.09	2.29	2.30	−0.01
January–June 1876	−1.19	1.01	2.50	−1.49
July–December 1876	−1.07	1.13	1.76	−0.63
January–June 1877	−1.22	0.98	1.36	−0.38
July–December 1877	−1.21	0.99	0.84	0.15
January–June 1878	−1.32	0.88	0.40	0.48
July–December 1878	−2.20	0.00	0.10	0.10

* $\frac{1}{6}\sum_{j=1}^{6} [i_{sp}(j) - i_{gr}(j)] = d.$

† The average of monthly exchange rate closings for the period was used to measure the current gold price of greenbacks. The 6s of 1881 were redeemable June 1, 1881.

Source: Calomiris (1985).

For the later period, no comparable greenback-denominated government bonds exist for comparison. Yields on low-risk, greenback-denominated railroad bonds and coin-denominated government bonds are available, however, though time varying default risk differentials and splicing of different railroads' yields introduce potential errors into the measurement of expected deflation. Calomiris (1985, chapter 3) constructs a measure of expected appreciation, under the assumption of constant default risk differentials among government bonds and highest-quality railroad bonds of similar maturity, for the period from 1869 to 1878, when the redemption of government bond principal in gold was a virtual certainty.[17]

The risk-adjusted yield differential thus calculated (reported in Table 5)

[17] Government credibility was established by the actual redemption of bond principal in gold, as well as by the Act of March 18, 1869 guaranteeing payment in gold, and the Supreme Court decision in Veazie Bank v. Fenno which supported the constitutionality of gold clauses.

indicates a consistent expectation of appreciation throughout the period. Expected and actual greenback appreciation are close for much of the period. Of course, whenever imputed expected appreciation is greater than actual, this reflects either time-varying default risk or measurement error, since no one would have expected appreciation beyond the parity level.

There is a slight negative trend in the imputed forecast error series (column (4) of Table 5) which may reflect peculiarities in the splicing of the series, or an unpredictable trend in policy.[18] The large value of 1.53 in column (4) for the first half of 1869 is consistent with the fact that 1869 was a turning point in the government's commitment to the redemption of bond principal in gold. Most of the subsequent entries in column (4) are relatively close to zero, which indicates that deflationary expectations were generally accurate, and the risk premium differential was fairly constant.

The large negative value of −1.49 for early 1876 is consistent with Unger's (1964) description of the political controversy and consequent forecast error regarding the future of resumption policy prior to the election of 1876. The first half of 1876 was the time of greatest challenge to the timely resumption of specie convertibility stipulated by the Resumption Act of 1875. The Democrats were divided between "hard"- and "soft"-money advocates. The desire to maintain party unity and to attract soft-money independents led to a tolerance of the soft-money minority in the Democrat-controlled Congress. Repeated attempts by soft-money Democrats to force consideration of the repeal of the Resumption Act prior to the election were thwarted by procedural rules and then finally by the nomination of the hard-money candidate Tilden. The repeal movement failed to force the issue prior to the election in an attempt to extract a price for party unity. Tilden's empty promises to postpone resumption and a party platform pledging the same were not viewed as credible commitments. The nomination of Tilden in July had effectively put to rest any true threat of a postponement of resumption. Even the house bill calling for postponement which passed August 5, 1876 was nothing more than a political ploy; it was kept vague deliberately and passed with a vote of 106 to 86, with 93 abstentions.

The old demand notes

Further evidence that the current specie value of greenbacks and other assets reflected expectations of resumption policy and long-run backing comes from Mitchell (1903). To bolster his argument that exchange rates were governed by fiscal news, Mitchell cites exchange rates between the demand notes of 1861 and the greenbacks of 1862. The demand notes were identical to the greenbacks in every respect, except that they were

[18] One thing this trend in errors does not support is Fels' (1959) conjecture that railroad defaults in 1873, which were important in the failure of Jay Cooke & Co., led to a general distrust of railroad securities. If Fels were right, one would expect, *ceteris paribus*, a positive trend in column (4).

acceptable for the payment of customs duties at par with gold, while greenbacks were not. Mitchell notes that this special tariff-backing allowed the demand notes to trade at a premium relative to greenbacks, as shown in Table 6. It is important to note that tariff backing was not immediate; until all demand notes had been paid in, agents had to value demand notes based on *expectations* of par valuation with gold, since not all demand notes could be redeemed immediately in payment of duties. Thus it was *expected* backing that distinguished demand notes from greenbacks.[19]

Debt funding policy as news

The conversion in the late 1860s of short-term paper-denominated government debt into long-term funded securities denominated in coin substantially reduced the potential benefit to the government of depreciating the currency. In mid-1865 government debt was split roughly evenly between obligations payable in lawful money and those payable only in coin. By mid-1867 coin-denominated securities out-numbered paper securities more than three to one, and by mid-1869 interest-bearing debt denominated in legal tender was less than 3 percent of total debt. There was some initial doubt regarding the government's intention to repay the principal of its coin-denominated debt in specie, but this was resolved in early 1869 when a combination of actual principal payments in specie, legislation mandating payment in specie, and a Supreme Court ruling made

TABLE 6
Relative Depreciation of United States Notes and Old Demand Notes At Various Dates in 1862 *and* 1863

Date	*Currency Value*		*Gold Value*	
	Gold	*Old Demand Notes*	*Currency*	*Old Demand Notes*
		1862		
April 12	$101\frac{7}{8}$	100	98·1	98.1
19	$101\frac{9}{16}$	100	98.4	98.4
26	$101\frac{9}{16}$	100	98.4	98.4
May 3	$102\frac{5}{8}$	100	97.4	97.4
10	$103\frac{5}{16}$	$100\frac{1}{4}$	96.8	97.0
17	$103\frac{1}{16}$	$100\frac{5}{8}$	97.0	97.6
24	$103\frac{1}{2}$	$100\frac{5}{8}$	96.6	97.2
31	$103\frac{9}{16}$	$100\frac{5}{8}$	96.6	97.2

[19] Because demand note supply was less than the sum of future tariff payments, the parity of gold and demand notes in payment of duties created a market parity between the two through arbitrage. The discounting of demand notes probably reflects the possibility of a future change in tariff payment parity. This discount explains why the demand notes were used instead of gold in payment of duties until their supply was exhausted. For more discussion of tax arbitrage constraints see Adam Smith (1776), p. 311; and Calomiris (1985).

TABLE 6 (*continued*)

Date	Currency Value: Gold	Currency Value: Old Demand Notes	Gold Value: Currency	Gold Value: Old Demand Notes
		1862		
June 7	$104\frac{1}{16}$	101	96.1	97.1
14	$105\frac{11}{16}$	103	94.6	97.5
23	$107\frac{3}{8}$	103	93.1	95.9
26	$100\frac{1}{8}$	$104\frac{1}{8}$	91.7	95.8
July 5	$109\frac{11}{16}$	$105\frac{1}{4}$	91.2	96.0
12	$114\frac{3}{16}$	$107\frac{1}{4}$	87.6	93.9
19	$118\frac{3}{8}$	108	84.5	91.2
26	$117\frac{1}{4}$	$106\frac{1}{2}$	85.3	90.8
August 2	$115\frac{1}{8}$	$105\frac{1}{4}$	86.9	91.4
9	$112\frac{11}{16}$	$105\frac{1}{2}$	88.7	93.6
16	$114\frac{9}{16}$	$107\frac{1}{2}$	87.3	93.8
23	$115\frac{1}{2}$	108	86.6	93.5
30	$115\frac{11}{16}$	$108\frac{1}{4}$	86.4	93.6
September 6	119	108	84.0	90.8
13	$118\frac{1}{8}$	$108\frac{3}{4}$	84.7	92.1
20	$116\frac{15}{16}$	$112\frac{1}{2}$	85.5	96.2
26	$120\frac{3}{8}$	$116\frac{1}{2}$	83.1	98.6
October 4	$122\frac{3}{4}$	$119\frac{1}{2}$	81.5	97.3
11	$128\frac{1}{8}$	$128\frac{3}{4}$	78.1	96.6
18	$130\frac{1}{8}$	129	76.8	99.1
25	$130\frac{5}{8}$	127	76.6	97.2
November 1	$130\frac{7}{16}$	$126\frac{1}{2}$	76.7	97.0
8	$132\frac{1}{4}$	126	75.6	95.3
15	$131\frac{7}{8}$	$126\frac{1}{2}$	75.8	95.9
22	$130\frac{5}{8}$	$124\frac{1}{4}$	76.6	95.1
29	$129\frac{1}{8}$	$124\frac{1}{2}$	77.5	96.4
December 6	$131\frac{1}{4}$	125	76.2	95.2
13	$131\frac{9}{16}$	$126\frac{1}{2}$	76.0	96.2
20	$123\frac{7}{16}$	$127\frac{1}{8}$	75.5	96.3
27	$132\frac{1}{4}$	129	75.6	97.5
		1863		
January 3	$134\frac{1}{8}$	129	74.6	96.2
10	$137\frac{13}{16}$	135	72.6	98.0
17	$147\frac{1}{4}$	143	67.9	97.1
24	$149\frac{3}{16}$	$144\frac{3}{4}$	67.0	97.0
February 7	$157\frac{1}{4}$	155	63.6	98.6
14	$155\frac{5}{8}$	151	64.3	97.0
21	$162\frac{3}{4}$	162	61.5	99.5
28	172	171	58.1	99.4
March 7	$155\frac{1}{8}$	153	64.5	98.6
14	$158\frac{1}{4}$	153	63.2	96.7

Sources: Data are from Mitchell (1903), p. 196, based on reported series in *Hunt's Merchants' Magazine*.

it clear that the principal of coin-denominated debt would not be paid with depreciated paper.[20]

Given the credibility of government debt repayment in coin and the reduction in the incentive to depreciate the currency which came from the changing debt composition, it follows that unanticipated changes in the composition of government debt may have been perceived as a component of news regarding the likelihood and timing of resumption. By reducing the amount of greenback-denominated debt, and consequently its incentive to depreciate the currency, the government may have signaled its intentions to redeem greenbacks in gold.

In order to investigate this proposition, I construct a vector autoregressive (VAR) model to measure the contributions of unpredictable changes in government debt composition and other variables in explaining movements in exchange rates, prices, and monetary aggregates.[21]

[20] The fact that the government always paid interest on bonds in gold and redeemed bond principal in gold ten years before greenback resumption indicates strong preferential treatment for bondholders. A reason for discrimination by the government in favour of bondholders over currencyholders may be that the bond market is a more competitive forum for funding. That is, if bondholders have access to many government bond issues, governments with poor reputations will find they face high interest costs, and perhaps, as Stiglitz and Weiss (1981, 1983) would suggest, increasing quantity constraints in bond markets. Thus there are strong incentives for a government to maintain its reputation among bondholders. If the elasticities of substitution between a government's currency issues and other media of exchange are smaller, the government may wish to ensure bond redemption first, and in some instances may even choose not to redeem currency when it has the ability to do so.

In their recent paper, "Suspension and the Financing of the Civil War: A Critique of Newcomb and Mitchell" (1984), Rolnick and Wallace conjecture that resumption expectations may have depended only on overall government fiscal expectations and, hence, suspension may have constituted only a change in numeraire relative to government finance without suspension but with the same overall fiscal uncertainty. I take exception to this view because it fails to distinguish between government commitments to bondholders and fiduciary currencyholders during and after the War. History often distinguished between the two. For example, bondholders received full value for their assets after the Revolution, whereas moneyholders received 1 percent of the promised value of their paper assets.

Hammond (1961) suggests that some of the original motivation for issuing notes to finance the Civil War was to prevent losses to holders of outstanding bonds. Bankers on the whole supported the issuing of greenbacks, though it is not clear whether they did so as a means to enhance liquidity or to protect the value of their bond holdings.

[21] Mitchell (1903, 1908) and Thompson (1972) compare actual fluctuations in the specie value of greenbacks with events they define as news. Mitchell claims that a variety of items constituted news relevant for resumption expectations: information on battles, government fiscal policy, and Treasury reports. He rejects the quantity theory approach to prices and exchange rates citing the endogeneity of money and the lack of correspondence between money and prices. He challenges what would now be called the elasticities approach to exchange rates and claims that "... the supply and demand for gold, instead of controlling were themselves controlled by the premium." He understands interest rate arbitrage and the consequent importance of London interest rates. Perhaps most important, Mitchell emphasizes that greenbacks were the liability of the government and that their value was determined as that of any private liability—by the credibility of the issuer.

> Greenbacks were notes of the government of the U.S., and as such their value—like the value of the notes of a private person—depended on the credit of the issuer. If confidence in the government's ability ultimately to redeem its notes had been entirely destroyed, the

I include the following monthly data series in the reduced-form model: the exchange rate; the U.S. wholesale price index; the British wholesale price index; Frickey's (1947) production index for communication and transportation; total government debt net of gold in the Treasury; the ratio of coin- to greenback-denominated debt; deposits of banks in New York, Boston, and Philadelphia; the interest rate on double-name choice commercial paper; the outstanding stock of greenbacks; and the outstanding stock of national bank notes.[22] Given the random-walk character of nominal variables, the model is estimated in first-differences. All variables enter as first-differences of logarithms except the commerical paper rate and the ratio of coin- to greenback-denominated debt which enter as simple differences.

The estimation equations derive series of predicted values and shocks for each variable using six lags of each endogenous variable and monthly dummies for the period 1867 through 1878. In simulation, the system of equations is solved simultaneously to derive the percentage contribution of shocks from each variable to the forecast variance of the others and the responses of all variables to shocks which originate in each series. Both the

---

Footnote 21 (*continued*)

> paper money would have depreciated to the level finally reached by the confederate currency. On the other hand, if the credit of the government had suffered no diminution, its notes would have depreciated little, if at all. Fluctuations between these two limits—par and zero—followed the varying estimates which the community was all the time making of the government's present and prospective ability to meet its obligations. [Mitchell (1903), p. 199]

Thompson (1972) extends Mitchell's discussion of resumption expectations and adds to it more formal statistical tests. Thompson finds a positive correspondence between exchange rate volatility and the extent of news. Thompson's results, however, are of limited usefulness because they are based on arbitrarily defined events seen with the benefit of hindsight, and because the definition of volatility employed implies inefficiency in the exchange market. *Ex ante,* news is virtually impossible to identify. In deciding what constitutes news the informed researcher and the contemporaneous press on which he draws will look for news where there is much to be explained, much the same way *The Wall Street Journal* seems to explain all market events *ex post* with an R^2 of unity.

A further weakness in Thompson's analysis derives from his attempt to reconcile the Friedman–Schwartz approach to exchange rates with Mitchell's asset-pricing approach. Thompson distinguishes between long- and short-run effects. He views the evidence of correspondence in prices and exchange rates as support for the Friedman–Schwartz approach to exchange rate determination, in which money is the "fundamental," long-run determinant of exchange rates and prices. News explains only departures from the "correct" path. In other words, Thompson's definition of volatility implicitly equates volatility with irrationality.

[22] Monthly U.S. prices are the Warren–Pearson wholesale price index. Greenbacks, national bank notes, government debt statistics, and deposits (for New York, Boston, and Philadelphia banks) are from *Hunt's Merchants' Magazine* and the *Commercial and Financial Chronicle*. A monthly price index for Britain was computed using eleven individual commodity prices from *The Economist* and price weights from Gayer, Rostow, and Schwartz (1953). All data, except the Frickey index and the Warren–Pearson index, are end-of-the-month. While measurement error no doubt enters in each of the series due to their partial coverage of relevant data, estimates using first-differences should eliminate "drift" caused by errors in the measurement of levels.

decomposition of forecast variance and the response patterns to shocks depend on assigning the estimated residuals—which are correlated across variables—to particular variables in the system. The orthogonalization of contemporaneous shocks that one chooses may alter, for example, the relative percentage contribution of one variable's disturbances to another's forecast variance.

I assign the following order of priority among residuals: greenbacks (DLG), outstanding net debt (DLNET), the ratio of coin- to greenback-denominated debt (DRINC), the exchange rate (DLEX), the commercial paper rate (DCPR), the U.S. wholesale price index (DLWP), deposits (DLDEP), national bank notes (DLN), production (DLPROD), and the British price index (DLUK). This ordering reflects the fact that initial note supply adjustment took longer than a month (due to bond purchase and note delivery lags), as well as the view that asset prices respond to common shocks before commodity prices, and the desire to place greenbacks supply and fiscal news prior to the exchange rate in order to measure the impact of innovations in these series on the exchange rate.[23] Varying the relative order of monetary aggregates, price indexes, the interest rate, and the exchange rate has little effect on the simulation results discussed below.

Table 7 reports F-tests of the inclusion of a variable's lagged values in each predicting equation, the correlation matrix of residuals, and the forecast variance decomposition for each variable. Only the long-run (forty-month) forecast variance decomposition is reported, but typically six-month decompositions are close to the forty-month figures because convergence to long-run responses occurs rapidly.

The high marginal significance levels for *F*-tests in the exchange rate equation supports the random-walk hypothesis of exchange rate movements. The government debt ratio proves to be one of the most important determinants of exchange rate movements; unpredictable innovations in this series lead to reductions in the exchange rate and price level; they explain 8.56 percent of the forecast variance of the exchange rate, and 8.03 percent of the forecast variance of the price level. Another important influence on the exchange rate is unpredictable changes in the production index. One way to explain their importance is as an indicator of prosperity, and hence, increased government budget surpluses.

Exchange rate disturbances prove a relatively significant and important determinant of wholesale prices, deposits and bank notes, which is consistent with the theoretical view of the exchange rate as the nominal anchor of the system. In contrast, shocks to money are unimportant for the determination of the exchange rate or price level. The high correlation (0.39) between disturbances in U.S. and British wholesale prices and the

[23] In order to issue notes banks had first to purchase and deposit bonds and await the delivery of the government-printed bank notes. Complaints frequently were made of bureaucratic delays. See Unger (1964), pp. 99 ff; Friedman and Schwartz (1963), p. 169, footnote 55; *Hunt's Merchants' Magazine*, 1868, p. 138.

TABLE 7
VAR Results

Lagged Endogenous Variables	*F-Tests Contemporaneous Variables* DLG	DLNET	DRINC	DLEX	DCPR	DLWP	DLDEP	DLN	DLPROD	DLUK
DLG	0.002	0.691	0.761	0.357	0.027	0.531	0.087	0.712	0.384	0.935
DLNET	0.279	0.055	0.005	0.883	0.297	0.976	0.141	0.973	0.659	0.436
DRINC	0.287	0.979	0.687	0.937	0.153	0.952	0.217	0.980	0.643	0.467
DLEX	0.297	0.126	0.472	0.970	0.288	0.129	0.140	0.031	0.795	0.930
DCPR	0.000	0.923	0.802	0.440	0.096	0.912	0.042	0.693	0.310	0.902
DLWP	0.981	0.043	0.118	0.813	0.243	0.529	0.678	0.726	0.924	0.648
DLDEP	0.358	0.915	0.644	0.653	0.003	0.690	0.004	0.391	0.775	0.758
DLN	0.208	0.743	0.670	0.985	0.756	0.196	0.346	0.000	0.731	0.833
DLPROD	0.247	0.398	0.214	0.390	0.126	0.272	0.315	0.036	0.047	0.988
DLUK	0.265	0.092	0.180	0.558	0.824	0.467	0.118	0.109	0.395	0.655

Correlation Matrix

	DLG	*DLNET*	*DRINC*	*DLEX*	*DCPR*	*DLWP*	*DLDEP*	*DLN*	*DLPROD*	*DLUX*
DLG	1.00									
DLNET	−0.04	1.00								
DRINC	0.09	−0.92	1.00							
DLEX	0.00	−0.14	0.02	1.00						
DCPR	0.09	0.19	−0.15	−0.12	1.00					
DLWP	0.02	0.07	−0.10	0.10	0.19	1.00				
DLDED	−0.21	−0.16	0.18	0.19	−0.49	−0.06	1.00			
DLN	−0.04	0.02	0.04	−0.10	0.13	0.02	−0.07	1.00		
DLPROD	−0.13	−0.09	0.02	−0.11	−0.03	−0.09	0.13	−0.03	1.00	
DLUK	0.25	−0.18	0.16	−0.11	0.05	0.39	0.02	−0.09	0.05	1.00

Decomposition of Forecast Variance (*40 month*)
(*Columns sum to* 100 *percent*)

	DLG	*DLNET*	*DRINC*	*DLEX*	*DCPR*	*DLWP*	*DLDEP*	*DLN*	*DLPROD*	*DLUK*
DLG	45.85	1.84	3.05	3.32	10.20	1.62	6.40	2.41	5.05	6.40
DLNET	3.59	62.96	53.55	3.01	5.60	3.50	8.33	1.25	6.92	4.31
DRINC	8.94	3.23	9.73	8.56	10.99	8.03	7.34	3.06	7.74	7.56
DLEX	6.94	5.82	6.13	62.99	5.42	9.67	7.27	8.77	3.87	2.56
DCPR	11.97	1.35	2.44	4.49	44.54	4.16	16.62	3.78	6.46	2.64
DLWP	1.60	5.33	4.00	1.24	2.73	54.46	2.32	1.47	4.60	15.66
DLDEP	2.72	2.48	3.25	2.94	7.34	3.16	37.74	2.54	4.33	4.23
DLN	9.38	4.07	4.17	1.64	4.19	8.56	3.23	66.13	3.62	4.35
DLPROD	3.87	5.90	6.30	8.93	4.37	3.25	5.00	5.18	51.74	2.01
DLUK	5.52	7.01	7.39	2.88	4.62	3.57	5.74	5.41	5.68	50.29

Data are monthly from March 1867 to December 1878.

Equations are estimated with 69 degrees of freedom. All variables except DRINC and DCPR are first-differences of logs. Six lags are used in estimation. Definitions follow:

DLG = greenbacks
DLNET = government debt net of Treasury gold
DRINC = ratio of gold- to greenback- denominated debt (differenced)
DLEX = exchange rate
DCPR = commercial paper rate
DLWP = U.S. wholesale price index
DLDEP = bank deposits at New York, Philadelphia, and Boston
DLN = national bank notes
DLPROD = U.S. production index
DLUK = constructed British wholesale price index

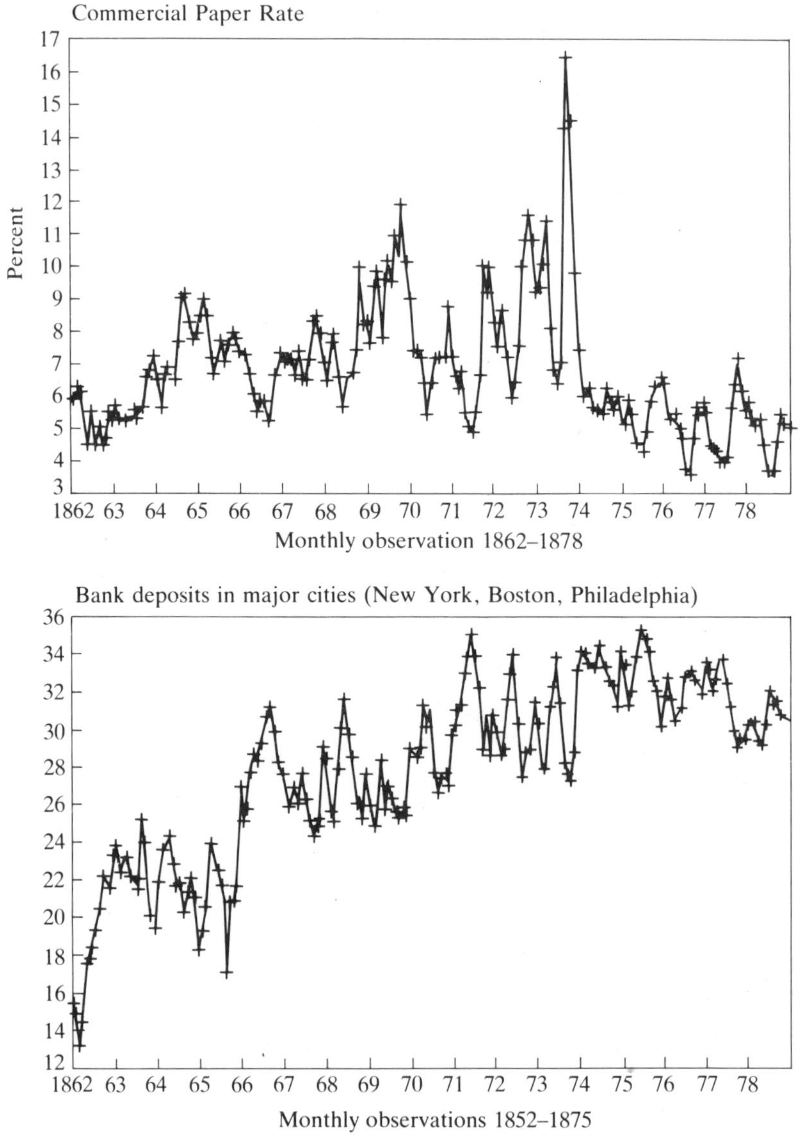

FIG. 3. Commercial paper rate and bank deposits

importance of U.S. shocks for British prices (or vice versa, when the orthogonalization reverses the ordering of price shocks) is supportive of close short-run price linkages across countries.[24]

[24] The significance and importance of commercial paper rate changes for greenbacks reflects the one-time increase in greenbacks supply in response to the Panic of 1873.

The market for real paper money

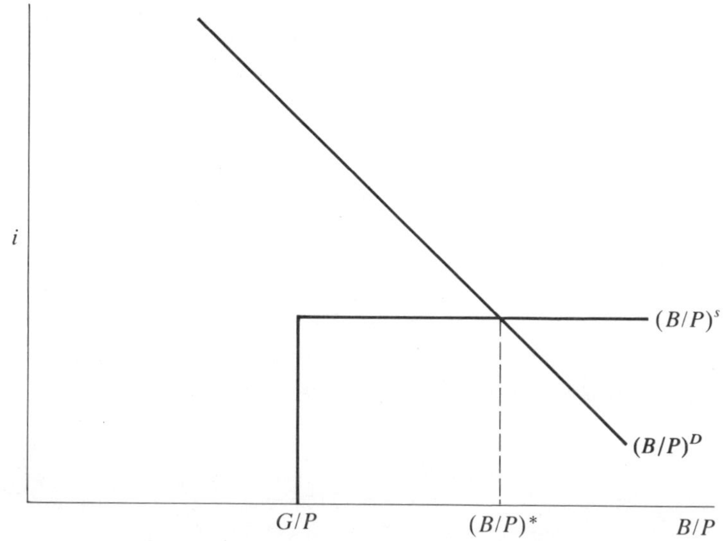

FIG. 4. The market for real paper money

IV. Concluding remarks

This paper argues in favor of the basic approach taken by Mitchell and others who concentrate on expectations of government fiscal and resumption policies during the Greenback Era as the main determinants of exchange rates and prices, and through them, money. The arguments used in favor of this approach include theoretical propositions regarding exchange rate determination and the infra-marginal role of greenbacks supply in determining the money stock, as well as empirical analysis of the importance of fiscal news for exchange rates.

The picture which emerges from these arguments and facts is roughly as follows: During the Greenback Era the United States was an open economy with a freely floating exchange rate that responded efficiently to changing perceptions of the future gold value of government paper. All classes of money—specie, bills, and deposits—adjusted to these changes in the price of gold, and hence those of other commodities, in order to satisfy real money demand. Thus the descriptive historical accounts of Mitchell, Studenski and Krooss, and Thompson are preferable to that of Friedman and Schwartz.

Aside from explaining variations in nominal variables from 1862 through 1878, this asset-pricing approach, with its emphasis on fiscal news, is useful for understanding both the onset of suspension in December 1861 and the successful resumption of parity at the beginning of 1879. In the first instance, the threat of British entry in the War due to the Trent Affair, the bad fiscal news of Chase's Report of December 1861, Chase's proposal to remedy the fiscal crisis by regulating the banking system, and the fact that the bad fiscal news came at a time when banks held large inventories of government loans, together led to the need for banks—and then the government—to suspend specie parity.[25] Similarly, it was the sound fiscal footing on which the government had placed itself by 1878 that made attempted resumption credible and successful.[26]

Northwestern University, USA.

APPENDIX: MEASURING RENTS FROM NOTE ISSUES

In his 1873 *Annual Report,* the Comptroller of the Currency, John Jay Knox, published calculations of the profitability to national banks from buying bonds and issuing notes during the suspension. Knox estimated profits at between 1 and $2\frac{1}{2}$ percent, depending on which region the bank was located. Knox noted that banks suffer an additional loss due to the difference between the market and face values of the bond at the date of maturity, but he did not include this in his calculation. In paper terms, one can write the *ex ante* profit rate to maturity per unit of bond purchase as:

$$s + \pi^e = Y - (0.9)\tau i_l - 0.009, \qquad (1)^*$$

where Y is the nominal annual yield to maturity on government bonds, i_l is the long-run yield on alternative uses of capital, and τ is the proportional greenback reserve requirement on notes. The 0.9 coefficient reflects the 111 percent ratio of bond reserves to notes, while the -0.009 intercept reflects the 1 percent federal tax per year on notes outstanding.

Government bonds were payable in coin rather than paper, but given that government bonds were not being held only by banks, arbitrage kept the real yield on government bonds close to that of other bonds, adjusting for default risk. Thus one can use paper railroad bond yields, adjusted for default risk, to derive *ex ante* paper yields on government bonds (see Calomiris, 1985).

Cagan (1965) modifies this approach to calculating the profitability of note issue. As Cagan points out, if banks can buy more bonds rather than make loans with the notes they receive initially, and issue further notes on these bonds, then the rate of return on note issuing should be taken as a ratio of bank capital diverted, not as a ratio of the total amount invested in bonds. Cagan (1965, p. 87) shows that leverage L is bounded by $BP/(BP-90)$, where BP is the purchase price of government bonds per \$100 in face value, and 90 reflects the number of notes which can be issued per \$100 in face value. This implies a revised version of the long-run nominal profit rate calculation:

$$s + \pi^e = L[Y - (0.9)\tau i_l - 0.009]. \qquad (2)^*$$

Some authors object to Cagan's assumption that banks could use notes to purchase bonds. Such objections are based on the claim that bond brokers or their banks would return notes to the bank of issue (see James (1976), p. 362). This is tantamount to challenging a bank's ability to determine its circulation. Of course, in the *aggregate,* given the independently determined

[25] See Studenski and Krooss (1963), pp. 142–43; Mitchell (1903), pp. 19–43.

[26] Consistent with their view that the money supply, rather than government credibility, determined the price level and exchange rate, Friedman and Schwartz (1963) consider resumption an "accomplishment of omission, as it were, not of commission" (p. 82).

price level and real demand, the nominal supply of notes would be demand determined, but individual banks would act as price takers in determining their own note supply. Interest rates would adjust to keep the sum of individual supplies equal to the desired aggregate and the Cagan form of the profit condition should hold in equilibrium. It is difficult to see why individual banks would not be able to increase their circulation by purchasing bonds as easily as they would by making loans.

REFERENCES

BOX, GEORGE E. P. and JENKINS, GWILYM M. *Time Series Analysis: Forecasting and Control.* Holden-Day (1976).

CAGAN, PHILLIP, *Determinants and Effects of Changes in the Stock of Money, 1875–1960.* National Bureau of Economic Research (1965).

CALOMIRIS, CHARLES W. and HUBBARD, R. GLENN. "Price Flexibility, Credit Rationing, and Economic Fluctuations: Evidence from the U.S., 1879–1914." Working paper (1986).

CALOMIRIS, CHARLES W. and HUBBARD, GLENN R. "Price Flexibility, Credit Rationing, and Economic Fluctuations: Evidence from the U.S., 1879–1914." Working paper (1986).

——. "Evaluating Theories of International Adjustment Under the Classical Gold Standard." NBER Working paper No. 2206 (April 1987).

Commerical and Financial Chronicle. W. B. Dana & Company, 1865–1878.

DELONG, J. BRADFORD and SUMMERS, LAWRENCE H. "The Changing Cyclical Variability of Economic Activity in the United States." NBER Working paper No. 1450 (September 1984).

DEWEY, DAVIS RICH. *Financial History of the United States.* Longmans, Green and Company (1903).

The Economist. Economist Newspaper, Ltd., 1862–1878.

FELS, RENDIGS. *American Business Cycles, 1865–1897.* University of North Carolina Press (1959).

FRICKEY, EDWIN. *Production in the United States, 1860–1914.* Harvard University Press (1947).

FRIEDMAN, MILTON and SCHWARTZ, ANNA J. *A Monetary History of the United States, 1867–1960.* Princeton University Press (1963).

GAYER, ARTHUR D., ROSTOW, W. W. and SCHWARTZ, ANNA J. *The Growth and Fluctuation of the British Economy, 1790–1850.* Oxford University Press (1953).

HAMMOND, BRAY. "The North's Empty Purse, 1861–1862." *American Historical Review,* Vol. LXVII, No. 1 (October 1961).

Historical Statistics of the United States, 1789–1945, First Edition. U.S. Department of Commerce (1949).

Hunt's Merchants' Magazine. William B. Dana, 1862–1870.

JAMES, JOHN, A. "The Conundrum of the Low Issue of National Bank Notes." *Journal of Political Economy.* Vol. 84 (April 1976).

KNOX, JOHN, J. *Annual Report of the Comptroller of the Currency.* 1873.

LESTER, RICHARD A. *Monetary Experiments: Early American and Recent Scandinavian.* Princeton University Press (1939).

MACAULAY, FREDERICK R. *The Movements of Interest Rates, Bond Yields and Stock Prices in the United States since 1856.* National Bureau of Economic Research (1938).

MCCLOSKEY, DONALD N. and ZECHER, J. RICHARD. "The Success of Purchasing Power Parity: Historical Evidence and its Implications for Macroeconomics." In *A Retrospective on the Classical Gold Standard, 1821–1931.* Michael D. Bordo and Anna J. Schwartz, editors. National Bureau of Economic Research (1985).

MITCHELL, WESLEY CLAIR. *A History of the Greenbacks.* The University of Chicago Press (1903).

——. *Gold, Prices, and Wages Under the Greenback Standard. University of California Publications in Economics,* Vol. I (March 1908).

OFFICER, LAWRENCE H. "The Floating Dollar in the Greenback Period: A Test of Theories of Exchange Rate Determination." *Journal of Economic History* XLI (September 1981).

ROLL, RICHARD. "Interest Rates and Price Expectations During the Civil War." *Journal of Economic History,* XXXII (June 1972).

ROLNICK, ARTHUR J. and WALLACE, NEIL. "Suspension and the Financing of the Civil War: A Critique of Newcomb and Mitchell. Federal Reserve Bank of Minneapolis Working Paper No. 265 (November 1984).

RUSSEL, ROBERT R. *The Fallacies of Monetarism.* Beimer Printing Company, Kalamazoo, MI (1976).

SACHS, JEFFREY. "The Changing Cyclical Behavior of Wages and Prices: 1890–1976." *American Economic Review* 70 (March 1980).

SARGENT, THOMAS J. and WALLACE, NEIL. "Some Unpleasant Monetarist Arithmetic." *Quarterly Review* 5. Federal Reserve Bank of Minneapolis (Fall 1981).

SMITH, ADAM. *The Wealth of Nations.* Edwin Canaan, editor. Modern Library (1937).

STIGLITZ, JOSEPH E. and WEISS, ANDREW. "Credit Rationing in Markets with Imperfect Information." *American Economic Review* Vol. 71 (June 1981).

——, "Incentive Effects of Terminations: Applications to the Credit and Labor Markets." *American Economic Review* Vol. 73 (December 1983).

STUDENSKI, PAUL and KROOSS, HERMAN E. *Financial History of the United States,* Second Edition. McGraw Hill (1963).

THOMPSON, GERALD RICHARD. "Expectations and the Greenback Rate, 1862–1878." University of Virginia, Ph.D. dissertation.

UNGER, IRWIN. *The Greenback Era: A Social and Political History of American Finance, 1865–1879.* Princeton University Press (1964).

Oxford Economic Papers 40 (1988), 751–781

BANKING PANICS AND BUSINESS CYCLES*

By GARY GORTON

I. Introduction

The nearly universal experience of banking panics has led many governments to regulate the banking industry. Economists, too, have increasingly focused on panics as evidence of bank uniqueness. Yet, competing theories to explain banking panics have never been tested. Are banking panics caused by the same relations governing consumer behavior during nonpanic times? Are panics random events, or are panics associated with movements in expected returns, in particular, with movements in perceived risk which are predictable on the basis of prior information? If so, what is the relevant information? Using newly constructed data this study addresses these questions by examination of the seven panics during the U.S. National Banking Era (1863–1914). Depositor behavior under subsequent monetary regimes is also examined. In all, one hundred years of depositor behavior are examined.

A common view of panics is that they are random events, perhaps self-confirming equilibria in settings with multiple equilibria, caused by shifts in the beliefs of agents which are unrelated to the real economy. An alternative view makes panics less mysterious. Agents cannot discriminate between the riskiness of various banks because they lack bank-specific information. Aggregate information may then be used to assess risk, in which case it can occur that all banks may be perceived to be riskier. Consumers then withdraw enough to cause a panic. While the former hypothesis is not testable, it suggests that panics are special events and implies that banks are inherently flawed. The latter hypothesis is testable; it suggests that movements in variables predicting deposit riskiness cause panics just as such movements would be used to price such risk at all other times. This hypothesis links panics to occurrences of a threshold value of some variable predicting the riskiness of bank deposits.

* The comments and assistance of Andy Abel, Robert Barro, Phillip Cagan, Bob DeFina, Mike Dotsey, Mark Edwards, Stanley Engerman, Lauren Feinstone, Claudia Goldin, Jack Guttentag, Robert King, Erv Miller, Jeremy Siegel, Alan Stockman, John Taylor, Steve Zeldes, two anonymous referees, and the University of Pennsylvania Macro Lunch Group, were helpful and greatly appreciated. They are not responsible for errors. The research assistance of Earl Pearsall, Elaine Ross, and Wendy Tann was invaluable for this work, as was the programming assistance of Steve Franklin, and Wells Vinton. Thanks to Robert Avery for help with the Tobit program, CRAWTRAN. This study was initiated while the author was at the Federal Reserve Bank of Philadelphia. The study was completed using the Philadelphia Fed's computers, thanks to Richard Lang. The views expressed in this paper are not necessarily those of the Federal Reserve Bank of Philadelphia or the Federal Reserve System.

The thrust of this paper is to differentiate between these two hypotheses. Since the former hypothesis imposes no restrictions on the data, this will, needless to say, be difficult. I, therefore, focus attention on the second hypothesis. The analysis is conducted along two lines. A reduced-form equation describing the behavior of the deposit-currency ratio is studied, and correlations in the data using only the panic dates are studied.

The results suggest that banking panics can be explained by the economic theory explaining consumer behavior during nonpanic times. Banking panics during the U.S. National Banking Era were systematic responses by depositors to changing perceptions of risk, based on the arrival of new information rather than random events. In fact, I show below that every time a variable predicting a recession reached a threshold level, a panic occurred. All the large movements in this variable exactly correspond to large movements in a consumption-beta-type measure of deposit riskiness. The risk measure also reaches a threshold or critical level at panic dates. Panics did not occur at other times. The interpretation is intuitive. Consumers know that during recessions they will want to dissave, drawing down bank accounts. But, banks, like other firms, tend to fail during recessions. When consumers forecast a coming recession they withdraw deposits in advance to avoid losses due to bank failure.

Thus, the analysis confirms that there is something special about panics, but not in the way suggested by theories of self-fulfilling panics or random shifts of depositor beliefs. Rather, depositor behavior during panics is accurately described by a model which characterizes their behavior at other times. But, the information arriving about a coming recession (while noisy) reaches a critical level; this is "special."

The panics of the 1930s, however, cannot be ascribed to the same pattern of consumer behavior. An estimated counterfactual shows that had the downturn of the thirties come during the National Banking Era, losses to depositors would have been four to five times lower; the number of banks that failed during the thirties was roughly twenty-five times what it would have been had the pre-Federal Reserve System institutions been in place. The banking panics during the Great Depression were, thus, special events. Those panics occurred without the private deposit insurance supplied by private bank clearinghouses or the deposit insurance supplied publicly afterwards.

II. Banking panics: description and theories

A bank panic occurs when depositors demand such a large-scale transformation of deposits into currency that, at the contracted for exchange rate (of a currency dollar for a deposit dollar), the banking system can only respond by suspending convertibility of deposits into currency, issuing clearinghouse loan certificates, or both.[1] Table 1 lists the recessions and panics during the National Banking Era, the declines in output as measured by pig iron production, and the increases in the currency-deposit ratio. Also shown are the losses to depositors and the numbers of banks failing. Notice that the banking panics tended to occur just after business cycle peaks. Also, losses on deposits and the number of failures seem small considering that the panics were generalized events which literally involved all banks and depositors.

TABLE 1
National Banking Era Panics

NBER Cycle Peak-Trough	*Panic Date*	$\%\Delta\left(\frac{C}{D}\right)^*$	*%Δ Pig Iron*†	*Loss Per Deposit $*†	*% and # Nat'l Bank Failures*†
Oct. 1873–Mar. 1879	Sept. 1873	14.53	−51.0	0.021	2.8 (56)
Mar. 1882–May 1885	Jun. 1884	8.8	−14.0	0.008	0.9 (19)
Mar. 1887–Apr. 1888	No Panic	3.0	−9.0	0.005	0.4 (12)
Jul. 1890–May 1891	Nov. 1890	9.0	−34.0	0.001	0.4 (14)
Jan. 1893–Jun. 1894	May 1893	16.0	−29.0	0.017	1.9 (74)
Dec. 1895–Jun. 1897	Oct. 1896	14.3	−4.0	0.012	1.6 (60)
Jun. 1899–Dec. 1900	No Panic	2.78	−6.7	0.001	0.3 (12)
Sep. 1902–Aug. 1904	No Panic	−4.13	−8.7	0.001	0.6 (28)
May 1907–Jun. 1908	Oct. 1907	11.45	−46.5	0.001	0.3 (20)
Jan. 1910–Jan. 1912	No Panic	−2.64	−21.7	0.0002	0.1 (10)
Jan. 1913–Dec. 1914	Aug. 1914	10.39	−47.1	0.001	0.4 (28)

* Percentage change of ratio at panic date to previous year's average.
† Measured from peak to trough.
Data sources provided in Appendix.

Two fundamentally different types of theories have been advanced to explain banking panics. The first type of theory, in its traditional form (e.g., Noyes (1909), Gibbons (1968), Kindleberger (1978)), views panics as random manifestations of "mob psychology" or "mass hysteria" rooted in individual and collective psyches. The modern version of the theory that panics are random events is articulated by Diamond and Dybvig (1983), and Waldo (1985). In these models depositors' expectations about the value of deposits are linked to extraneous variables because of an exogenously

[1] Of the seven panics during the National Banking Era five involved suspension of convertibility (1873; 1890, 1893, 1907, 1914) and six involved the issuance of clearinghouse loan certificates (1873, 1884, 1890, 1893, 1907, 1914). During the Panic of 1895 issuance of the loan certificates was authorized, but none were actually issued. Clearinghouse loan certificates are explained in Gorton (1985B) and Gorton and Mullineaux (1986). This definition is much more precise than others which include the nebulous idea of "periods of financial stringency." See, for example, Sprague (1915) and Kemmerer (1910). To be clear, a *bank run* refers to a situation in which depositors at a *single* bank seek to exchange their deposits for currency. A *banking panic* refers to the situation in which depositors at *all* banks want to withdraw currency.

imposed first-come-first-served rule for bank repurchases of their deposits, in which case the return a depositor receives depends on his place in line at the bank. If the face value of the deposits is larger than the liquidation value of the bank's assets, and there is such a first-come-first served rule, then there exist panic equilibria in which the banking system collapses in panic. Hence, in the Diamond and Dybvig model, for example. "... anything that causes [depositors] to anticipate a run will lead to a run." Possible causes include "a bad earnings report, a commonly observed run at some other bank, a negative government forecast, or even sunspots" (p. 410). I will subsequently refer to these alleged panic-causing events as "sunspots."

The second type of theory advanced to explain panics argues that panics are systematically related to the occurrence of other events which change perceptions of risk. If there is an information asymmetry between banks and depositors because bank assets and liabilities are nontraded, for example, then depositors might not be able to accurately assess the risk of individual bank's liabilities. They may be forced to use aggregate information. There are three versions of this theory, differentiated by what the relevant aggregate information is taken to be. These theories are: (i) panics are caused by extreme seasonal fluctuations (referred to here as "the Seasonal Hypothesis"); (ii) panics are caused by the (unexpected) failure of a large (typically financial) corporation (referred to as "the Failure Hypothesis"); (iii) panics are caused by major recessions (referred to as "the Recession Hypothesis"). As discussed below, these three hypotheses are not mutually exclusive.

The view that panics are manifestations of seasonal "crises" or seasonal "stringency" was first put forth by Jevons (1884) with reference to England, and later, by Andrew (1906) and Kemmerer (1910) for the United States. Kemmerer identified the seasons when the money market was most "strained" as the periods of the "spring revival" (March, April, May), and the crop-moving period of the fall (September, October, November). He points out that, of the six panics prior to 1910 (the date his work was published), four occurred in the fall and two occurred in the spring. In each case, Kemmerer cites high interest rates, depressed stock prices, and the failure of specific firms as the seasonal effects precipitating panics. He concluded that "the evidence ... points to a tendency for the panics to occur during the seasons normally characterized by a stringent money market" (p. 232). Andrew (1906) expresses a similar view, and Miron (1985) presents a modern articulation of this traditional view.

The Failure Hypothesis cites the unexpected failure of a large, typically financial, institution as the immediate cause of panics.[2] The argument of the

[2] The failures cited by contemporary observers of panics and subsequent researchers are as follows: 1873: Jay Cooke and Co.; 1884: Grand and Ward; 1890; Decker, Howell and Co.; 1893: The National Cordage Co.; 1907: The Knickerbocker Trust Co.; 1914: the closing of the stock exchange. Details can be found in the *Commercial and Financial Chronicle* and in many secondary sources.

Failure Hypothesis appears to be that because of an information externality such failures created distrust in the future solvency of all banks, leading to withdrawals as depositors sought to avoid expected capital losses on deposits. Since there are many examples of failures of large firms which did not result in panics, a failure *per se* cannot be the cause of a panic. Writers arguing the Failure Hypothesis generally point to the economic context in which the failure occurs. In general, the economic context of the failure cited is a recession.

The Recession Hypothesis emphasizes that panics occurred as features of severe recessions, presumably because depositors expected large numbers of banks to fail during recessions. During the National Banking Era every major business cycle downturn was accompanied by a banking panic. During this period seven of the eleven cycles (in the NBER chronology) contain panics (see Table 1). Writers articulating the Recession Hypothesis include Mitchell (1941) and Fels (1959). Mitchell, for example, argues that, "when prosperity merges into crisis ... heavy failures are likely to occur, and no one can tell what enterprises will be crippled by them. The one certainty is that the banks holding the paper of bankrupt firms will suffer delay and perhaps a serious loss on collection" (p. 74). Like Mitchell, Fels (1959, p. 224) sees panics as "primarily endogenous" parts of the business cycle. Gorton (1985A, 1987A) presents a model of the Recession Hypothesis.

The central common element of all these theories of banking panics is the hypothesized existence of an information asymmetry between banks and depositors which creates the possibility of (information) externalities which change perceptions of the risk of bank deposits, sometimes to the point of panic (e.g., Diamond and Dybvig (1983), Gorton (1987A)). Different explanations of banking panics differ on what variables change perceived risk, but agree that because of the information asymmetry the banking system cannot respond by adjusting the rate of return on deposits. Instead, if there is a panic, the banking system responds to the change in perceived risk by suspending convertibility of deposits into currency rather than adjusting the rate of return. (See Gorton (1985A).) This is because, due to the information asymmetry and consequent externalities, either the change in perceived risk is unrelated to "fundamentals" or it is not possible to credibly raise the rate of return.

III. The deposit-currency ratio

The view that panics are random events places no testable restrictions on the data. Consequently, the basic strategy of analysis followed here is to empirically examine a description of depositor behavior and test whether this description explains depositor behavior at panic dates. In this section the model to be examined is discussed and the hypotheses to be tested are explained. As Miron (1986) points out, data limitations severely constrain the sophistication of models of panics which can be feasibly tested. This section first presents some theoretical motivation for a subsequent, basically ad hoc, model which will be estimated.

Consider the behavior of a representative consumer who lives in a Baumol-Tobin economy where consumption goods must be purchased with currency and where "trips" to the bank are costly. Let the number of trips chosen be m_t; let X_t be real consumption, and let p_t be the price level. Under the usual Baumol–Tobin assumptions, currency (C) and deposit holdings (D) during period t are defined as follows:[3]

$$C_t \equiv X_t(1/m_t)p_t; \qquad D_t \equiv X_t(1-1/m_t)p_t;$$
$$\bar{C}_t = (\tfrac{1}{2})C_t; \qquad \bar{D}_t = (\tfrac{1}{2})D_t;$$

These definitions follow Baumol-Tobin in imposing a binding cash-in-advance constraint on the consumer. For simplicity deposits are the only way of saving.

The representative consumer finances current consumption (X_t) and "trips" (m_t) with last periods' savings and income:

$$\underset{m_t}{\text{MAX}}: E_t\left\{\sum_{i=t}^{\infty} \beta^{i-t} U(X_i) \mid I_t\right\} \qquad \text{(I)}$$

subject to:

$$X_t + \alpha m_t \leqslant (1 - r_{dt-1} - \pi_{t-1})\frac{\bar{D}_{t-1}}{p_t} + Y_{t-1}$$

where:

- α is the real cost of a trip;
- r_{dt-1} is the real rate of return promised *ex ante* by banks on an average balance deposit dollar held during $t-1$;
- π_{t-1} is the real capital loss on an average balance deposit dollar;
- Y_{t-1} is real income earned during $t-1$;
- β is the subjective rate of time preference;
- I_t is the information set available at time t.

The budget constraint requires current consumption and current "trip" costs to be financed by income earned (Y_{t-1}) and the return on savings, which is the realized return on the average deposits held last period ($\bar{D}_{t-1}$). Since the cash-in-advance constraint is assumed binding, choice of m_t determines current consumption and, simultaneously, choice of savings (through choice of $\bar{D}_t$).

The first order condition for problem (I) is:

$$\alpha U'_{X_t} = E_t\{\beta U'_{X_{t+1}}(1 + r_{dt} - \pi_t)(\tfrac{1}{2})(X_t)(1/m_t)^2 \mid I_t\} \qquad (1)$$

[3] The usual assumptions are that "trips" are evenly spaced and that deposits are only drawn down when currency balances are exhausted. See Tobin (1956). Notice, also, that it is without loss of generality that the possibility of writing checks, i.e., using deposits as a medium of exchange, is not allowed. This could be included without changing the basic equation.

which is a stochastic Euler equation. Similar equations have been extensively studied, e.g., Lucas (1978). In this case, solving (1) for m_t and using the above definitions, the relation is a money demand function.

Let utility exhibit constant relative risk aversion where A is the coefficient of relative risk aversion. Then, solving (1) for m_t and using the solution in the above definitions, the deposit-currency ratio is obtained:

$$\left[\frac{\bar{D}_t}{\bar{C}_t}+1\right]^2 = E_t\left\{\beta\left(\frac{X_{t+1}}{X_t}\right)^{-A}\frac{(\frac{1}{2})X_t}{\alpha}(1+r_{dt}-\pi_t) \mid I_t\right\} \tag{2}$$

Or, alternatively, letting $S_t \equiv \beta(X_{t+1}/X_t)^{-A}(\frac{1}{2})(1/\alpha)X_t$, the deposit-currency ratio can be expressed as:

$$\left[\frac{\bar{D}_t}{\bar{C}_t}+1\right]^2 = E_t\{S_t \mid I_t\}E_t\{(1+r_{dt}-\pi_t) \mid I_t\}$$
$$+ \mathrm{COV}\,(S_t; (1+r_{dt}-\pi_t) \mid I_t) \tag{3}$$

Equation (3) is the basic description of the deposit-currency ratio to be studied. In (3) the deposit-currency ratio is a function of expectations about the rate of return on demand deposits, the intertemporal terms-of-trade, S_t, and the covariance between the two. An important feature of (3) is the specification that the covariance is not time invariant. It depends on the depositor's information. The task is to determine the information on which the expected rate of return and covariance are conditioned, and what, if any, information variables can be identified as causing changes in either the expected rate of return or covariance, such that the deposit-currency ratio declines to the extent of panic. The model does not explain panics, but offers a simple way of embedding the previous discussed models in a single, testable, framework.

The empirical model

Equation (3) contains a number of unobservable parameters. In particular, A, α, and β are not observable. There are, also, severe data problems. For the nineteenth century, there are no data on the promised rate of return (r_{dt}), the capital loss (π_t), consumption, or demand deposits. Data on currency are incomplete. An additional problem is that the data are not evenly spaced, as explained below. In principle, equation (2) could be estimated using the method of moments (Hansen and Singleton (1982)), ignoring the data problems by using proxies and constructed data. The fact that no consumption data is available, and that the banking data is unevenly spaced seem particularly troublesome. The proxy for consumption data is pig iron production, discussed below. Nothing can be done about the uneven data spacing, except to insure that, as far as possible, data are at the same, if unevenly spaced, dates. Given these problems the moment condition, implied by (2), is likely to be misspecified.

These considerations lead to the empirical strategy adopted here. In particular, most of the analysis is conducted using nonparametric methods, after projecting various measures of the covariance and rate of return on possible information variables to get expected values. However, some *ad hoc* versions of equation (3) will also be analyzed. Given the use of pig iron production as a proxy for consumption, the resulting equation is best viewed as a reduced form. It is worth stressing, in defense of this approach, that since there are many ways of constructing the different variables required, the reasons why different combinations of constructed variables produce robust results are laid bare.

A basic version of the *ad hoc* model to be estimated is:

$$\left[\frac{\bar{D}_t}{\bar{C}_t}+1\right]^2 = \alpha_0 + \alpha_1 t + \alpha_2 t^2 + \alpha_3(1 + r_{dt} - \pi_t^2) + \alpha_4 \,\mathrm{COV}_t^e + \mu t \tag{4}$$

$$\alpha_3 \equiv \mathrm{EXP}\,[\beta_1 \ln(X_{t+1}/X_t) + \beta_2 \ln X_t]$$

$$\begin{aligned} \pi_t &= \mathbf{Z}_t\boldsymbol{\gamma} + \varepsilon_t \quad \text{if} \quad Z_t\gamma + \varepsilon_t > 0 \\ &= 0 \qquad\qquad\; \text{if} \quad Z_t\gamma + \varepsilon_t \leqslant 0 \end{aligned} \tag{5}$$

$$\begin{aligned} \mathrm{COV}_t \equiv (X_{t+1} - X_t)\pi_t &= \mathbf{W}_t\boldsymbol{\delta} + u_t \quad \text{if} \quad Z_t\gamma + \varepsilon_t > 0 \\ &= 0 \qquad\qquad\; \text{if} \quad Z_t\gamma + \varepsilon_t \leqslant 0 \end{aligned} \tag{6}$$

The total expected rate of return on demand deposits consists of two components, the "promised" component (r_{dt}) and the expected capital loss component (π_t^e). The promised component is known at time t because it is contractually agreed upon by banks and depositors *ex ante*. Since demand deposits never earn capital gains, the capital loss component (π_t), realized at the end of period t, is constrained, in (5), to be positive or zero. Hence, equation (5) will be estimated using Tobit methods. The expected capital loss, estimated from (5), then enters equation (4). In equation (5) $\mathbf{Z}_t$ is a matrix of predictors of the capital loss.

Perceived risk is taken as the estimated value of COV_t from equation (6) and entered into equation (4).[4] In an abuse of terminology, the representative depositor's conditional forecast of how consumption and losses on deposits will covary is indicated as "expected covariance," COV_t^e. As shown, the asymmetry of the contract, namely that $\pi_t \geqslant 0$, must be taken into consideration when estimating (6). Note that equation (6) forecasts only part of the covariance term, the expected product of the change in consumption and the capital loss. The term $1 + r_{dt}$ is not included, and the cross product of the means is not present. The cross product of the means of the change in consumption and the capital loss term can be computed

[4] Joint estimation of the model, (4)–(6), is not econometrically feasible because of the truncation of (5), and the affect of that truncation on (6). Gorton (1987B) reports on some joint estimates of (4) and (6) when the truncation of (5)'s affects on (6) are ignored. No results, subsequently reported, seem to turn on this issue.

separately. This requires predicting X_{t+1}. Computing the covariance is difficult because of the data problems mentioned above. In fact, none of the relevant data are available. The basic strategy adopted in this paper is to compute a weighted capital loss, as in (6), as a proxy. While Gorton (1987B) contains many other results, results reported here all use variations of equation (6). In equation (6), $\mathbf{W}_t$ is a matrix of predictors, possibly different from $\mathbf{Z}_t$.

Note that while next period's consumption, X_{t+1}, appears in (4), the model does not contain an equation predicting next period's consumption.[5] As discussed below, pig iron production is used as a proxy for consumption. Pig iron production can be directly substituted for consumption. Or it may be reasonable to think of current pig iron production as the best estimate of next period's consumption. Subsequently, both possibilities are investigated.

Finally, equation (4) contains time trends because data limitations require that deposits be restricted to nationally chartered bank deposits, a declining fraction of total deposits (which include state banks).[6]

Data considerations

The covariance term is constructed as the weighted loss on deposits, where the weights are the difference in consumption. Pig iron production is used in place of consumption. In what follows a great deal of attention is focused on the covariance term so it is worth briefly discussing each of its components in detail

Consumption data for the nineteenth century are not available at observation intervals of less than a year. The available annual data are constructed. One possibility would have been to distribute the annual series across months using related series. This would mean using related monthly series to distribute a constructed series. In fact, one of the few monthly series available is pig iron production. Consequently, the second possibility of using pig iron in place of consumption was chosen.

How reasonable a proxy is pig iron production? Berry (1978) presents constructed annual personal consumption expenditures in constant dollars (see Berry's Table 7B). Gallman has also constructed annual estimates of the value of goods flowing to consumers (in constant 1860 prices). Gallman's estimates are unpublished, but are described in Gallman (1966). The correlation between Berry's annual consumption series and the annual average pig iron production, i.e., the average of monthly values, is 0.9270. The correlation between Gallman's annual consumption series and the average annual pig iron production is 0.8877. If, instead of averaging monthly pig iron values to obtain an average annual value, the last value is used, then the correlations are 0.8600 and 0.8260 between pig iron and the

[5] Subsequent reported results were not changed when next period's consumption was predicted with an ARIMA model.

[6] The time trend squared is included because the dependent variable is squared.

Berry and Gallman series, respectively. Thus, pig iron production is a very good proxy for real consumption.[7]

There are no data on the capital losses on deposits. The proxy for actual capital losses during the pre-1914 period is the "loss on assets compounded or sold under order of court" for national banks placed in the hands of receivers (see Appendix). In other words, when a bank failed, court appointed receivers would liquidate the bank over a period of years (sometimes ten or so years). Each year in which an asset was sold at some amount below book value, a loss was recorded. This stream of losses was assigned to the date the bank was closed as the capital loss of deposits.

During a banking panic banks suspend convertibility of deposits into currency. Banks' liabilities, however, continued to circulate in the form of loan certificates and certified checks. (See Gorton (1985B) and Gorton and Mullineaux (1986).) During the period of suspension these bank liabilities exchanged at small discounts against government currency. These discounts represent losses to depositors during suspension periods. Below inclusion of such losses does not change any results.

Hypothesis testing using the model

The model, (4)–(6), will be used to test three types of hypotheses, First, are banking panics systematic events? The basic claim that panics are systematic events requires testing the hypothesis that the characterization of the deposit-currency ratio estimated using all nonpanic observations (significantly) holds at the panic dates. If panics are random events caused by extraneous events such as sunspots, then the behavior of the deposit-currency ratio at panic dates should *not* be described by relations which hold at other dates. *From this point of view, economic theories of causal relations are not at issue.* Rather, the question is whether a set of correlations which significantly hold at nonpanic dates also hold at panic dates. If the correlations hold at panic dates, panics will be described as *systematic* events.

A stronger type of claim concerns hypothesized economic behavior, the second type of claim to be examined. In particular, are banking panics predictable? The above model is one of risk averse depositors who seek to optimally smooth consumption intertemporally. The model hypothesizes that losses on deposits which come during periods when depositors want to dissave will be given a lot of weight in utility terms. On the other hand, losses on deposits which occur during periods of rising consumption will be given little weight in utility terms. With respect to panics, if depositors expect a coincidence of declining consumption and high capital losses on

[7] Data on pig iron production apparently doesn't exist beyond the series reported in Macaulay (1938). His last observation is dated January 1936. *Historical Statistics of the United States,* however, reports a series on pig iron shipments. The correlation between pig iron shipments and total real consumption over 1929–1970 is 0.7360.

deposits, then they will seek to withdraw deposits in advance of those periods. They do this in order to avoid the capital loss which they expect to occur during the period in which they expect to dissave. In other words, panics should not only be systematic, but should be *associated with movements in perceived risk predictable on the basis of prior information.* This hypothesis then requires that the predictors of COV_t not include contemporaneous information (unlike the first claim, above). In this case, panics will be said to be *predictable.*

The third, and final, type of claim concerns what is contained in the information set upon which expectations are conditioned. What type of news causes panics? If panics are systematic, and perhaps predictable, then which of the variables predicting π_t and COV_t are important at all points in time and, *if important at all points in time, which are important at panic dates*? In other words, conditional on panics being, at least, systematic, which of the predictors of the capital loss, π_t, and risk, COV_t, are important at panic dates. *Notice that this excludes predictors which are important at panic dates, but not at other dates.* This restriction, then, tests for "sunspots," if "sunspots" are events which do not occur at all dates. Below, however, the first two claims are re-examined by checking whether predictors found to be unimportant as predictors of COV are important at panic dates.

The three hypotheses that panics are predictable are given empirical form by including in the Z_t and W_t matrices of (5) and (6) variables (and lags) capturing seasonal effects, failures, and recessions. These variables are taken to be exogenous, and, in fact, are exogenous by Granger-causality tests (see Gorton (1987B)). The seasonal Hypothesis is represented by the rate of interest on commercial paper (from Macaulay (1938)). Short-term interest rates had strong seasonals during the pre-Fed period (e.g., Kemmerer (1910), Sargent (1971), Shiller (1980)). The inclusion of short-term interest rates is intended to capture the notion of "seasonal stringency" or "seasonal crisis." The Recession Hypothesis is represented by a leading economic indicator, liabilities of failed nonfinancial businesses.[8]

The Failure Hypothesis emphasizes the unanticipated failure of large, usually financial, institutions. This notion is the hardest to quantify. The Failure Hypothesis is represented by unanticipated capital losses on deposits, i.e., the residuals from the Tobit estimation of capital losses (see Gorton (1987B)). This measure seems close to what the failure hypothesis maintains, but it limits attention to national banks and ignores completely the idea that the failure of specific institutions is what counts.

The variables chosen to capture the content of each hypothesis are not pure representations. All three hypotheses, for example, involve business

[8] The liabilities of failed businesses led peaks by one cycle phase, and led troughs by two cycle phases (Burns and Mitchell (1946)). Neftci (1979) has shown how the predictive ability of leading indicators can be evaluated by applying a test for Granger causality. By such a test the liabilities of failed businesses does not lead pig iron production, but does lead the risk measure.

failures, and short-term interest rates reflect more than seasonals. To some extent these effects can be disentangled. Failed business liabilities and short-term interest rates can be deseasonalized. It is, therefore, possible to test whether failed business liabilities have an impact on the risk measure independent of seasonal movements. Similarly, it is possible to test for effects of interest rates independent of seasonals.

IV. Analysis of the national banking era

The National Banking Era (1865–1914) is examined first because this period preceded the existence of the Federal Reserve System and the Federal Deposit Insurance Corporation, two institutions which may be expected to affect depositor behavior. During the National Banking Era national (though not state) banks were required to report a variety of information to the Comptroller of the Currency five times a years. The Comptroller *Reports* provide most of the data to test the hypotheses of the previous section.

An important drawback to using the Comptroller *Reports* is that information was recorded five times a year (at "call dates"). These reporting dates were not the same every year, but fell in different months. The observations, then, are not evenly spaced.[9] *In what follows the data are treated as if they were evenly spaced.* Aslo, the information is limited to national banks. All data are described in the appendix. The fact that virtually every series is constructed or proxied has some potentially important implications discussed in particulars later.[10]

The first step in estimating the model of the currency-deposit ratio is estimation of the capital loss on deposits, equation (5), the fitted value of which enters equation (6). The expected capital loss series is the predicted value from an equation estimated using Tobit analysis due to the truncated distribution of π_t. The equation used in what follows contains a constant term, two lags of the capital loss, the contemporaneous and nine lags of the liabilities of failed businesses, and the contemporaneous and four lags of both pig iron production and the interest rate on commercial paper. The results are not sensitive to specification of this equation and details may be found in Gorton (1987B). In fact, subsequent results are not changed significantly, if, instead of predicted values of the capital loss, actual future capital losses are used. *The reason is that panics are not associated with spikes in the capital loss series. There are many dates at which capital losses are much higher*! There is, thus, prior evidence that the timing of the capital

[9] This was precisely the intention of the Comptroller, who while monitoring banks attempted to keep the call dates from being predictable.

[10] The fact that virtually every data series is constructed, proxied, or interpolated raises a large number of issues and makes the possible combinations of estimates very large. Many of the issues are discussed in Gorton (1987B) which is a large companion appendix to this text. In the text here only the sensitive issues are discussed.

losses with respect to changes in consumption, and not just the level of losses, is important.

Estimates of perceived risk

The results of estimating equation (6) are all contained in Gorton (1987B). Here those results are summarized. Subsequently, predicted values of COV_t will be used so the importance of equation (6) lies in what variables are important predictors of perceived risk (COV_t). In this regard, the results are basically robust to how COV_t is defined, and to whether data are deseasonalized or not.[11] The best fits are achieved with ten lags of COV, nine lags of the liabilities of ailed nonfinancial businesses, and four lags of the commercial paper rate.[12] The R-squared's are all in the range of 0.30. (Estimated coefficients, unimportant for purposes here, can be found in Gorton (1987B).[13])

[11] Recall that since pig iron is being used as a proxy for consumption, as discussed in the main text, there is the question of the appropriate empirical definition of COV_t. Recall that throughout we are restricting attention to definitions in which the cross product of the means component of COV is ignored. Possible definitions are: (1) $COV_t \equiv (X_{t+1} - X_t)(r_{dt} - \pi_t)$; (2) $COV_t \equiv (X_{t+1} - X_t)\pi_t$; (3) $COV_t \equiv (X_t - X_{t-1})(r_{dt} - \pi_t)$; (4) $COV_t \equiv (X_t - X_{t-1})\pi_t$. The main text argued that the last definition is the appropriate definition. The results discussed in the text are basically robust to which definition is used, though the R^2 in the case of the third definition is more than twice the other cases, whether data are deseasonalized or not, and whether contemporaneous predictors are included or not. The high R^2 does not occur in the case of definition (2), though definitions (1) and (2) give similar results. The likely reason is the way r_{dt} was constructed. See Gorton (1987B) for the full set of results.

[12] When tests for whether panics are systematic events, as defined in the main text, contemporaneous values of the liabilities of failed businesses and the commerical rate are also included. Contemporanoeus values are excluded when analyzing whether panics are predictable on the basis of prior information.

[13] A typical example is as follows:

$$\begin{aligned}
COV_t = {} & \underset{(0.002)}{0.004} + \underset{(0.074)}{0.049}COV_{t-1} - ,\underset{(0.074)}{0.185}COV_{t-1} + \underset{(0.073)}{0.006}COV_{t-3} \\
& + \underset{(0.070)}{0.074}COV_{t-4} - \underset{(0.070)}{0.102}COV_{t-5} + \underset{(0.070)}{0.089}COV_{t-6} + \underset{(0.070)}{0.001}COV_{t-7} \\
& + \underset{(0.070)}{0.020}COV_{t-8} + \underset{(0.068)}{0.013}COV_{t-9} - \underset{(0.067)}{0.128}COV_{t-10} - \underset{(1.56)}{1.44}BLIA_t \\
& - \underset{(1.7)}{4.34}BLIA_{t-1} + \underset{(1.8)}{1.09}BLIA_{t-2} - \underset{(1.81)}{7.33}BLIa_{t-3} - \underset{(1.79)}{1.1}BLIA_{t-4} \\
& + \underset{(1.77)}{2.9}BLIA_{t-5} - \underset{(1.77)}{2.2}BLIA_{t-6} + \underset{(1.77)}{3.46}BLIA_{t-7} - \underset{(1.76)}{2.77}BLIA_{t-8} \\
& + \underset{(1.67)}{4.81}BLIA_{t-9} - \underset{(0.025)}{0.011}COMP_t - \underset{(0.027)}{0.105}COMP_{t-1} \\
& + \underset{(0.028)}{0.091}COMP_{t-2} - \underset{(0.028)}{0.057}COMP_{t-3} + \underset{(0.027)}{0.041}COMP_{t-4}
\end{aligned}$$

$R^2 = 0.28$; $SSE = 0.0026$; $F = 2.89$; $df = 186$.

BLIA ≡ Liabilities of failed businesses; COMP ≡ interest rate on commercial paper. This example uses nondeseasonalized data.

In all cases, the liabilities of failed businesses variables, deseasonalized or not, are always jointly significant. When short-term interest rates are added to the equation, the liabilities variables, deseasonalized or not, remain jointly significant. Seasonality, as captured by the interest rate variables are always jointly significant. But, notably, when the interest rate on commerical paper is deseasonalized, the interest rates are not jointly significant!

Unanticipated capital losses (representing the Failure Hypothesis) do not appear in any of the final equations used because this variable and lagged values were never jointly significant. There is the possibility that the failure of a single institution occurring in conjunction with business failures is what is important, but attempts to separate these effects did not improve the predictive power of the equation.[14]

It is perhaps important to point out that the information used to predict COV and capital losses on deposits separately was available to agents living during the National Banking Era. The liabilities of failed businesses were published as were interest rate data. In addition, the telegraph, invented in the 1840s, had spread nationwide by the National Banking Era.

Test results for the deposit-currency ratio equation

The main results of interest are estimates of the nonlinear deposit-currency ratio equation, (4), using predicted perceived risk measures, and expected capital loss measures from the Tobit procedure. Table 2 presents a sample of the results. Table 2 considers a variety of different COV predictions. In Table 2, rows (1), (2) and (5) use nondeseasonalized data to predict COV; the remaining rows use deseasonalized data. Rows (1)–(4) use contemporaneous variables, as well as lags, to predict COV; rows (5) and (6) only use lagged variables.[15]

Consider the first hypothesis to be examined: that panics are systematic events. Table 2 addresses this issue by including a dummy variable for the panic dates. If the estimated model cannot explain panics then the dummy variable should be significant. But, the dummy is not significant.[16] The implication is that nothing is happening at panic dates which is not being explained by the model. This conclusion is very strong. It does not depend

[14] The contemporaneous liabilities of failed businesses, proxying for both effects, would be mismeasured. OLS estimates, columns (1), (2), and (4), would then be biased and inconsistent. Columns (3) and (5) address this potential problem by using instrumental variables. The instruments were the current value and four lags of loans and discounts at national banks and the current value and four lags of Frickey's Index of Production for Transportation and Communication. (See Gorton (1987B) for details.) Inspection of Table 2 does not reveal any important differences when the instruments are used, but subsequently the Failure Hypothesis is reexamined, and the measures of perceived risk estimated using instruments.

[15] Rows (1) and (3) use instruments to predict COV, as discussed above in footnote 14.

[16] The dummy variable is set to one at the panic dates and zero otherwise. The panic dates *in the data* are: December 26, 1873; June 20, 1884; December 19, 1890; July 12, 1893; October 6, 1896; December 3, 1907; September 12, 1914. The results are not sensitive to perturbations of these dates. The dummy variable was not significant in any functional specification attempted. In a log-linear deposit-currency ratio equation, reported on in Gorton (1987B), dummies for the individual panic dates were never significant, individually or as a group. The nonlinear estimation procedure would not converge when individual panic dummies were included.

TABLE 2
Deposit-Currency Ratio Test Results, 1870–1914

$$\left[\frac{D_t}{C_t}+1\right]^2 = \alpha_0\text{Dummy} + \alpha_1 + \alpha_2 t + \alpha_3 t^2 + \text{Exp}\,[\alpha_4 \ln (X_{t+1}/X_t) + \alpha_5 \ln X_t](1 + r_{dt} - \pi_t^e) + \alpha_6\,\text{COV}_t^e$$

	α_0	α_1	α_2	α_3	α_4	α_5	α_6	R^2	σ
1)	0.6349	3.74	−0.0084	0.0002	−0.1971	0.9789	85.99	0.9686	0.4681
	(0.5731)	(0.151)	(0.0029)	(0.00002)	(0.2619)	(0.0304)	(19.89)		
2)	0.5495	3.737	−0.0081	0.0002	−0.1901	0.982	110.34	0.9689	0.4660
	(0.5530)	(0.15)	(0.0029)	(0.00002)	(0.2601)	(0.0303)	(24.26)		
3)	−0.4526	3.689	−0.0079	0.0002	−0.066	0.9881	53.15	0.9668	0.4820
	(0.5044)	(0.1555)	(0.0030)	(0.00002)	(0.2668)	(0.0303)	(21.14)		
4)	−0.5260	3.696	−0.0076	0.0002	−0.0849	0.9882	87.35	0.9673	0.4778
	(0.4918)	(0.1534)	(0.0029)	(0.00002)	(0.2623)	(0.030)	(27.61)		
5)	0.3765	3.729	−0.0080	0.0002	−0.1440	0.9831	101.69	0.9684	0.4690
	(0.5485)	(0.5485)	(0.0029)	(0.00002)	(0.2612)	(0.0303)	(24.42)		
6)	−0.7739	3.712	−0.008	0.0002	−0.0315	0.9844	90.93	0.9671	0.4792
	(0.4888)	(0.1553)	(0.003)	(0.00002)	(0.2661)	(0.0307)	(30.68)		

Standard errors are in parentheses. Dummy = 1 at panic dates and zero otherwise.

on the definition of COV, on whether data are deseasonalized, on whether contemporaneous predictors of COV are used, or on the functional specification of the deposit-currency equation. (See Gorton (1987B).)

The evidence is also strong that panics are predictable on the basis of prior information. In Table 2, the perceived risk variable is significant in all equations. In particular, it is significant when the contemporaneous predictors of COV are omitted as in rows (5) and (6). This means that if, on the basis of prior information, COV_t^e is negative, then depositors shift from deposits to currency in order to avoid the capital loss which they expect to occur when consumption is declining.[17] This conclusion is slightly sensitive to the definition of COV_t.[18]

The final caveat concerns the functional form of the deposit-currency ratio equation in the face of the multitude of data assumptions that have been made. Unfortunately, because of the presence of the time trends in the deposit-currency equation, White (1981, 1982) specification tests are inappropriate.[19] The results here are robust to a number of other specifications, however. (See Gorton (1987B).)

[17] There is an important data timing problem, discussed subsequently in the main text, which slightly colors these results. The quarterly liabilities of failed businesses observations were assigned to the nearest call date (and the missing value estimated) because of seasonals. In order to avoid mixing up seasons, the resulting series sometimes assigns future values to the current date and sometimes past values. This means that, strictly speaking, including the contemporaneous business liabilities variable as a predictor of COV_t is not inconsistent with the hypothesis that panics are predictable on the basis of prior information.

[18] In particular, when r_{dt} is included, the perceived risk measure is not significant. See Gorton (1987B).

[19] One possible way to circumvent the problem is to first detrend the data and then test the functional specification. This biases the test in favor of rejection since the White test is now testing the joint hypothesis of correct specification of the detrending function and correct specification of the deposit-currency ratio equation. Gorton (1987B) reports the results of this procedure. In general, the joint hypothesis of correct specification is not accepted.

Considering the multitude of assumptions about data construction, variable definition, and specification of functional form, and the fact that many of the usual tests cannot be conducted, the robustness of the results is, perhaps, more suspect than usual.[20] Nevertheless the robustness of the results is worth stressing. It seems difficult to argue that there is something special about panics in the sense that the above specification of consumer behavior does not capture behavior during panics. However, the next section re-analyzes the data by concentrating on the panic dates, and avoiding, at least, the specification of the deposit-currency ratio equation. In that sense, the tests in the next section are nonparametric. Such tests also allow for a more precise, and intuitive, sense of what is happening during a banking panic.

V. The timing and severity of panics

In this section the actual panic dates are the focus of attention. By focusing on the panic dates it is possible to identify anything "special" which may have occurred. To confirm the above hypotheses, it should be the case that the special event is a large change, a spike, in a variable predicting COV, which in turn, causes a change in the deposit-currency ratio. The special event is the arrival of information which causes depositors to reassess the riskiness of deposits, and to withdraw currency from banks as a consequence. In this section, the channel of causation is analyzed. It is shown that panics did correspond to spikes in the predictors of deposit riskiness, but in a rational way.

The hypotheses that panics are systematic and predictable have testable implications for the timing and severity of panics. With respect to the timing of panics, the hypotheses imply that *at the panic dates* there should be specific, identifiable, movements in the predictors of risk which result in movements in perceived risk and, hence, in the deposit-currency ratio. *Movements in the predictors at panic dates should imply that the perceived risk variable achieves some critical (negative) value at the panic dates. Also, the movements in the risk predictors and in perceived risk should occur at*

[20] Entering the perceived risk measure into the deposit-currency ratio equation imposes a set of restrictions on the manner in which the predictors of the risk measure are allowed to influence the deposit-currency ratio. If the measure of perceived risk is appropriate, then the imposition of the restrictions should not significantly worsen the fit of the deposit-currency ratio equation. It is well-known that such cross-equation restrictions can be tested (e.g., Barro (1981)). In effect, the test is for whether there is additional information in the predictors of COV_t which affects the deposit-currency ratio through some channel other than perceived risk. Unfortunately, this type of test is inappropriate here because it is not possible to impose the restriction that $\pi_t \geq 0$, i.e., that there are no capital gains to deposits. That is, the truncated value of COV_t, shown in (6), cannot be imposed. Gorton (1987B) discusses this issue in greater detail and conducts some experiments concerning its importance. It turns out to be important, so the cross-equation restriction tests are not conducted.

panic dates and not at other dates. If such movements occurred at other dates, then there should have been panics at those dates.[21]

At the panic dates the magnitudes of the movement of variables can be tested. In effect, the flow of information through the channel of perceived risk at panic dates can be tested. If the information in the predictors of risk is accurate, then the severity of the panic should be related, through the perceived risk measure, to measures of the information content of the predictors. The larger the movement in the predictors, and hence the larger the movements in perceived risk, the larger should be the movements in the deposit-currency ratio.

In addition, if the movements in the predictors are accurate, then the size of these movements, and the associated movements in perceived risk, should be statistically related to the magnitude of downturns in income, rises in capital losses, and the risk measure. The size of the movement in the deposit-currency ratio should be related, through the channel of perceived risk, to the size of income declines and to capital losses. Each of the three hypotheses about what the relevant predictive information is can be examined with respect to the above implications for the predictors of risk.

Tests of timing relations

At a panic date the perceived risk variable should achieve a critical or threshold value not achieved at other dates. Using five different measures of perceived risk, Table 3 lists the number of times the perceived risk measure achieved a lower value *before* the panic date (i.e., previous business cycle peak to panic date) and after the panic date (i.e., panic date to subsequent business cycle trough).[22] As a reference, the first column of the table lists the number of data points between the previous peak and the panic date (labelled "before") and between the panic date and the subsequent trough (labelled "after"). The results are quite striking: negative spikes in the perceived risk measures tend to occur at panic dates.

Is there a threshold value of perceived risk which, when reached, results in a panic? The evidence, while sensitive to the perceived risk measure, supports the existence of such a critical value. In the case of the first perceived risk measure, $COV_t^e(1)$, for example, there are a total of four values lower (i.e., "more" negative) than those occurring at the panic

[21] This statement, however, is subject to an important caveat. Following panic dates deposits may be perceived as even riskier, as depositors get more information, but depositors have already withdrawn their deposits, the banking system has suspended convertibility, or depositors have converted their deposits into clearinghouse loan certificates. On clearinghouse loan certificates see Gorton (1985B), Gorton and Mullineaux (1986), and Cannon (1910).

[22] The five measures of perceived risk all define $COV_t \equiv (X_t - X_{t-1})\pi_t$, where X_t is pig iron production at date t, and π_t is the capital loss on deposits at date t. See footnote 11. All the equations use the lags of COV, nine lags of the liabilities of failed businesses, and four lags of the commercial paper rate. In Table 3, $COV_t^e(1)$ $COV_t^e(2)$, and $COV_t^e(3)$ use nondeseasonalized data, $COV_t^e(4)$ and $COV_t^e(5)$ use deseasonalized data. $COV_t^e(5)$ was estimated jointly with the deposit-currency ratio equation. The estimated equations are provided in Gorton (1987B).

TABLE 3
Timing of Measures of Perceived Risk†

Panic of	# DataPoints Before	After	$COV_t^e(1)$ Before*	After	$COV_t^e(2)$ Before	After	$COV_t^e(3)$ Before	After	$COV_t^e(4)$ Before	After	$COV_t^e(5)$ Before	After
1873	0	26	0	0	0	0	0	0	0	2	0	0
1884	13	4	3	1	6	3	1	1	1	1	1	1
1890	2	2	0	1	1	1	0	0	1	1	0	0
1893	2	4	0	1	0	1	0	1	0	1	0	0
1896	4	3	0	0	0	1	0	0	0	0	0	0
1907	2	2	0	1	0	1	0	0	0	0	0	0
1914	8	2	1	1	2	1	0	0	0	0	0	0

† The five measures, $COV_t^e(1)$, $COV_t^e(2)$, etc., are defined in footnote 22.

* Number of times the perceived risk measure is lower, i.e., "more negative," than the value at the panic date, from previous peak to panic date (Before), and from panic date to subsequent trough (After).

dates, three associated with the Panic of 1884. $COV_t^e(2)$ also has some problem with the Panic of 1884. The last three perceived risk measures indicate that spikes do, indeed, tend to occur at the panic dates. It is rare for there to be a spike in the perceived risk variable before or after the panic.

What causes the large negative values or spikes in the perceived risk measure at panic dates? Do these spikes correspond to identifiable movements or spikes in the predictor variables? In order to test these implications for the three hypotheses, measures of the information content of the (contemporaneous) predictors of perceived risk are needed. Three measures of the liabilities of failed businesses are used in subsequent tests. The first measure attempts to capture the new information in the liabilities of failed businesses, movements in the variable not predictable on the basis of prior information (its own history). This measure is unanticipated changes in the liabilities of failed business (UNLIA), measured by the residuals from an estimated ARIMA model (see Gorton (1987B)). The second measure is the cyclic component of the liabilities of failed businesses series (CCBUS), measured as the log of the observation minus the mean of the logged series. The third measure, using deseasonalized data, is the observation minus the mean of the series (DECC).

The commercial paper rate is examined by looking at deviations from seasonals. In other words, at panic dates the observed rate of interest should be higher than the expected seasonal movement. Such a deviation is intended as a measure of "seasonal stringency." The unanticipated losses on deposits, intended to capture the Failure Hypothesis, are also re-examined.

First, the timing of movements in the liabilities of failed businesses predictor is examined. Table 4 lists the largest positive values of unanticipated increases in the liabilities of failed businesses (UNLIA) and the largest positive values of the cyclical component of liabilities of failed businesses (CCBUS for nondeseasonalized data; DECC for deseasonalized data). *In each case there are no positive shocks larger than those listed in the table.* For each measure of the information in the liabilities variable, the values listed are equal to or higher than the lowest value at a panic date.

The results in Table 4 are striking: panics tend to correspond to the largest values of the liabilities shocks. By the CCBUS measure, every time a shock greater than or equal to 0·8264 occurred after a business cycle peak, there was a panic. Also, the panics correspond to the first large shock following the latest business cycle peak. There are some exceptions. For example, by the UNLIA measure, the shock in November 1887 did not cause a panic, while a smaller one did in June 1884.[23]

[23] The Panic of 1895–96 was the mildest panic of those discussed and constitutes a borderline case. The New York Clearing House Association authorized the use of loan certificates on December 23, 1895, but no member banks applied for them. In late August 1896 the loan certificate process was again activated in response to panic conditions. (See New York City Clearing House Loan Committee *Minutes.*) The *Commercial and Financial Chronicle* describes September to December 1895 and December 1896 as "panicky periods". Spikes in the liabilities variable in October 1896 would then be accurate since December 1896 is not a data point.

TABLE 4
Timing of Liabilities of Failed Businesses Shocks

NBER Chronology Peak Trough	*Largest Values of UNLIA*	*Largest Values of CCBUS*	*Largest Values of DECC*	*Panic Date*
	(Sep. 1873:1.1474)			
Oct. 1973–Mar. 1879	Dec. 1873:1.5028	Dec. 1873:1.4012	Dec. 1987:0.08187	Dec. 1873
	(Feb. 1874:1.272)*	(Feb. 1874:1.1511)	(Feb. 1874:0.05181)*	
	(Oct. 1878:0.7587)	(Mar. 1878:0.9397)	Jun. 1878:0.04086)	
	(Oct. 1883:0.782)			
Mar. 1882–May 1885	Jun. 1884:1.0535	Jun. 1884:0.9653	Jun. 1884:0.07631	Jun. 1884
Mar. 1887–Apr. 1888	Nov. 1887:1.307	Nov. 1887:0.8223		No Panic
Jul. 1890–May 1891	Dec. 1890:1.1249	Dec. 1890:1.0216	Dec. 1890:0.03956	Dec. 1890
Jan. 1893–Jun. 1894	Jul. 1893:1.4340	Dec. 1893:1.3323	Jul. 1893:0.11365	Jul. 1893
			(Jul. 1895:0.03313)	
Dec. 1895–Jun. 1897	Oct. 1896:0.8780	Oct. 1896:0.8264	Jul. 1896:0.03255	Oct. 1896
			(Jul. 1897:0.03579)	
Jun. 1899–Dec. 1900			Jun. 1900:0.03383	No Panic
Sep. 1902–Aug. 1904				No Panic
May 1907–Jun. 1908	Dec. 1907:0.8712	Dec. 1907:0.9308	Dec. 1907:0.03183	Dec. 1907
	(Feb. 1908:0.8763)*			
Jan. 1910–Jan. 1912	Mar. 1910:1.041	Mar. 1910:0.8236	Jun. 1911:0.03615	No Panic
		(Apr. 1913:0.8736)	(Jun. 1913:0.0482)	
		(Jan. 1914:0.8618)	(Mar. 1914:0.0396)	
		(Jun. 1914:1.1558)	(Jun. 1914:0.0940)	
Jan. 1913–Dec. 1914	Mar. 1914:0.7545	(Jun. 1914:1.1558)	Sep. 1914:0.0434	Sept. 1914
		Sep. 1914:0.9958	(Dec. 1914:0.0986)	
		(Dec. 1914:0.9863)		
		(Mar. 1914:0.9535)		

*During suspension.

The deviation of the commercial paper rate from its seasonals is positive at all the panic dates, but there are *larger* deviations at many other dates. In fact, at 33 nonpanic dates there are positive deviations higher than the lowest positive deviation at a panic date. Nor is there any particular (e.g., business cycle) pattern to the seasonal shocks. This evidence suggests that seasonality in interest rates is not important for panics, though it is important for movements in perceived risk and, hence, the deposit-currency ratio over the whole cycle.

The results for unanticipated losses on deposits are similar to those for seasonal deviations in the commercial paper rate. At three of the panic dates there were no unanticipated losses on deposits. At eight nonpanic dates the unanticipated losses were higher than the *highest* unanticipated loss at a panic date. There are many cases of positive unanticipated losses, with no apparent pattern. By this measure the Failure Hypothesis again seems unimportant. The timing evidence with respect to the predictors of perceived risk suggests that for panics the liabilities of failed businesses is the important variable. Banks hold claims on firms, and when firms begin to fail in sufficiently large numbers, it signals the onset of a recession and a panic is likely to occur.

Remarkably, the data support the notion of a critical or threshold value of the liabilities of failed businesses variable, and a threshold value of the perceived risk measure, at the panic dates. The seemingly anomalous event of a panic appears to be no more anomalous than recessions.

Severity tests

While strongly suggestive, the timing of variables discussed above does not constitute a test. However, Spearman's rank correlation coefficient can be used to test the implications of the systematic hypothesis for timing and severity. The rank correlation test is important because it can check that the above hypotheses explain panics when the data are unconstrained by nonpanic relations. The test is conducted by ranking the measures of the information content of the predictors, the perceived risk measures, the currency-deposit ratio, measures of the severity of recessions, and measures of losses on deposits. The Spearman rank correlation coefficient can then be used to test whether the correlations between the movements of these variables *at the specified dates* are significant.

The results are presented in Table 5. The Spearman rank correlation coefficients are shown for seventeen variables which were ranked at eleven dates.[24] The first three variables are measures of the severity of the eleven

[24] Seven of the dates were the panic dates. The remaining four dates correspond to the remaining four business cycles during the National Banking Era. These four dates were selected according to the largest spikes in the measures of the information in the liabilities variable. The dates used were: December 26, 1873; June 20, 1884; October 5, 1887; December 19, 1890; July 12, 1893; October 6, 1896; June 29, 1900; January 22, 1904; December 3, 1907; March 29, 1910; September 12, 1914.

TABLE 5
Spearman Rank Correlation Coefficients

	Eckler (Overall)	Eckler (Pig Iron)	Achinstein (Amplitude)	% ΔM	% $\Delta \frac{C}{D}$	UNLIA	CCBUS	DECC	Losses	Total Losses	Post-panic Losses	RES	DECOMP	$COV^e(1)$	$COV^e(2)$	$COV^e(3)$	$COV^e(4)$
	(1)	(2)	(3)	(4)	(5)	(6)	(7)	(8)	(9)	(10)	(11)	(12)	(13)	(14)	(15)	(16)	(17)
(1)		0.90	0.818	0.564	0.609	0.888	0.618	0.582	0.818	0.935	0.913	0.782	0.445	0.636	0.591	0.718	0.636
(2)			0.827	0.50	0.755	0.867	0.668	0.527	0.627	0.909	0.873	0.605	0.455	0.70	0.618	0.691	0.60
(3)				0.65	0.632	0.877	0.682	0.609	0.782	0.944	0.914	0.536	0.591	0.709	0.618	0.645	0.536
(4)					0.564	0.862	0.736	0.755	0.691	0.818	0.764	0.482	0.464	0.445	0.336	0.445	0.409
(5)						0.872	0.70	0.273	0.391	0.914	0.879	0.282	0.727	0.836	0.755	0.773	0.682
(6)							0.65	0.491	0.605	0.956	0.962	0.268	0.482	0.591	0.555	0.536	0.436
(7)								0.673	0.545	0.949	0.91	0.345	0.482	0.809	0.673	0.673	0.60
(8)									0.436	0.60	0.509	0.345	0.264	0.518	0.30	0.355	0.345
(9)										0.791	0.782	0.682	0.527	0.627	0.573	0.664	0.727
(10)											0.989	0.473	0.718	0.759	0.736	0.755	0.709
(11)												0.382	0.627	0.636	0.664	0.645	0.645
(12)													0.355	0.491	0.364	0.582	0.391
(13)														0.855	0.891	0.818	0.80
(14)															0.918	0.882	0.827
(15)																0.982	0.873
(16)																	0.855
(17)																	

The rank correlation can range from −1 (completely uncorrelated) to +1 (perfectly correlated). The correlation is significant at the 5% level if the calculated coefficient is higher than 0.553, and at the 1% level if the calculated coefficient is higher than 0.684.

Columns (1)–(3) are measures of the severity of the eleven recessions during the National Banking Era. Column (1) is an overall measure from Eckler (1933). Column (2), also from Eckler (1933), is a measure based only on pig iron production. Column (3) is a measure of the amplitude of each cycle from Achinstein (1961). Columns (4) and (5) are the percentage changes in the money stock and currency-deposit ratio from the selected date through the trough. Columns (6), (7), and (8) are the measures of the liabilities variable, UNLIA, CCBUS, and DECC, respectively. Column (9) is the loss per deposit dollar at the selected date, while column (10) is the loss per deposit dollar from peak through the trough (Total Losses). Column (11) is the loss per deposit dollar from selected date through the trough (Post-panic Losses). Column (12) is the unanticipated loss on deposits measure (RES). Column (13) is the deviation from the seasonal for the rate of return on commercial paper (DECOMP). Columns (14)–(17) are four measures of perceived risk. (See footnote 26.)

recessions during the National Banking Era. Columns (4) and (5) are the percentage changes in the money stock and currency-deposit ratio for the selected dates through the subsequent recession.[25] Columns (9)–(11) are measures of losses on deposits. Columns (14)–(17) are four measures of perceived risk.[26] The notes to the table explain the other variables.

The results in Table 5 broadly confirm the earlier conclusion that panics are systematic. The nondeseasonalized measures of failed business liabilities (UNLIA, CCBUS) are significantly correlated with the measures of risk which do not use deseasonalized data ($COV^e(1)$, $COV^e(2)$). The cyclical component, CCBUS, is significantly correlated with all the measures of perceived risk.[27] The deviations of the commercial paper rate from its seasonals (DECOMP) are significantly correlated with all the measures of perceived risk, though not with any measure of the liabilities variable. The unanticipated losses on deposits (RES) are correlated with one measure of perceived risk, $COV^e(3)$.

The business cycle aspect of panics is also revealed again. The percentage change in the currency-deposit ratio is significantly correlated with all the measures of perceived risk. Both the currency-deposit ratio and the perceived risk measures are significantly correlated with the measures of recession and losses on deposits.

The results of this section confirm the earlier conclusion that panics are systematic. The stronger hypothesis that panics are predictable is problematic. Causal inferences would be stronger if it could unambiguously be stated that panics are predictable on the basis of *prior* information, rather than on the basis of contemporaneous information. But there is an important data timing problem. The quarterly liabilities of failed businesses observations were assigned to the nearest call date (and the missing value estimated) because of seasonals. The resulting series then sometimes assigns future values to the current date and sometimes past values.[28] If the contemporaneous value of the liabilities variable is omitted in equations (5)

[25] Results are unaffected if percentage changes are computed from peak to trough.

[26] The four measures of perceived risk correspond to the first four measures described in footnote 22. Gorton (1987B) contains similar results using other measures of perceived risk.

[27] Notice, however, that seasonality in the liabilities variable seems important. The nondeseasonalized measure (UNUA, CCBUS) are significantly correlated with the measures of risk, but the deseasonalized liabilities measure (DECC) is *not* significantly correlated with any of the perceived risk measures.

[28] Three dates are relevant: the actual date of the panic; the dating of the Comptroller's *Reports*; the assignment of the quarterly liabilities of failed businesses variable. The call date in the Comptroller's *Reports* immediately *after* the panic date is assigned to the panic in the data (though "immediately after" varies by up to almost three months). At these call dates, corresponding to the panics, the liabilities variable is dated *after*, but in the same month, in four cases, and before, in the immediately proceeding month in two cases. These were the closest assignments. In the case of the Panic of 1873 the liabilities variable was estimated from railroad bond defaults (see Gorton (1987B)). The problem is further complicated by the fact that the liabilities variable is cumulative over the quarter.

and (6), estimates of equation (4) are basically unaffected, but the analysis *at the panic dates* using only lags of the liabilities variable to predict COV_t results in insignificant correlations.[29] The problem seems to be that the liabilities observations lagged once are "too far away." In short, the data are not fine enough to adequately draw stronger inferences.

VI. The federal reserve system, deposit insurance, and panics

The Federal Reserve System, begun in 1914, and deposit insurance, initiated in 1934, were both introduced primarily to prevent banking panics. This section examines the effects of these two monetary regimes on depositor behavior by estimating the model over these subsequent periods. All data, estimated equations, and test statistics for this section are detailed in Gorton (1987B).

The period 1873–1934

The introduction of the Federal Reserve System significantly altered depositor behavior. Both the perceived risk equations and the deposit-currency ratio equations exhibit significant structural changes after 1914.[30] A more precise sense of the difference made by the existence of the Federal Reserve System may be obtained by examining the timing of the measures of the information content of the liabilities of failed businesses variable during the period of 1914–1934. Table 6 lists the largest liabilities shocks for the peak to trough phase of the business cycles during this period. The table presents two measures. The unanticipated liabilities measure (UNLIA) was estimated over the period 1873–1934 and is, thus, comparable with the earlier period (Table 4). The cyclical component of the liabilities shock (CCBUS) was computed as the logged value minus the mean of the logged value over the years 1914–1934.

Examining the table, the UNLIA shock in June 1920 was large enough to have precipitated a panic had it come during the National Banking Era, but there was no panic under the Federal Reserve system. The UNLIA shock in December 1929 also did not precipitate panic, though it would have during the National Banking Era. The December 1929 shock coincides wih the stock market crash since October 1929 is not a data point. By the other measure, CCBUS, which is not comparable with the earlier period, there is also a spike in December 1929.

[29] More accurately, the perceived risk estimates are often zero at several panic dates, so that there is no way to rank them and conduct the tests. In the one case where this is not true, however, the perceived risk measure is significantly correlated with the percentage change in the currency-deposit ratio. See Gorton (1987B).

[30] Tests for structural change after the introduction of the Federal Reserve System, and deposit insurance in 1934, were done on the equations predicting COV_t, the deposit-currency ratio equation, and a log-linear deposit-currency ratio equation. The evidence favored the existence of structural change under all data definitions, using the usual Chow tests.

TABLE 6
Timing Relations During the Period 1914–1934

Peak-Trough	*UNLIA Shock*	*CCBUS Shock*	*Panic*
Aug. 1918–Mar. 1919	Nov. 1918 0.2435	No Positive Shocks	No Panic
Jan. 1920–July 1921	June 1920 1.1341	Mar. 1921 0.7767	No Panic
May 1923–July 1924	Nov. 1923 0.5199	Mar. 1924 1.1473 (Oct. 1923 0.9392)	No Panic
Oct. 1926–Nov. 1927	Apr. 1927 0.2685	Mar. 1927 0.6584	No Panic
Aug. 1929–Mar. 1933	Dec. 1929 0.7687	Dec. 1929 0.7775	Oct. 1930
		Jan. 1931 1.1157	Mar. 1931
		Jan. 1932 1.1392	Jan. 1933
		Feb. 1932 1.0074	
		Mar. 1932 1.1061	
		Apr. 1932 1.1817	
		Jan. 1933 0.9366	

UNLIA was estimated over the period 1873–1934. CCBUS was estimated over 1914–1934.

Notably, the timing of the UNLIA shocks in June 1920 and December 1929 are the same as the pre-Fed era. Both shocks come just following the business cycle peaks. Simple tests on processes generating the failure liabilities do *not* reject the null hypothesis of no structural change (see Gorton (1987B)). In other words, the introduction of the Federal Reserve System did not alter the process driving failure liabilities. Depositor behavior changed. In deposit-currency ratio equations over the 1914–1934 sample period, measures of perceived risk are always insignificant though the perceived risk equations perform *best* over this period (see Gorton (1987B)). The panics of the 1930s happened in October 1930, March 1931, and January 1933, *well after* the business cycle peak. So the existence of the Fed did prevent a panic in June 1920, but only altered the timing of the later panic.

The period 1914–1972

The introduction of deposit insurance again significantly altered depositor behavior. Both the perceived risk equations and the currency-deposit ratio equations exhibit significant structural changes after 1934. Following the introduction of deposit insurance there were several cases of large failed business liabilities shocks, none of which precipitated panics. Like the results for the 1914–1934 period, the perceived risk measure is insignificant in the deposit-currency ratio equation estimated over the 1935–1972 sample period. Over the 1914–1934 period the sign on the perceived risk measure is positive as it is over the pre-Fed period. That is, in response to an expected coincidence of capital losses on deposits with declining consumption, i.e.,

$COV_t < 0$, depositors reduced their deposit-currency ratios. However, over the 1935–1972 sample period the sign on the perceived risk measure is consistent with the success of deposit insurance. Expecting to dissave during recessions, when the perceived risk measure is negative, depositors increased their deposit-currency ratios.

VII. The 1920s and 1930s without the Fed

What would have happened during the 1920s and 1930s if the Federal Reserve System had not come into existence? This question can be partly answered if it is assumed that depositors would have reacted to the liabilities of failed businesses signal during the 1920s and 1930s in the same way as during the National Banking Era. Recall that tests of the null hypothesis that the process generating the liabilities variable is not stable over the 1873–1934 sample period are rejected. As previously indicated, the UNLIA shock estimated over the period 1873–1934 is appropriate for the counterfactual. According to this UNLIA series (see Table 6), there would have been a panic in June 1920, and another panic in December 1929. These panics would have followed the timing pattern of the panics during the National Banking Era. The June 1920 spike comes shortly after the business cycle peak of January 1920 (the trough was July 1921). The December 1929 spike follows the August 1929 peak (trough: March 1933).

To construct the counterfactual, two further reduced form equations must be estimated to characterize the effects of depositor responses to changes in perceived risk during panics. Using the observations on the seven panics during the National Banking Era, the percentage of failing banks in the system and the percentage losses on deposits can be predicted using the UNLIA shock. The estimated reduced form relations are:

$$\begin{gathered}\%\mathrm{FAIL}_t = 0.010023\ \mathrm{UNLIA}_t \\ (0.0027) \\ R^2 = 0.6973 \qquad \mathrm{DW} = 1.7019 \qquad \mathrm{d.f.} = 6\end{gathered} \tag{7}$$

$$\begin{gathered}\%\mathrm{LOSS}_t = 0.062942\ \mathrm{UNLIA}_t \\ (0.0204) \\ R^2 = 0.6129\ \mathrm{DW} = 1.7097\ \mathrm{d.f.} = 6.\end{gathered} \tag{8}$$

Standard errors are in parentheses. The observations on losses and failures are cumulative from the panic date through the trough date, divided by total deposits and total number of national banks, respectively, at the panic date.

Table 7 compares the actual percentages of failures and losses, from the panic dates through the troughs, with the values predicted using (7) and (8). For the actual percentages of banks failing from December 1929 through March 1933, two numbers are listed. The first uses the Federal Reserve System's definition of suspension which is not strictly comparable (see Gorton (1987B)). The second number, in the case of National Banks,

TABLE 7
Actual and Predicted Losses and Failures, 1920s and 1930s

	Failures		
Date	Predicted *% of National Banks Failing*	Actual *% of National Banks Failing*	Actual *% of All Banks Failing*
June 1920	1.137	0.27	0.91*
Dec. 1929	0.77	26.24; 13.36	36.08; 30.76

	Losses	
Date	Predicted *Losses at National Banks (%)*	Actual *Losses at National Banks (%)*
JUne 1920	7.14	0.42
Dec. 1929	4.84	18.407

* Covers the period Jan. 1921–July 1921 and uses the number of all banks in June 1921 as the base. Data on all banks begin in 1921.

All data described in Gorton (1987B).

uses the number of receiverships closed during 1930–1933. The second number, in the case of all banks, uses the number of banks which did not reopen after the March 1933 banking holiday (2, 132), instead of the Federal Reserve number for suspensions during March 1933 (3,460) (see Gorton (1987B)). Neither of these measures is strictly comparable. The two numbers, however, are the upper and lower limits. The loss measures, however, are comparable.

Table 7 shows that *if there had been a panic in June 1920, the percentages of banks failing and losses on deposits would have been higher than those which actually happened.*[31] *However, if there had been a panic in December 1929, failure and loss percentages would have been an order of magnitude lower.* Losses and failures from June 1920 through the trough (July 1921) were lower than predicted perhaps because there was no panic. Between December 1929 and April 1933, there were three panics which came near the trough (October 1930; March 1931; Jaunary 1933). Losses and failures, however, were much higher than predicted. Table 7 indicates that the magnitudes of the losses and failures during the 1930s cannot be explained by the relations operating prior to the existence of the Federal Reserve System. The existence of the Federal Reserve System altered depositors'

[31] Moreover, prior to 1920 state bank failure rates were about three times the rates for National banks (Bremer (1935)). This would increase the differences between the actual and predicted values for June 1920.

perceptions of risk, as indicated by the insignificance of the perceived risk measures in the deposit-currency ratio equations estimated over the 1914–1934 sample period (see Gorton (1987B)).

VIII. Conclusion

The results of this study are a set of stylized facts about banking panics, which, while extremely important since their reoccurrence motivated bank regulation, are not well understood. The main stylized fact is that panics are systematic (as previously defined) events linked to the business cycle. Panics turn out not be mysterious events after all. The evidence favors the conclusion that panics were a manifestation of consumption smoothing behavior on the part of cash-in-advance constrained agents. Panics seem to have resulted from changes in perceived risk predictable on the basis of prior information. The recession hypothesis best explains what prior information is used by agents in forming conditional expectations. Banks hold claims on firms and when firms begin to fail, a leading indicator of recession (when banks will fail), depositors reassess the riskiness of deposits.

Depositors panic when the liabilities signal is strong enough. In fact, during the National Banking Era, whenever the information measure of the liabilities of failed businesses reached a "critical" level, so did perceptions of risk and there was a banking panic. In this sense panics were special events. The cyclical behavior of the liabilities variable made panics an integral part of the pre-1914 business cycle.

As with all statistical inference, the above results cannot reject the notion that there exists an unknown variable(s) causing simultaneous increases in the currency-deposit ratio, risk, and the liabilities of failed businesses. *However, we can say that the influence of such unknown factors must happen the same way at panic and nonpanic dates, which is not consistent with sunspot theories of panics.* Sunspot theories argue that there is something special going on at the panic dates which does not occur at other dates, i.e., sunspots, but this is not consistent with the above evidence.

Could the causality be reversed in the above conclusions? Might it not be the case that depositors panic because of sun spots, run the banks, and thereby, cause the banker to call in loans, causing firms to fail? This scenario can be eliminated for three reasons. First, capital losses on demand deposits do not Granger-cause the liabilities of failed businesses, but liabilities of failed businesses do Granger-cause losses on deposits.[32] In other words, the mechanism of causality running from depositors withdrawing currency from "illiquid" banks and causing businesses to fail is not

[32] In regressions with ten lags of each variable, the F statistic for the liabilities variable with capital losses on deposits as the dependent variable was 2.11 (d.f. = (11, 184)), significant at the 5% level. In other words, the liabilities variable Granger-causes losses. The reverse test results in an F statistic of 0.38. Losses on deposits do not cause business failures.

present, at least when all dates are examined. Second, the response of banks to panics was not to liquidate loans, but to issue circulating private money which insured depositors against the failure of individual banks. (See Gorton (1985B, 1987A).) Finally, call loans do not seem to have been sizable enough to be the mechanism, and do not seem to have been loaned to nonfinancial businesses, in general. (See Myers (1931).)

At the panic dates the important shock seems to be the liabilities of failed businesses (with a seasonal component). This result was the basis of the counterfactual about the 1920s and 1930s. After 1914 the private insurance arrangements of commercial bank clearinghouses were replaced by the Federal Reserve System (see Gorton (1985B)). The counterfactual reveals the inadequacies of drawing policy conclusions about private market failures from the experience of the Great Depression. The evidence suggests that the private insurance arrangements of clearinghouses compare favorably to the Federal Reserve System in responding to banking panics.

The Wharton School, University of Pennsylvania, USA

APPENDIX

Gorton (1987B) contains complete details of data sources and data construction methods, as well as further results. The basic data sources are as follows. Currency in the hands of the public and demand deposit data are from the *Annual Report* of the Secretary of the Treasury, Friedman and Schwartz (1963), *Survey of Current Business*(Supplements), *Banking and Monetary Statistics,* and the *Annual Statistical Digest* of the Federal Reserve System. The liabilities of failed businesses series is from *Finanical Review* and from *Survey of Current Business,* for the later period. Pig iron production is from Macaulay (1938). Capital losses on demand deposits are constructed from the Comptroller *Reports* and from FDIC *Annual Reports.* Data on bank suspensions are from the Federal Reserve *Bulletin,* September 1937. Earlier data on the number of national banks failing are from the Comptroller *Report* of 1925 and 1935.

REFERENCES

ACHINSTEIN, ASHER (1961), "Economic Fluctuations," Chapter 6 of Seymour Harris, ed., *American Economic History* (New York; McGraw-Hill Book Company).

ANDREW, A. P. (1906), "The Influence of the Crops on Business in America," *Quarterly Journal of Economics,* XX.

BARRO, R. J. (1981), "Unanticipated Money Growth and Economic Activity in the United States," Chapter 5 of *Money, Expectations, and Business Cycles* (New York; Academic Press).

BERRY, THOMAS Senior (1978), *Revised Annual Estimates of American Gross National Product,* Preliminary Annual Estimates of *Four Major Components of Demand, 1789–1889,* Bostwick Paper No. 3 (The Bostwick Press).

BREMER, C. D. (1935), *American Bank Failures* (New York; Columbia University Press).

BURNS, ARTHUR, and MITCHELL, WESLEY (1946), *Measuring Business Cycles* (New York; National Bureau of Economic Research).

CAGAN, PHILLIP (1965), *Determinants and Effects of Changes in the Stock of Money, 1875–1960* (New York; National Bureau of Economic Research).

CANNON, J. G. (1910), *Clearing Houses* (National Monetary Commission, S. Doc. 491, 61st Cong. 2nd sess.).

CHOW, GREGORY and LIN, AN-LOH (1971), "Best Linear Unbiased Interpolation, Distribution, and Extrapolation of Time Series by Related Series," *Review of Economics and Statistics* 53(4) (November).

DIAMOND, D. and DYBVIG, P. (1983), "Bank Runs, Deposit Insurance, and Liquidity," *Journal of Political Economy,* Vol. 91, No. 3 (June).

ECKLER, A. R. (1933), "A Measure of the Severity of Depressions, 1873–1932," *Review of Economic Statistics* (May), XV, 75–81.

FELS, RENDIGS (1959), *American Business Cycles, 1865–1897* (University of North Carolina Press).

FRIEDMAN, M. and SCHWARTZ, A. J. (1963), *A Monetary History of the United States, 1867–1960* (Princeton University Press).

——, (1970), *Monetary Statistics of the United States* (New York; National Bureau of Economic Research).

GALLMAN, ROBERT E. (1966), "Gross National Product in the United States, 1834–1909," In *Output Employment and Productivity in the United States after 1800*, Studies in Income and Wealth, Volume 30, by the Conference on Research in Income and Wealth, National Bureau of Economic Research (Columbia University Press).

GIBBONS, J. S. (1968), *The Banks of New York, Their Dealers, the Clearing House, and the Panic of 1857* (New York; Greenwood Press; reprint of 1859 original).

GORTON, G. (1985A), "Bank Suspension of Convertibility," *Journal of Monetary Economics* 15(2) (March).

—— (1985B), "Clearing Houses and the Origin of Central Banking in the U.S.," *Journal of Economic History,* 45(2) (June).

—— (1987A), "Incomplete Markets and the Endogeneity of Central Banking," Rodney L. White Center for Financial Research Working Paper #16–87, The Wharton School, University of Pennsylvania.

—— (1987B), "Banking Panics and Business Cycles: Data Sources, Data Construction, and Further Results," The Wharton School, University of Pennsylvania, mimeo.

GORTON, GARY and DONALD J. MULLINEAUX (1987), "The Joint Production of Confidence: Endogenous Regulation and 19th Century Commercial-Bank Clearinghouses," *Journal of Money, Credit, and Banking,* Vol. 19, No. 4 (November).

HANSEN, L. P. and K. J. SINGLETON (1982), "Generalized Instrumental Variables Estimation of Nonlinear Rational Expectations Models," *Econometrica* 50, 1269–1286.

JEVONS, STANLEY W. (1884), *Investigations in Currency and Finance* (London).

KEMMERER, EDWIN W. (1910), *Seasonal Variations in the Relative Demand for Money and Captial in the United States* (Washington, D.C.; Government Printing Office).

KINDLEBERGER, CHARLES P. (1978), *Manias, Panics, and Crashes, a History of Financial Crises* (New York; Basic Books).

KLEIN, BENJAMIN (1974), "Competitive Interest Payments on Bank Deposits and the Long-Run Demand for Money," *American Economic Review* (Dec.), LXIV, No. 6, 931–49.

LUCAS, ROBERT (1978), "Asset Prices in an Exchange Economy," *Econometrica.*

MACAULAY, F. (1938), *The Movements of Interest Rates, Bond Yields, and Stock Prices in the United States Since 1856* (New York; National Bureau of Economic Research).

MIRON, J. A. (1985), "Financial Panics, the Seasonality of the Nominal Interest Rate, and the Founding of the Fed," *American Economic Review* 76(1) (March 1986), 125–140.

MITCHELL, WESLEY C. (1941), *Business Cycles and Their Causes* (Berkeley; University of California Press).

MYERS, MARGARET (1931), *The New York Money Market*, Volume 1 (New York; Columbia University Press).

NEFTCI, S. (1979), "Lead-Lag Relations, Exogeneity and Prediction of Economic Time Series," *Econometrica* (January), 104–13.

NOYES, A. D. (1909), *Forty Years of American Finance* (New York; G. P. Putnam's and Sons).

SARGENT, T. J. (1971), "Expectations at the Short End of the Yield Curve: An Application of Macaulay's Test," in *Essays on Interest Rates,* edited by J. Guttentag (New York; Columbia University Press and National Burea of Economic Research).

SHILLER, R. J. (1980), "Can the Fed Control Real Interest Rates," in *Rational Expectations and Economic Policy,* edited by Stanley Fischer (Chicago; University of Chicago Press).

SPRAGUE, O. M. W. (1915), "The Crisis of 1914 in the United States," *American Economic Review* (Sept.).

—— (1910), *History of Crises Under the National Banking System* (National Monetary Commission, S. Doc. No. 538, 61st Cong., 2nd sess.).

TOBIN, J. (1956), "The Interest-Elasticity of Transactions Demand for Cash," *Review of Economics and Statistics* 38 (August), 241–47.

WALDO, DOUGLAS (1985), "Bank Runs, the Deposit-Currency Ratio and the Interest Rate," *Journal of Monetary Economics* 15(3) (May), p. 269–278.

WHITE, H. (1981), "Consequences and Detection of Misspecified Nonlinear Regression Models," *Journal of the American Statistical Association* 76, 419–33.

—— (1982), "Maximum Likelihood Estimation of Misspecified Models," *Econometrica* 50, 1–25.